CORPORATE CONTROLLER'S

HANDBOOK OF

FINANCIAL MANAGEMENT

SECOND EDITION

Joel G. Siegel, Ph.D., CPA
Jae K. Shim, Ph.D.
Nicky A. Dauber, MS, CPA

PRENTICE HALL

W9-AKW-947

Library of Congress Cataloging in Publication Data

ISBN 0-13-079657-3

ATTENTION: CORPORATIONS AND SCHOOLS
Prentice Hall books are available at quantity discounts with bulk purchase for educational, business, or sales promotional use. For information, please write to: Prentice Hall Special Sales, 240 Frisch Court, Paramus, New Jersey 07652. Please supply: title of book, ISBN, quantity, how the book will be used, date needed.

PRENTICE HALL
Paramus, NJ 07652

A Simon & Schuster Company

On the World Wide Web at http://www.phdirect.com

Prentice Hall International (UK) Limited, *London*
Prentice Hall of Australia Pty. Limited, *Sydney*
Prentice Hall Canada, Inc., *Toronto*
Prentice Hall Hispanoamericana, S.A., *Mexico*
Prentice Hall of India Private Limited, *New Delhi*
Prentice Hall of Japan, Inc., *Tokyo*
Simon & Schuster Asia Pte. Ltd., *Singapore*
Editora Prentice Hall do Brasil, Ltda., *Rio de Janeiro*

WHAT THIS SUPPLEMENT WILL DO FOR YOU

This supplement updates the main volume of *Corporate Controller's Handbook of Financial Management, Second Edition.* It includes current developments in financial management, accounting, and taxes. These developments take the form of recent trends in finance, new technology or software applications, and new authoritative accounting requirements. The following are some of the areas which have been updated:

- New pronouncements of the Financial Accounting Standards Board in the areas of earnings per share, segmental reporting, stock compensation plans, impairment of assets including loans, asset transfers, capital structure, and comprehensive income.
- Updates to leases, pensions, accounting for income taxes, and divestitures.
- Environmental reporting and disclosures.
- Updates for new tax laws affecting business decisions.
- Expansion of various tax areas such as corporate liquidation.
- Electronic funds transfer.

The following are new chapters which take into account recent developments and/or provide for more comprehensive coverage of corporate finance:

- The Use of Computer Software in Managerial Accounting.
- Internet & World Wide Web.
- Intranets.
- Business Law.
- Total Quality Management (TQM) and Quality Costs.

- Risk Management and Analysis.
- Reengineering and Outsourcing the Business.
- Forecasting & Financial Planning.
- Financial & Earnings Forecasting.
- Cash Flow Forecasting.
- Interest Rate Forecasting.
- Forecasting Foreign Exchange Rates.
- Evaluation of Forecasts.
- Forecasting Tools and Software.
- Management Analysis of Operations.
- Financial Derivative Products and Financial Reengineering.

Like the main volume, the contents of this supplement are clear, concise and to the point. Use the cumulative Index at the back of this work to locate topics covered in this work or the main volume. Use the two works as your handy "how to" reference tool.

SUPPLEMENT CONTENTS

The Use of Computer Software in Managerial Accounting*

Computer software is available for most areas of managerial accounting, including cost systems, activity-based costing (ABC), forecasting, budgeting and planning, inventory evaluation, material requirement appraisal, project management, capital budgeting, risk analysis, linear programming, and flow-charting. There are stand-alone packages, templates, and spreadsheet add-ins. The purpose of this chapter is to alert you to software useful in managerial accounting, including their features, applications, and suitability to meet a particular company's needs.

PLANNING AND BUDGETING

In the areas of planning and budgeting, many useful software exist.

Planet Corporation's *Business Maestro* generates operational and strategic business plans, while its *Budget Maestro* accounts for projects and evaluates trends in human resources and related costs.

Orange Systems' *ALCIE* provides capacity planning, purchasing job shop control, inventory management, and distribution.

Comshare's *Commander Budget* does budgeting with the use of spreadsheets and prepares management reports. It performs multidimensional analysis, analyzes budgeted figures and how they impact on the business, performs variance analysis, looks at "what-if" scenarios, performs

---

*This chapter was coauthored by Anique A. Qureshi, Ph.D., CPA, CIA, associate professor of accounting and information systems at Queens College.

exception analysis, and prepares management reports. It has application interfaces to financial databases.

Adaytum Software's *Planning* integrates budgeting links between cost centers, expense/sales, production plans, and cash flow analysis. Variance analysis is performed.

KCI Computing's *Control* is multidimensional and dynamic in handling budgets, planning models, consolidations, foreign currency translation, and cost allocations.

SAS Institute's *CFO Vision* software does costing by project, job, customer, and business segment. It performs financial consolidations, reporting, and analysis. It examines the reasons behind the figures and improves the timeliness and availability of business reporting.

Design Data Systems' *DDS Financial* integrates financial distribution, project management, and sales force modules.

TM1 software does multidimensional budgeting, forecasting, and reporting. It looks at various pricing scenarios, and evaluates the consequences of budget options.

Walker Interactive's *Business Framework Series* is used for budgeting, planning, forecasting, and analysis of cost and profitability.

Software 2000 Incorporated's *Infinium Financial Manager* performs purchase management, order processing, inventory control, quality control, and master production scheduling. It also does financial analysis, cost allocation, budgeting, specialized reporting, project management and currency management.

M-USA Business Systems' *Pacioli 2000* has modules for inventory control, job costing, budgeting, project control, cash management, assembly control and sales history.

Alcar is a strategic planning and appraisal software for Fortune 1000 companies. Users can assess if a plan or acquisition can be sufficiently funded by internal cash flow or outside financing.

Arbor Software's *Essbase* is a multidimensional database for business planning, evaluation, and management reporting.

Big Software's *Big Business* is a business management system integrating sales, marketing, inventory, and finance. It monitors inventory and tracks customers.

Synex Systems' *F9 Universal* software integrates budget reports.

Chief financial officers may use *CFO Spreadsheet Applications,* a spreadsheet template, for selecting optimal alternative capital investments and to manage cash flows.

Budget Express is a spreadsheet add-in facilitating "what-if" analysis comparing current to future values based on inputted changes. It makes the preparation of budgets and forecasts easy. For instance, by automatically totaling columns and rows, and calculating summary information by month, quarter, and year.

Pro Plan is a template used for financial planning and reporting. It prepares such financial statements as the income statement, balance sheet, and statement of cash flows. Ratio reports are also generated.

Profit Planner is a template used to project sales, cost of sales, operating expenses, assets, liabilities, and stockholders' equity. The financial figures for a company are compared to industry averages.

What-if Solver is an optimization add-in used to solve optimization problems subject to various constraints.

SRC Software's *Advisor Series* includes decision support, planning and forecasting, currency translations, and international consolidations. It handles complex budgeting and financial reporting situations.

Microcompass Systems' *QL Financials* is a software containing budget management, sales and purchase ordering, and inventory management. It has multicurrency features.

Social Systems' *Simplan* is used for integrated, multipurpose planning and budgeting. It can be used for revenue forecasting, econometric modeling, and time series analysis. In projecting sales, variables to be considered include selling price, units, availability of materials, interest rates, and market share.

Comshare's *Interactive Financial Planning System* (IFPS) is a multipurpose, interactive financial modeling system aiding in constructing, solving, and asking "what-if" questions of financial models. Interrelationships of data are considered. The output is in the form of spreadsheet. Data inputted into the model include revenue, selling price, volume, growth rate, variable cost, fixed cost, gross margin, contribution margin, net present value, internal rate of return, departmental figures, assets, working capital and market position. Alternative options to result in a desired outcome may also be presented. Information may be summarized in final form in terms of department, geographic region, product line, service line, customer, and supplier. IFPS has statistical functions that may be performed such as moving average, regression, and autocorrelation. Leading and lagging variables may be considered such as estimating future cash collections based on prior credit sales. There is a sampling routine based on examining the population considering the probability distribution. Sensitivity analysis (considering the effect of changing a variable on an outcome) is another feature of IFPS. There is also a goal seeking mode. Variables are analyzed as to their overall contributions. The software has graphic capabilities.

EXPRESS is used for financial planning and analysis including pro forma financial statements and risk analysis. There are statistical and analytical features such as percent difference, sorting, maximum-minimum, and leads and lags. Statistical functions include regression, cluster analysis, factor analysis, exponential smoothing, deseasonalization, and time series. There are graphic displays.

Ferox Microsystems' *ENCORE! PLUS* performs analytical functions and risk evaluation.

Micro Data Base's *GURU* is an expert system shell used to prepare reports, statistical analysis, and data management. The software provides managerial and financial advice for routine decisions.

Financial modeling for profit planning and budgeting can be done using a powerful spreadsheet program such as *Lotus 1-2-3, VP Planner, Javelin, Excel, SuperCalc, Quattro Pro, Educom Financial Planning Model* (EFPM), *XSIM, Empire, Foresight, Orion,* and *Venture.*

Ernst and Young's *Prosper* performs corporate financial planning and analysis of financial data. It prepares budgets and cash flow reports along with various visual presentations. It also performs investment analysis.

Smart Shop's *Cash Wise* prepares and evaluates cash flow projected statements to meet a company's strategic planning needs. It responds to "what-if" scenarios.

FuziWare Inc's *FuziCalc* is a unique spreadsheet that allows the decision maker to benefit from the structure of quantitative decision analysis, without forcing the user to provide very precise numerical inputs. The spreadsheet is based on the fuzzy set theory and fuzzy logic; it takes the computational complexity out of fuzzy arithmetic. Its primary strength is in modeling under uncertainty. As a spreadsheet, *FuziCalc* offers only the very basic features. Many features that one is accustomed to in conventional spreadsheets are lacking in *FuziCalc*. Most users will probably want *FuziCalc* to supplement, rather than replace, their conventional spreadsheet. *FuziCalc* is easy to use and offers powerful features to model decision making under uncertainty.

FORECASTING AND STATISTICS

There are numerous software for forecasting financial and nonfinancial information. Further, a spreadsheet template can produce sales and market forecasts for new products and services based on historical data.

Spreadware's *Pro Forma* prepares and analyzes pro forma financial statements. It tracks cash inflows and outflows, and conducts "what-if" evaluation among alternatives. Variance analysis is performed.

Business Matters Incorporated's *Cashe* is a comprehensive business forecasting and modeling software product. Financial planning is made easier through built-in formulas and linked relationships which may be adjusted with changing information. In-depth analysis is performed including that for changes in assumptions or scenarios. External factors are taken into account when forecasting such as changing interest rates. Analysis of variances, break-even, and risk evaluations are performed. It allows for the modification of business assumptions so financial forecasts may be reviewed, updated, and compared easily.

Geneva's *Statistical Forecasting* is a stand-alone package of forecasting data series over a specified time period (e.g., monthly). It includes linear and nonlinear regressions and exponential smoothing techniques.

Tomorrow is a forecasting software based on a mix of exponential smoothing and regression. Data used may be in up to 30 separate ranges. Seasonality adjustments are made. Forecasts may be made in different time series such as revenue by different geographic areas.

Forecast! GFX is a software for doing time series analyses (adjusted for seasonality), exponential smoothing, moving average, and decomposition. Trend applications are used to appraise data moving toward a lower limit. There is a multiple regression feature for a maximum of 10 explanatory variables used to explain a dependent variable.

Forecast Pro uses artificial intelligence in forecasting data while *Forecast Plus* uses artificial intelligence to evaluate data, and then selects an appropriate forecasting method among 13 available ones. There is optimization of smoothing constants and excellent graphics features.

ForeCalc is an add-in forecasting program. It can take historical data in a spreadsheet and, using exponential smoothing, determine the optimal projection based on the best fit of the data. The software also provides confidence limits. Information may be graphically displayed. Seasonal factors are considered in the model.

Sibyl/Runner is an interactive, stand-alone forecasting package allowing for data appraisal. It recommends the appropriate forecasting method for the given facts, compares results, and provides various accuracy measures.

Stat Plan IV is stand-alone software using statistics to solve business problems. It is very useful in management decision making. Data may be evaluated by range, standard deviation, mean, correlation, analysis of variance, and statistical significance. The forecasting methods include regression, autocorrelation, and exponential smoothing. Data may be graphically plotted including comparing actual to budget figures. Applications include trend depictions, financial modeling, and market appraisal.

Smart Forecasts automatically selects the best statistical technique to use based on the facts in a particular case. The approach allows for flexibility based on desired changes of the user via the program's *EYEBALL* utility. For example, the revenue projection is changed as changes are made in selling price, promotion plan, and consumers' disposal income. Forecasting may be in the form of moving averages and exponential smoothing. Seasonality can be adjusted, such as by using time series decomposition. It considers up to 60 variables.

Micro TSP involves econometric forecasting including descriptive statistics, multiple regression, and exponential smoothing.

Infordata Systems' *INQUIRE* is a special-purpose package used for decision support. Its features include query, data retrieval, and report generation.

Pendock Mallorn's *Pro-Forma Plus* is a financial forecasting model for preparing financial projections. "What-if" analysis for alternative assumptions is provided. It does variance, ratio, and break-even analysis.

General purpose statistical software include such packages as Statistical Package for Social Scientists (SPSS), Systat, Statgraphics, Statistical Analysis System (SAS), Statpack, and Minitab.

PROJECT PLANNING AND EVALUATION

Deltek Systems' *Costpoint* does project and activity accounting. It tracks by project costs and hours, compares estimates to actual for each task level, allocates costs, computes project revenue and profitability, tracks backlogs and purchase commitments, manages material, plans procurements, and fosters inventory control.

Concepts Dynamic's *CDI Project Control System* keeps track, manages, and reports revenue, cost, and time by major project.

Power Cerv's *INTERGY* software has features for order processing, purchasing, and project management.

Ross Systems' *The Renaissance CS Financials* monitors, projects and controls financial results. It includes features of purchase order, currency management, inventory control, budgeting, and bid tracking.

ProSoft Corporation's *Carpe Diem* software generates electronic timesheets and cost reports.

Marsh Software Systems' *Axiom Project Manager* tracks projects and performs job costing functions. There is an interface to financial software.

GBA Systems' *Pedigree Software* has modules for project accounting management and for preventive maintenance control.

Design Data Systems' *DDS Work Order Management* is for order entry and project reporting.

Design Data's *SQL*TIME* is software for project scheduling including scheduling for personnel and capital resources. It also resolves scheduling conflicts.

Open Systems' *Traverse* is an international accounting business software.

Proposed projects may be evaluated using the *Project Evaluation Toolkit* template. It uses various capital budgeting methods such as discounted cash flow analysis. Alternative scenarios may be appraised by changing variables such as cost or revenue projections, changes in timing of cash flows, and changes in beginning or interim dates.

CapPlans is a template appraising a proposed project using capital budgeting techniques such as payback period, internal rate of return, and net present value. It can forecast cash flows for up to 15 years. It prepares graphs and managerial reports. Sensitivity analysis routines are also included.

Computer Associates' *CA Masterpiece* performs job and project costing, inventory control, and time recording.

JBA International's *System 21* does costing by project and job, warehousing, work order processing, production control, manufacturing routing and scheduling, capacity planning, and analysis of material requirements.

J.D. Edward's *One World* does job- and project-cost accounting, time recording, warehouse management, production control, master production scheduling, routing, materials requirements planning, capacity requirements planning, and manufacturing control.

Oracle's *Financials* includes applications for job and project costing, work-order processing, production control and scheduling, bills of materials routing, plant capacity, and appraisals of materials.

FTP Software's *Group Works* enables efficient project organization, management, and execution. It performs scheduling assignments, tracks deadlines, assigns tasks, sets priorities, and monitors project status. The software also makes problem-solving suggestions.

CAPITAL BUDGETING

Worth It Software's *Worth It* does capital budgeting and analysis. It aids in the capital expenditure management process. The software is used to budget acquisitions by business units, project future operating changes, highlight negative trends, and appraise alternative investment plans and compare relative costs.

RISK ANALYSIS

Corporate risk may be analyzed using the spreadsheet add-in *@Risk*. It examines the effect of changing circumstances on the company's profitability, competitive reaction, and market position. Sampling methods are used for "what-if" analysis. The software indicates the degree of acceptability of the particular risk and recommends ways to reduce such risk including contingency plans.

Business Foundations' *Internal Operations Risk Analysis* appraises a company's areas of risk. It is an expert system developed around more than 150 interview questions. Based on the answers to the questions, the software prepares analytical and management reports summarizing the strengths and weaknesses in the company's operations. A risk rating (high, medium, low) is assigned to risk categories. It recommends for problem areas corrective steps. There is an upgrade for industry-specific situations.

Pleier and Associates' *ADM Plus* also performs risk management.

COST ACCOUNTING SYSTEMS

Maxwell Business Systems' *Job Cost Accounting and Management Information System* (JAMIS) is a job costing system. The software keeps track of employee hours worked, distributes (allocates) labor cost to the responsible unit, keeps track of department or product costs, distinguishes between direct labor and indirect labor, and manages inventory. Job costs are broken down into 100 different transactions. Since the software tracks all costs, it can also perform activity-based accounting because the jobs can be expressed in terms of activities or tasks. The activities can further be divided into subactivities or subtasks. Costs may be broken down by operation or function (e.g., buying materials). Costs may also be identified by division or department. JAMIS can also be used to budget by cost type (e.g., labor, materials and supplies). Costs may be tracked by project or contract for multiple years. It has time-based budgeting. It makes automated retroactive rate adjustments. The system supports contract types, cost classes, and job budgeting.

SouthWare Innovations' *Excellence Series* has features for job costing, contract management, service management and wholesale distribution.

Manufacturing Management Systems' *Quite-A-Profit* performs competitive pricing, target costing, and earnings appraisal by product or service.

Peachtree Accounting has a module for *Job Costing* to track and report the revenue, cost, and profit for individual jobs and projects.

Macola Software's *Progression Series Accounting and Distribution Software* has modules for job costing, inventory management, and shop floor control. It prepares many management reports, including those analyzing inventory and manufacturing operations.

Lawson Software's *Activity Manager* performs activity-based management and costing. It performs multi-dimensional data analysis, offers "what-if" scenarios, does cost allocations, performs inventory control, and aids in warehousing.

Abacus Data Systems' *ADAMS 4GL* aids in warehousing, shop-floor control, inventory control and management, work-order management, and customer analysis.

Prosoft's Inc's *Contractor Cost Accounting Package* offers speed and flexibility. The system is fully integrated and each module interacts with others. It offers modules for General Ledger, Accounts Payable, Job Costing, Payroll, Accounts Receivable, and Purchase Orders. Accounts are user-defined and can be referenced and accessed by name or by number. You can customize the program and its reports to suit your needs.

3C Software's *Impact* allows you to set up the system to use any cost accounting method—ABC, Traditional, Machine Based, Job, Direct, Japanese, JIT, or your own hybrid—so you can control how costs are calculated. It allows you to define the methodology, calculations, variables, products, processes, and reports. *Impact* contains an integrated, full-featured query and report writer which allows reports to be generated quickly and easily. Typical reports include: Product Cost Sheets, Product Pricing Sheets, Variance Reports, Inventory Valuations, Budgets and Forecasts, Profitability Reports, and other customized reports to meet cost reporting requirements.

ACTIVITY-BASED COSTING (ABC)

Activity-Based Costing (ABC) records cost based on manufacturing or service activities. Costs are assigned by activity and linked to the related products and services. Besides using spreadsheets for this purpose, there exists specialized software unique to ABC.

Price Waterhouse's *Activa* is activity-based software providing cost management for manufacturing and service companies. It does forecasting and simulation, product and service costing, activity-based budgeting, performance measurement reporting, profitability analysis, and valuing products and processes. It can manage information across multiple periods for multiple locations. For multinational companies, it can provide information in multiple currencies.

Armstrong Laing's *Hyper ABC* provides ABC costing information. It provides multidimensional cost object analysis which allows the user to evaluate business across customers, products, services, and distribution channels. It compares budget to actual figures for variance determination. "What-if" analysis is performed such as for the effects of changing variables on volume.

Sapling Software's *Net Prophet* does activity-based costing, constraint checking, capacity planning, "what-if" evaluation, scenario playing, and process analysis. It has flexible reporting, model validation, and graphic features.

ABC Technologies' *Oros EIS With Power Play* and *Oros 3.0* provide data warehousing, target costing, and process yield. They provide a picture of activity-based information through active charts, graphs, and crosstable formats. *Oros* does analysis of profitability and performance.

ICMS Software's *CMS-PC* software has spreadsheet-style screens for activity-based product costing. There is an activity dictionary database. The project manager helps with activity interview questions.

Syspro Impact Software's *IMPACT* ABC module appraises pre-production manufacturing and sales costs. There is online cost inquiry and simulated cost recovery.

Applied Computer Services' *PROFILE* ABC software performs analysis of activity data, profitability evaluation, appraisal of staffing requirements, reengineering, and makes activity-based management decisions.

Deloitte and Touche's *Strategic Cost Management* software assigns costs to activities, operations, products, and services. It manages cross-functional processes and involves "what-if" decision making.

Com MIT Systems' *Com MIT-ABC* tracks, collects, and allocates costs based on activities and cost drivers. "What-if" alternatives are evaluated.

Lead Software's *Activity Analyzer* involves product costing by activity and process. It tracks cycle time, capacity, cost drivers, rates, and manpower.

Automatic Consulting's *Cost Accounting System for Service Organizations* (CASSO) evaluates costs at the activity, work group and product levels.

There are many other software packages that may be used in activity-based costing including KPMG Peat Marwick's *Profit Manager,* Deloitte and Touche's *TR/ACM,* Coopers and Lybrand's *AB Cost Manager,* VanDeMark Products' *Alpha Cost,* Polaris Systems' *e3 System,* ABC Technologies' *Easy ABC,* and Marcam Corporation's *Prism.*

APPRAISAL OF INVENTORY

SQL Financials International's *Purchasing Control* is used to control the purchasing processes. It provides information about purchase orders, items, vendors, receipts, invoices, and payments.

Computer Associates' *ACCPAC* is a financial management software including order entry, inventory control, and job costing.

Lawson Software's *Insight Business Management System* includes supply chain and procurement, materials distribution, and audit controls.

Inventory Analyst is a template for computing economic order quantity, reorder point, and optimal inventory levels. Inventory history is depicted as a basis to predict future trends. It incorporates such forecasting techniques as moving average, exponential smoothing, and time series. Seasonal factors are incorporated.

Computron Software's *Computron Financials* does inventory stock control and time recording.

Dun & Bradstreet's *Smart Stream* does inventory stock control, warehousing, accounting for manufacturing processes, production scheduling and routing, and materials requirements planning.

Syspro Impact Software's *Impact Encore* does materials and resource planning to aid in cutting costs and improving delivery and quality. It has a purchase order system and can handle activity-based costing. It aids in tracking items through the production process.

Open Systems' *Accounting Software* inventory module features alternative costing and pricing methods including matrix pricing for customers. It can perform physical and cycle counts based on specified criteria. It also determines the level of inventory requiring a reorder. The package also has sales order functions.

Fourth Shift Corporation's *Manufacturing Software System* keeps track of inventory and manufacturing.

Best Ware's *MYOB* software's inventory module provides a listing of items, restocking information, and backorder listing.

EXECUTIVE MANAGEMENT GAMES

Computerized management games provide an excellent learning tool in making financial and managerial decisions so as to develop analytical and strategic abilities. The management game is a type of mathematical model and simulation. Simulation is designed to simulate a system and to generate a series of quantitative and financial results regarding system operations. In management games, participants make decisions at various stages in an attempt to better comprehend the external simulated environment. The games allow for a better understanding of the interrelationships of the various functions within the business and how such interactions affect overall performance. Some good management games are *PERT-SIM* for project planning and control, *Westinghouse Simulation Exercise* for distribution and logistics, *IBM Production Manpower Decision Model* for production and manpower scheduling, *MARKSIM* for marketing decision making, *X-Otol* for distribution analysis, Green and Sisson's *Materials Inventory Management Game* for inventory planning, and *FINASIM* for financial management simulation. (PERT stands for Program Evaluation and Review Technique which refers to the sequence of steps to complete a long-term project in the minimum time.) Other executive management games are Harvard University's *Harvard Business Game,* K. Goosen's *Management Accounting Game,* R. Schrieber's *Top Management Decision Game,* Carnegie Mellon's *COGITATE,* and R. Barton's *IMAGINIT Management Game.*

LINEAR PROGRAMMING

Linear programming is the allocation of limited capital and human resources to maximize gain or minimize cost. *Linear Interactive and Discrete Optimization* (LINDO) can be used to obtain optimal solutions.

What's Best! is a linear programming software aiding in determining the optimal allocation of limited capital, human, and financial resources. It considers time constraints and is ideal for management decision making. The objective of the software is to maximize revenue or minimize cost.

FLOWCHARTING

Flowcharts are diagrams that use standardized symbols, interconnected with flow lines, to visually represent complex procedures and data flow. People generally understand pictures better than words, and visual representation of data can often enhance understanding. Accountants can use flowcharts to document and understand the processing of information through the accounting system. Flowcharting software allows users to illustrate policies, processes, and procedures with diagrams. Typical flowcharting packages allow users to create diagrams for process and data flows, hierarchy charts, fishbone diagrams, structure charts, cause and effect diagrams, and organizational charts. Most packages contain templates or specialized libraries for symbols typically used by accountants and other professionals. It is also possible to create a custom library composed of frequently used shapes.

Micrografx Inc's *ABC FlowCharter* is a powerful and easy-to-use package. You can "drag and drop" hundreds of shapes from its extensive template library.

HavenTree Software Ltd.'s *EasyFlow* is a specialized drawing program. It uses the "drag and drop" approach to flowcharting. The user selects shapes from a palette and drops them into the appropriate place in the work area. *EasyFlow* comes with excellent documentation and tutorials.

Clear Software's *allCLEAR* takes a unique approach to flowcharting. To create a flowchart in *allCLEAR,* you write a script in the form of an outline. The punctuation in the script determines how the flowchart will look. The script approach makes it easy to create and modify even complicated flowcharts. However, the script approach greatly restricts the user's ability to customize flowcharts.

Patton & Patton Software Corp's *Flow Charting* is a good choice for the flowcharting beginner. It is a specialized drawing program and utilizes the drag and drop approach to flow charting. It comes with an excellent tutorial.

Aldus Corp.'s *IntelliDraw* is a powerful diagramming and illustration package. It is not exclusively a flowcharting package. *IntelliDraw* is ideal if you work with many types of drawings, and flowcharting is just one of your many needs.

Micrografx Inc.'s *ABC SnapGraphics* is a general purpose drawing and illustration package. It offers an easy-to-use interface and makes extensive use of drag and drop capabilities. It is ideal for an individual that prefers ease of use over esoteric features.

Shapeware Corp's *Visio* offers users a choice of drag and drop or script approach. Drawing flowcharts with *Visio* is very similar to manually drawing flowcharts. *Visio* works with computerized versions of plastic stencils that include cutouts for various symbols.

INTERNET AND WORLD WIDE WEB

There are many online databases of interest to financial managers. These can be used to obtain information in making corporate decisions. These databases offer accounting, audit, tax, finance, economic, management, marketing, production, regulatory, and legal information. The most important online databases available on the Internet are discussed in this chapter. Online databases improve decision making and analysis, allow management to improve their appraisal and evaluation of financial information, add value to the company by creating new products and services through information exchange and processing, and perform searches of relevant information.

Electronic databases may be classified by presentation methodology. The methodologies include text, number, image (video), audio, electronic services, and software. In a text-based database, the user performs searches using text phrases in order to find specific information. Text-based databases include bibliographic, directory, dictionary, full text, and others. Numeric databases are used mostly for transactions and for obtaining statistical data. Multimedia audio and graphical databases are gaining popularity. Bulletin board services are another form of online database which have a wide variety of data which can be downloaded.

The World Wide Web (Web) portion of the Internet has a rapidly growing number of online business databases. These databases use multimedia graphical and audio features with hypertext links to other data and resources. Users need a Web browser (such as Netscape's Navigate or Microsoft's Internet Explorer) in order to read a graphical Web database. Web online business databases are an important resource because they link to other Internet resources including text files, Telnet (standard Internet protocol for remote terminal connection service), Gophers (a distributed information service that makes available hierarchical collections of information across the Internet), Usenet newsgroups, and other portions of the Internet.

COMMERCIAL ONLINE SERVICES

This section discusses those commercial online services of interest and assistance to financial managers in performing their duties. They include:

- **Lexis/Nexis** (800-346-9759). This service uses its own research software to search in specific industries including public relations and law. It is the most popular database of legal data including case decisions and previous testimony of expert witnesses. In addition to case records, files of state and federal codes and regulations are available on everything from banking to hazardous waste. This includes law review and journal articles. It has a collection of U.S. patents and public records data including corporate reports filed with government agencies. Individual libraries exist on Lexis such as a bankruptcy library. There are also electronic editions of basic legal reference tools such as the *Martindale-Hubbell Law Directory*. Also, Lexis contains the *American Law Reports*, which is a useful legal research tool. The Lexis online service allows you to search geographically and narrow your search by state.

- **West's Law Tax.** Provides legal and tax information.

- **Total Online Tax and Accounting Library** (800-862-4272). An online service available from the American Institute of CPAs. It includes the National Automated Accounting Research System (NAARS) which provides information contained in the annual reports of companies, showing how they handle their accounting, reporting, and disclosure matters.

U.S. GOVERNMENT'S STAT-USA ONLINE SERVICE

The U.S. government provides online information of interest to corporate financial managers. Timely business and economic information from over fifty Federal agencies is available. STAT-USA/Internet provides over 300,000 reports and statistical series online, including press releases, trade leads, and reports that are released on a daily or weekly basis. Financial managers interested in obtaining access for multiple users should call 202-482-1986. STAT-USA databases include:

- **Bureau of Economic Analysis (BEA) Economic Information.** An authoritative online news release source for Survey of Current Business issues, and for detailed data files from BEA's national, regional, and international economic accounts.

- **Bureau of Economic Analysis, U.S. Department of Commerce.** Gross domestic product press release with corporate profits, economic indicators summary text file; leading, coincident, and lagging indexes release; and personal income and outlays.

- **Bureau of the Census, U.S. Department of Commerce.** New construction, durable goods, shipments and orders, new home sales, housing starts, manufacturing and trade inventories and sales, advance retail sales, shipments, inventories and orders, and U.S. international trade in goods and services.

- **Bureau of Labor Statistics, U.S. Department of Labor.** The Employment Situation, Consumer Price Index, Producer Price Index, and Productivity and Cost Preliminary.

- **Economic Bulletin Board/Lite Edition.** This is a comprehensive Internet source for government-sponsored economic releases and business leads. It provides in-depth analyses of markets, products, exports, and economic trends.

- **Federal Reserve Board.** This provides commentary on current economic conditions, industrial production and capacity utilization, bank credit, consumer credit, foreign exchange rates, interest rates, and money stock data.

- **The Global Business Opportunities Service.** This is an international marketplace for U.S. businesses, providing procurement opportunities from all over the world.

- **The Census Bureau's Merchandise Trade Export and Import Statistics.** This makes available information on commodities by country.

- **The Economic Bulletin Board.** This provides late-breaking business developments and provides in-depth analyses of markets, products, and economic trends.

ONLINE BUSINESS DATABASES

Online databases that financial managers can access to obtain information in rendering business and financial decisions include:

- **Access Business Online.** This is an all-in-one business center. It offers financial executives headline news, press releases, links to financial markets, company profiles, upcoming trade shows and seminars, and search capability of vendors in various industries. Exec-U-Net is an excellent tool for business executives to communicate with other business executives and senior professionals. There is a provision for import/export exchange and world wide finance.

- **Advertising and Marketing Intelligence.** A bibliographic database abstracting articles from advertising, marketing, and media publications. It includes information on products and services. It is updated daily. Information may be obtained by calling (201) 267-2268.

- **FinanceNET ... FASAB.** The Federal Accounting Standards Advisory Board provides up-to-date information on issues in financial management and accounting.
- **Internal Auditing World Wide Web.** Comprehensive web sites for internal auditors.
- **Kaplan's Audit Net Resource List.** A directory of accounting and auditing resources, updated monthly.
- **Moody's Investors Service.** A corporate financial service available online through Dialog (212) 553-0546.
- **National Automated Accounting Research System (NAARS).** Contains the full text, including footnotes and auditor's report, of the financial statements of over 4,200 company annual reports. NAARS also includes the complete text of a wide variety of authoritative accounting literature, such as Statements on Auditing Standards (SAS), Accounting Research Bulletins (ARBs), and Accounting Standards Executive Committee (ASEC) position papers and issue papers.
- **Netsurfer Focus.** Contains guidance on computer and network security.
- **New York State Society of CPAs' Luca Online.** A database of accounting, auditing, and tax information.
- **Rutgers Accounting Web.** Has a link to nearly every accounting-related site on the Internet. The Rutgers web server acts as a web site for the American Institute of CPAs, Institute of Management Accountants, Institute of Internal Auditors, Financial Accounting Standards Board, and American Accounting Association, among others. There is a database on "Improving Business Reporting," that can be accessed through the AICPA web site. The Institute of Management Accountants offers case studies in management accounting practices and techniques such as implementing activity-based costing. Hundreds of accounting firms can be accessed at this web site.

INTERNET SERVICES AND THE WORLD WIDE WEB

Databases available through the Internet use four types of internet services. They are Gopher, Telnet, Anonymous File Transfer Protocol, and the World Wide Web.

Gophers use a series of menus to easily access any type of textual information available on the Internet. While there are some stand-alone Gopher services, the wide majority interconnect with other Gopher services allowing simple information access. A Gopher's ease of use results from a simple standard menu interface. A Gopher search may be a document that can be read and saved, or a database that is searched according to a user-supplied keyword.

Telnet allows users to access and log in to a remote Internet computer site and then run the computer software at that site. Telnet is the Internet standard protocol for remote terminal connection service. It uses a series of commands to communicate with other computers. On the Internet, Telnet acts as the intermediary between your computer (the local computer) and the other computer (referred to as the remote computer). To reach a particular computer, a user would have to enter a Telnet address and then "Telnet" to the remote computer.

File transfer protocol (FTP) allows Internet users to copy computer files from a remote server to the user's computer. Anonymous file transfer protocol allows a user to retrieve documents, files, programs, and archived data from anywhere on the Internet. By using the special user identification of "anonymous" the network user will bypass local security checks and will have access to publicly accessible files on the remote system without having to establish a user ID and password.

The Web accesses all parts of the Internet, and allows information to be presented in creative multimedia formats using video, color graphics, animation, sound, and hypertext links between other text and databases with data downloading capabilities. Web browser software is necessary to use the Web.

Online databases available on the Internet of interest to financial managers are as follows:

- **Advertising Law Internet Site.** This site provides a guide to Federal Trade Commission regulations on advertising, guides to state business opportunity laws, and privacy concerns about customer mailing lists (http://www.webcom.com/^lewrose/home.html).

- **Asia Pacific Business and Marketing Resources.** This site contains information on business and management in Asia. Other resources include market reports for specific countries (gopher.hoshi.cic.sfu.ca:70/11/dlam/business).

- **Canadian Business Infoworld.** A Canadian business directory including business resources (http://csclub.uwaterloo.ca/u/nckwan).

- **Commerce Information Locator Service.** Assists the user in finding business, economic, scientific, and technical information (http://www.fedworld.gov).

- **Commercial Sites Index.** A directory of commercial services, products, and information on the Internet (http://www.directory.net).

- **Construction and Engineering Industries.** This construction network offers Internet access and a bulletin board service for members of the architecture, engineering, and construction industries (http://www.aecnet.com).
- **Dun and Bradstreet Information Services.** This site contains information on global and technical marketing, credit/risk assessment including predicting slow payers, managing vendors, company history, business background of management, purchasing, planning, and operations review (http://www.dbisna.com).
- **EXPO Guide Home Page.** This is an index of trade shows, searchable by date, location, or keyword (http://www.expoguide.com).
- **Federal Reserve Board.** Contains flow of funds tables, industrial production and capacity utilization, and money stock measure and components (gopher://town.hall.org:70/11/other/fed).
- **Franchise Source.** Directory of franchise opportunities searchable by initial investment category or type of business (http://www.axxs.com/source.html).
- **Insurance Industry.** An insurance industry information news page which compiles reports pertaining to property and casualty coverage (http://www.newspage.com).
- **International Trade Law Project.** Provides information for legal research on international trade law (http://ananse.irv.uit.no/trade_law/nav/trade.html).
- **Internet Bankruptcy Library.** This site offers frequently asked questions on bankruptcy filings, news updates, a directory of international bankruptcy professionals, and pointers related to bankruptcy issues (http://bankrupt.com).
- **Internet Business Center.** An extensive site providing detailed information on every aspect of electronic business, especially marketing (http://www.tig.com).
- **Internet Business Opportunity Showcase.** An advertising space intended to match entrepreneurs with potential investors (http://www.clark.net/pub/ibos).
- **Internet Law Library, Code of Federal Regulations.** Gives partial access to, and search capabilities for, federal regulations (http://www.pls.com:8001/his/cfr.html).
- **Internet Marketing Archives.** A fully indexed, searchable entry form of the Internet Marketing List (http://www.popco.com/hyper/internet-marketing).

- **McNeil's Tax Sites.** Contains a comprehensive list of tax resources including domestic and foreign tax laws (http:www.best.com/-ftmexpat/html/taxsites.html).

- **NAFTA Watch.** A forum for NAFTA-inspired business opportunities in Mexico (http://www.aescon.com/naftam/index.htm).

- **National Bureau of Economic Research Home Page.** This site contains information on the bureau with links to online data, major programs and projects, and publications. The database has links to other sites with economic data (http:nber.harvard.edu/).

- **National Locator and Data.** A database of reports on such subjects as commercial credit reports, corporate records, compensation claims, and public records (http://www.iu.net/hodges).

- **Overseas Business Reports.** Provides information on the economic environment of various countries. The database contains information on trade agreements, economic outlook, government attitude towards trade, economic policy, fees, customs, recent trends, and list of organizations and contacts (gopher:umslvama.umsl.edu:70/11/library/govdocs/obr).

- **SEC EDGAR.** This searchable Securities Exchange Commission online database provides access to financial information on all publicly-traded companies. This site includes Daily SEC News and Digest, and rule-making proposals and final rules. SEC forms are also available (http://www.sec.gov/edgarhp.html).

- **STO's Internet Patent Search System.** Provides search forms for determining patent class using the Manual of Classification or the Index to Classification, retrieve patent titles using class/subclass code, and/or retrieve patent abstracts using a patent number (http://sunsite.unc.edu/patents/intropat.html).

- **The Construction Site.** Provides the construction industry with information on advertising, legal matters, and trade secrets (http://www.constr.com).

- **Thomas Register Supplier Finder.** Allows one to search for product or service information and vendors that offer them (http://www.thomasregister.com).

- **U.S. Census Bureau.** Contains tables and narrative interpretations for census summaries of manufacturers, retail, service, and wholesale industries (http://www.census.gov).

- **U.S. Copyright Law.** Provides copyright information including regulations, law, and court decisions (http://www.law.cornell.edu:80/topics/copyright.html).

- **U.S. Patent Law.** Provides information on patents including regulations, law, and court decisions (http:/www.law.cornell.edu:80/topics/patent.html).

- **United States Patent and Trademark Office.** Provides keyword searching of index of trademark goods and services, as well as trademark and patent application advice. It includes information on patent law, software patents, and information security (http://www.uspto.gov).

- **University of Michigan Statistics.** Provides access to U.S. Department of Commerce statistical files containing information on employment, export, gross national product, etc. (gopher://una.hh.lib.umich.edu:70/11/ebb).

CD-ROM BUSINESS DATABASES

The financial manager may wish to refer to various CD-ROM business databases to obtain information in making prudent decisions. Most of these databases have multimedia features. They include the following:

- **Research Institute of America Tax Service.** A comprehensive database of tax information including Internal Revenue Service regulations and rules, and case law.

- **The National Economic Social and Environmental Data Bank.** This includes information on socio-economic programs and trends in the United States. It covers business statistics, capital and equipment, consumer expenditures, economic conversion, employment statistics, energy information, financial statistics, government policy statements and analysis, pollution data, overseas industrial production statistics, and commodity information. There are projections and indicators included in some areas.

- **The National Trade Data Bank.** This provides export opportunities by industry, country, and product; foreign companies or importers looking for specific products; how-to market guides; demographic, political, and socio-economic conditions in hundreds of countries; and much more. The database includes information on agricultural commodity production and trade, export information, capital markets and export financing, country reports on economic and social policies and trade practices, energy production, supply and inventories, exchange rates, export licensing information, guides to doing business in foreign countries, international trade directory, international finance assistance, international trade regulations/agreements, employment and productivity, maritime and shipping information, market research reports, overseas contacts, overseas and domestic industry information, trade opportunities, U.S. export regulations, U.S. import and export statistics by country and commodity, and world minerals production.

- **U.S. Global Trade Outlook.** This site contains updated statistics for many industries including tracking industry shipments, employment, capital investment, imports, and exports.

FAXBACK SERVICES

A faxback service delivers specified documents directly to your fax machine. Most faxback services offer an index of documents. They include the following:

- **AMERI-FAX** (202-482-1495). It provides documents on the North American Free Trade Agreement (NAFTA). It is useful for financial managers interested in Mexican, Canadian, and Latin American markets.
- **BISNIS Fax Retrieval System** (202-501-3144). It provides a fax retrieval service for the Russian Federation, including business contacts, import and export documents, periodicals, electronic databases, trade overviews, banking, tariff schedules, trade shows, and related items.
- **Canada Business Service Centre Faxback System** (604-775-5515). It includes business information about Canada such as agriculture, business startup and management, communications, environment, marketing and strategic alliances, research and development, science and technology, taxation, trade, and government programs.
- **Eastern Europe Flashfax** (202-482-5745). It provides information on Eastern Europe, including current trade and business opportunities, sources of financing, multilateral development, venture capital, pending trade events, and country information.
- **Export Hotline** (617-248-9393). It provides reports on countries and industries including industry analyses and marketing strategies.
- **Faxlink Information Service** (613-944-6500). It provides data about Canadian business contacts, government programs, industry sector profiles, and newsletters.
- **Japan Export Promotion Hotline** (202-482-4565). It provides information about doing business in Japan including how to build business relationships, Japanese distribution system business negotiations, direct marketing, Japanese beer market, trademark registration, customs

clearance and regulations, Japanese banking, and construction and reconstruction opportunities.

- **NAFTA FACTS** (202-482-4464). It includes coverage of NAFTA provisions, rules of origin and customs information, tariff schedules, and doing business in Mexico and Canada.
- **STAT-USA/FAX** (202-482-0005). A source for current business, economic, and international trade information.
- **The USTR Fax Service** (202-395-4809). It provides trade press releases, reports, treaties, and announcements from the Office of the U.S. Trade Representative. It provides trade policies regarding various nations and regions of the world. It is a tool for understanding difficulties in certain regions and assessing new trade opportunities resulting from changes in international trade policies. It explains the General Agreement on Trade and Tariffs (GATT).
- **Trade Information Center Hotline** (202-501-3144). This provides general export information, information on specific U.S. government export programs, alternative trade finance options, trade leads, national trade data bank locations, and a national export directory by state and industry.

INTRANETS

Intranets are internal company networks that use the infrastructure and standards of the Internet and the World Wide Web. In other words, it is a *small version* of the Internet. Since intranets use Internet technology, there is ready access to external data. Intranets are in effect internal Web sites. An intranet is an important tool to use in business. An intranet is developed and used by a company. An intranet is of relatively minor cost and time to develop. It is fairly easy to install and flexible in use. What is developed for one platform may be used for others. If you already have a traditional network, it may be easily converted into an intranet structure.

Financial managers must be familiar with the intranet structure and organization because it raises managerial advisory consulting, accounting, tax, audit, control, and security issues and concerns. Managers, customers, employees, stockholders, potential investors, creditors, loan officers, government agent representatives (SEC, IRS), and other interested parties can access the database or information in a company through *Web browsers (interfaces)* such as Netscape's Navigator and Microsoft's Internet Explorer. When a company sets up an intranet so that it can be accessed by someone outside the company (e.g., vendors), it is referred to as an extranet.

Management may set up an intranet to improve operating efficiencies and productivity and to reduce operating costs (e.g., distribution expenses), time, and errors. Of course, keeping information on the intranet current takes time and resources. Controls must exist to prevent unauthorized access of the company's data through the Internet. One control device is the development and use of firewalls (barriers) to *protect* the company's intranet by unauthorized traffic from entering the intranet and misusing it to alter accounting and financial information, stealing assets, obtaining confidential information, or committing other inappropriate or fraudulent acts. Further, add-on security tools are available to restrict usage by users such as preventing them from doing certain things or viewing certain "restricted" data.

In an intranet, one protocol connects all users to the Web server. Intranets run on standard protocols supported by any computer.

APPLICATION FEATURE SET

Intranets offer the following application feature set:

- easy navigation (internal home page has links to data)
- rapid prototyping (measurable in hours or days)
- can be tied to "legacy" information sources (e.g., groupware databases)
- accessible via most computing platforms
- scaleable (start small, build as requirements allow)
- extensible to media types (video, audio, interactive applications)
- can integrate distributed computing strategy (localized web servers residing near the content author)

There are many advantages to this feature set including:

- Inexpensive in dollars or infrastructure to establish
- More timely than traditional information (paper) delivery
- More efficient utilization of computing resources
- Open platform architecture means large (and increasing) number of add-on applications
- Allows companies to evolve from a "calendar" or "schedule" based publishing strategy to one of an "event-driven" or "needs-based" publishing strategy
- Reduction in costs and time of content development, duplication, distribution, and usage

PRACTICAL APPLICATIONS

The uses of intranets (and extranets) by companies are unlimited, including:

- Furnishing outside CPAs with accounting, audit, and tax information.
- Providing marketing and sales information to current and prospective customers.
- Providing information to salespersons in the field and managers at different branches (e.g., sales and profit reports).
- Furnishing resource needs and reports to suppliers.

- Communicating corporate information to employees such as company policies and forms, operating instructions, job descriptions, human resource data and documents, business plans, newsletters, and fringe benefit packages.
- Assisting in employee training and development.
- Transferring to government agencies (e.g., Department of Commerce, SEC, IRS) relevant information.
- Furnishing current and prospective investors with profitability, growth, and market value data.
- Providing lenders and creditors with useful liquidity and solvency data.
- Providing project, proposal and scheduling data to participating companies in joint ventures (e.g., Boeing and McDonnell Douglas).
- Providing press releases and product/service announcements.
- Giving legal information to outside attorneys involved in litigation matters.
- Providing trade associations with input for their surveys.
- Furnishing information to outside consultants (e.g., investment management advisors, pension planners).
- Providing insurance companies with needed information to draft or modify needed insurance protection.
- Furnishing economic statistics about the company to economic advisors.
- Facilitating database queries and document requests.
- Providing spreadsheets, database reports, tables, checklists, and graphs to interested parties.
- Displaying e-mail.

An intranet requires Web application development for its internal network such as appropriate Web servers. For quick response time, there should be a *direct connection* to the server. Web browsers may be used to achieve cross-platform viewing and applications for a wide variety of desktops used within the company. The use of Web technology (e.g., Web servers) allows each desktop having a Web browser to access corporate information over the existing network. Therefore, employees in different divisions of the company located in different geographic areas (e.g., buildings) can access and use centralized and/or scattered information (cross section).

There are many client/server applications within and among companies, such as cross-platform applications. The major element in an intranet is the Web server software which runs on a central computer and serves as a clearinghouse for all information. Web servers for the intranet are available from many vendors including:

- IBM (800-426-2255). Internet Connection Server for MVS.
- Microsoft (800-426-9400). Internet Information Server (comes with Microsoft's NT Server).
- Netscape (415-528-2555). Fast Track and Commerce Server for Windows NT.
- Lotus (800-828-7086). InterNotes Web Publisher.
- CompuServe (800-848-8199). Spry Web Server for Windows NT.
- Quarterdeck (800-683-6696). Web Server and Web Star for Windows 95/NT.

The authors believe that advantages of the Microsoft's Windows NT Server are higher security and easier capability to upgrade to more powerful hardware at a later date as application needs increase.

Further, there are many intranet tool vendors such as Illustra Information Technologies (http://www.illustra.com). Telephone number (510) 652-8000) and Spider Technologies (http://www.w3spider.com). Telephone number (415) 969-7149). For example, the authors recommend as an intranet tool Frontier Technologies' Intranet Genie which includes a fairly secure Web server, HTML authoring instructions and guidelines (discussed below), Web browser, and e-mail functions. Regardless of the operating system used by the client (e.g., Windows, Unix, Macintosh), many intranet tools are available.

HYPERTEXT MARKUP LANGUAGE (HTML)

The authors recommend the use of a Hypertext Markup Language (HTML) in developing intranets because it is an *easier* Graphical User Interface (GUI) to program than window environments such as Motif or Microsoft Windows. HTML is a good integrating tool for database applications and information systems. It facilitates the use of hyperlinks and search engines enabling the easy sharing of identical information among different responsibility segments of the client company. Intranet data usually goes from back-end sources (e.g., mainframe host) to the Web server to users (e.g., customers) in HTML format.

COMMON GATEWAY INTERFACE (CGI)

The majority of Web applications run through a mechanism in the Web server referred to as the common gateway interface (CGI). CGI is used to connect users to databases. Most CGI programs are written in TCL or Perl (a scripting language). However, due to the fact that these languages involve printing a source code of the Web server, there is an unsecured situation from a control and security standpoint. Other deficiencies are relative slowness in applications, non-existence or inadequate debuggers, and maintenance problems. The authors suggest considering other languages for the CGI such as C or C++.

The authors recommend the following for CGI business applications:

1. In developing Web applications for intranets, code management tools are needed to enable different participants in a corporate project or activity to communicate and work together. You must also use tools for database design, modeling, and debugging. In this connection, the following Web sites, among others, provide helpful information to financial managers:

   a. Basic HTTP

      (http://www.w3.org/hypertext/www/protocols/http/http2.html)

   b. HTML Browser List

      (http://www.w3org/hypertext/www/clients.html)

   c. Web Server Comparison Chart

      (http://www.proper.com/www/servers-chart.html)

   d. HTML Specs from the WWW Consortium

      (http://www.w3.org/hypertext/www/markup/markup.html)

   e. Introduction to CGI

      (http://hoo.hoo.ncsa.uiuc.edu/docs/cgi:/overview.html)

2. Do not commit to a particular server or browser because new technological developments require flexibility on your part. Therefore, you should set up your system so that it may accommodate many servers and browsers.

3. Make sure your HTML user interface is separated from the database and application logic.

SETTING UP AN INTRANET

Intranet applications can start small and grow. This feature allows companies to experiment with an Intranet pilot to publish a limited amount of content on a single platform, and appraise the results. If the pilot shows promise, additional content can be migrated to the intranet server.

SITE CONTENT

Key database applications include customer records, product information, inventory, technical problem tracking, investment information, training material, employee data, geographic reporting, salesperson performance, credit analysis, financial analysis, manufacturing schedules, and call reports. The financial manager can gain timely access to a wide variety of information residing in a variety of original forms and sources such as databases and spreadsheets.

Business Law

CONTRACTS

While the corporate controller is not ordinarily trained in legal matters, he or she is often relied upon to recognize situations requiring the need for legal counsel. When contracts are drawn, the controller is often consulted on accounting and other business matters. The area of contracts therefore represents an area with which the controller needs some basic familiarity.

By definition, a contract is a legally enforceable agreement, and is governed by (1) Article 2 of the Uniform Commercial Code (UCC) if the contract pertains to the sale of tangible personal property (i.e., goods), and (2) common law if the subject matter covered by the contract is real estate, services or intangibles.

Types of Contracts

Essentially, there are nine types of contracts:

1. An *executory* contract is based on conditions that have not yet been fully performed by both parties to the contract.
2. An *executed* contract is created when both parties have fully performed the conditions required by the contract.
3. An *express* contract involves an agreement expressed in words, whether spoken or written.
4. An *implied* contract is a contract that is inferred as a result of the acts or conduct of the parties involved.
5. A *bilateral* contract arises when one promise is given in exchange for another.

6. A *unilateral* contract involves an offer of a promise and an act that is committed as a result of reliance on the promise.

7. A *quasi*-contract represents an obligation created by law in order to prevent unjust enrichment.

8. A *void* contract is a contract without any legal obligations on the part of each party.

9. A *voidable* contact is a contract that may be avoided or ratified by one or more of the parties.

Elements of Contracts

The four elements required for a contract are agreement, consideration, legality, and capacity of the parties.

Agreement involves an offer and acceptance. The terms of an offer must be definite and must demonstrate an intent to incur a legal obligation. To be valid, an offer must be communicated to the offeree by the offeror (or his or her agent) and is deemed to be effective when the offeree receives it. The offeree may accept an offer until it is terminated. In general, an offer will terminate if (1) the offer has expired (i.e., it is not accepted within the time specified or within a reasonable period of time, if no time is stipulated), (2) the offer is revoked at any time prior to acceptance, (3) the offer is rejected, (4) a counter-offer is made, (5) either party dies or becomes disabled, (6) the subject matter of the offer is destroyed, or (7) the subject matter of the offer subsequently becomes illegal. In connection with point "2," it should be noted that certain offers are irrevocable. An option contract, which is irrevocable, involves an offer supported by consideration; therefore, it cannot be withdrawn prior to the expiration of the stated period of time, or a reasonable period of time if no time is specified. A firm offer, which is also irrevocable, involves a merchant who makes a written offer to buy or sell goods and specifies that the offer will remain open for a specified period. Finally, in a unilateral contract, even though the act necessary to accept the offer has not been completed, performance has begun, and the offer becomes irrevocable.

Acceptance of the offer must be unequivocal. Accordingly, the offeree cannot alter or qualify the provisions of the offer. Acceptance may be effected by any reasonable means of communication, unless a specific means of acceptance is stipulated by the offeror. Acceptance is generally effective upon dispatch (e.g., when mailed).

As noted, consideration is a necessary element of a contract. As such, both parties to the contract must give consideration. For consideration to exist, there must be legal sufficiency (i.e., something of value) and a bargained-for exchange. It should be noted, however, that some types of transactions do not require consideration for enforcement. For example, promissory estoppel, also known as the doctrine of detrimental reliance, prevents the promisor from pleading lack of consideration for his or her promise where he or she has induced the promisee to make a substantial change of position in reliance thereon. In addition, no consideration is necessary in order to modify contracts for the sale of goods.

The subject matter of a contract must be legal. An agreement will be illegal and unenforceable when formation or performance of an agreement is criminal, tortious, or otherwise opposed to public policy. In these circumstances, the contract is void.

Capacity of the parties is also necessary for a contract to be valid. While a contract made by a minor is voidable at his or her election, it may be ratified upon reaching majority. Further, a contract made by a legally insane person is generally voidable. Where one has been legally declared insane, attempted contracts are void. Lastly, with respect to an intoxicated individual, a contract is voidable if the degree of intoxication was such that the individual did not realize he or she was entering into a contract.

The Statute of Frauds

Pursuant to the statute of frauds, to be enforceable, certain executory contracts must be in writing and signed by the party to be charged with performance. The written contract may be formal or informal and may be set forth in one or more documents, but must clearly indicate the parties, specify the subject matter and essential terms, and include the signature of the party against whom enforcement is sought. The contracts covered by the statute of frauds include, but are not limited to:

1. Contracts involving the sale of goods with a price of at least $500.
2. Contracts involving the sale of investment securities.
3. Contracts conveying an interest in real property.
4. Contracts that cannot be performed within one year after the contract is made.
5. Contracts of guaranty.

Needless to say, there are exceptions to the statute of frauds. For example, with respect to sales of real property, under the doctrine of part performance, an oral contract is enforceable if the buyer makes full or partial payment, and either (1) the buyer takes possession of the property (with the seller's approval), or (2) valuable and permanent improvements have been made to the property by the buyer. With respect to the sale of goods, an oral contract will fall outside the statute of frauds if the contract covers specially manufactured goods. A written contract is also unnecessary with respect to goods that have been accepted or for which payment has been made. Finally, it should be obvious that the statute of frauds in not applicable when a party admits in court that a contract was in fact made.

The Parol Evidence Rule

Any written or oral evidence that is not contained in the written contract is known as parol evidence. The parol evidence rule stipulates that no parol evidence of any prior or contemporaneous agreement will be allowed to change or otherwise modify any of the terms or provisions of an existing written agreement. The parol evidence rule, however, is sometimes inapplicable. For example, the rule does not apply (1) to contracts that are partly written and partly verbal, (2) to an obvious clerical or typographical error, or (3) when it is necessary to explain terms that are ambiguous.

Conclusion

The controller should be able to recognize when a contract exists. Accordingly, he or she must understand the basic elements of a contract. Further, the controller needs to be cognizant of the statute of frauds and the parol evidence rule. Not being a legal expert, the controller should contact the appropriate legal counsel if he or she perceives that (1) a contract has been breached, (2) a contract is not valid, or (3) a modification to a contract is being attempted.

SALES

Generally accepted accounting principles require that a sale be afforded accounting recognition upon its execution.

In general, the concepts of contract law are applicable to sales. It should be obvious that the seller is required to deliver the full agreed-upon quantity to the buyer. Unless otherwise stipulated, if a carrier is involved, the seller's delivery obligation depends on the pertinent shipment terms (i.e., F.O.B. shipping point or F.O.B. destination point). The place of delivery is deemed to be the seller's place of business, however, if no carrier is involved. The buyer is of course entitled to full delivery and has the right to reject delivery of a partial or excess quantity. Upon acceptance, however, the buyer will be responsible for those items accepted. In general, the buyer has the right to examine goods prior to accepting them or paying for them. However, with respect to Collect on Delivery (C.O.D.) sales, payment by the buyer is necessary before inspection. Said payment does not constitute acceptance and any nonconforming goods may be rejected.

Remedies for Breach

The various remedies for breach of a sales contract are dependent upon which party caused the breach.

Seller. If the buyer causes the breach, the seller may generally withhold delivery. If a down-payment was received by the seller, and a liquidating damages clause is not included in the contract, then the seller is entitled to keep the smaller of 20% of the purchase price or $500. The excess down-payment must therefor be returned to the buyer.

A breach on the part of the buyer also entitles the seller to stop delivery of goods in transit or in possession of a third party.

Further, the seller may reclaim goods if demand is made within ten days of receipt by an insolvent buyer.

In situations where the seller has attempted to deliver nonconforming goods, the seller has the right to notify the buyer of an intent to cure and deliver conforming goods within the time limits specified in the original contract.

With respect to manufactured goods, the seller is permitted to complete manufacture of unfinished goods, identify them to the contract, and sell them, or cease their manufacture and sell the remainder for scrap. In any event the seller is entitled to recover the difference between the contract and selling prices.

Finally, in certain instances, the seller may either cancel the contract or sue for the contract price and/or damages. Legal counsel should of course be consulted if a lawsuit is contemplated.

Buyer. If the seller effectuates the breach, the buyer may reject the goods if they are nonconforming. The seller must be given notice, and if the buyer is a merchant, the buyer is required to follow the seller's reasonable instructions pertaining to the rejected goods.

When goods are not in conformity with the contract, and the nonconformity decreases the value of the goods, the buyer may generally revoke acceptance.

Alternatively, the remedy of "cover" may be available. In situations where the buyer procures the same or similar goods from another vendor, the buyer may be entitled to recover the difference between the cost of cover and the contract price, increased by any incidental damages, but reduced by any expenses saved as a result of the seller's breach.

In lieu of suing for cover, the buyer may be entitled to sue for damages. In these instances, the measure of damages is the difference between the market price at the time the buyer learned of the breach and the contract price, increased by any incidental damages, but reduced by any expenses saved as a result of the seller's breach.

INVESTMENT SECURITIES

There are two types of investment securities; those that are "certificated," and those that are "uncertificated." Only certificated securities are negotiable.

To be certificated, an investment security must be registered to a specific party or be in bearer form. A registered security states the name of the party entitled to the security or the rights it represents. Accordingly, the issuer must maintain books to record its transfer.

To be a bona fide purchase of an investment security, the purchase must be made (1) for value, (2) in good faith, and (3) without notice of any adverse claim. Investment securities should be carefully safeguarded because stolen securities, that are properly endorsed, may actually be transferred to a bona fide purchaser who takes them free of the prior party's title claim.

The transfer of a certificated security to a purchaser for value carries with it the implied warranties that the transfer is effective and rightful, the security is genuine and has not been materially altered, and the transferor is unaware of any facts that might impair the security's validity.

Endorsement of a security, by itself, does not constitute a transfer; delivery of the security on which the endorsement appears must take place for a transfer to be consummated.

The controller should also be aware that the statute of frauds is applicable to contracts involving the sale of securities; accordingly, the contract must generally be in writing.

Sometimes, no matter how tight controls are, investment securities may be lost, stolen, or accidentally destroyed. In these instances, the owner is entitled to a replacement certificate provided that (1) a request for a replacement is made before the issuer becomes aware that the security has been transferred to a bona fide purchaser, (2) a sufficient indemnity bond is filed with the issuer, and (3) all reasonable requirements of the issuer are met.

EMPLOYMENT REGULATIONS

This chapter is intended to expand on the business law concepts briefly mentioned on pages 703 and 704 of the main text. An awareness of the provisions contained in this chapter will enable the controller to interface with responsible individuals in the personnel department.

The Federal Occupational and Safety Health Act (OSHA)

The Occupational and Health Administration of the Department of Labor is authorized to administer and enforce the Act. Their objective is to promote safety in the work environment.

The Act, while not applicable to federal, state, and local governments, applies to virtually all private employers.

Under the Act, a general duty is imposed on employers to furnish a work environment that is "free from recognized hazards that are causing or are likely to cause death or serious physical harm" to employees. It should be noted, however, that an employer's liability under the Act arises only where the employer actually knew or should have known of danger. In addition to complying with the general standards of the Act, employers must also comply with certain industry-specific OSHA standards.

Workplace inspections, which are conducted without prior notification, represent the Act's simple means of enforcing compliance. To be legal, however, inspections are generally subject to employer permission. Alternatively, where the government has probable cause, a search warrant may be secured.

Employers are subject to both civil and criminal penalties for violations of the Act's provisions. Civil penalties as high as $1,000 per violation may be imposed; a $10,000 penalty may be imposed for repeated violations. An employer deemed to be a willful violator may be fined up to $10,000 and/or imprisoned for up to six months.

Finally, it is illegal to fire an employee who reveals an OSHA violation.

The Federal Fair Labor Standards Act (FLSA)

FSLA requires that employers pay a minimum hourly wage; further, employers must generally pay an overtime rate equal to time-and-a-half for work in excess of 40 hours per week. The Act, however, exempts professionals, administrative employees, executives and outside sales workers from the minimum wage and overtime provisions.

In addition, the Act regulates the employment of children in nonagricultural positions. Under the Act, children under the age of 14 may generally not be employed. However, they may be employed for newspaper delivery, acting, and working for their parents. Children between the ages of 14 and 15 may be employed to a limited extent outside of school hours in nonhazardous work. Finally, a child who is either 16 or 17 years old may be employed to perform nonhazardous tasks.

The Equal Pay Act

The Equal Pay Act makes it illegal for an employer to discriminate on the basis of gender by paying different wages for substantially equal work. The Act does, however, permit payment of different wages based on seniority, merit, quantity or quality of work, or any other factor not relating to gender. Should an employer violate the Act, it may be directed to discontinue its illegal pay structure and it may be required to provide back pay to any injured employees.

The Civil Rights Act of 1964 (CRA)

CRA makes it illegal for an employer to discriminate on the basis of race, color, religion, gender, or national origin. The Act also prohibits sexual harassment but not discrimination based on sexual preference. The Act is applicable to entities that employ 15 or more employees for 20 weeks in the current or preceding year. After enactment, the Act was modified to include The *Pregnancy Discrimination Act Amendment* which forbids employment discrimination based on pregnancy, childbirth, or related medical conditions. It should be noted that employment discrimination based on gender, religion, and national origin (but not race) is allowable if the employer can show it to be a bona fide occupational qualification. Employment practices dependent on seniority systems and work-related merit are also permitted. Violations of CRA may entitle victims to up to two years' back pay in additional to recovery of reasonable legal fees. Reinstatement, injunctive relief, and affirmative action represent possible equitable remedies.

Age Discrimination in Employment Act (ADEA)

The Act, which is applicable to nonfederal employers with 20 or more employees, forbids employment discrimination based solely on age. ADEA is applicable to all employees at least 40 years old; the Act also contains a prohibition against mandatory retirement of nonmanagerial employees based on age. Subsequent to enactment, the ADEA was amended to ban age discrimination with respect to employee benefits. The Act does, however, allow age discrimination where justified by a bona fide seniority system, a bona fide occupational qualification, or a bona fide employee benefit plan. Injured individuals may seek injunctive relief, affirmative action, and back pay.

Rehabilitation Act of 1973

The Rehabilitation Act of 1973 was enacted to prevent discrimination on the basis of handicap by any employer that is the recipient of federal assistance or contracts. While employers subject to the Act are required to make reasonable efforts to accommodate the handicapped, they are not required to hire or promote handicapped persons who are unable to perform the job after reasonable accommodations are made. Persons with physical and mental handicaps are covered by the Act while persons with alcohol or drug abuse problems are not.

Americans with Disabilities Act (ADA)

ADA, which is applicable to entities employing 15 or more individuals, prevents an employer from employment discrimination against qualified individuals with disabilities. A qualified individual with a disability is an individual who is able to perform the essential job function, with or without reasonable accommodation. A disabled person is an individual with or without a history of a physical or mental impairment that substantially limits one or more major life activities. In this connection, ADA affords protection to persons afflicted with cancer and HIV infections; recovering alcoholics and drug addicts are also protected. The Act bars employers from asking job applicants about disabilities but does allow inquiry about the applicant's ability to perform job-related tasks. Prospective employees are also protected by the Act's prohibition of pre-employment medical exams. However, if such exams are required of all other job applicants, the employer is not barred. The Act does afford protection to an employer as well. Accordingly, an employer may refuse to hire or promote a disabled person in situations where (1) accommodation would present an undue hardship, (2) the disabled person cannot fulfill job-related criteria that cannot be reasonably accommodated and (3) the disabled person would represent a direct threat to the health of other individuals.

Comprehensive Omnibus Budget Reconciliation Act of 1985 (COBRA)

COBRA mandates that employers allow voluntarily or involuntarily terminated (and certain disabled) employees to continue their group-health insurance coverage for a period not to exceed to 18 (if disabled, up to 29) months following termination. The terminated employee must, however, bear the expense of the premiums. COBRA applies to nongovernmental entities (1) employing at least 20 individuals and (2) offering an employer-sponsored health plan to employees. An employee's spouse and minor children must also be given the right to continue their group-health coverage.

Worker Adjustment and Retraining Notification Act (WARN)

WARN, which is applicable to employers of more than 100 employees, requires that employees be given 60 days notice of plant closures or mass layoffs. A plant closing is defined as the permanent or temporary closing of a single plant or parts of a plant but only if at least 50 employees will lose their jobs within a specified 30-day period. A mass layoff arises when the jobs of at least 500 employees are terminated during a 30-day period, or the jobs of at least one-third of the employees are terminated at a given site, if that one-third equals at least 50 employees.

The Family and Medical Leave Act (FMLA)

FMLA, which is applicable to entities with at least 50 employees, requires an employer to provide 12 weeks unpaid leave each year for medical or family reasons. While on leave, an employee is entitled to continued medical benefits, and upon return, an employee is entitled to the same or equivalent job.

SECURED TRANSACTIONS

A secured transaction is defined as any transaction that is aimed at creating a security interest in personal property or fixtures. When an agreement between a debtor and creditor has been reached, whereby the creditor shall have a security interest, a security agreement results. The security agreement must be in writing, signed by the debtor, and must delineate any collateral, if the agreement pertains to a nonpossessory interest.

When an interest in personal property or fixtures that secures payment or performance of an obligation exists, by definition, a security interest is created. Security interests may be either possessory or nonpossessory. Attachment must occur in order for rights of a secured party to be enforceable against the debtor. Perfection is necessary in order to make the security interest effective against most third parties.

In order for attachment to occur, (1) the secured party must have collateral pursuant to an agreement with the debtor (or the debtor must have signed a security agreement delineating collateral), (2) the creditor gives value, which may be any consideration that would support a simple contract, and (3) the debtor is afforded property rights in collateral.

Once the security interest has attached, perfection is said to have occurred. In general, the filing of a financing statement with the appropriate public official accomplishes perfection. The content of the financing statement is usually governed by state law, but generally includes, at a minimum, the names and addresses of the secured party and debtor, specification of the collateral, and (3) the signature of the debtor.

Perfection may also be accomplished by attachment alone, without filing, through the use of a purchase money security interest (PMSI) in consumer goods. This form of perfection provides protection against a debtor's other creditors and a debtor's trustee in bankruptcy.

Finally perfection is achieved when the creditor is in possession of the collateral. This means of perfection is useful for a security interest in goods, instruments, negotiable documents, and letters of credit. In the case of negotiable instruments, this is the only acceptable means of perfection.

It should be understood that there are two types of secured transactions; namely, a secured credit sale and a secured loan transaction. The former concerns a sales transaction in which the creditor is involved either as a seller or a money lender. The creditor takes a purchase money security interest (PMSI). Possession and risk of loss pass to the buyer, but the creditor retains a security interest in the goods until he or she has been paid in full. In the case of the latter, there is no sale of goods. Rather, the creditor lends money while simultaneously accepting a debtor-pledged security interest in collateral.

Essentially, there are four types of collateral; i.e., goods, negotiable instruments, intangibles and fixtures.

Goods include consumer goods, inventory and equipment. Consumer goods consist of items that are used or purchased for use primarily for personal, family, or household purposes. Inventory, on the other hand, includes goods held for sale or lease, including unfinished goods. A security interest in inventory may result in a "floating lien," whereby the lien attaches to inventory in the hands of the dealer as it is received by the dealer. Equipment, it should noted, may also be subject to a "floating lien."

Negotiable instruments include commercial paper, documents of title and investment securities.

Intangibles include both accounts receivable and contract rights.

Perfecting a Security Interest

As previously noted, to accomplish perfection, a financing statement must be filed with an appropriate public official. In instances where conflicting interests exist, the order of perfection is crucial and will decide priority, regardless of attachment. The first security interest to attach is afforded priority in cases where none of the conflicting security interests have been perfected.

If, within a ten-day period, before or after the debtor takes possession of the collateral, a purchase money security interest in noninventory collateral is filed, the creditor will be protected as of the day on which the security interest was created (i.e., the day on which the debtor takes possession of the collateral) against any nonpurchase money security interest previously filed during the ten-day period. Creditor protection also applies to previously filed floating liens. In the event that the security interest is perfected after the ten-day period, the secured party will be afforded protection as of the date of filing but will not be able to secure protection against previously perfected non-PMSI.

A PMSI in inventory takes priority over conflicting security interests (i.e., previously perfected non-PMSI) but only if both (1) the PMSI-holder perfected the interest in the inventory on or before the date the inventory was received by the debtor and (2) the PMSI-holder furnished written notice (before the debtor takes possession of the inventory) indicating the acquisition of the interest and describing the secured inventory to all holders of conflicting security interests that previously filed a financing statement pertaining to the same type of inventory.

A filing will be necessary to protect against an innocent, nonmerchant purchaser from the consumer/debtor, even though no filing is required in order to perfect a purchase money security interest in consumer goods.

The written financing statement needed to perfect a security interest must generally include the names and addresses of both the debtor and the creditor. Only the debtor must sign the statement. The financing statement must also describe the collateral covered, and is effective for a five year period commencing on the date filed. In order to extend the original five-year period for another five-years, a continuation statement, signed by the secured party, is necessary and must be filed by the secured party within the six-month period prior to the original statement's expiration date.

Rights of Parties upon Default

The secured party may, upon default by the buyer/debtor, have the right to repossess the goods without going through legal channels. Alternatively, the secured party may sell the goods and apply the proceeds to any outstanding debt.

The secured party generally will be protected against subsequent creditors and most other third parties if a security interest has been perfected. However, holders in due course will defeat the claims of any and all secured parties. Furthermore, a buyer in the ordinary course of business is not controlled by a seller-created security interest, even in instances where the security interest was perfected and the buyer was conscious of it. This is quite prevalent where inventory has been pledged as collateral.

Upon default, the secured party may exercise a privilege to notify the obligor on accounts receivable, contract rights, instruments, etc., to directly remit remuneration.

While the debtor has right to redeem collateral prior to disposition, the creditor has right to retain goods. However, unless the debtor had relinquished rights after default, the creditor must give the debtor written notice about his or her intention(s). Furthermore, except in cases involving consumer goods, the creditor must send this notice to all other interested secured parties. If the creditor receives an objection to his or her retention within a 21-day period following the sending of this notice, then the creditor is required to dispose of the property.

If the debtor has satisfied at least 60% of the obligation, and the collateral consists of consumer goods with a PMSI, then the creditor is forced to sell the collateral within 90 days of the collateral's repossession, unless the debtor has relinquished his or her rights after default. Any excess debt owed, plus repossession costs, must be returned by the secured party to the debtor.

When, for value and without knowledge of any defects in the sale, a good faith purchaser acquires collateral that was disposed of after default, the acquisition is free of any subordinate (but not superior) security interests. Finally, the debtor has no right to redeem collateral sold to a good-faith purchaser.

SURETYSHIP AND CREDITOR'S RIGHTS

Suretyship involves situations where one party agrees to be unconditionally liable for the debt or default of another party.

The parties involved in suretyship include the surety or guarantor (i.e., the party, whether compensated or not, who is responsible for the debt or obligation of another), the creditor (i.e., the party who is owed the debt or obligation), the debtor or principal debtor (i.e., the party whose obligation it is). It should be noted that co-sureties may exist. If this is the case, more than one surety is obligated for the same debt, although each co-surety may not be liable for the same amount nor may they be aware of each other's existence.

Since guaranty of collection imposes only a secondary liability upon the guarantor, the creditor must initially attempt collection from the debtor before attempting collection from the guarantor. It should be noted that, except in instances where collection is subject to some condition, guaranty and suretyship are synonymous terms.

Under the Statute of Frauds discussed earlier, a promise of guaranty must be set forth in writing and signed by the guarantor in order to be enforceable. On the other hand, a surety agreement does not have to be set forth in writing.

While the surety/guarantor need not receive consideration, consideration is needed to support the surety/guarantor's promise, and is usually represented by the creditor's granting of the loan.

Surety's Rights against Debtor or Co-Sureties

Once payment is made by the surety to the creditor, the surety is entitled to seek indemnification or reimbursement from the debtor.

In situations involving co-sureties, once the surety has made payment to the creditor, one co-surety may seek a proportionate share from any other co-sureties.

A co-surety's share of the principal debt is calculated by multiplying the amount of principal debt by a fraction, the numerator of which is the amount for which the co-surety is liable and the denominator of which is the total amount of liabilities for all co-sureties.

In the event that a co-surety is released by a creditor, any remaining co-sureties will be liable, but only to the extent of their proportionate share.

After the creditor is paid by the surety, the surety stands in the shoes of the creditor; this is known as subrogation.

If the debtor defaults, the surety may seek relief from the courts. The courts may order the debtor to pay the creditor. A surety may seek similar relief against co-sureties. This equitable right of the surety against the debtor is known as exoneration.

Defenses of a Surety

In general, a surety may raise any defense that may be raised by a party to an ordinary contract. As such, a surety may claim mutual mistake, lack of consideration, undue influence and creditor fraud.

On the other hand, a surety may not claim such defenses as death, insolvency, or bankruptcy of the debtor. The statute of limitations is similarly barred as a defense.

Another possible defense arises when the surety is not advised by the creditor about matters material to the risk when the creditor reasonably believes that the surety does not possess knowledge of such matters.

A defense also arises if the surety does not consent to material modification of the original contract. There is, however, a difference between a noncompensated surety and a compensated surety. The former is completely discharged automatically. The latter is discharged only to the extent that the material modification results in the surety sustaining a loss.

The release of the debtor by the creditor without the surety's consent may also be claimed as a defense. However, if the creditor specifically reserves his or her rights as against the surety, the reservation of rights will be effective and the surety shall remain liable pursuant to the original promise.

When the security is released or its value is impaired by the creditor, the surety is discharged but only to the extent of the security released or impaired.

Finally, the debtor's tender of payment to the creditor may be used as a defense.

Rights of the Creditor

The rights of the creditor, like the defenses of the surety, depend on the facts and circumstances of the events giving rise to the suretyship.

When improvements are made to real property and the provider is not paid for labor or materials, the creditor has the right to place a mechanic's lien on the property.

Pursuant to writ of execution, which is a postjudgment remedy, a court directs the sheriff to (1) seize and sell a debtor's nonexempt property and (2) apply the proceeds to the costs of execution and the creditor's judgment.

A writ of attachment, on the other hand, is a prejudgment remedy whereby the sheriff is directed to seize the debtor's nonexempt property. The seized property is then sold to pay the judgment, but only if a judgment against the debtor is secured. This remedy is not obtained easily and requires the creditor to post a bond sufficient to cover court costs and damages for a possible wrongful attachment action by the debtor.

Alternatively, a creditor may wish to secure a writ of garnishment. This course of action may be a prejudgment or postjudgment remedy. The writ of garnishment is aimed at a third party, such as a bank or employer, holding debtor-owned funds. The third party is directed to pay a regular portion of those funds to the creditor. The federal government's desire to prevent abusive and excessive garnishment resulted in enactment of The Consumer Credit Protection Act. Under the Act, a debtor may retain the larger of 75 percent of the weekly disposable earnings, or an amount equal to 30 hours of work at the federal minimum wage rate.

An assignment for the benefit of creditors is also a viable option. Under this option, a debtor voluntarily transfers property to a trustee who then sells the property and applies the sale proceeds on a pro-rata basis to the creditors of the debtor.

It should be noted that a homestead exemption is afforded to a debtor in bankruptcy. Accordingly, the debtor is permitted to retain a family home, or a portion of the proceeds from the sale of a family home, free from the claims of unsecured creditors and trustees. However, the protection of the homestead exemption is not available to tax liens, liens for labor or materials pertinent to real property improvements, and contract obligations for the purchase of real property.

Finally, if a debtor transfers property to a third party with the intent of defrauding the debtor's creditors, and the property becomes unavailable to the debtor's creditors, a fraudulent conveyance has taken place, and is voidable at the option of the debtor's creditors.

Federally-Enacted Statutes

The federal government passed the Truth-in-Lending Act (TLA) to require that creditors disclose finance charges and credit extension charges. TLA also sets limit on garnishment proceedings. Further, a consumer who uses his or her principal residence as security for credit purposes is given the right to cancel the transaction within three business days of the credit-transaction date, or the date the creditor provided the debtor with a required notice of the right to cancel, whichever is later. In general, TLA applies to consumer credit purchases up to $25,000. The $25,000 limit is not applicable, however, where the creditor maintains a security interest in the principal dwelling of the debtor.

TLA was later amended to include the Consumer Leasing Act (CLA) to expand its disclosure requirements to leases of consumer goods of up to $25,000. The provisions of CLA, however, are not applicable to real estate leases or leases between consumers.

Another amendment to TLA is the Fair Credit and Charge Card Disclosure Act, that requires disclosure of credit terms on credit and charge card solicitations and applications.

In an effort to ensure that there is no discrimination in the extension of credit, the Equal Credit Opportunity Act was enacted. Under the Act, it is illegal to discriminate on the basis of race, color, national origin, religion, age, gender, marital status, or receipt of income from public assistance programs.

By virtue of the Fair Credit Billing Act (FCBA), payment may be withheld by a credit card customer for supposedly defective products. FCBA regulates credit billing and establishes a mechanism enabling consumers to challenge and correct billing errors.

Finally, the Fair Debt Collection Practices Act may be useful as it affords protection to consumer-debtors from abusive, deceptive, and unfair practices by debt collectors.

DOCUMENTS OF TITLE

The controller should have a basic knowledge of documents of title because they indicate ownership of goods and emanate from shipment or storage of goods. Documents of title may be sold, transferred, or even pledged as collateral, and include bills of lading issued by a carrier to evidence the receipt of shipment, and warehouse receipts used to evidence receipt of goods by persons hired to store goods.

It should be understood that there is a difference between a negotiable document and a nonnegotiable document. In the case of the former, the document states that goods are to be delivered to "bearer" or to the "order of" a named person. Accordingly, the goods are required to be delivered to the holder of the document. A negotiable document of title is not, however, payable in money, as commercial paper is. In the case of the latter, goods are consigned to a specified person, and therefore delivery must be made to the specified person. A nonnegotiable document, also known as a straight bill of lading, represents a receipt for the goods rather than a document of title.

Transfer or Negotiation

Transfer of nonnegotiable documents is in essence an assignment, whereby the assignee is effectively subject to all defenses that are available against the assignor.

The rules applicable to negotiable documents are much more complex and depend on whether the document is order paper or bearer paper.

With respect to order paper, which is negotiable by endorsement and delivery, a transferee of an order document which was not endorsed has a right to obtain such endorsement. It should be noted that the endorsement of a document of title does not render the endorser liable for any default by the bailee or by previous endorsers.

An endorser does however warrant to the immediate purchaser (1) the genuineness of the document, (2) that the transferor has no knowledge of any fact that would impair the validity of the document and (3) that the transferor's negotiation is rightful and fully effective with respect to the document's title and the goods represented by the document.

Bearer paper, on the other hand is negotiable by delivery alone.

To be "duly negotiated," a document must be properly negotiated to a holder who, in the regular course of business or financing and not in settlement or payment of a money obligation, has purchased the document in good faith, for value, and without notice of defenses.

To secure proper negotiation of order paper, the transferor must obtain a document with proper consent of the owner, and with the owner's endorsement.

Warehouse Obligations

Goods should only be delivered to the person possessing the negotiable document, which is required to be surrendered for cancellation.

Further, a warehouse has the right to refuse delivery of the goods until payment for the goods has been made.

Finally, a completed warehouse receipt, issued with blanks and purchased in good faith, entitles the purchaser to recover from the warehouse that issued the incomplete document.

CORPORATIONS

By definition, a corporation is a separate legal entity that possesses certain powers stipulated in its charter or by governing statutes.

Classification of Corporations

There are eight classifications of corporations: public, private, domestic, foreign, publicly held, closely held, S corporation, and professional.

> A *public corporation* is a corporation that is formed for governmental purposes.
>
> A *private corporation* essentially includes all other corporations, whether publicly held or not.
>
> A *domestic corporation* is a corporation organized under the laws of a particular state.
>
> A *foreign corporation* is a corporation deemed to be "foreign" with respect to every state other than the state of incorporation.
>
> A *closely held corporation* is a corporation, the stock of which is owned by a small number of persons, who are quite commonly related to each other.
>
> A *publicly held corporation* is a corporation, the stock of which (1) is owned by a large number of persons and (2) widely traded through one of the stock exchanges.
>
> A *professional corporation* is a corporation enabling professionals, including certified public accountants, to operate utilizing the corporate form.
>
> An *S corporation,* as discussed in Chapter 42, is a corporation that (1) has satisfied certain IRS requirements and (2) is electing to be taxed essentially like a partnership.

Parties to a Corporation

If the decision is made to form a publicly held corporation, the services of a promoter are usually necessary. The promoter is responsible for developing ideas pertinent to the corporation, securing stock subscribers, and entering into contracts on behalf of the corporation to be established. While corporations are generally not legally bound by contracts until a preincorporation contract is assumed by the formed corporation, promoters are generally deemed to be personally liable on contracts.

An incorporator is an important party as well, since he or she is the individual charged with devising the formal application needed to create the corporation. Corporate existence only begins upon the State's issuance of the certificate of incorporation.

The stockholders are the owners of the corporation's stock. They are empowered to elect directors who will manage the entity, vote on important issues, inspect books and records, and receive financial statements. Since stockholders, as owners, share in the corporation's profits, they are entitled to receive dividends declared at the discretion of the board of directors. Stockholders may force the board to make dividend payments only when directors are found to have abused their judgment regarding dividend declaration. It should be noted that a dividend received by a stockholder during the period of a company's insolvency must be returned to the corporation.

One the greatest advantages of the corporate form, from the stockholders' point of view, is that stockholders are generally not liable beyond their investment. The courts may, however, "pierce the corporate veil," and hold the stockholders liable if, among other circumstances, the Courts determine that the corporation (1) was established in order to perpetrate a fraud or (2) is undercapitalized.

Directors, elected by the stockholders are charged with establishing the corporation's essential policies of the corporation and electing corporate officers. Since directors are employed in a fiduciary capacity, they are liable for negligence but not errors in judgment. Stockholders may commence a derivative action to cure any damage done by the directors. Directors acting in a representative capacity, however, are entitled to corporate indemnification with respect to acts performed on behalf of the corporation. While directors have the discretion to declare dividends, they will be held to be personally liable for illegal dividends; i.e., dividend payments made during the corporation's period of insolvency, or dividend payments that force the corporation into insolvency, or dividend payments made from an unauthorized account.

The corporate officers are responsible for managing the daily operations of the corporation, and their rights and powers are governed by agency law and are limited by the corporation's charter and bylaws. Corporate officers, appointed by the board of directors, while liable for negligent acts, are entitled to indemnification for acts performed within the scope of their authority, so long as they acted in good faith.

Powers and Rights of a Corporation

A corporation's sources of power include the corporation's charter and bylaws as well as relevant statutes. A corporation is normally empowered to borrow and lend money, enter into contracts, acquire and dispose property, have perpetual existence, and have exclusive use of its legal corporate name.

Dissolution or Termination of Corporations

While a corporation normally is afforded perpetual existence, there are circumstances that enable a corporation to terminate its existence. Termination may be accomplished by voluntary or involuntary dissolution.

In order to dissolve voluntarily, the board of directors must approve a corporate resolution. Approval generally requires a majority vote on the part of stockholders possessing stock with voting rights. A special shareholders' meeting is needed and all shareholders must be provided written notice of the purpose, time, date, and location of the special meeting.

Involuntary dissolution, on the other hand, may result from an administrative hearing on the part of the secretary of state, or from a judicial proceeding prompted by either a shareholder or corporate creditor.

To force an involuntary dissolution based on an administrative hearing, the secretary of state must prove that the corporation has failed to comply with state laws. Accordingly, the corporation's failure to file required annual reports or pay taxes may result in an involuntary dissolution.

A court may also force a corporation to dissolve. To do so, it must prove that the corporation fraudulently obtained its charter, the corporation was involved in ultra vires acts (i.e., those abusing or in excess of its authority), the board of directors was involved in an illegal or fraudulent act, or the assets of the corporation are being wasted or misapplied. A court forced dissolution may also result when either (1) the shareholders are deadlocked and have failed to elect directors for at least two consecutive annual meetings or (2) the directors are deadlocked, the shareholders cannot break the deadlock, and irreparable damage is threatened or being suffered by the corporation.

Consolidation or Merger

From a legal standpoint, a consolidation involves joining two or more corporations in order to form a new entity with the assets and liabilities of the old corporations. A merger, on the other hand, occurs when one corporation absorbs another. The corporation absorbed is accordingly terminated, while the other corporation (i.e., the survivor) continues its existence. The survivor logically assumes the liabilities of the corporation absorbed in the merger.

In order to effectuate a consolidation or merger, the board of directors of each corporation must ratify a formal plan, which must then be submitted to the stockholders of each corporation for their approval. Approval constitutes the consent of a majority of each corporation's voting shareholders, following due notice of a special shareholders' meeting. Furthermore, each voting shareholder must be given a copy of the merger or consolidation plan.

Any dissenting shareholders must be provided an appraisal remedy; i.e., they must be given the value of the shares immediately prior to the action to which the dissenter objects plus accrued interest, if any. In order to obtain an appraisal remedy, a dissenting shareholder must (1) file a written notice of dissent with the corporation prior to the vote of the shareholders,

(2) vote against the proposed transaction, and (3) demand in writing that an appraisal remedy be made after the shareholders' vote of approval.

Finally, articles of consolidation or merger must be filed with the absorbing corporation's state of incorporation. The merger or consolidation is effective only when this document is filed.

It should be noted that a short-form merger is often permitted when a merger of a subsidiary into a parent corporation is desired. To qualify, a parent corporation must own at least 90 percent of the outstanding shares of each class of stock in a subsidiary. It is interesting to note that only the approval of the parent corporation's board of directors is necessary. It is not necessary to secure the approval of either the shareholders of each corporation or the board of directors of the subsidiary corporation. Additionally, only the shareholders of the subsidiary corporation need be given an appraisal remedy.

BANKRUPTCY

A knowledge of bankruptcy is essential given today's economic conditions and competitive markets. This section is designed to update and expand on the material contained on pages 989 and 990 in the main text. From a legal standpoint, the primary basis for bankruptcy is insolvency in the equity sense as opposed to balance sheet insolvency. Accordingly, the entity must be unable to pay debts as they become due as opposed to merely having an excess of liabilities over assets.

Bankruptcy Reform Act of 1994

The Bankruptcy Reform Act of 1994 essentially contains two chapters applicable to corporations.

Chapter 7 permits the voluntary or involuntary liquidation of a debtor's nonexempt assets, the distribution of the proceeds to creditors, and the discharge of the remaining business and/or personal debt of the debtor. While Chapter 7 relief is available to corporations, a discharge of indebtedness is not available if the debtor is a corporation, since the limited liability of shareholders would preclude the need for a discharge. Under Chapter 7, it should be apparent that the business no longer continues to operate.

Chapter 11, on the other hand, is quite different. Chapter 11 relief, which is generally available if the entity is eligible for relief under Chapter 7, enables reorganization by the entity's business debtors, in order to keep the financially troubled business in operation. Fraud, incompetence, or gross mismanagement, however, will prevent the desired continuity.

A petition under Chapter 11 may be voluntary or involuntary, and insolvency in the balance sheet sense is not a condition precedent. The filing of a voluntary petition by an eligible debtor operates as an order for relief, effectively eliminating the need for a formal hearing.

Appointment of a committee of unsecured creditors follows an order of relief. The parties holding the seven largest unsecured claims against the debtor usually sit on the committee.

Under Chapter 11, the debtor usually remains in possession and control of the business. However, a trustee may be appointed by the Court for cause, which includes, but is not limited to, fraud on the part of the debtor or incompetence of the debtor.

The right to file a reorganization plan during the first 120 days following the order for relief rests with the debtor, unless the court has appointed a trustee. If the creditors do not accept a timely filed plan, then no other party is permitted to file a plan for reorganization during the first 180 days after the order for relief. Thereafter, however, a plan for reorganization may be filed by one or more interested parties.

In order to be effective, each class of creditors must accept the proposed plan for reorganization. Confirmation by the Bankruptcy Court is then required. Acceptance by a class of creditors requires approval by creditors holding at least two-thirds of the debt owed to that class of creditors and holding more than one-half of the allowed claims for that class.

Upon confirmation by the court, a final decree is entered, resulting in the discharge of the debtor from most pre-confirmation debts.

An expedited reorganization process is available to a qualified small business, which is defined as a business whose aggregate noncontingent liquidated secured and unsecured debts are less than $2 million. The expedited process enables elimination of creditor committees and affords the debtor the exclusive right to file a reorganization plan within 100 days.

Bankruptcy Petitions

A bankruptcy petition must be filed in order to begin bankruptcy proceedings. If the debtor files the petition, it is said to be a voluntary petition. A voluntary petition generally lists the entity's creditors, exempt property, and a description of financial condition. Upon filing a voluntary petition, an order for relief is entered.

If the creditors of the entity file the petition, it is referred to as an involuntary petition. The debtor, of course, has the right to contest the petition in court. An order for relief, however, is entered only after a court hearing.

Three petitioning creditors are required when the debtor has 12 or more creditors; only one creditor is required if the debtor has less than 12 creditors. In either situation, the petition must allege unsecured debts of at least $10,000 owed by the debtor to the petitioning creditors.

If the petition is opposed by the debtor, the court may enter an order of relief only if (1) the debtor is not paying debts as they mature, or (2) within 120 days before the petition is filed, to enforce a lien against the property, a receiver took possession of substantially all of the debtor's property.

A successful contest of an involuntary bankruptcy petition by the debtor may result in the court granting a judgment for (1) costs, (2) reasonable attorney's fees, and (3) compensatory damages. The debtor may also be awarded punitive damages should the court determine that the petition was filed in bad faith.

Priority of Claims

The priority of a claim depends on whether it is a secured claim or an unsecured claim. A creditor with a perfected secured claim against specific property of the debtor is afforded first priority to the proceeds from that property. To the extent that the proceeds of the sale of the secured asset are not sufficient to fully discharge the claim of the secured party, the creditor is considered to be an unsecured creditor.

After secured claims are satisfied, unsecured creditors are entitled to any remaining assets. Since some unsecured claims are given priority, they must be paid in full before payment is made to subordinate claims. In the event that a debtor's assets are not sufficient to fully pay unsecured creditors with the same priority, payments must be made on a pro-rata basis.

The general order of priority applicable to nonsecured claims is (1) administrative expenses, (2) debt obligations incurred after commencement of an involuntary bankruptcy case, but before the order for relief or appointment of a trustee, (3) unsecured claims for wages earned within 90 days before the filing of a bankruptcy petition or cessation of business, whichever is first, limited to $4,000 for each employee, (4) contributions to employee benefit plans based on services rendered within 180 days before the filing of the bankruptcy petition, but limited to $4,000 per employee, (5) deposits with the debtor to the extent of $1,800 per individual for the purchase, rental, or lease of property or personal services, for family or household use, (6) taxes, and (7) general creditor claims.

Discharge of Debt

While a discharge in bankruptcy generally discharges debt, certain obligations are not. Some of the more common debts that are not discharged include taxes in general, unlisted debts and debts where the creditor notice did not stipulate the debtor's name, address, and taxpayer identification number, debts for fraud, embezzlement, or larceny, liability for injury that was willful and malicious, fines and penalties, debts surviving an earlier bankruptcy proceeding, and loans used to pay federal taxes.

Discharge of debt will be denied if the debtor, within a one-year period before the petition is filed, or during the hearing of the case, (1) directly or indirectly transferred, destroyed, or concealed property, (2) concealed, destroyed, falsified, or failed to preserve any records necessary for determining financial condition, (3) committed fraud, refused to testify, or attempted bribery in connection with the bankruptcy, (4) failed to explain satisfactorily any loss or deficiency of assets, (5) refused to obey a lawful court order, (6) has been granted a discharge in a case commenced within six years before the date of the filing of the petition, or (7) executed a court-approved written waiver of discharge after the order for relief.

It should be noted that under certain conditions, a debtor and a creditor may agree to honor a discharged debt. The agreement is known as a reaffirmation agreement.

ENVIRONMENTAL LAW

Violation of environmental law may subject the corporation to stiff criminal and civil fines and penalties. As a valued member of management, the controller should possess some basic knowledge of relevant federal statutes pertinent to environmental law.

Federal statutes have been enacted to extend common law liability for nuisance (i.e., unreasonable interference with use and enjoyment of another's land) and trespass (i.e., the intentional and unlawful entry upon another's land).

The Environmental Protection Agency (EPA) is a federal administrative agency that is charged with administering federal laws designed to protect the environment.

The National Environmental Policy Act (NEPA) requires the federal government to consider the "adverse impact" of proposed legislation, rule-making, or other federal government action on the environment before the action is set in motion. Under the law, an environmental impact statement must be prepared in connection with all proposed federal legislation or major federal action that significantly impacts the quality of the human environment.

The Clean Air Act, which regulates air quality, specifically addresses (1) national ambient air quality standards, (2) stationary sources of air pollution, (3) mobile sources of air pollution, and (4) toxic air pollutants.

The Clean Water Act enables the EPA to establish water quality criteria in order to regulate the concentrations of permissible pollutants in a body of water and limit the amount of pollutants that are discharged from a particular source. Enforcement of the Act is delegated to individual states.

The Noise Control Act enables the EPA to establish noise standards for new products. Under the Act, the EPA (with the Federal Aeronautics Administration) is empowered to establish noise limits for new aircraft and to regulate, with the assistance of the Department of Transportation, noise emissions from trucks.

The Resource Conservation and Recovery Act (RCRA) authorizes the EPA to identify hazardous wastes. Further, the Act authorizes the EPA to regulate entities that generate, treat, store, and dispose of wastes deemed to be hazardous.

Finally, The Comprehensive Environmental Response, Compensation, and Liability Act (CERCLA), often referred to as the "Superfund" law, mandates that the EPA identify hazardous waste sites. The EPA must the rank the identified sites according to the severity of the environmental risk they pose.

Should the EPA have to clean up a hazardous site, it may recover the cost of the cleanup from one or more responsible parties.

FINANCIAL STATEMENT REPORTING: THE INCOME STATEMENT

FINANCIAL ACCOUNTING STANDARDS BOARD STATEMENT NUMBER 130

FASB Statement No. 130 (Reporting Comprehensive Income) requires companies to report comprehensive income and its elements in a full set of financial statements. FASB Statement Number 130 keeps the current reporting requirements for net income, but it considers net income a major element of comprehensive income. A restatement of previous years' financial statements is needed when presented for comparative purposes.

Comprehensive income applies to the change in equity (net assets) arising from either transactions or other occurrences with nonowners. Excluded are investments and withdrawals by nonowners. Comprehensive income is comprised of two components: net income and other comprehensive income. Other comprehensive income relates to all items of comprehensive income excluding net income. Thus, net income plus other comprehensive income equals total comprehensive income. Other comprehensive income includes the following:

- Foreign currency items including translation gains and losses, and gains and losses on foreign currency transactions designated as hedges of a net investment in a foreign entity.

- Unrealized losses or gains on available-for-sale securities.
- Minimum pension liability adjustments applying to the amount by which the additional pension liability exceeds the unrecognized prior service cost.
- Changes in market value of a futures contract that is a hedge of an asset reported at fair value.

FASB Statement Number 130 provides flexibility on how comprehensive income may be shown in the financial statements. There are three allowable options of reporting other comprehensive income and its components as follows:

1. Below the net income figure in the income statement, or
2. In a separate statement of comprehensive income beginning with net income, or
3. In a statement of changes in equity as long as such statement is presented as a primary financial statement. It cannot appear only in the footnotes.

Options 1 and 2 are income-statement-type formats while option 3 is a statement-of-changes-in-equity format. Options 1 and 2 are preferred.

A sample presentation under option 1 within the income statement follows:

Statement of Income and Comprehensive Income

Net Income		$600,000
Other Comprehensive Income:		
Foreign currency translation loss	($50,000)	
Unrealized gain on available-for-sale securities	70,000	
Minimum pension liability adjustment	(10,000)	
Total Other Comprehensive Income		10,000
Total Comprehensive Income		$610,000

Under the second option a separate statement of comprehensive income is presented. The reporting follows:

Income Statement

Net Income	$600,000

Statement of Comprehensive Income

Net Income		$600,000
Other Comprehensive Income:		
Foreign currency translation loss	($50,000)	
Unrealized gain on available-for-sale securities	70,000	
Minimum pension liability adjustment	(10,000)	
Total Other Comprehensive Income		10,000
Total Comprehensive Income		$610,000

Under the third option comprehensive income and its components are presented in the comprehensive income column as part of the statement of changes in equity. An illustrative format of the comprehensive income column follows:

Comprehensive Income:

Net income		xx
Other comprehensive income:		
Foreign currency items	xx	
Unrealized loss or gain on available-for-sale securities	xx	
Minimum pension liability adjustment	xx	
Total other comprehensive income		xx
Total comprehensive income		xx

In the stockholders' equity section, "accumulated other comprehensive income" is presented as one amount for all items and listed for each component separately.

The components of other comprehensive income for the period may be presented on a before-tax basis with one amount for the tax impact of all the items of other comprehensive income.

A reclassification adjustment may be required so as not to double count items reported in net income for the current period which have also been considered as part of other comprehensive income in a prior period. An example is the realized gain on an available-for-sale security sold in the current year when a holding gain was also included in other comprehensive income in a prior year. Reclassification adjustments may also apply to foreign currency translation. The reclassification adjustment applicable to a foreign exchange translation only applies to translation gains and losses realized from the sale or liquidation of an investment in a foreign entity.

Reclassification adjustments may be presented with other comprehensive income or in a footnote. The reclassification adjustment may be shown on a gross or net basis (except the minimum pension liability adjustment must be presented on a net basis).

Example 1. On January 1, 19X1, a company purchased 1,000 shares of available-for-sale securities having a market price per share of $100. On December 31, 19X1, the available-for-sale securities had a market price of $150 per share. On January 1, 19X2, the securities were sold at a market price of $130 per share. The tax rate is 30%.

The unrealized gain or loss included in other comprehensive income is determined below:

	Before Tax	Tax Effect at 30%	Net of Tax
19X1 (1,000 × $50*)	$50,000	$15,000	$35,000
19X2 (1,000 × $20**)	(20,000)	(6,000)	(14,000)
Total gain	$30,000	$9,000	$21,000

*$150 - $100 = $50
**$150 - $130 = $20

The presentation in the income statement for 19X1 and 19X2 follows:

	19X1	19X2
Net Income:		
Gross realized gain on available-for-sale securities		$30,000
Tax expense		9,000
Net realized gain		$21,000
Other Comprehensive Income:		
Unrealized gain or loss after tax	$30,000	$(9,000)
Reclassification adjustment net of tax		(21,000)
Net gain included in other comprehensive income	$30,000	$(30,000)
Total effect on comprehensive income	$30,000	$(9,000)

In interim financial statements issued to the public, FASB Statement Number 130 requires a business to present total comprehensive income. However, it is not required for interim reporting to present the individual components of other comprehensive income.

DISCLOSURES ASSOCIATED WITH OPERATIONS

Disclosure should be made of a company's major products and services including principal markets by geographic area. The information enables a proper evaluation of the entity's nature of operations. Further, AICPA Statement of Position (SOP) Number 94-6 mandates disclosure of major risks and uncertainties facing the entity. The SOP also requires disclosure in the significant accounting policies footnote that the financial information presented is based on management's estimates and assumptions. Reference should be made that actual results may differ from such estimates.

SERVICE SALES REVENUE

A transaction often involves both the sale of a product and a service. It is thus necessary to determine if the transaction should be classified primarily as a product transaction or a service transaction, or a combination of both.

For transactions having both a product and service element, the following applies:

- A transaction should be classified as primarily a service transaction if the inclusion or exclusion of the product would not change the total price of the transaction.
- If the inclusion or exclusion of the service would not alter the total transaction price, then the transaction should be classified as primarily a product transaction.
- If the inclusion or exclusion of the service or product would change the total transaction price, then the transaction should be split and the product component should be accounted for separately from the service element.

The following four methods should be used to recognize revenue from service activities:

- The specific performance method is used when performance involves a single action and the revenue is recognized when that action occurs.
- The proportional performance method is used when performance relates to a series of actions. If the transaction involves an unspecified number of actions over a stated time period, an equal amount of revenue should be recognized at fixed intervals. If the transaction relates to a specified number of similar actions, an equal amount of revenue should be recorded when each action is completed. If the transaction relates to a given number of dissimilar or unique actions, revenue

enue should be recognized at fixed intervals. If the transaction relates to a specified number of similar actions, an equal amount of revenue should be recorded when each action is completed. If the transaction relates to a given number of dissimilar or unique actions, revenue should be recognized based upon the following ratio: direct costs involved in a single action ÷ total estimated direct costs of the transaction × total revenue for the entire transaction.

- The completed performance method is used to recognize revenue when completing the final action is so critical that the entire transaction should be considered incomplete without it.
- The collection method is used to recognize revenue when there is significant uncertainty with regard to the collection of revenue. Revenue is not recognized until cash is received.

The three major cost categories that arise from service transactions are:

- Initial direct costs are incurred to negotiate and obtain a service agreement. They include commissions, credit investigation, legal fees, and processing fees.
- Direct costs arise from rendering the service such as labor charges and the cost of materials.
- Indirect costs are all the costs needed to perform the service, but cannot be classified as either initial direct costs or direct costs. Indirect costs include rent, depreciation, selling and administrative costs, allowance for bad debts, and the costs to negotiate transactions that are not consummated.

Indirect costs are expensed as incurred. Initial direct costs and direct costs are expensed only when the related revenue is recognized using either the specific performance or completed performance method. In other words, initial direct costs and direct costs should be recorded as prepaid assets and expensed once the service has been rendered. The same accounting treatment is used to expense initial direct costs under the proportional performance method; that is, initial direct costs are recorded as prepaid assets and expensed when the revenue is recognized. On the other hand, direct costs should be expensed as incurred when the proportional performance method is used. This is done because of the close relationship between the direct costs incurred and the completion of the service. If the collection method is used, both initial direct costs and direct costs are expensed as incurred.

A loss may be incurred in a service transaction. A loss should be recognized when initial direct costs and estimated total direct costs exceed the estimated revenue. The loss is first applied to reduce the prepaid asset and any remaining loss is charged against the estimated liability account.

A service transaction may involve initiation and/or installation fees. The fees are usually nonrefundable. If one can objectively determine the value of the right or privilege granted by the initiation fees, then the fees should be recognized as revenue and the associated direct costs should be expensed on the initiation date. On the contrary, if the value cannot be determined, the fees should initially be deemed unearned revenue, a liability account. Revenue should be recognized from such initiation fees using one of the service revenue recognition methods.

The accounting afforded to equipment installation fees depends upon whether the customer can buy the equipment independent of the installation. If equipment may be bought independent of installation, then the transaction is considered a product transaction and installation fees are treated as part of the product transaction. On the contrary, if both the equipment and installation are essential for service and the customer cannot buy the equipment separately, then the installation fees should be treated as unearned revenue. Unearned revenue should be recognized and the cost of installation and equipment should be amortized over the estimated service period.

CONTRACT TYPES

There are various types of construction contracts including time- and materials, unit price, fixed-price, and cost-type. Time- and materials contracts reimburse the contractor for direct labor and direct material costs. Unit price contracts provide payment to the contractor based on the amount of units completed. Fixed-price contracts are not usually subject to adjustment such as due to increasing construction costs. Cost-type contracts may either be cost without a fee or cost plus a fee. The fee is usually based on a profit margin. However, the fee may be based on some other factor such as total expected costs, uncertainty in estimating costs, project risk, economic conditions, etc. The contract costs should never be more than its net realizable value, otherwise the contract would not be financially feasible. A loss is recognized when accumulated cost exceeds net realizable value.

Contracts which are very similar may be grouped for accounting purposes. Similarity may be indicated by a similar project management, single customer, conducted sequentially or concurrently, interrelated, and negotiated as a package deal. The segmenting of a contract is segregating the larger unit into smaller ones for accounting purposes. By breaking up a unit, revenues are associated with different components or phases. In consequence, different profitability margins may apply to each different unit or phase.

Segmenting of a project may be indicated when all of the following criteria are satisfied:

- The project may be segregated into its components.
- A contract bid price exists for the entire project and its major components.
- Customer approval is received.

Even if all of these conditions are not met, the project may still be segmented if all of the following exist:

- Segregation is logical and consistent.
- Risk differences are explainable.
- Each segment is negotiated.
- Cost savings arise.
- Stability exists.
- Similarity exists in services and prices.
- Contractor has a track record.

An addition or modification made to an existing contact arising from an option clause is accounted for as a separate contract if any of the following applies:

- Price of the new product or service is distinct.
- Product or service is similar to that in the original contract but differences do exist in contract pricing and cost.
- Product or service is materially different than the product or service provided for in the initial contract.

A claim is an amount above the contract price that a contractor wants customers to pay because of customer errors in specifications, customer delays, or other unanticipated causes resulting in higher costs to the contractor. The contractor may recognize additional revenue because of these claims if justification exists and the amount is determinable. The revenue is recognized only to the extent that contract costs related to the claim have been incurred. As per AICPA Statement of Position 81-1, the following benchmarks exist to establish the ability to record the additional revenue:

- Additional costs incurred were not initially expected when the contract was signed.

- The claim has a legal basis.
- The claim is verifiable and objective.
- Costs are determinable.

If the above conditions are not met, a contingent asset should be disclosed.

CONTRACT COSTS

Costs incurred to date on a contract include pre-contract costs and costs incurred after the contract date. Pre-contract costs include learning costs for a new process, design fees, and any other expenditures likely to be recouped after the contract is signed. After the contract, the pre-contract costs are considered contract costs to date.

Some pre-contract costs, such as for materials and supplies, may be deferred to an asset called Deferred Contract Costs in anticipation of a specific contract as long as recoverability is probable. If recoverability is not probable, the pre-contract costs must be immediately expensed. If excess goods are produced in anticipation of future orders, related costs may be deferred to inventory if the costs are considered recoverable.

After the status of a contract bid has been determined (accepted or rejected) a review should be conducted of the pre-contract costs. If the contract has been approved, the deferred pre-contract costs are included in contract costs. If the contract is rejected, the pre-contract costs are immediately expensed unless there are other related contracts pending that might recoup these costs.

Back charges are billable costs for work performed by one party that should have been performed by the party billed. Such an agreement is usually stipulated in the contract. Back charges are accounted for by the contractor as a receivable from the subcontractor with a corresponding reduction in contract costs. The subcontractor accounts for the back charge as contract costs and as a payable.

GOVERNMENT CONTRACTS

On cost-plus-fixed fee government contracts, fees should typically be accrued as billable. If an advance payment is received, it should not offset receivables unless the payment is for work-in-process. If any amounts are offset, disclosure is required.

If a government contract is subject to renegotiation, a renegotiation claim to which the contractor is accountable for should be charged to sales ernment should be shown under current assets unless a long delay in payment is anticipated. A termination claim should be accounted for as a sale. A subcontractor's claim arising from the termination should be included in the contractor's claim against the government. Assume a contractor has a termination claim receivable of $800,000 of which $200,000 applies to the contractor's obligation to the subcontractor. In this situation, a liability should be accrued for $200,000. The termination claim is reduced by any inventory applying to the contract that the contractor is retaining. Disclosure should be provided of the terms of terminated contracts.

Direct costs are included in contract costs such as material, labor, and subcontracting costs. Indirect costs are allocated to contracts on an appropriate basis. Allocable costs include quality control, insurance, contract supervision, repairs and maintenance, tools, and inspection. Learning and startup costs should be charged to existing contracts. The entry for an expected loss on a contract is to make a loss provision.

REVENUE RECOGNITION WHEN A RIGHT OF RETURN EXISTS

A reasonable estimate of returned merchandise may be impaired if the products are not similar, lack of previous experience in estimating returns because the product is new or circumstances have changed, a long time period exists for returns, and the product has a high degree of obsolescence.

Example 2. On March 1, 19X5, product sales of $1,000,000 were made. The cost of the goods is $600,000. A 60-day return privilege exists. The anticipated return rate of goods is 10%. On April 15, 19X5, a customer returns goods having a selling price of $80,000. The criteria to recognize revenue when the right of return exits have been satisfied. The journal entries follow:

March 1, 19X5

Accounts Receivable	1,000,000	
Sales		1,000,000
Cost of Sales	600,000	
Inventory		600,000
Sales Returns	100,000	
Allowance for Sales Returns		100,000
$1,000,000 \times 10\% = $100,000		
Inventory	40,000	
Cost of Sales		40,000

$100,000 \times 40\%$ (gross profit rate) = \$40,000

April 15, 19X5

Allowance for Sales Returns	80,000	
Accounts Receivable		80,000
Cost of Sales	8,000	
Inventory		8,000*
*Inventory assumed returned (\$100,000 × 40%)		$40,000
Less: Amount returned (\$80,000 × 40%)		32,000
Adjustment to inventory		$ 4,000

SOFTWARE REVENUE RECOGNITION

As per AICPA Statement of Position 97-2, revenue should be recorded when the software contract does not involve major production, change, or customization as long as the following conditions exist:

1. The contract is enforceable.
2. The software has been delivered.
3. Receipt of payment is probable.
4. The selling price is fixed or known.

Separate accounting is required for the service aspect of a software transaction if the following conditions exist:

1. The services are required for the software transaction.
2. A separate provision exists in the contract covering services so a price for such services is provided for.

A software contract may include more than one component such as upgrade, customer support subsequent to sale, add-ons, and return or exchange provision. The total selling price of the software transaction should be allocated to the contractual components based on their fair values. If fair value is not ascertainable, revenue should be deferred until it is determinable or when all components of the transaction have been delivered. NOTE: The four revenue criteria stipulated above must be met before any allocation of the fee to the contractual elements may be made. Additionally, the fee for a contractual component is ascertainable if the element is sold separately.

the fee for a contractual component is ascertainable if the element is sold separately.

WARRANTY AND MAINTENANCE REVENUE

Extended warranty and product maintenance contracts are often provided by retailers as separately priced services in addition to the sale of their products. Any warranty or maintenance agreements that are not separately priced should be accounted for as contingencies. Services under contracts may be provided at fixed intervals, a certain number of times, or as required to keep the product operational.

Revenues and incremental direct cost from separately priced extended warranty and product maintenance contracts should be initially deferred. Revenue should be recorded on a straight line basis over the contract period. The associated incremental direct costs should be expensed proportionately to the revenue recognized. Incremental direct costs arise from obtaining the contract. Other costs, such as the cost of services rendered, general and administrative costs, and the costs of contracts not consummated, should be expensed as incurred.

Losses from these contracts should be recognized when the anticipated costs of rendering the service plus the unamortized portion of acquisition cost exceeds the corresponding deferred revenue. To ascertain loss, contracts should be grouped in a consistent manner. Losses are not recognized on individual contracts but instead apply to a grouping of similar contracts. Loss is recognized by initially reducing unamortized acquisition costs. If this is insufficient, a liability is recorded.

CONTRIBUTIONS

FASB Statement Number 116 applies to the accounting and reporting for contributions received and contributions made. Cash, other monetary and nonmonetary assets, services, or unconditional promises to give assets or services qualify as contributions. Contributions may involve either donor imposed restrictions or donor imposed conditions. If the donor restricts the way a contribution is to be used (such as to build a research laboratory), it is considered a restriction and the revenue from such a contribution and any associated costs are recognized immediately. However, if the donor imposes a condition, such as, the donee must obtain matching funds, that condition must be met before revenue may be recognized.

A donor may make an unconditional or conditional promise. An unconditional promise exists if the donor has no right to take back the donated asset and the contribution would be available after some stated time period or on demand. Unconditional promises to give contributions are recognized immediately. A conditional promise is contingent upon the happening of a future occurrence. If that event does not take place, the donor is not obligated by the promise. A vague promise is considered conditional. Conditional promises are recorded only when its terms are met. A conditional promise may be treated as an unconditional promise if the possibility that the condition will not be satisfied is remote.

There must be supporting evidence to substantiate that a promise has been made. Such evidence includes information about the donor (e.g., donor's name and address), the amount the donor commits to give such as in a public announcement, when the amount promised will be given, and to whom the promise to give was made. The donor may have taken certain actions relying on the promise. The donor may have made partial payments. A recorded promise should be at the fair market value of the consideration. If the amount will be collected beyond one year, a discounted cash flow calculation may be made. If discounting is done, the interest is accounted for as contribution income, not interest income.

Contributed services should be recognized if specialized skills are rendered by the donor and those skills would have been purchased by the donee if they were not donated. Contributions received should be recorded at fair value by debiting the asset and crediting revenue. Quoted market prices or market prices for similar assets, appraisal by independent experts, or valuation techniques such as discounted cash flows, should be used to compute fair value. The value of contributed services should be based on quoted market prices for those services.

Disclosures are required in the financial statements of recipients of contributions. For unconditional promises to give, the amount of receivables due within one year, in one to five years, and more than five years should be disclosed along with the amount expected to be uncollected. For conditional promises to give, disclosure is required of promised amounts along with a description of the promise. Promises with similar characteristics may be grouped. Disclosure should be made of the nature and degree of contributed services, limitations or conditions set by the donor, and the programs or activities benefiting from contributed services. Companies are encouraged to disclose the fair value of services received but not recorded as revenue.

The donor should record an expense and a corresponding decrease in assets, or an increase in liabilities, at fair value, in the year in which the contribution is made. If fair value differs from carrying value, a loss or gain on disposition is recorded.

ADVERTISING COSTS

American Institute of CPAs' Statement of Position 93-7 (Reporting on Advertising Costs) requires the expensing of advertising as incurred when the advertising program first occurs. However, the cost of direct-response advertising may be deferred if the major purpose of the promotion is to elicit sales to customers who respond specifically to the advertising and for which future benefit exists. For example, the former condition is satisfied if the response card is specially coded. The latter condition is met if the resulting future revenues exceed the future costs to be incurred. The deferred advertising is amortized over the expected benefit period using the revenue method (current year revenue to total revenue). The cost of a billboard should also be capitalized and amortized. Advertising expenditures incurred after revenue is recognized should be accrued. These advertising costs should be expensed when the related revenues are recognized.

RESTRUCTURING CHARGES

Securities and Exchange Commission Staff Accounting Bulletin Number 67 requires restructuring charges to be expensed and presented as a component in computing income from operations.

In general, an expense and liability should be accrued for employee termination benefits in a restructuring. Disclosure should be made of the group and number of workers laid off.

An exit plan requires the recognition of a liability for the restructuring changes incurred if there is no future benefit to continuing operations. The expense for the estimated costs should be made on the commitment date of the exit plan. Expected gains from assets to be sold in connection with the exit plan should be recorded in the year realized. These gains are not allowed to offset the accrued liability for exit costs. Exit costs incurred are presented as a separate item as part of income from continuing operations. Disclosures associated with an exit plan include the terms of the exit plan, description and amount of exit costs incurred, activities to be exited from, method of disposition, expected completion date, and liability adjustments.

EARNINGS PER SHARE

FASB Statement Number 128 (Earnings Per Share) covers the computation, reporting and disclosures associated with earnings per share. The pronouncement makes some major changes in the computation of earnings per share as previously existed under APB Opinion Number 15. Presentation of both basic and diluted earnings per share is mandated.

warrants, and their equivalents. Diluted earnings per share should not assume the conversion, exercise, or contingent issuance of securities having an antidilutive effect (increasing earnings per share or decreasing loss per share) because it violates conservatism.

BASIC EARNINGS PER SHARE

Basic earnings per share equals net income available to common stockholders divided by the weighted average number of common shares outstanding. Common stock equivalents are no longer presented in this computation. When a prior period adjustment occurs that causes a restatement of previous years' earnings, basic EPS should be restated.

Example 3. The following data are presented for a company:

Preferred stock, $10 par, 6% cumulative, 30,000 shares issued and outstanding	$300,000
Common stock, $5 par, 100,000 shares issued and outstanding	$500,000
Net income	$400,000

The cash dividend on the preferred stock is $18,000 (6% × $300,000).
Basic EPS equals $3.82 as computed below.
Earnings available to common stockholders:

Net income	$400,000
Less: Preferred dividends	(18,000)
Earnings available to common stockholders	$382,000

Basic EPS = $382,000/100,000 shares = $3.82

Example 4. On January 1, 19X3, David Company had the following shares outstanding:

6% Cumulative preferred stock, $100 par value	150,000 shares
Common stock, $5 par value	500,000 shares

During the year, the following took place:

- On April 1, 19X3, the company issued 100,000 shares of common stock.
- On September 1, 19X3, the company declared and issued a 10% stock dividend.
- For the year ended December 31, 19X3, the net income was $2,200,000.

Basic earnings per share for 19X3 equals $2.06 ($1,300,000/632,500 shares) computed below.

Earnings available to common stockholders:

Net income	$2,200,000
Less: Preferred dividend (150,000 shares x $6)	(900,000)
Earnings available to common stockholders	$1,300,000

Weighted-average number of outstanding common shares is determined as follows:

1/1/19X3 - 3/31/19X3 (500,000 x 3/12 x 110%)	137,500
4/1/19X3 - 8/31/19X3 (600,000 x 5/12 x 110%)	275,000
9/1/19X3 - 12/31/19X3 (660,000 x 4/12)	220,000
Weighted average outstanding common shares	632,500

DILUTED EARNINGS PER SHARE

If potentially dilutive securities exist that are outstanding, such as convertible debt, convertible preferred stock, stock options, or stock warrants, then both basic and diluted earnings per share must be shown.

FASB Statement Number 128 retains the "if converted method" to account for convertible securities in earnings per share determination. The pronouncement also retains the "treasury stock method" to account for stock options and warrants.

If options are granted as part of a stock-based compensation agreement, the assumed proceeds from the exercise of the options under the treasury stock method includes deferred compensation and the ensuing tax benefit that would be credited to paid-in capital arising from the exercise of the options.

The denominator of diluted earnings per share equals the weighted average outstanding common shares for the period plus the assumed issue of common shares arising from convertible securities plus the assumed shares issued because of the exercise of stock options or stock warrants, or their equivalent.

Table 1 shows in summary form the earnings per share fractions.

Table 1. Earnings Per Share Fractions

BASIC EARNINGS PER SHARE = Net Income Available to Common Stockholders/Weighted Average Number of Common Shares Outstanding

DILUTED EARNINGS PER SHARE = Net Income Available to Common Stockholders + Net of Tax Interest and/or Dividend Savings on Convertible Securities/Weighted Average Number of Common Shares Outstanding + Effect of Convertible Securities + Net Effect of Stock Options

---

Example 5. Assume the same information as in the prior example dealing with basic earnings per share for David Company. Assume further that potentially diluted securities outstanding include 5% convertible bonds (each $1,000 bond is convertible into 25 shares of common stock) having a face value of $5,000,000. There are options to buy 50,000 shares of common stock at $10 per share. The average market price for common shares is $25 per share for 19X3. The tax rate is 30%. Diluted earnings per share for 19X3 is $1.87 ($1,475,000/787,500 shares) as computed below.

Income for diluted earnings per share:		
Earnings available to common stockholders		$1,300,000
Interest expense on convertible bonds		
($5,000,000 × .05)	$250,000	
Less: Tax savings ($250,000 × .30)	(75,000)	
Interest expense (net of tax)		175,000
Income for diluted earnings per share		$1,475,000
Shares outstanding for diluted earnings per share:		
Weighted average outstanding common shares		632,500
Assumed issued common shares for convertible bonds		
(5,000 bonds × 25 shares)		125,000
Assumed issued common shares from exercise of option	50,000	
Less: Assumed repurchase of treasury shares		
(50,000 × $10 = $500,000/$25)	(20,000)	30,000
Shares outstanding for diluted earnings per share		787,500

Basic earnings per share and diluted earnings per share (if required) must be disclosed on the face of the income statement. A reconciliation is required of the numerators and denominators for basic and diluted earnings per share.

SUPPLEMENT TO CHAPTER 6

Financial Statement Reporting: The Balance Sheet

LOANS RECEIVABLE

FASB Statement Number 91 (Accounting for Nonrefundable Fees and Costs Associated With Originating or Acquiring Loans and Initial Direct Costs of Leases) applies to both the incremental direct costs of originating a loan, and internally incurred costs directly related to loan activity. Loan origination fees are netted with the related loan origination costs and are accounted for in the following manner:

- For loans held for resale, the net cost is capitalized and recognized at the time the loan is sold.
- For loans held for investment, the net cost is capitalized and amortized over the loan period using the interest method.

Loan commitment fees are initially deferred and recognized in earnings as follows:

- If the commitment is exercised, the fee is recognized over the loan period by the interest method.
- If the commitment expires, the fee is recognized at the expiration date.

- If, based upon previous experience, exercise of the commitment is remote, amortize the fee over the commitment period using the straight-line method.

IMPAIRMENT OF LOANS

FASB Statement Number 114 (Accounting by Creditors for Impairment of a Loan) provides that a loan is a contractual obligation to receive money either on demand or at a fixed or determinable date. Loans include accounts receivable and notes if their maturity date exceeds one year. If it is probable that some or all of the principal or interest is uncollectible, the loan is deemed impaired. A loss on an impaired loan is recorded immediately by debiting bad debt expense and crediting a valuation allowance.

Determining the Value of an Impaired Loan

The loss on an impaired loan is the difference between the investment in loan and the discounted value of future cash flows using the effective interest rate on the original loan. In general, the investment in loan is the principal plus accrued interest. In practical terms, the value of a loan may be based on its market price, if available. The loan value may also be based on the fair value of the collateral, less estimated selling costs, if the loan is collateralized and the security is expected to be the only basis of repayment.

Example 1. On December 31, 2000, Debtor Inc. issues a five-year, $100,000 note at an annual interest rate of 10% payable to Creditor Inc. The market interest rate for the loan is 12%. The discounted value of the principal is $56,742 (based on a principal of $100,000 discounted at 12% for 5 years). The discounted value of the interest payments is $36,048 (based on annual interest of $10,000 for 5 years discounted at 12%). Thus, the discounted value of the loan is $92,790 ($56,742 plus $36,048). Discount on Notes Receivable is $7,210 ($100,000 less $92,790). The discount will be amortized using the effective interest method. Creditor Inc. records the note as follows:

Notes Receivable	100,000	
Discount on Notes Receivable		7,210
Cash		92,790

On December 31, 2002, Creditor Inc. determines that it is probable that Debtor Inc. will only be able to repay interest of $8,000 per year (rather than $10,000 per year) and $70,000 (rather than $100,000) of face value at maturity. This loan impairment requires the immediate recognition of a loss. The discounted value of future cash flows discounted for 3 years at 12% for $70,000 is $49,824, and for $8,000 is $19,215. Therefore, the total present value of future cash flows is $69,039 ($49,824 plus $19,215). On 12/31/02, the carrying value of the investment in loan is $95,196. As a result, the impairment loss is $26,157 ($95,196 less $69,039). The journal entry to record the loss is:

Bad Debts	26,157	
Allowance for Bad Debts		26,157

Interest income from an impaired loan may be recognized using several methods including cash-basis, cost-recovery, or a combination.

If the creditor's charging off of some part of the loan results in recording an investment in an impaired loan below its present value of future cash flows, no additional impairment is to be recorded.

In determining the collectibility of a loan, consideration should be given to the following:

- Financial problems of borrower
- Borrower is in an unstable or unhealthy industry
- Regulatory reports
- Compliance exception reports
- Amount of loan
- Prior loss experience
- Lack of marketability of collateral

A loan is not considered impaired when the delay in collecting is insignificant.

Disclosures

The following should be disclosed either in the body of the financial statements or in the footnotes:

- The creditor's policy of recognizing interest income on impaired loans, including the recording of cash receipts.
- The average recorded investment in impaired loans, the related interest revenue recognized while the loans were impaired, and the amount of interest revenue recognized using the cash basis while the loans were impaired.

- The total investment in impaired loans including (1) the amount of investments for which a related valuation allowance exists and (2) the amount of investments for which a valuation allowance does not exist.

DONATION OF FIXED ASSETS

FASB Statement Number 116 (Accounting for Contributions Received and Contributions Made) requires a donated fixed asset to be recorded at its fair market value by debiting the fixed asset and crediting contribution revenue.

According to FASB Statement 116, the company donating a nonmonetary asset recognizes an expense for the fair value of the donated asset. The difference between the carrying value and the fair value of the donated asset is a gain or loss.

Example 2. Hartman Company donates land costing $100,000 with a fair value of $130,000. The journal entry is:

Contribution Expense	130,000	
Land		100,000
Gain on Disposal of Land		30,000

If a company pledges unconditionally to give an asset in the future, accrue contribution expense and a payable. However, if the pledge is conditional, an entry is not made until the asset is transferred.

IMPAIRMENT OF FIXED ASSETS

FASB Statement Number 121 (Accounting for the Impairment of Long-Lived Assets and for Long-Lived Assets to be Disposed Of) states that a noncurrent asset is considered impaired if the total (undiscounted) expected future cash flows from using it is below its carrying value. (In ascertaining whether asset impairment has occurred, its carrying value should include any associated goodwill.) If this recoverability test for asset impairment is satisfied, an impairment loss must be computed as the excess of the asset's book value over its fair value. Fair value is the amount at which the asset could be purchased or sold between willing participants; fair value is not based on a forced or liquidation sale. Possible methods to determine fair market value include the market price in an active market, price of similar assets, or value based on a valuation technique (e.g., present value of future cash flows, options pricing model).

If the fair market value is not determinable and the discounted value of future cash flows is used, the asset should be grouped at the lowest level at which the cash flows are separately identifiable.

An impairment loss is charged against earnings with a similar reduction in the recorded value of the impaired fixed asset. After impairment, the reduced carrying value becomes the new cost basis for the fixed asset. Thus, the fixed asset cannot be written up for a subsequent recovery in market value. Therefore, the impaired loss cannot be restored. Depreciation is based on the new cost basis.

In the event that the impaired asset is to be disposed of instead of being kept in service, the impaired asset should be recorded at the lower of cost or net realizable value.

An impairment may arise from a major change in how the asset is used, a decline in market value, continued expected losses from the asset, excess construction costs over expected amounts, adverse business conditions, or legal problems.

Example 3. A company has a fixed asset with a cost of $1,000,000 and accumulated depreciation of $200,000. In applying the recoverability test to ascertain if an impairment has taken place, it is determined that the total (undiscounted) expected future net cash flows is $840,000. No impairment exists because the undiscounted future expected net cash flows ($840,000) is more than the carrying value of the asset ($800,000).

Example 4. Assume the same data as in the prior example except that the total (undiscounted) future net cash flows is $700,000. The recoverability test now shows an impairment loss because the total (undiscounted) cash flows ($700,000) is less than the book value ($800,000) of the fixed asset. Assuming the fixed asset has a fair market value of $680,000, the impairment loss equals $120,000 (book value of $800,000 less fair market value of $680,000). The journal entry to record the impairment is:

Loss on Impairment of Fixed Asset	120,000	
Accumulated Depreciation		120,000

The following must be footnoted in connection with impaired fixed assets:
- Identifying the asset impaired
- Amount of loss
- Method used to determine fair market value
- Cause of impairment
- Business segment experiencing the impairment in asset value

If an impaired asset is to be disposed of instead of used, the impaired asset is presented at the lower of cost or net realizable value (fair value less cost to sell). The selling costs include brokerage commissions and transfer fees. However, insurance, security services, utility expenses and costs to protect or maintain the asset are usually not deemed selling costs in determining net realizable value. The present value of costs to sell may be used when the fair value of the asset is based on the discounted cash flows and the sale is expected to take place after one year.

If the asset is to be disposed of shortly, the net realizable value is a better measure of the cash flows that one can expect to receive from the impaired asset. Assets held for disposal are not depreciated. Conceptually, these assets are more like inventory because they are expected to be sold in the near term.

STOCK-BASED COMPENSATION

FASB Statement Number 123 (Accounting for Stock-Based Compensation) applies to stock option plans, nonvested stock, employee stock purchase plans, and stock compensation awards that are to be settled by cash payment.

Stock Option Plans

Employers may account for stock option plans using either the "intrinsic value" method or the "fair value" method.

The "intrinsic value" method is the one in place before FASB Statement Number 123. It is already discussed in the main volume. The "fair value" method under FASB Statement Number 123 is discussed in this supplement.

Under the fair value method, fair value is computed by using an option-pricing model that takes into account several factors. A popular option pricing model is Black and Scholes. It is used to compute the equilibrium value of an option. The model provides insight into the valuation of debt relative to equity. This model may be programmed into computer spreadsheets and some pocket calculators. The Black-Scholes model makes it possible to determine the present value of hypothetical financial instruments. Some assumptions of this model are that 1) the stock options are freely traded and 2) the total return rate (considering the change in price plus dividends) may be determined based on a continuous compounding over the life of the option. Under FASB Statement Number 123 the option life is the expected time period until the option is exercised rather than the contractual term. By reducing the option's life its value is reduced. It is a random variable derived from a normal bell curve distribution. The Black-Scholes model was developed based on European-style options exercisable only at expiration. However, most employee stock options are American-style and are exercisable at any time during the option life once vesting has taken place. The

Black-Scholes model uses the volatility expected for the option's life. NOTE: Difficulties arise in determining option values when there is an early option exercise and variability in stock price and dividends. The Black-Scholes model may also be used in valuing put options by modifying computations. See chapter on Financial Derivatives Products and Financial Engineering for more information on Black-Scholes.

Other models may be used for option pricing such as the more complicated binomial model.

Before the current value of an option may be computed, consideration must be given to its expiration value.

Compensation expense is based on the fair value of the award at the grant date, and is recognized over the period between the grant date and the vesting date, in a way similar to the intrinsic value method.

Under the fair value method, the stock option is accounted for in a similar way as the journal entries under the intrinsic value method, except the fair value of the option would be recognized as deferred compensation and amortized over the period from the grant date to the date the option is initially exercisable.

Note: Non-compensatory stock option plans may also exist. Such plans are characterized by having stock offered to employees on some basis (e.g., equally, percent of salary), participation by full-time employees, a reasonable time period for the exercise of the options, and the discount to employees to buy the stock is not better than that afforded to company stockholders. If any of these criteria are not satisfied, than the plan is compensatory in nature. The objective of a non-compensatory plan is to obtain funds and to have greater widespread ownership in the company among employees. It is not primarily designed to provide compensation for services performed. Therefore, no compensation expense is recognized.

Nonvested Stock

Nonvested stock is stock that cannot be sold currently because the employee who was granted the shares has not yet satisfied the vesting requirements to earn the right to the shares. The fair value of a share of nonvested stock awarded to an employee is measured at the market price per share of non-restricted stock on the grant date unless a restriction will be imposed after the employee has a vested right to it, in which case the fair value is approximated considering the restriction.

Employee Stock Purchase Plans

An employee stock purchase plan allows employees to buy stock at a discount. It is noncompensatory if the discount is minor (5% or less), most full-time employees may participate, and the plan has no option features.

Stock Compensation Awards Required to Be Settled by Paying Cash

Some stock-based compensation plans require an employer to pay an employee, either on demand or at a particular date, a cash amount based on the appreciation in the market price of the employer's stock. A ceiling stock price may be established depending on the plan. The compensation cost applicable to the award is the amount of change in stock price.

Disclosures

The following should be disclosed regarding the fair value method to account for stock options as well as for stock-based compensation plans in general:

- Weighted-average grant date fair value of options and/or other equity instruments granted during the year.
- A description of the method and assumptions used to estimate fair value of options.
- Major changes in the terms of stock-based compensation plans.
- Amendments to outstanding awards.

Tax Aspects

Compensation expense is deductible for tax reporting when paid but deducted for financial reporting when accrued. This results in interperiod income tax allocation involving a deferred income tax credit. If for some reason reversal of the temporary difference does not occur, a permanent difference exists which does not impact profit. The difference should adjust paid-in-capital in the year the accrual occurs.

SUPPLEMENT TO CHAPTER 8

ACCOUNTING AND DISCLOSURES

SEGMENTAL DISCLOSURES

FASB Statement Number 131 (Disclosures About Segments of an Enterprise and Related Information) requires that the amount reported for each segment item should be based on what is used by the "chief operating decision-maker" in formulating a determination as to how much resources to assign to a segment and how to appraise the performance of that segment. The term "chief operating decision maker" may apply to the chief executive officer or chief operating officer or to a group of executives. *Note:* The reference of "chief operating decision-maker" may apply to a function and not necessarily to a specific person(s).

Revenue, gains, expenses, losses, and assets should only be allocated to a segment if the chief operating decision maker considers it in measuring a segment's earnings for purposes of making a financial or operating decision. The same is true with regard to allocating to segments eliminations and adjustments applying to the company's general purpose financial statements. Any allocation of financial items to a segment should be rationally based.

In measuring a segment's earnings or assets, the following should be disclosed for explanatory purposes:

- Measurement or valuation basis used.
- Differences in measurements used for the general-purpose financial statements relative to the financial information of the segment.

- A change in measurement method relative to prior years.
- A symmetrical allocation meaning an allocation of depreciation or amortization to a segment without a related allocation to the associated asset.

Segmental information is required in annual financial statements. Some segmental disclosures are required in interim financial statements.

Segmental Attributes

An operating segment is a distinct revenue-producing component of the business for which internal financial data are produced. Expenses are recognized as incurred in that segment. *Note:* A start-up operation would qualify as an operating segment even though revenue is not being earned. An operating segment is periodically reviewed by the chief operating decision-maker to evaluate performance and to determine what and how much resources to allocate to the segment.

A reportable segment requiring disclosure is one which is both an operating segment and meets certain percentage tests discussed in the next section.

An aggregation may be made of operating segments if they are similar in terms of products or services, customer class, manufacturing processes, distribution channels, legal entity, and regulatory control.

Percentage Tests

A reportable segment satisfies one of the following criteria:

- Revenue including unaffiliated and intersegment sales or transfers is 10% or more of total (combined) revenue of all operating segments.
- Operating profit or loss is 10% or more of total operating profit of all operating segments.
- Assets are 10% or more of total assets of all operating segments.

After the 10% tests have been made, additional segments may be reported on if they do not satisfy the 10% tests until at least 75% (constituting a substantial portion) of total revenue of all operating segments have been included. As a practical matter, no more than 10 segments (upper limit) should be reported because to do otherwise would result in too cumbersome or detailed reporting. In this case, combined reporting should be of those operating segments most closely related.

If a segment does not meet the 10% test for reportability in the current year but met the 10% test in prior years and is expected to be reportable in future years, it should still be reported in the current year.

If a segment passes the 10% test in the current year because of some unusual and rare occurrence, it should be excluded from reporting in the current year.

Reconciliation

A company does not have to use the same accounting principles for segmental purposes as that used to prepare the consolidated financial statements. There must be a reconciliation between segmental financial data and general purpose financial statements. The reconciliation is for revenue, operating profit or loss, and assets. Any differences in measurement approaches between the company as a whole and its segments should be explained. If measurement practices have changed over the years regarding the operating segments, that fact should be disclosed and explained. The business must describe its reasoning and methods in deriving the composition of its operating segments.

Restatement

If the business structure changes, this may require a restatement of segmental information presented in prior years to aid in comparability. If restatement occurs, appropriate footnote disclosure should be made.

Disclosures

Disclosure should be provided of major sources of foreign revenue constituting 10% or more of total revenue. Further, disclosure is necessary if a foreign area constitutes 10% or more of total operating profit or loss, or of total assets. The foreign area and the percentage derived therein should be disclosed.

Disclosure should exist of the dollar sales to major customers comprising of 10% or more of total revenue. A single customer may refer to more than one customer if under common control (e.g., subsidiaries of a parent). A single customer may also be defined as government agencies.

Information about foreign geographic areas and customers are required even if this information is not used by the business in formulating operating decisions.

Disclosure should be made of major contracts to other entities and governments.

Disclosure should be made of how reporting segments were determined (e.g., customer class, products or services, geographic areas). Disclosure should be given identifying those operating segments that have been aggregated. The following should be disclosed for each reportable segment:

- Types of products and services.
- Revenue to outside customers as well as intersegment revenue.
- Operating profit or loss.
- Total assets.
- Capital expenditures.
- Depreciation, depletion and amortization.
- Major noncash revenues and expenses excluding that immediately above.
- Interest revenue and interest expense.
- Extraordinary and unusual items.
- Equity in earnings of investee.
- Tax effects.

Example 1. A company reports the following information for its reportable segments:

Segment	Total Revenue	Operating Profit	Identifiable Assets
1	$500	$50	$200
2	250	10	150
3	3,500	200	1,950
4	1,500	100	900
Total	$5,750	$360	$3,200

The revenue test is $10\% \times \$5,750 = \$575$. Segments 3 and 4 satisfy this test.

The operating profit (loss) test is $10\% \times \$360 = \$36$. Segments 1, 3 and 4 satisfy this test.

The identifiable assets test is $10\% \times \$3,200 = \$320$. Segments 3 and 4 satisfy this test. Therefore, the reportable segments are 1, 3 and 4.

DISCLOSURE OF CAPITAL STRUCTURE INFORMATION

FASB Statement Number 129 (Disclosure of Information About Capital Structure) requires footnote disclosure regarding the rights and privileges of common and preferred stockholders such as dividend preferences, participation privileges, conversion terms, unusual voting rights, sinking fund requirements, and terms for additional issuances. In a liquidation situation, footnote information must be made of liquidation preferences such as dividend arrearages and liquidation values for preferred stock. In the case of redeemable stock, disclosure must be made of redemption requirements for each of the next five years.

RELATED PARTY DISCLOSURES

FASB Statement Number 57 deals with disclosures for related party transactions. Such transactions occur when a transacting party can significantly influence or exercise control of another transaction party because of a financial, common ownership, or familial relationship. It may also arise when a nontransacting party can significantly impact the policies of two other transacting parties. Related party transactions include those involving:

- Joint ventures.
- Activities between a subsidiary and parent.
- Activities between affiliates of the same parent company.
- Relationships between the company and its principal owners, management, or their immediate families.

Related party transactions often occur in the ordinary course of business and may include such activities as granting loans or incurring debt, sales, purchases, services performed or received, guarantees, allocating common costs as the basis for billings, compensating balance requirements, property transfers, rentals, and filing of consolidated tax returns.

Related party transactions are presumed not to be at arm's length. They are usually not derived from competitive, free-market dealings. Some possible examples follow:

- A "shell" company (with no economic substance) purchases merchandise at inflated prices.
- A lease at "bargain" or excessive prices.
- Unusual guarantees or pledges.
- A loan at an unusually low or high interest rate
- Payments for services at inflated prices.

Related party disclosures include the following:

- Nature and substance of the relationship.
- Amount of transaction.

- Terms of transaction.
- Year-end balances due or owed.
- Any control relationships that exist.

DISCLOSURES FOR DERIVATIVES

The Securities and Exchange Commission requires certain disclosures for the accounting and reporting for derivatives including financial instruments and commodities. Derivative commodity instruments include futures, forwards, options and swaps. These disclosures include:

- The types and nature of derivative instruments to be accounted for.
- The accounting method used for derivatives such as the fair value method, accrual method, and deferral method. Disclosure should be made where gains and losses associated with derivatives are reported.
- The risks associated with the derivatives.
- Distinguishment of derivatives used for trading or nontrading purposes.
- Derivatives used for hedging purposes including explanation.

INFLATION INFORMATION

FASB Statement Number 89 (Financial Reporting and Changing Prices) permits an entity to voluntarily disclose inflation information so management and financial statement readers can better evaluate the impact of inflation on the business. Selected summarized financial information should be presented based on current costs and adjusted for inflation (in constant purchasing power) for a five-year period. The Consumer Price Index for All Urban Consumers may be used. Inflation disclosures include those for sales and operating revenue stated in constant purchasing power, income from continuing operations (including per share amounts) on a current cost basis, cash dividends per share in constant purchasing power, market price per share restated in constant purchasing power, purchasing power gain or loss on net monetary items, inflation adjusted inventory, restated fixed assets, foreign currency translation based on current cost, net assets based on current cost, and the Consumer Price Index used.

ENVIRONMENTAL REPORTING AND DISCLOSURES

Companies are faced with federal and local compliance requirements regarding environmental issues. Environmental laws provide rigorous specifications with which companies must comply. The costs of compliance could significantly increase a company's expected cost of projects and processes. Failure to abide by environmental dictates could result in substantial costs and risks including civil and criminal prosecution and fines. The company must police itself to avoid legal defense fees and penalties. An effective compliance program, such as having preventive and detective controls, is crucial in minimizing environmental risks. The corporate manager must be assured that appropriate accounting, reporting, and disclosures for environmental issues are being practiced by the firm.

Legislation

The Environmental Protection Agency (EPA) enforces Federal laws regulating pollution, sold waste disposal, water supply, pesticide and radiation control and ocean dumping. EPA regulations require adherence to specific pollution detection procedures, such as leak testing, and installation of corrosion protection and leak detection systems applicable to underground storage tanks.

The Clean Air Act of 1963 concentrates on issues such as acid rain, urban smog, air-borne toxins, ozone-depleting chemicals and other air pollution problems. The Clean Water Act established controls of water pollution and wetlands preservation.

The Environmental Response Compensation and Liability Act (Superfund) relates to uncontrolled or abandoned hazardous waste disposal sites. Companies must disclose emergency planning, spills or accidents of hazardous materials, and when chemicals are released into surrounding areas. The chemicals must be disclosed to prospective buyers, employees, and tenants.

To go from a reactive position (the company just complies with regulations) to a proactive policy (the company envelops environmental concerns into its daily business practices), the entity must formulate financial information to complement technical and scientific data. Further, environmental expenditures have to be segregated so as to improve decision making and accountability for environmental responsibilities. There should be an appraisal model for setting priorities as the basis for resource allocations.

Accounting and Reporting

Securities and Exchange Commission Staff Accounting Bulletin Number 92 deals with how environmental liabilities are determined, future contingencies, "key" environmental factors, and disclosures of environmental problems. Depending on the circumstances a liability and/or footnote disclosure would be required. Examples are:

- Information on site remediation projects such as current and future costs, and remediation trends. Site remediation includes hazard waste sites.
- Contamination due to environmental health and safety problems.
- Legal and regulatory compliance issues such as with regard to cleanup responsibility.
- Water or air pollution.

Environmental problems should be addressed immediately to avoid significant future costs including additional cleanup costs, penalties, and legal fees.

Environmental costs should be compared to budgeted amounts, and variances may be computed and tracked. Forecasted information should be changed as new information is available. Internal controls must be established over the firm's environmental responsibility, including internal checks, safeguarding of assets, and segregation of duties.

A financial analysis of environmental costs should be conducted by analyzing cost trends over the years within the company, comparisons to competing companies, and comparisons to industry averages. Additionally, comparisons should be made between projects within the company.

Environmental costs should be allocated across departments, products, and services. Environmental cost information is useful in product and service mix decisions, pricing policies, selecting production inputs, appraising pollution prevention programs, and evaluating waste management policies.

KEY FINANCIAL ACCOUNTING AREAS

LEASES

Transfer of Lease Receivable

The lessor may transfer a lease receivable. The gain on sale equals the cash received less both the portion of the gross investment sold and unearned income related to the minimum lease payments.

Example 1. A lessor has on its books a lease receivable with an unguaranteed residual value. Unlike guaranteed residual value, unguaranteed residual value does not qualify as a financial asset. The lessor sells an 80% interest in the minimum lease payments for $100,000. The lessor keeps a 20% interest in the minimum lease payments and a 100% interest in the unguaranteed residual value. Other information follows:

Minimum lease payments		$110,000
Unearned income in minimum lease payments		75,000
Gross investment in minimum lease payments		185,000
Add: Unguaranteed residual value	7,000	
Unguaranteed income in residual value	13,000	
Gross investment in residual value		20,000
Gross investment in lease receivable		$205,000

The journal entry for the sale of the lease receivable is:

Cash	100,000
Unearned income ($75,000 × 80%)	60,000
Lease receivable ($185,000 × 80%)	148,000
Gain	12,000

Related Parties

In a related party lease where substantial influence exists, the lease should be accounted for based on its economic substance rather than its legal form. If substantial influence is absent, the related party lease should be classified and accounted for as if the participants were unrelated.

FASB Statement Number 13 requires that a parent must consolidate a subsidiary whose principal business operations is leasing property from a parent or other affiliates.

A related party lease agreement involving significant influence may require consolidation accounting for the lessor and lessee if all of the following conditions are present:

- Most of the lessor's activities apply to leasing assets to one specific lessee.
- The lessee incurs the risks and rewards applicable with rented property along with any related debt. This may occur if the lease agreement gives the lessee control and management over the leased property, the lessee guarantees the lessor's debt or residual value of the leased item, and the lessee has the right to purchase the property at a lower than fair value price.
- The lessor's owners do not have a significant residual equity capital investment at risk.

If the consolidation conditions are not met, combined financial statements instead of consolidated financial statements may be appropriate.

FASB Statement Number 57 requires disclosure of the nature and degree of leasing transactions among related parties.

Money-Over-Money Lease

A money-over-money lease occurs when an entity manufactures or purchases an asset, leases it to the lessee, and receives nonrecourse financing exceeding the cost of the asset. The collateral for the borrowing is the leased asset and any future rental derived therefrom. The lessor is prohibited from offsetting the asset (in an operating lease) or the lease receivable (in other than an operating lease) and the nonrecourse obligation unless a legal right of setoff exists. The leasing and borrowing are considered separate transactions.

Business Combinations

A business combination by itself has no bearing on lease classification. In a purchase transaction, the acquirer may assign a new value to a capitalized lease because of the allocation of acquisition price to the net assets of the acquired entity. However, provided the lease terms are not modified, the lease should be accounted for using the original terms and classification. A similar treatment is afforded under the pooling-of-interest method in that the new lease would retain its classification.

With respect to a leveraged lease when the purchase method is used the following guidelines are followed:

- The classification continues as a leveraged lease.
- The net investment in the leveraged lease should be recorded at fair market value including tax effects.
- The usual accounting for a leveraged lease should be practiced.

Disposal of a Business Segment

The expected costs directly associated with a disposal of a business segment decision includes future rental payments less amounts to be received from subleases. The difference between the unamortized cost of the leased property and the discounted value of the minimum lease payments to be received from the sublease is recognized as a gain or loss.

PENSION PLANS

Employers Having More Than One Defined Benefit Plan

If an employer has more than one pension plan, it has to prepare separate calculations of pension expense, fair value of plan assets, and liabilities for each plan.

The employer is prohibited from offsetting assets or liabilities of different pension plans unless a legal right exists to use the assets of one plan to pay the debt or benefits of another plan.

Disclosures may be combined for all pension plans kept by the employer with the following exceptions:

- U.S. pension plans may not be aggregated with foreign pension plans unless there exist similar assumptions.
- A minimum pension asset of one plan may not be used to offset a minimum pension liability of another, and vice versa.

Multiemployer Plans

A multiemployer plan typically includes participation of two or more unrelated employers. It often arises from a collective-bargaining contract with the union. The plan is typically administered by a Board of Trustees. In this instance, plan assets contributed by one employer may be used to pay employee benefits of another participating employer. Hence, the assets are combined for all employers and are available and unrestricted to pay benefits to all employees irrespective of whom they are employed by. In other words, there is no segregation of assets in a particular employer's account or any restrictions placed on that employer's assets. An example is a plan contributed to by all employers employing the members of a particular union regardless of whom the employees work for. Retirees of different employers receive payment from the same combined fund. An example is the teamster's union.

In a multiemployer plan, the employer's pension expense equals its contribution to the plan for the year. If a contribution is accrued, the employer must record a liability.

If an employer withdraws from the multiemployer plan, it may incur a liability for its share of the unfunded benefit obligation of the plan. If an employer would probably incur a liability if it withdraws from the plan and the amount is reasonably ascertainable, a loss must be accrued with a concurrent liability. However, if the loss is reasonably possible, only footnote disclosure is needed.

Footnote disclosure for employers involved with a multiemployer plan include:

- A description of the plan including employees covered.
- The benefits to be provided.
- Nature of matters affecting the comparability of information for the years presented.
- Pension expense for the period.

Multiple-Employer Plans

These plans have similarities to multiemployer plans. They also consist of two or more unrelated employers. However, multiple-employer plans are in effect aggregated single-employer plans that are combined so that assets of all may be totaled so as to lower administrative costs. The assets are merged so as to improve the overall rate of return from investing them. In many instances, participating employers may use different benefit formulas for their respective pension contributions. Each employer in the plan accounts for its particular interest separately. An example of such an arrangement is when businesses in an industry have their trade group handle the plans of all the companies. Each company retains its responsibilities only for its own workers. Multiple-employer plans are typically not associated with collective-bargaining agreements.

Annuity Contracts

An employer may sign a valid and irrevocable insurance contract to pay benefit obligations arising from a defined benefit plan. Annuity contracts are used to transfer the risk of providing employee benefits from the employer to the insurance company.

If the annuity contracts are the basis to fund the pension plan and to pay plan obligations, the employer's insurance premium is the pension expense for the period covering all currently earned benefits. In this instance, the company and plan do not report plan assets, accumulated benefit obligation, or a projected benefit obligation. On the contrary, if the annuity contracts only cover part of the benefit obligation, the employer is liable for the uncovered obligation.

In a participating annuity contract, the insurer pays the employer part of the income earned from investing the insurance premiums. In most instances, income earned (e.g., interest, dividends) reduces pension expense. A disadvantage to the employer of a participating contract is that it costs more than one which is nonparticipating due to the participation privilege. This additional cost applicable to the participation right should be recognized as a pension plan asset. Therefore, except for the cost of participation rights, pension plan assets exclude the cost of annuity contracts. In later years, fair value should be used in valuing the participation right included in plan assets. In the event that fair value may not be reasonably determined, the asset should be recorded at cost with amortization based on the dividend period stipulated in the contract. However, unamortized cost cannot exceed the net realizable value of the participation right. If the terms of the participating annuity contract is such that the employer retains all or most of the risk applicable to the benefit obligation, the purchase of this contract does not constitute a settlement of the employer's obligations under the pension plan.

Insurance contracts other than annuity contracts are considered investments. They are reported as pension plan assets and reported at fair value.

Fair value may be in terms of conversion value, contract value, cash surrender value, etc., depending on the circumstances.

The definition of an annuity contract is *not* met if one or more of the following exist:

- There exists uncertainty as to whether the insurance company will be able to pay its debts due to financial difficulties.
- There is a captive insurance company, meaning that the insurance entity has as its major client the employer or any of its associated parties.

An employer has to record a loss when it assumes the obligation to pay retirees because the insurance company is financially unable to do so. The loss is recorded at the lower of any gain associated with the original insurance contract or the amount of benefit assumed. An unrecognized additional loss should be treated as an amendment to the pension plan.

Employee Retirement Income Security Act (ERISA)

The Act generally provides for full vesting of pension benefits if an employee has worked for 15 years. Past service costs must be funded over a period not more than 40 years.

Employer's Accounting for Postemployment Benefits

FASB Statement Number 112 provides authoritative guidance in accounting and reporting for postemployment benefits. The pronouncement relates to benefits to former or inactive employees, their beneficiaries, and dependents after employment, but before retirement. Former or inactive employees include individuals on disability and those that have been laid off. However, individuals on vacation or holiday or who are ill are not considered inactive.

Postemployment benefits are different from postretirement benefits. Postemployment benefits may be in cash or in kind and include salary continuation benefits, supplemental unemployment benefits, severance benefits, disability related benefits, job training and counseling benefits, life insurance benefits, and healthcare benefits.

An accrual is made for postemployment benefits if the following conditions are met:

- The amount of benefits is reasonably determinable.
- Benefits apply for services already rendered.
- Payment of benefits is probable.
- Benefit obligations vest or accumulate.

PROFIT SHARING PLANS

A profit sharing plan may be discretionary (contributions are at the discretion of the Board of Directors) or nondiscretionary (contributions are based on a predetermined formula and depend on attaining a specified earnings level). In a discretionary plan, an accrual of expense is made when set by the Board. The entry is to debit profit sharing expense and credit accrued profit sharing liability. In a nondiscretionary arrangement, an accrual is made when required under the plan terms.

INCOME TAX ACCOUNTING

Multiple Tax Jurisdictions

The determination for federal reporting purposes may differ from that of local reporting requirements. As a result, temporary differences, permanent differences, and loss carrybacks or carryforwards may differ between federal and state and/or city reporting. If temporary differences are significant, separate deferred tax computations and recording will be required.

Tax Status Changes

The impact of any change in tax status affecting a business requires an immediate adjustment to deferred tax liabilities (or assets) and to income tax expense. An example of a tax status change requiring an adjustment on the accounts is a company opting for C corporation status. There should be a footnote describing the nature of the status change and its impact on the accounts.

Business Combinations

In a business combination accounted for under the purchase method the costs assigned to the acquired entity's net assets may differ from the valuation of those net assets on the tax return. This may cause a temporary difference arising in either a deferred tax liability or deferred tax asset reported on the acquirer's consolidated financial statements.

The amortization of goodwill for tax purposes is over a mandatory 15-year period while for books goodwill may be amortized over a 40-year period. This gives rise to a temporary difference. Negative goodwill may also result in a temporary difference arising from the difference of depreciation expense for book and tax purposes.

A company may have unrecognized tax benefits applicable to operating losses or tax credits arising from a purchase business combination. This may give rise to other similar tax advantages after the combination date. The tax benefits realized should be apportioned for book reporting between pre- and post-acquisition tax benefits.

Under the pooling-of-interest method, if the combined entity will be able to use an operating loss or tax credit carryforward, the deferred tax benefits should be recognized when previous year's financial statements are restated.

In some cases, a pooling-of-interests is taxable requiring a step up of the net assets of a combining company for tax reporting. The difference between the stepped-up basis and the book value of net assets on the books constitutes a temporary difference.

Separate Financial Statements of a Subsidiary

If separate financial statements are prepared, the consolidated income tax expense should be allocated to each of the subsidiaries.

Employee Stock Ownership Plans

Retained earnings is increased for the tax benefit arising from deductible dividends paid on unallocated shares held by an ESOP. However, dividends paid on allocated shares are includable in income tax expense.

Quasi Reorganization

The tax benefits applicable with deductible temporary differences and carryforwards on the date of a quasi-reorganization should usually be recorded as an increase in paid-in-capital if the tax benefits will occur in later years.

COST-VOLUME-PROFIT ANALYSIS AND LEVERAGE

BREAK-EVEN AND COST-VOLUME-REVENUE ANALYSIS FOR NONPROFIT ORGANIZATIONS

By definition, the goal of a nonprofit entity is *not* to earn a profit. The nonprofit organization's objective is to render as much suitable service as possible with as little human and physical services, as needed. Ideally, the performance in a nonprofit organization is to break even. This means that, by and large and on a short-term basis, revenues should equal costs. If you generate a surplus, a possibility is that you may not receive the same amount from the funding agency as last year. On the other hand, if you produce a deficit, you may run into insolvency, a danger for survival. Further, chances are that you may not be able to borrow money from the bank, as not-for-profit entities often can, because of your weak financial stance. One thing is clear; over the long run, nonprofit entities cannot survive without reserves and cannot sustain persistent deficits.

Cost-volume-revenue (CVR) analysis, together with cost behavior information, helps nonprofit managers perform many useful analyses. CVR analysis deals with how revenue and costs change with a change in the service level. More specifically, it looks at the effects on revenues of changes in such factors as variable costs, fixed costs, prices, service level, and mix of services offered. By studying the relationships of costs, service volume, and revenue, nonprofit management is better able to cope with many planning decisions.

Break-even analysis, a branch of CVR analysis, determines the break-even service level. The break-even point—the financial crossover point where revenues exactly match costs—does not show up in financial reports, but nonprofit financial managers find it an extremely useful measurement in a variety of ways. It reveals which programs are self-supporting and which are subsidized.

Questions Answered by CVR Analysis

CVR analysis tries to answer the following questions:

(a) What service level is (or what units of service are) required to break even?

(b) How would changes in price, variable costs, fixed costs, and service volume affect a surplus?

(c) How do changes in program levels and mix affect aggregate surplus/deficit?

(d) What alternative break-even strategies are available?

Analysis of Revenues. Revenues for nonprofit entities are typically classified into the following categories:

- Grants from governments.
- Grants from private sources.
- Cost reimbursements and sales.
- Membership fees.
- Public contributions received directly or indirectly.
- Legacies and memorials.
- Other revenues such as investment income (e.g., interest, dividends).

For managerial purposes, however, each type of revenue is grouped into its fixed and variable parts. Fixed revenues are those that remain unchanged regardless of the level of service, such as gifts, grants, and contracts. In colleges, for example, donations, gifts, and grants have no relationship to enrollment. Variable revenues are the ones that vary in proportion to the volume of activity. Examples are cost reimbursements and membership fees. In colleges, tuition and fees are variable in relation to the number of students. Different nonprofit entities may have different sources of revenue: variable revenue only, fixed revenue only, or a combination of both. In this chapter, we will cover all three cases in treating break-even and CVR questions.

Analysis of Cost Behavior. For external reporting purposes, costs are classified by managerial function (such as payroll, occupancy, and office), and also by programs and supporting services. A model functional classification is *IRS Form 990 Part II—Statement of Functional Expenses,* an excerpt from which is shown below.

IRS Form 990

Line No.	Functional expense category
26	Salaries and wages
27	Pension plan contributions
28	Other employee benefits
29	Payroll taxes
30	Professional fundraising fees
31	Accounting fees
32	Legal fees
33	Supplies
34	Telephone
35	Postage and shipping
36	Occupancy
37	Equipment rental and maintenance
38	Printing and publications
39	Travel
40	Conferences, conventions, meetings
41	Interest
42	Depreciation, depletion, etc.
43	Other expenses (itemize)

For managerial purposes (such as planning, control, and decision making), further classification of costs is desirable. One such classification is by behavior. Depending on how a cost will react or respond to changes in the level of activity, costs may be viewed as variable or fixed. This classification is made within a specified range of activity, called the relevant range. The relevant range is the volume zone within which the behavior of variable costs, fixed costs, and prices can be predicted with reasonable accuracy.

Typical activity measures are summarized below.

Measures of the Service Level

Nonprofit Types	Units of Service
Hospital or health care	Bed-days, patient contact hours, patient-days, service hours
Educational	Number of enrollments, class size, full-time equivalents (FTE) hours
Social clubs	Number of members served

Variable Costs. Variable costs vary in total with changes in volume or level of activity. Examples of variable costs include supplies, printing and publications, telephone, and postage and shipping.

Fixed Costs. Fixed costs do not change in total regardless of the volume or level of activity. Examples include salaries, accounting and consulting fees, and depreciation.

The following table shows the fixed-variable breakdown of IRS Form 990 functional expenses.

IRS Form 990 Line No.	Expense Category
	FIXED COSTS
26	Salaries and wages
27	Pension plan
28	Other benefits
29	Payroll taxes
30	Fund-raising fees
31	Accounting fees
32	Legal fees
36	Occupancy
37	Equipment rental/maintenance
41	Interest
42	Depreciation
43	Other
	VARIABLE COSTS
33	Supplies
34	Telephone
35	Postage and shipping

38	Printing and publications
39	Travel
40	Conferences, meetings
43	Other

Types of Fixed Costs—Program-Specific or Common. Fixed costs of nonprofit entities are subdivided into two groups. Direct or program-specific fixed costs are those that can be directly identified with individual programs. These costs are avoidable or escapable if the program is dropped. Examples include the salaries of the staff whose services can be used only in a given program, and depreciation of equipment used exclusively for the program. Common fixed costs would continue even if an individual program were discontinued.

CVR Analysis with Variable Revenue Only

For accurate CVR analysis, a distinction must be made between costs as either variable or fixed. In order to compute the break-even point and perform various CVR analyses, note the following important concepts.

Contribution Margin (CM). The contribution margin is the excess of revenue(R) over the variable costs (VC) of the service. It is the amount of money available to cover fixed costs (FC) and to generate surplus. Symbolically, CM = R – VC.

Unit CM. The unit CM is the excess of the unit price (P) over the unit variable cost (V). Symbolically, unit CM = P – V.

CM Ratio. The CM ratio is the contribution margin as a percentage of revenue, i.e.,

$$\text{CM ratio} = \frac{\text{CM}}{\text{R}} = \frac{\text{R} - \text{VC}}{\text{R}} = 1 - \frac{\text{VC}}{\text{R}}$$

The CM ratio can also be computed using per-unit data as follows:

$$\text{CM ratio} = \frac{\text{Unit CM}}{\text{P}} = \frac{\text{P} - \text{V}}{\text{P}} = 1 - \frac{\text{V}}{\text{P}}$$

Note that the CM ratio is 1 minus the variable cost ratio. For example, if variable costs are 40 percent of revenue, then the variable cost ratio is 40 percent and the CM ratio is 60 percent.

Example 1. To illustrate the various concepts of CM, assume that Los Altos Community Hospital has an average revenue of $250 per patient day. Variable costs are $50 per patient day. Total fixed costs per year are $650,000. Expected number of patient days is 4,000. The projected statement of revenue and expenditures follows:

	Total	Per Unit	Percentage
Revenue (4,000 days)	$1,000,000	$250	100%
Less: Variable costs	200,000	50	20
Contribution margin	$ 800,000	$200	80%
Less: Fixed costs	650,000		
Net income	$ 150,000		

From the data listed above, CM, unit CM, and the CM ratio are computed as:

$$CM = R - VC = \$1,000,000 - \$200,000 = \$800,000$$
$$Unit\ CM = P - V = \$250 - \$50 = \$200$$

$$CM\ ratio = \frac{CM}{R} = \frac{\$\ 800,000}{\$1,000,000} = 1 - \frac{\$\ 200,000}{\$1,000,000}$$
$$= 0.8 = 80\%$$

$$or = \frac{Unit\ CM}{P} = \frac{\$200}{\$250} = 0.8 = 80\%$$

Break-Even Analysis

The break-even point represents the level of revenue that equals the total of the variable and the fixed costs for a given volume of output service at a particular capacity use rate. Generally, the lower the break-even point, the higher the surplus and the less the operating risk, other things being equal. The break-even point also provides nonprofit managers with insights into surplus/deficit planning. To develop the formula for the break-even units of service, use the following variables:

R = Total revenue

P = Price or average revenue per unit

U = Units of service

VC = Total variable costs

V = Unit variable cost

FC = Total fixed costs

To break even means: Total revenue − total costs = 0

$$R - VC - FC = 0 \text{ or } PU - VU - FC = 0$$

To solve, factor U out to get $(P - V)U - FC = 0$
Rearrange as $(P - V)U = FC$ and divide by $(P - V)$ to isolate U.

$$U = \frac{FC}{(P - V)}$$

In words,

$$\text{Break-even point in units} = \frac{\text{Fixed costs}}{\text{Unit CM}}$$

If you want break-even point in dollars, use

$$\text{Break-even point in dollars} = \frac{\text{Fixed Costs}}{\text{CM ratio}}$$

Example 2. Using the same data as given in Example 1, where unit CM = $250 - $50 = $200 and CM ratio = 80%, we get:

Break-even point in units = $650,000/$200 = 3,250 patient days
Break-even point in dollars = $650,000/0.8 = $812,500

Or, alternatively,

3,250 patient days × $250 = $812,500. The hospital needs 3,250 patient days to break even.

Graphical Approach in a Spreadsheet Format. The graphical approach to obtaining the break-even point is based on the so-called *break-even (B-E) chart* as shown in Figure 1. Sales revenue, variable costs, and fixed costs are plotted on the vertical axis while volume, x, is plotted on the horizontal axis. The break-even point is the point where the total revenue line intersects the total cost line. The chart can effectively report surplus potentials over a wide range of activity and therefore can be used as a tool for discussion and presentation.

The *surplus-volume (S-V) chart* as shown in Figure 2, focuses on how surplus varies with changes in volume. Surplus is plotted on the vertical axis, while units of output are shown on the horizontal axis. The S-V chart provides a quick condensed comparison of how alternatives on pricing, variable costs, or fixed costs may affect surplus (or deficit) as volume changes. The S-

V chart can be easily constructed from the B-E chart. Note that the slope of the chart is the unit CM.

Determination of Target Surplus Volume. Besides determining the break-even point, CVR analysis determines the volume to attain a particular level of surplus. The formula is:

$$\text{Target surplus level} = \frac{\text{Fixed costs plus target surplus}}{\text{Unit CM}}$$

Example 3. Using the same data as given in Example 1, assume the hospital wishes to accumulate a surplus of $250,000 per year. Then, the target surplus service level would be:

$$\frac{\$650,000 + \$250,000}{\$250 - \$50} = \frac{\$900,000}{\$200} = 4,500 \text{ patient days}$$

Figure 1. Break-Even Chart

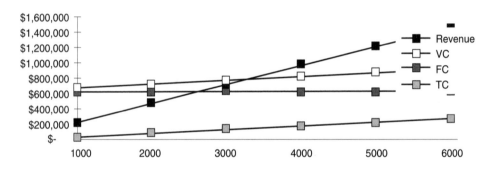

Figure 2. Surplus-Volume (S-V) Chart

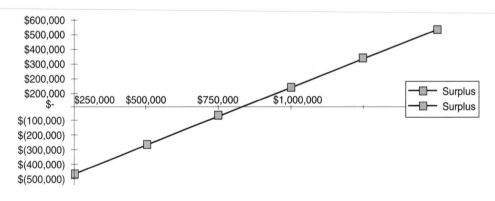

Margin of Safety. The margin of safety is a measure of difference between the actual level of service and the break-even service level. It is the amount by which revenue may drop before deficits begin, and is expressed as a percentage of expected service level:

$$\text{Margin of safety} = \frac{\text{Expected level} - \text{Break-even level}}{\text{Expected level}}$$

The margin of safety is used as a measure of operating risk. The larger the ratio, the safer the situation since there is less risk of reaching the break-even point.

Example 4. Assume that Los Altos Hospital projects 4,000 patient days with a break-even level of 3,250. The projected margin of safety is

$$\frac{4,000 - 3,250}{4,000} = 18.75\%$$

Example 5. A nonprofit college offers a program in management for executives. The program has been experiencing financial difficulties. Operating data for the most recent year are shown below.

Tuition revenue (40 participants @$7,000)	$280,000
Less variable expenses (@$4,000)	160,000
Contribution margin	$120,000
Less fixed expenses	150,000
Operating deficit	$(30,000)

The break-even point is $150,000/($7,000 - $4,000) = 50 participants.

Example 6. In Example 5, the dean of the school is convinced that the class size can be increased to more economical levels without lowering the quality. He is prepared to spend $15,000 per year in additional promotional and other support expenses. If that is the case, the new break-even point is 55 participants ($165,000/($7,000 - $4,000).

To generate a surplus of $30,000, the school must get 60 participants [$150,000 + $30,000)/$3,000].

Some Applications of CVR Analysis and What-If Analysis. The concepts of contribution margin and the contribution income statement have many applications in surplus/deficit planning and short-term decision making. Many "what-if" scenarios can be evaluated using them as planning tools, especially utilizing a spreadsheet program such as *Microsoft Excel* or *Lotus 1-2-3*. Some applications are illustrated below using the same data as in Example 1.

Example 7. Recall from Example 1 that Los Altos Hospital has unit CM =$250 - $50 = $200, CM ratio = 80%, and fixed costs of $650,000. Assume that the hospital expects revenues to go up by $250,000 for the next period. How much will surplus increase?

Using the CM concepts, we can quickly compute the impact of a change in the service level on surplus or deficit. The formula for computing the impact is:

$$\text{Change in surplus} = \text{Dollar change in revenue} \times \text{CM ratio}$$

Thus:

$$\text{Increase in surplus} = \$250,000 \times 80\% = \$200,000$$

Therefore, the income will go up by $200,000, assuming there is no change in fixed costs. If we are given a change in service units (e.g., patient days) instead of dollars, then the formula becomes:

$$\text{Change in surplus} = \text{Change in units} \times \text{Unit CM}$$

Example 8. Assume that the hospital expects patient days to go up by 500 units. How much will surplus increase? From Example 1, the hospital's unit CM is $200. Again, assuming there is no change in fixed costs, the surplus will increase by $100,000, as computed below.

$$500 \text{ additional patient days} \times \$200 \text{ CM per day} = \$100,000$$

Example 9. Referring back to Example 5, another alternative under consideration is to hold the present program without any change in the regular campus facilities instead of in rented outside facilities that are better located. If adopted, this proposal will reduce fixed costs by $60,000. The variable costs will decrease by $100 per participant. Is the move to campus facilities advisable if it leads to a decline in the number of participants by 5?

	Present		Proposed
S(40 × $7,000)	$280,000	(35 × $7,000)	$245,000
VC(40 × $4,000)	160,000	(35 × $3,900)	136,500
CM	$120,000		$108,500
FC	150,000		90,000
Surplus	$(30,000)		$ 18,500

The answer is yes, since the move will turn into a surplus.

CVR Analysis with Variable and Fixed Revenues. Many nonprofit organizations derive two types of revenue: fixed and variable. In this situation, the formulas developed previously need to be modified. The following example illustrates this.

Example 10. ACM, Inc., a mental rehabilitation provider, has a $1,200,000 lump-sum annual budget appropriation to help rehabilitate mentally ill clients. The agency charges each client $600 a month for board and care. All the appropriation must be spent. The variable costs for rehabilitation activity average $700 per patient per month. The agency's annual fixed costs are $800,000. The agency manager wishes to know how many patients can be served.

Let U = units of service = number of clients to be served.

We set up: Total revenue - Total expenses = 0

Lump sum appropriation + R - VC - FC = 0
Lump sum appropriation + PU - VU - FC = 0
$1,200,000 + $7,200 U - $8,400 U - $800,000 = 0
($7,200 - $8,400)U = $800,000 - $1,200,000
$$-\$1,200\ U = -\$400,000$$
$$U = \$400,000/\$1,200$$
$$U = 333 \text{ clients}$$

Alternatively, you may use the following formula:

$$\text{Break-even point in units} = \frac{\text{Fixed costs - Fixed revenue}}{\text{Unit CM}}$$

Thus,

$$\text{Break-even number of patients} = \frac{\$800,000 - \$1,200,000}{-\$1,200}$$
$$= \$400,000/\$1,200 = 333 \text{ clients}$$

We will investigate the following two "what-if" scenarios:

Example 11. In Example 10, suppose the manager of the agency is concerned that the total budget for the coming year will be cut by 10 percent to $1,080,000. All other things remain unchanged. The manager wants to know how this budget cut affects the next year's service level. Using the formula yields:

$$\text{Break-even number of clients} = \frac{\$800,000 - \$1,080,000}{-\$1,200}$$

$$U = -\$280,000 / -\$1,200$$

$$U = 233 \text{ clients}$$

Example 12. In Example 10, the manager does not reduce the number of patients served despite a budget cut of 10 percent. All other things remain unchanged. How much more does he or she have to charge clients for board and care? We let V = board and care charge per year and set up

$$\$1,200,000 + \$7,200\,U - \$8,400\,U - \$800,000 = 0$$

$$(\$7,200 - \$8,400)U = \$800,000 - \$1,200,000$$

$$-\$1,200\,U = -\$400,000$$

$$U = \$400,000 / \$1,200$$

$$U = 333 \text{ clients}$$

$$\$1,080,000 + 333V - \$8,400\,(333) - \$800,000 = 0$$

$$333V = \$2,797,200 + \$800,000 - \$1,080,000$$

$$333V = \$2,517,200$$

$$V = \$2,517,200 / 333 \text{ clients}$$

$$V = \$7,559$$

Thus, the monthly board and care charge must be increased to $630 (7,559/12 months).

Use of Spreadsheet Software. "What-If" scenarios can be easily analyzed using popular spreadsheet software such as *Microsoft Excel, Lotus 1-2-3*, or *QuattroPro*. Examples 11 and 12 can be solved using the GoalSeek command. For example, in Excel, you find this command under Tools Bar.

CVR Analysis with Fixed Revenue Only. Some nonprofit entities may have only one source of revenue, typically a government budget appropriation. In this case, the break-even formula becomes:

$$\text{Break-even points in units} = \frac{\text{Fixed revenue} - \text{Fixed costs}}{\text{Unit variable cost}}$$

Example 13. A social service agency has a government budget appropriation of $750,000. The agency's main mission is to assist disabled people who are unable to seek or hold jobs. On the average, the agency supplements each individual's income by $6,000 annually. The agency's fixed costs are

$150,000. The agency CEO wishes to know how many people could be served in a given year. The break-even point can be computed as follows:

$$\frac{\$750{,}000 - \$150{,}000}{\$6{,}000} = 100$$

Example 14. In Example 13, assume that the CEO is concerned that the total budget for the year will be reduced by 10 percent to a new amount of 90%($750,000) = $675,000. The new break-even point is:

$$\frac{\$675{,}000 - \$150{,}000}{\$6{,}000} = 88 \text{ (rounded)}$$

The CEO has the options of cutting the budget in one or more of three ways: (1) cut the service level, as computed above, (2) reduce the variable cost, the supplement per person, and (3) seek to cut down on the total fixed costs.

Program Mix Analysis

Previously, our main concern was to determine program-specific break-even volume. But as we are aware, most nonprofit companies are involved in multiservice, multiprogram activities. One major concern is how to plan aggregate break-even volume, surplus, and deficits. Break-even analysis and cost-volume-revenue analysis require additional computations and assumptions when an organization offers more than one program. In multiprogram organizations, program mix is an important factor in calculating an overall break-even point. Different rates and different variable costs result in different unit CMs. As a result, break-even points and Cost-Volume-Revenue relationships vary with the relative proportions of the programs offered, called the *program mix.*

When the product is defined as a package, the multiprogram problem is converted into a single-program problem. The first step is to determine the number of packages that need to be served to break even. The following example illustrates a multiprogram, multiservice situation.

Example 15. The Cypress Counseling Services is a nonprofit agency offering two programs: psychological counseling (PC) and alcohol addiction control (AAC). The agency charges individual clients an average of $10 per hour of counseling provided under the PC program. The local Chamber of Commerce reimburses the company at the rate of $20 per hour of direct service provided under the AAC. The nonprofit agency believes that this billing variable rate is low enough to be affordable for most clients and also high enough to derive clients' commitment to the program objectives. Costs of administering the two programs are given below.

	PC	AAC
Variable costs	$4.6	$11.5
Direct fixed costs	$120,000	$180,000

There are other fixed costs that are common to the two programs, including general and administrative and fund raising, of $255,100 per year. The projected surplus for the coming year, segmented by programs, follows:

	PC	AAC	Total
Revenue	$500,000	$800,000	$1,300,000
Program mix in hours	(50,000)	(40,000)	
Less: VC	(230,000)	(460,000)	(690,000)
Contribution margin	$270,000	$340,000	$610,000
Less: Direct FC	(120,000)	(180,000)	(300,000)
Program margin	$150,000	$160,000	$310,000
Less: Common FC			(255,100)
Surplus			$54,900

First, based on program-specific data on the rates, the variable costs, and the program mix, we can compute the package (aggregate) value as follows:

Program	P	V	Unit CM	Mix*	Package CM
PC	$10	$4.6	$5.4	5	$27
AAC	20	11.5	8.5	4	34
Package total					$61

*The mix ratio is 5:4 (50,000 hours for PC and 40,000 hours for AAC).

We know that the total fixed costs for the agency are $555,100. Thus, the package (aggregate) break-even point is

$$\frac{\$555,100}{\$61} = 9,100 \text{ packages}$$

The agency must provide 45,500 hours of PC (5 × 9,100) and 36,400 hours of AAC (4 × 9,100) to avoid a deficit. To prove,

	PC	AAC	Total
Revenue	$455,000 (a)	$728,000 (b)	$1,183,000
Program mix in hours	(45,500)	(36,400)	
Less: VC	(209,300) (c)	(418,600)(d)	(627,900)
Contribution margin	$245,700	$309,400	$ 555,100
Less: Direct FC	(120,000)	(180,000)	(300,000)
Program margin	$125,700	$129,400	$ 255,100
Less: Common FC			(255,100)
Surplus			$ 0

(a) 45,500 × $10   (c) 45,500 × $4.60
(b) 36,400 × $20   (d) 36,400 × $11.50

Example 16. Assume in Example 15 that 56,000 hours of PC services are budgeted for the next period. The agency wants to know how many hours of AAC services are necessary during that period to avoid an overall deficit. The answer is 29,729 hours, as shown below.

Direction: Set surplus = 0 and PC units of service = $56,000 and let Goal Seeking determine ACC units of service.

Input Data	PC	AAC
Rates	$ 10	$ 20
Units of service (Hours)	56,000	29,729
Variable cost per unit	$ 4.6	$ 11.5

Contribution Statement of Surplus or Deficit

	PC	AAC	Total
Revenue	$560,000	$594,588	$1,154,588
Less: Variable Costs	257,600	341,888	599,488
Contribution margin	$302,400	$252,700	$ 555,100
Less: Direct fixed costs	120,000	180,000	300,000
Program margin	$182,400	$ 72,700	$ 255,100
Less: Common fixed costs			255,100
Surplus			$ (0)

Management Options

Cost-volume-revenue analysis is useful as a frame of reference, as a vehicle for expressing overall managerial performance, and as a planning device via break-even techniques and "what-if" scenarios. In many practical situations, management will have to resort to a combination of approaches to reverse a deficit, including:

1. Selected changes in volume of activity.
2. Planned savings in fixed costs at all levels.
3. Some savings in variable costs.
4. Additional fund drives or grant seeking.
5. Upward adjustments in pricing.
6. Cost reimbursement contracts.

All these approaches will have to be mixed to form a feasible planning package. Many nonprofit managements fail to develop such analytical approaches to the economics of their operations. Further, the accounting system is not designed to provide information to investigate cost-volume-revenue relations.

THE USE OF CAPITAL BUDGETING IN DECISION MAKING

COMPARING PROJECTS WITH UNEQUAL LIVES

A replacement decision typically involves two mutually exclusive projects. When these two mutually exclusive projects have significantly different lives, an adjustment would be necessary. We discuss two approaches: (1) the replacement chain (common life) approach and (2) the equivalent annual annuity approach.

The Replacement Chain (Common Life) Approach

This procedure extends one or both projects until an equal life is achieved. For example, Project A has a 6-year life, while Project B has a 3-year life. Under this approach, the projects would be extended to a common life of 6 years. Project B would have an adjusted NPV equal to the NPV_B plus the NPV_B discounted for 3 years at the project's cost of capital. Then the project with the higher NPV would be chosen.

Example 1. Sims Industries, Inc. is considering two machines to replace an old machine. Machine A has a life of 10 years, will cost $24,500, and will produce net cash savings of $4,800 per year. Machine B has an expected life of 5 years, will cost $20,000, and will produce net cash savings in operating costs of $6,000 per year. The company's cost of capital is 14 percent. Project A's NPV is

$$NPV_A = PV - I = \$4,800 \; PVIFA_{10,14} - \$24,500$$
$$= \$4,800(5.2161) - \$24,500 = \$25,037.28 - \$24,500$$
$$= \$537.28$$

Project B's extended time line can be set up as follows:

0	1	2	3	4	5	6	7	8	9	10
-200	60	60	60	60	60	60	60	60	60	60
						-200			(in hundredths)	

$$\text{Adjusted } NPV_B = PV - I = \$6,000 \; PVIFA_{10,14} - \$20,000 \; PVIF_{5,14} - \$20,000$$
$$= \$6,000(5.2161) - \$20,000(0.5194) - \$20,000$$
$$= \$31,296.60 - \$10,388.00 - \$20,000$$
$$= \$908.60$$

Or, alternatively,

$$NPV_B = PV - I = \$6,000 \; PVIFA_{5,14} - \$20,000$$
$$= \$6,000(3.4331) - \$20,000$$
$$= \$20,598.60 - \$20,000$$
$$= \$598.60$$

$$\text{Adjusted } NPV_B = NPV_B + NPV_B \text{ discounted for 5 years}$$
$$= \$598.60 + \$598.60 \; PVIF_{5,14}$$
$$= \$598.60 + \$598.60(0.5194)$$
$$= \$598.60 + \$310.91$$
$$= \$909.51 \text{ (due to rounding errors)}$$

The Equivalent Annual Annuity (EAA) Approach. It is often cumbersome to compare projects with different lives. For example, one project might have a 4-year life versus a 10-year life for the other. This would require a replacement chain analysis over 20 years, the lowest common denominator of the two lives. In such a case, it is often simpler to use an alternative approach, the *equivalent annual annuity method.*

This procedure involves three steps:

1. Determine each project's NPV over its original life.
2. Find the constant annuity cash flow or EAA, using

The Use of Capital Budgeting in Decision Making

$$\frac{\text{NPV of each project}}{\text{PVIFA}_{n,i}}$$

3. Assuming infinite replacement, find the infinite horizon (or perpetuity) NPV of each project, using

$$\frac{\text{EAA of each}}{\text{cost of capital}}$$

Example 2. From Example 1, $\text{NPV}_A = \$537.28$ and $\text{NPV}_B = \$598.60$. To obtain the constant annuity cash flow or EAA, we do the following:

$$\text{EAA}_A = \$537.28/\text{PVIFA}_{10,14} = \$537.28/5.2161 = \$103.00$$
$$\text{EAA}_B = \$598.60/\text{PVIFA}_{5,14} = \$598.60/3.4331 = \$174.36$$

Thus, the infinite horizon NPVs are as follows:

Infinite horizon $\text{NPV}_A = \$103.00/0.14 = \$735.71$
Infinite horizon $\text{NPV}_B = \$174.36/0.14 = \$1,245.43$

The Concept of Abandonment Value

The notion of abandonment value recognizes that abandonment of a project before the end of its physical life can have a significant impact on the project's return and risk. This distinguishes between the project's economic life and physical life. Two types of abandonment can occur:

1. Abandonment of an unprofitable asset.
2. Sale of the asset to some other party who can extract more value than the original owner.

Example 1. ABC Company is considering a project with an initial cost of $5,000 and net cash flows of $2,000 for next three years. The expected abandonment cash flows for years 0,1,2, and 3 are $5,000, $3,000, $2,500, and $0. The firm's cost of capital is 10 percent. We will compute NPVs in three cases.

Case 1. NPV of the project if kept for 3 years.
$$\text{NPV} = \text{PV} - \text{I} = \$2,000 \ \text{PVIFA}_{10,3} = \$2,000(2.4869) - \$5,000$$
$$= -\$26.20$$

Case 2. NPV of the project if abandoned after Year 1

$$\text{NPV} = \text{PV} - \text{I} = \$2,000 \text{ PVIF}_{10,1} + \$3,000 \text{ PVIF}_{10,2} - \$5,000$$
$$= \$2,000(0.9091) + \$3,000(0.9091) - \$5,000$$
$$= \$1,818.20 + \$2,727.30 - \$5,000 = -\$454.50$$

Case 3. NPV of the project if abandoned after Year 2

$$\text{NPV} = \text{PV} - \text{I} = \$2,000 \text{ PVIF}_{10,1} + \$2,000 \text{ PVIF}_{10,2} + \$2,500 \text{ PVIF}_{10,2} - \$5,000$$
$$= \$2,000(0.9091) + \$2,000(0.8264) + \$2,500(0.8264) - \$5,000$$
$$= \$1,818.20 + \$1,652.80 + \$2,066.00 - \$5,000 = \$537$$

The company should abandon the project after Year 2.

HOW INCOME TAXES AFFECT INVESTMENT DECISIONS

Income taxes make a difference in many capital budgeting decisions. The project which is attractive on a before-tax basis may have to be rejected on an after-tax basis and vice versa. Income taxes typically affect both the amount and the timing of cash flows. Since net income, not cash inflows, is subject to tax, after-tax cash inflows are not usually the same as after-tax net income.

How to Calculate After-Tax Cash Flows

Let us define:
  S = Sales
  E = Cash operating expenses
  d = Depreciation
  t = Tax rate

Then, before-tax cash inflows (or cash savings) = S − E and net income = S − E − d

By definition,

After-tax cash inflows = Before-tax cash inflows − Taxes = (S − E) − (S − E − d) (t)

Rearranging gives the short-cut formula:

After-tax cash inflows = (S - E) (1 - t) + (d)(t) or
= (S − E − d) (1 − t) + d

As can be seen, the deductibility of depreciation from sales in arriving at taxable net income reduces income tax payments and thus serves as a *tax shield.*

Tax shield = Tax savings on depreciation = (d)(t)

Example 1. Assume:

> S = $12,000
> E = $10,000
> d = $500 per year using the straight line method
> t = 30%

Then,

> After-tax cash inflow = ($12,000 - $10,000) (1 - .3) + ($500)(.3)
>   = ($2,000)(.7) + ($500)(.3)
>   = $1,400 + $150 = $1,550

> Note that a tax shield = tax savings on depreciation = (d)(t)
>   = ($500)(.3) = $150

Since the tax shield is *dt,* the higher the depreciation deduction, the higher the tax savings on depreciation. Therefore, an accelerated depreciation method (such as double-declining balance) produces higher tax savings than the straight-line method. Accelerated methods produce higher present values for the tax savings which may make a given investment more attractive.

Example 2. The Navistar Company estimates that it can save $2,500 a year in cash operating costs for the next ten years if it buys a special-purpose machine at a cost of $10,000. No residual value is expected. Depreciation is by straight-line. Assume that the income tax rate is 30%, and the after-tax cost of capital (minimum required rate of return) is 10%. After-tax cash savings can be calculated as follows:

Note that depreciation by straight-line is $10,000/10 = $1,000 per year. Thus,

> After-tax cash savings = (S - E) (1 - t) + (d)(t)
>   = $2,500(1 - .3) + $1,000(.3)
>   = $1,750 + $300 = $2,050

To see if this machine should be purchased, the net present value can be calculated.

> PV = $2,050 T4(10%, 10 years) = $2,050 (6.145)=$12,597.25

Thus, NPV = PV - I = $12,597.25 - $10,000 = $2,597.25

Since NPV is positive, the machine should be bought.

Capital Budgeting Decisions and the Modified Accelerated Cost Recovery System (MACRS)

Although the traditional depreciation methods still can be used for computing depreciation for book purposes, 1981 saw a new way of computing depreciation deductions for tax purposes. The current rule is called the *Modified Accelerated Cost Recovery System* (MACRS) rule, as enacted by Congress in 1981 and then modified somewhat in 1986 under the Tax Reform Act of 1986. This rule is characterized as follows:

1. It abandons the concept of useful life and accelerates depreciation deductions by placing all depreciable assets into one of eight age property classes. It calculates deductions, based on an allowable percentage of the asset's original cost (see Tables 1 and 2).

With a shorter asset tax life than useful life, the company would be able to deduct depreciation more quickly and save more in income taxes in the earlier years, thereby making an investment more attractive. The rationale behind the system is that this way the government encourages the company to invest in facilities and increase its productive capacity and efficiency. (Remember that the higher d, the larger the tax shield (d)(t)).

2. Since the allowable percentages in Table 1 add up to 100%, there is no need to consider the salvage value of an asset in computing depreciation.

3. The company may elect the straight line method. The straight-line convention must follow what is called the *half-year convention*. This means that the company can deduct only half of the regular straight-line depreciation amount in the first year. The reason for electing to use the MACRS optional straight-line method is that some firms may prefer to stretch out depreciation deductions using the straight-line method rather than to accelerate them. Those firms are the ones that just start out or have little or no income and wish to show more income on their income statements.

Example 1. Assume that a machine falls under a 3-year property class and costs $3,000 initially. The straight line option under MACRS differs from the traditional straight line method in that under this method the company would deduct only $500 depreciation in the first year and the fourth year ($3,000/3 years =$1,000; $1,000/2=$500). The table below compares the straight line with half-year convention with the MACRS.

Year	Straight line (half-year) Depreciation	Cost		MACRS %	MACRS deduction
1	$ 500	$3,000	×	33.3%	$ 999
2	1,000	3,000	×	44.5	1,335
3	1,000	3,000	×	14.8	444
4	500	3,000	×	7.4	222
	$3,000				$3,000

Example 2. A machine costs $10,000. Annual cash inflows are expected to be $5,000. The machine will be depreciated using the MACRS rule and will fall under the 3-year property class. The cost of capital after taxes is 10%. The estimated life of the machine is 4 years. The salvage value of the machine at the end of the fourth year is expected to be $1,200. The tax rate is 30%.

The formula for computation of after-tax cash inflows (S - E)(1 - t)+ (d)(t) needs to be computed separately. The NPV analysis can be performed as follows:

	Present value factor @ 10%	Present value
Initial investment: $10,000	1.000	$(10,000.00)
(S - E)(1 - t):		
$5,000 (1 - .3) = $3,500 for 4 years	3.170(a)	$11,095.00
(d)(t):		

Year	Cost		MACRS %	d	(d)(t)		
1	$10,000	×	33.3%	$3,330	$ 999	.909(b)	908.09
2	$10,000	×	44.5	4,450	1,335	.826(b)	1,102.71
3	$10,000	×	14.8	1,480	444	.751(b)	333.44
4	$10,000	×	7.4	740	222	.683(b)	151.63

Salvage value:
$1,200 in year 4: $1,200 (1 - .3) =

840(c)	.683(b)	573.72
Net present value (NPV)		$4,164.59

(a) Present value of an annuity of $1 = 3.170 (from Table A-4 in the Appendix).
(b) Present values of $1 obtained (from Table A-3 in the Appendix).
(c) Any salvage value received under the MACRS rules is a *taxable gain* (the excess of the selling price over book value, $1,200 in this example), since the book value will be zero at the end of the life of the machine.

Since NPV = PV - I = $4,164.59 is positive, the machine should be bought.

Example 3. A firm is considering the purchase of an automatic machine for $6,200. The machine has an installation cost of $800 and zero salvage value at the end of its expected life of five years. Depreciation is by the straight-line method with the *half-year convention*. The machine is considered a five-year property. Expected cash savings before tax is $1,800 per year over the five years. The firm is in the 40 percent tax bracket. The firm has determined the cost of capital (or minimum required rate of return) of 10 percent after taxes.

Year(s)		Having Cash Flows	Amount of Cash Flows	10% PV Factor	PV
Initial investment		Now	$(7,000)	1.000	$(7,000)
Annual cash inflows:					
$1,800					
× 60%					
$1,080		1-5	1,080	3.791	4,094

Depreciation deductions:

Year	Depreciation	Tax Shield at 40%				
1	$700	$280	1	280	0.909	255
2	1,400	560	2	560	0.826	463
3	1,400	560	3	560	0.751	421
4	1,400	560	4	560	0.683	382
5	1,400	560	5	560	0.621	348
6	700	280	6	280	0.564	158
Net Present Value						$(879)

The firm should not buy the automatic machine since its NPV is negative.

Example 4. The Wessels Corporation is considering installing a new conveyor for materials handling in a warehouse. The conveyor will have an initial cost of $75,000 and an installation cost of $5,000. Expected benefits of the conveyor are: (a) Annual labor cost will be reduced by $16,500, and (b) breakage and other damages from handling will be reduced by $400 per month. Some of the firm's costs are expected to increase as follows: (a) Electricity cost will rise by $100 per month, and (b) annual repair and maintenance of the conveyor will amount to $900.

Assume the firm uses the MACRS rules for depreciation in the five-year property class. No salvage value will be recognized for tax purposes. The conveyor has an expected useful life of eight years and a projected salvage value of $5,000. The tax rate is 40 percent. We will determine the project's NPV at 10 percent. Should the firm buy the conveyor?

Annual cash inflows are computed as follows:

$16,500	Reduction in labor cost
4,800	Reduction in breakage
-1,200	Increase in electricity costs
-900	Increase in repair and maintenance cost
$19,200	

Initial amount of investment is:

$75,000 + $5,000 = $80,000

Year(s)

		Having Cash Flows	Amount of Cash Flows	10% PV Factor	PV
Initial investment		Now	$(80,000)	1.000	$(80,000)
Annual cash inflow:					
	$19,200				
	× 60%				
After-tax cash inflow:	$11,520	1-8	11,520	5.335	61,459.20
Depreciation deduction:					

Year	Cost	MACRS	Depreciation	Tax Shield				
1	$80,000	20%	$16,000	$ 6,400	1	6,400	0.909	5,817.60
2	80,000	32	25,600	10,240	2	10,240	0.826	8,458.24
3	80,000	19.2	15,360	6,144	3	6,144	0.751	4,614.14
4	80,000	11.5	9,200	3,680	4	3,680	0.683	2,513.44
5	80,000	11.5	9,200	3,680	5	3,680	0.621	2,285.28
6	80,000	5.8	4,640	1,856	6	1,856	0.564	1,046.78
								$24,735.48

Salvage value, fully taxable since book value will be

zero:

$5,000					
× 60%					
$3,000		8	3,000	0.467	1,401.00
Net present value					$ 7,595.68

The Wessels Corporation should buy and install the conveyor since it brings a positive NPV.

Table 1 Modified Accelerated Cost Recovery System Classification of Assets

Property class

Year	3-year	5-year	7-year	10-year	15-year	20-year
1	33.3%	20.0%	14.3%	10.0%	5.0%	3.8%
2	44.5	32.0	24.5	18.0	9.5	7.2
3	14.8a	19.2	17.5	14.4	8.6	6.7
4	7.4	11.5a	12.5	11.5	7.7	6.2
5		11.5	8.9a	9.2	6.9	5.7
6		5.8	8.9	7.4	6.2	5.3
7			8.9	6.6a	5.9a	4.9
8			4.5	6.6	5.9	4.5a
9				6.5	5.9	4.5
10				6.5	5.9	4.5
11				3.3	5.9	4.5
12					5.9	4.5
13					5.9	4.5
14					5.9	4.5
15					5.9	4.5
16					3.0	4.4
17						4.4
18						4.4
19						4.4
20						4.4
21						2.2
Total	100%	100%	100%	100%	100%	100%

a Denotes the year of changeover to straight-line depreciation.

Table 2 MACRS Tables by Property Class

MACRS Property Class & Depreciation Method	Useful Life (ADR Midpoint Life) "a"	Examples of Assets
3-year property 200% declining balance	4 years or less	Most small tools are included; the law specifically excludes autos and light trucks from this property class.
5-year property 200% declining balance	More than 4 years to less than 10 years	Autos and light trucks, computers, typewriters, copiers, duplicating equipment, heavy general-purpose trucks, and research and experimentation equipment are included.
7-year property 200% declining balance	10 years or more to less than 16 years	Office furniture and fixtures and most items of machinery and equipment used in production are included.
10-year property 200% declining balance	16 years or more to less than 20 years	Various machinery and equipment, such as that used in petroleum distilling and refining and in the milling of grain, are included.
15-year property 150% declining balance	20 years or more to less than 25 years	Sewage treatment plants, telephone and electrical distribution facilities, and land improvements are included.
20-year property 150% declining balance	25 years or more	Service stations and other real property with an ADR midpoint life of less than 27.5 years are included.
27.5-year property Straight-line	Not applicable	All residential rental property is included.
31.5-year property Straight-line	Not applicable	All nonresidential real property is included.

"a" The term ADR midpoint life means the "useful life" of an asset in a business sense; the appropriate ADR midpoint lives for assets are designated in the Tax Regulations.

TOTAL QUALITY MANAGEMENT (TQM) AND QUALITY COSTS*

TOTAL QUALITY MANAGEMENT

In order to be globally competitive in today's world-class manufacturing environment, firms place an increased emphasis on quality and productivity. *Total quality management (TQM)* is an effort in this direction. Simply put, it is a system for creating competitive advantage by focusing the organization on what is important to the customer. Total quality management can be broken down into: "Total": that is the whole organization is involved and understands that customer satisfaction is everyone's job. "Quality": the extent to which products and services satisfy the requirements of internal and external customers. "Management": the leadership, infrastructure and resources that support employees as they meet the needs of those customers.

TQM is essentially an endless quest for perfect quality. It is a *zero-defects* approach. It views the optimal level of quality costs as the level where zero defects are produced. This approach to quality is opposed to the traditional belief, called *acceptable quality level (AQL),* which allows a predetermined level of defective units to be produced and sold. AQL is the level where the number of defects allowed minimizes total quality costs. The rationale behind the traditional view is that there is a tradeoff between prevention and appraisal costs and failure costs. Quality experts maintain that the optimal quality level should be about 2.5% of sales.

---

* This chapter was coauthored by Anique Qureshi, Ph.D., CPA, CIA, associate professor of accounting at Queens College, and an accounting professional.

Principles of TQM

Making a product right the first time is one of the principal objectives of TQM. Implementing a successful TQM program will in fact reduce costs rather than increase them. There is no question that better quality will result in better productivity. This is based on the principle that when less time is spent on rework or repair, more time is available for manufacturing, which will increase productivity.

When an organization maintains accurate records of its cost of quality, TQM will demonstrate that effective quality assurance geared towards prevention versus correction will pay for itself. A good example of this is the situation where it is possible to eliminate 100% inspection with a good statistical process control (SPC) program. Elimination of high reject rates results in fewer products being repaired, reworked or scrapped with the obvious reductions in cost.

Tying the cost of quality to TQM is necessary in order to motivate management who is cost motivated in both industry and government. In a TQM environment, management will start utilizing the cost data to measure the success of the program. The corporate financial planner can determine that overall product costs are being reduced by the TQM program. Given this success in the prevention of defects, the following failure costs will be reduced or eliminated:

1. Rework or repair
2. Inspection of rework
3. Testing of rework
4. Warranty costs
5. Returned material
6. Discounts, adjustments and allowances

It is quite obvious that the cost of prevention in TQM is minor when taken against the above listed failure costs.
A checklist of TQM features are as follows:

- A systematic way to improve products and services
- A structured approach in identifying and solving problems
- Long term
- Conveyed by management's actions
- Supported by statistical quality control
- Practiced by everyone

Elements of TQM

The principle elements of TQM are straightforward and embrace a commonsense approach to management. However, each of the individual elements must be integrated into a structured whole to succeed. The elements are as follows:

1. *A Focus on the Customer*

   Every functional unit has a customer, whether it be an external consumer or an internal unit. TQM advocates that managers and employees become so customer-focused that they continually find new ways to meet or exceed customers' expectations. We must accept the concept that quality is defined by the customer and meeting the customer's needs and expectations is the strategic goal of TQM.

2. *A Long-Term Commitment*

   Experience in the U.S. and abroad shows that substantial gains come only after management makes a long-term commitment, usually five years or more, in improving quality. Customer-focus must be constantly renewed to keep that goal foremost.

3. *Top Management Support and Direction*

   Top management must be the driving force behind TQM. Senior managers must exhibit personal support by using quality improvement concepts in their management style, incorporating quality in their strategic planning process, and providing financial and staff support.

4. *Employee Involvement*

   Full employee participation is also an integral part of the process. Each employee must be a partner in achieving quality goals. Teamwork involves managers, supervisors, and employees in improving service delivery, solving systemic problems, and correcting errors in all parts of work processes.

5. *Effective and Renewed Communications*

   The power of internal communication, both vertical and horizontal, is central to employee involvement. Regular and meaningful communication from all levels must occur. This will allow an agency to adjust its ways of operating and reinforce the commitment of TQM at the same time.

6. *Reliance on Standards and Measures*

   Measurement is the springboard to involvement, allowing the organization to initiate corrective action, set priorities and evaluate progress. Standards and measures should reflect customer requirements and changes that need to be introduced in the internal business of providing those requirements. The emphasis is on "doing the right thing right the first time."

7. *Commitment to Training*

Training is absolutely vital to the success of TQM. The process usually begins with awareness training for teams of top-level managers. This is followed by courses for teams of mid-level managers, and finally by courses for non-managers. Awareness training is followed by an identification of areas of concentration, or of functional areas where TQM will first be introduced. Implementing TQM requires additional skills training, which is also conducted in teams.

8. *Importance of Rewards and Recognition*

Most companies practicing TQM have given wide latitude to managers in issuing rewards and recognition. Here, a common theme is that individual financial rewards are not as appropriate as awards to groups or team members, since most successes are group achievements.

QUALITY COSTS

Costs of quality are costs that occur because poor quality may exist or actually does exist. More specifically, quality costs are the total of the costs incurred by (1) investing in the prevention of nonconformances to requirements; (2) appraising a product or service for conformance to requirements; and (3) failure to meet requirements.

Quality costs are classified into three broad categories: prevention, appraisal, and failure costs. *Prevention costs* are those incurred to prevent defects. Amounts spent on quality training programs, researching customer needs, quality circles, and improved production equipment are considered in prevention costs. Expenditures made for prevention will minimize the costs that will be incurred for appraisal and failure. *Appraisal costs* are costs incurred for monitoring or inspection; these costs compensate for mistakes not eliminated through prevention. *Failure costs* may be internal (such as scrap and rework costs and reinspection) or external (such as product returns due to quality problems, warranty costs, lost sales due to poor product performance, and complaint department costs. Market shares of many U.S. firms have eroded because foreign firms have been able to sell higher-quality products at lower prices.

Studies indicate that costs of quality for American companies are typically 20 to 30% of sales. Quality experts maintain that the optimal quality level should be about 2.5% of sales.

Two Different Views Concerning Optimal Quality Costs

There are two views concerning optimal quality costs:

1. the traditional view that uses an acceptable quality level
2. the world-class view that uses total quality control

Optimal Distribution of Quality Costs: Traditional View. The traditional approach uses an *acceptable quality level (AQL)* that permits a pre-determined level of defective units to be produced and sold. AQL is the level where the number of defects allowed minimizes total quality costs. The reasoning of the traditional approach is that there is a tradeoff between failure costs and prevention and appraisal costs. As prevention and appraisal costs increase, internal and external failure costs are expected to decrease. As long as the decrease in failure costs is greater than the corresponding increase in prevention and failure costs, a company should continue increasing its efforts to prevent or detect defective units.

Optimal Distribution of Quality Costs: World-Class View. The world-class view uses total quality control and views the optimal level of quality costs as the level where zero defects are produced. The zero-defects approach uses a quality performance standard that requires:

1. all products to be produced according to specifications and
2. all services to be provided according to requirements

Zero defects reflect a total quality control philosophy used in Just-in-Time (JIT) manufacturing. Figure 1 below illustrates the relationship between these two cost components under two different views.

QUALITY COST AND PERFORMANCE REPORTS

The principal objective of reporting quality costs is to improve and facilitate managerial planning, control, and decision making. Potential uses of quality cost information include:

(a) quality program implementation decisions
(b) evaluation of the effectiveness of quality programs
(c) strategic pricing decisions (For example, a reduction in quality costs might enable a firm to reduce its selling price, improve its competitive position, and increase market share.)

Figure 1

Traditional View

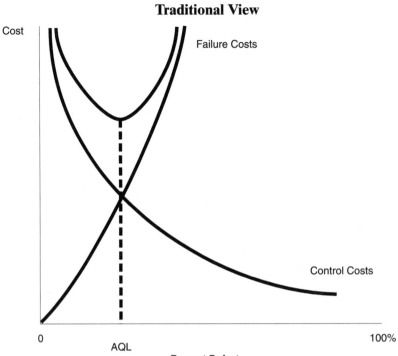

Cost

Failure Costs

Control Costs

0   AQL   100%

Percent Defects

World-Class View

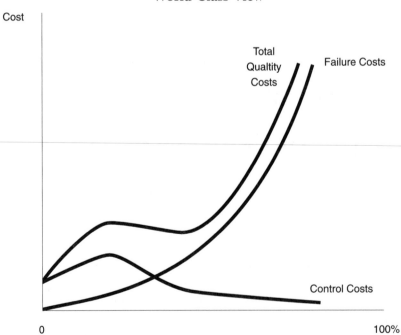

Cost

Total Qualtity Costs   Failure Costs

Control Costs

0   100%

Percent Defects

The control process involves comparing actual performance with quality standards. This comparison provides feedback that can be used to take corrective action if necessary. The first step in a quality cost reporting system is to prepare a detailed listing of actual quality costs by category. Furthermore, each category of quality costs is expressed as a percentage of sales. This serves two purposes: (a) it permits managers to assess the financial impact of quality costs, and (b) it reveals the relative emphasis currently placed on each category.

Figure 2 Quality Costs—General Description

Prevention Costs

The costs of all activities specifically designed to prevent poor quality in products or services. Examples are the costs of new product review, quality planning, supplier capability surveys, process capability evaluations, quality improvement team meetings, quality improvement projects, quality education and training.

Appraisal Costs

The costs associated with measuring, evaluating or auditing products or services to assure conformance to quality standards and performance requirements. These include the costs of incoming and source inspection/test of purchased material, in process and final inspection/test, product, process, or service audits, calibration of measuring and test equipment, and the costs of associated supplies and materials.

Failure Costs

The costs resulting from products or services not conforming to requirements or customer/user needs. Failure costs are divided into internal and external failure cost categories.

Internal Failure Costs

Failure costs occurring prior to delivery or shipment of the product, or the furnishing of a service, to the customer. Examples are the costs of scrap, rework, reinspection, retesting, material review, and downgrading.

External Failure Costs

Failure costs occurring after delivery or shipment of the product, and during or after furnishing of a service, to the customer. Examples are the costs of processing customer complaints, customer returns, warranty claims, and product recalls.

Total Quality Costs

The sum of the above costs. It represents the difference between the actual cost of a product or service, and what the reduced cost would be if there was no possibility of substandard service, failure of products, or defects in their manufacture.

Quality cost reports (Figure 3) can be used to point out the strengths and weaknesses of a quality system. Improvement teams can use them to describe the monetary benefits and ramifications of proposed changes. Return-on-investment (ROI) models and other financial analyses can be constructed directly from quality cost data to justify proposals to management. In practice, quality costs can define activities of quality program and quality improvement efforts in a language that management can understand and act on—dollars.

The negative effect on profits, resulting from product or service of less than acceptable quality or from ineffective quality management, is almost always dynamic. Once started, it continues to mushroom until ultimately the company finds itself in serious financial difficulties due to the two-pronged impact of an unheeded increase in quality costs coupled with a declining performance image. Management that clearly understands this understands the economics of quality.

In the quality cost report, quality costs are grouped into one of four categories:

1. prevention costs
2. appraisal costs
3. internal failure costs
4. external failure costs

In addition, each category of quality costs is expressed as a percentage of sales. There are four types of performance reports to measure a company's quality improvement. They are:

1. *Interim quality performance report.* It measures the progress achieved within the period relative to the planned level of progress for the period (see Figure 4).

2. *One-year quality trend report.* It compares the current year's quality cost ratio with the previous year's ratio. More specifically, it compares (1) the current year's variable quality cost ratio with the previous year's variable quality cost ratio, and the current year's actual fixed quality costs with the previous year's actual fixed quality costs (see Figure 5).

3. *Long-range quality performance report.* It compares the current year's actual quality costs with the firm's intended long-range quality goal (see Figure 6).

Activity-Based Management and Optimal Quality Costs

Activity-based management supports the zero-defect view of quality costs.

Activity-based management classifies activities as: (1) value-added activities and (2) nonvalue-added activities.

Quality-related activities (internal and external failure activities, prevention activities, and appraisal activities) can be classified as value-added and nonvalue-added.

Internal and external failure activities and their associated costs are nonvalue-added and should be eliminated.

Prevention activities that are performed efficiently are value-added. (Costs caused by inefficiency in prevention activities are nonvalue-added costs.)

Appraisal activities may be value-added or nonvalue-added depending upon the activity. For example, quality audits may serve a value-added objective.

Once the quality-related activities are identified for each category, resource drivers can be used to improve cost assignments to individual activities. Root or process drivers can also be identified and used to help managers understand what is causing the cost of the activities.

Using Quality Cost Information

The principal objective of reporting quality costs is to improve and facilitate managerial planning, control, and decision making.

Potential uses of quality cost information include:

1. quality program implementation decisions
2. evaluation of the effectiveness of quality programs
3. strategic pricing decisions (For example, improved reporting of quality costs might be used by managers to target specific quality costs for reductions. A reduction in quality costs might enable a firm to reduce its selling price, improve its competitive position, and increase market share.)
4. inclusion of quality costs in cost-volume-profit analysis (For example, overlooking quality cost savings results in a higher breakeven and possible rejection of a profitable project.)

The control process involves comparing actual performance with quality standards. This comparison provides feedback that can be used to take corrective action if necessary.

Figure 3

Allison Products
Quality Cost Report
For the Year Ended March 31, 19x2

	Quality Costs		Percentage of Sale(a)
Prevention costs:			
Quality training	$30,000		
Reliability engineering	79,000	$109,000	3.73%
Appraisal costs:			
Materials inspection	$19,000		
Product acceptance	10,000		
Process acceptance	35,000	$64,000	2.19%
Internal failure costs:			
Scrap	$40,000		
Rework	34,000	$74,000	2.53%
External failure costs:			
Customer complaints	$24,000		
Warranty	24,000		
Repair	15,000	$63,000	2.16%
Total quality costs		$310,000	10.62% (b)

(a) Actual sales of $2,920,000
(b) $310,000/$2,920,000 = 10.62 percent. Difference is rounding error.

Figure 4

Allison Products
Interim Standard Performance Report
For the Year Ended March 31, 19x2

	Actual Costs	Budgeted Costs(a)	Variance
Prevention costs:			
Quality training	$30,000	$30,000	$0
Reliability engineering	79,000	80,000	1,000 F
Total prevention	$109,000	$110,000	$1,000 F
Appraisal costs:			
Materials inspection	$19,000	$28,000	$9,000 F
Product acceptance	10,000	15,000	5,000 F
Process acceptance	35,000	35,000	0
Total appraisal	$64,000	$78,000	$14,000 F

Total Quality Management (TQM) and Quality Costs

Internal failure costs:			
Scrap	$40,000	$44,000	$4,000 F
Rework	34,000	36,500	2,500 F
Total internal failure	$74,000	$80,500	$6,500 F
External failure costs:			
Fixed:			
Customer complaints	$24,000	$25,000	$1,000 F
Variable:			
Warranty	24,000	20,000	(4,000) U
Repair	15,000	17,500	2,500 F
Total external failure	$63,000	$62,500	($500) U
Total quality costs	$310,000	$331,000	$21,000 F
Percentage of actual sales	10.62%	11.34%	0.72% F

(a) Based on actual sales
(b) Actual sales of $2,920,000

Figure 5

Allison Products
Quality Cost, One-Year Trend
For the Year Ended March 31, 19x2

	Actual Costs 19x2(a)	Budgeted Costs 19x1	Variance
Prevention costs:			
Quality training	$30,000	$36,000	$6,000 F
Reliability engineering	79,000	120,000	41,000 F
Total prevention	$109,000	$156,000	$47,000 F
Appraisal costs:			
Materials inspection	$19,000	$33,600	$14,600 F
Product acceptance	10,000	16,800	6,800 F
Process acceptance	35,000	39,200	4,200 F
Total appraisal	$64,000	$89,600	$25,600 F
Internal failure costs:			
Scrap	$40,000	$48,000	$8,000 F
Rework	34,000	40,000	6,000 F
Total internal failure	$74,000	$88,000	$14,000 F
External failure costs:			
Fixed:			
Customer complaints	$24,000	$33,000	$9,000 F

Variable:			
Warranty	24,000	23,000	(1,000) U
Repair	15,000	16,400	1,400 F
Total external failure	$63,000	$72,400	$9,400 F
Total quality costs	$310,000	$406,000	$96,000 F
Percentage of actual sales	10.62%	13.90%	3.29% F

(a) Based on actual sales = $2,920,000

Figure 6

Allison Products
Long-Range Performance Report
For the Year Ended March 31, 19x2

	Actual Costs	*Target Costs(a)*	*Variance*
Prevention costs:			
Quality training	$30,000	$14,000	($16,000) U
Reliability engineering	79,000	39,000	(40,000) U
Total prevention	$109,000	$53,000	($56,000) U
Appraisal costs:			
Materials inspection	$19,000	$7,900	($11,100) U
Product acceptance	10,000	0	(10,000) U
Process acceptance	35,000	12,000	(23,000) U
Total appraisal	$64,000	$19,900	($44,100) U
Internal failure costs:			
Scrap	$40,000	$0	($40,000) U
Rework	34,000	0	(34,000) U
Total internal failure	$74,000	$0	($74,000) U
External failure costs:			
Fixed:			
Customer complaints	$24,000	$0	($24,000) U
Variable:			
Warranty	24,000	0	(24,000) U
Repair	15,000	0	(15,000) U
Total external failure	$63,000	$0	($63,000) U
Total quality costs	$310,000	$72,900	($237,100) U
Percentage of actual sales	10.62%	2.50%	−8.12% U

(a) Based on actual sales of $2,920,000. These costs are value-added costs.

RISK MANAGEMENT AND ANALYSIS

Risk management involves identifying risk exposure, analyzing risk, measuring potential loss, determining the best insurance strategy (or whether to self-insure), cost projections and control, volatility of operations, timing of adverse events, claims adjustment, proper cost allocation, and the use of risk management software.

Risks facing a business may negatively affect its reputation, "bottom-line," cost and availability of financing, credit rating, market price of stock, regulatory or legislative changes, and elimination of barriers to entry.

An evaluation must be made of the tradeoff between risk and return. A higher risk mandates a higher rate of return to justify taking the extra risk.

A risk program must be in place. The program must have built-in flexibility to adjust, as conditions require. The program must conform to the goals, objectives, and policies of the business.

The company must have a workable contingency plan such as a recovery plan. Employees must be instructed what to do in such eventualities. Test runs should be practiced. Contingency plans must be updated periodically to incorporate new technologies, changing staff, and new areas of business activity.

Areas of risk must be identified and corrective action taken to reduce those risks. Unusually high risk will not only have negative effects on earnings but might also place in question the continuity of the operation.

Models and quantitative approaches including actuarial techniques may be used to appraise potential catastrophic losses, product/service liability, intellectual property losses, and business interruption. Probability distributions should be arrived at of expected losses based on the model or quantitative technique used.

APPRAISAL OF RISK

The "red flags" of undue risk must be identified and controlled. "Red flags" include poor employee training and performance, inadequate planning, fragmentation, poor communication, lateness, improper focus, failure to observe government regulations or laws (e.g., the federal Comprehensive Environmental Response, Compensation and Liability Act covering the release and disposal of hazardous substances and wastes), overconfidence, and "hostile" attitudes.

When appraising a particular situation, evaluate the risk profile, financial status, and acceptable risk exposure. What is the entity's risk tolerance level? To what extent does the risk of a situation exceed predetermined maximum risk levels? Has management received proper approval to undertake the high-risk level? Has proper planning been performed to take into account the adverse effects on the business if things do not work out? For example, if losses are incurred that significantly exceed the entity's traditional insurance program, the company might be permanently crippled. Examples include a business interruption resulting from a terrorist bombing, loss of a major vendor, misinterpretation of law, or a product recall.

In appraising risk, consideration must be given to the company's liquidity and solvency position to withstand loss. A determination must be made of the costs associated with various risks.

Risk should be evaluated and minimized. Risk may be reduced through the following means:

- Vertically integrate to reduce the price and supply risk of raw materials.
- Take out sufficient insurance coverage for possible asset and operating losses (including foreign risk protection). A lower trend in insurance expense to the asset insured may indicate inadequate coverage.
- Diversify activities, product/service line, market segments, customer bases, geographic areas, and investments.
- Sell to diversified industries to protect against cyclical turns in the economy.
- Sign a forward contract to take delivery of raw materials at fixed prices at a specified future date so the entity insulates itself from price increases.
- Enter into foreign currency futures contracts to lock in a fixed rate.
- Participate in joint ventures and partnerships with other companies. In so doing, obligations of the parties must be taken into account. For example, questions to be asked are: *Which company is to absorb most of the losses? What is our company's duties and exposure under the agreement?*

- Sell low-priced products as well as more expensive ones to protect against inflationary and recessionary periods.
- Change suppliers who prove unreliable.
- Take steps so the company is less susceptible to business cycles (e.g., inelastic demand products, negatively correlated products/services).
- Add products/services having different seasonal attractiveness and demand.
- Emphasize a piggyback product base (similar merchandise associated with the basic business).
- Balance the company's financing mix.

In analyzing the company's product/service line, determine:

- Extent of correlation between products. Positive correlation means high risk because the demand for all the products go in the same direction. Negative correlation minimizes the risk. No correlation means indifference between products.
- Product demand elasticity equal to the percentage change in quantity relative to the percentage change in price. Elastic demand means that a minor change in price has a significant impact on quantity demanded. This indicates higher risk. Inelastic product demand minimizes risk because a change in price will have little effect on quantity demanded.

In analyzing the risk associated with multinational companies, compute:

- Total assets in high-risk foreign countries to total assets.
- High-risk foreign revenue to total revenue. High-risk revenue is based on risk ratings of companies in published sources (e.g., International Country Risk Guide).
- High-risk foreign revenue to net income.
- Percentage of earnings associated with foreign government contracts.
- Fluctuation in foreign exchange rates.

TYPES OF RISK

The corporate financial manager needs to take into account the various types of risk the entity faces. For example, corporate risk may be in the form of overrelying on a few key executives or the underinsurance of assets. Industry risk may be the high technological environment, or an industry scrutinized under the "public eye," or a capital-intensive business. Moving toward a variable cost-oriented business may minimize industry risk. Economic risk includes susceptibility to the business cycle. This risk may be reduced by having a low-priced substitute for a high priced-one.

Social risk occurs when a company experiences customer boycott or discrimination cases. A way to reduce this risk is to be engaged in community involvement and sensitivity training.

A company must properly instruct its personnel not to intrude with electronic mail, slander others, or commit libel. The company must carefully train and monitor staff to guard against possible infractions causing employee lawsuits or federal/local government investigation.

Political risk applies to relations with U.S. and local government agencies and foreign governments when operations are carried out overseas. This risk may be reduced through lobbying efforts and avoiding activities and placing assets in high-risk foreign areas.

Environmental risk includes product lines and services susceptible to changes in the weather. Having counter-seasonal goods and services, or moving to another geographic location may reduce this risk. Multinational entities are susceptible to environmental risk, particularly in the former "Iron Curtain" countries. There are often problems with the land and resource use, including pollution and hazardous waste. The acquiring company must be cautious of not only the cleanup costs, but also associated penalties and fines. Prior to acquisition, the acquirer must be assured that there is a contract under which the seller will be responsible for all or part of the environmental obligations. A high-risk premium applies to corporate investments in countries with environmental problems. Insurance companies, for example, should reject potential clients that are not environmentally certified or fail to meet particular environmental norms. Banks need to be concerned with the collectibility of loans to companies with major environmental exposure. If a company is "dirty," it may have difficulty obtaining adequate insurance or loans. Further, the effect of impending government environmental laws on the business must be considered. Environmental problems and disasters may significantly hurt earnings.

Terrorism is also of concern to certain types of businesses. Security measures must be in place to guard against bombing.

A determination must be made as to how the risks facing a business interact. A model must consider alternative scenarios.

RISK ANALYSIS AND MANAGEMENT SOFTWARE

Software is available to assess, evaluate, and control the risks facing a company. A risk management information system (RMIS) includes hardware and software components. However, we consider here software availability, implications, benefits, and applications. The software selected should be that which offers a proper "fit" to the environment and circumstances of the company.

In deciding on the "right" software the financial manager should consider the company's requirements and expectations, corporate culture, report preparation needs, regulatory reporting mandates, product/service line, nature of operations, claims processing and administration, government compliance laws, business policies and procedures, insurance coverage, technological resources, employee background and experience, levels of communication, legal liability aspects, organizational structure, and work flow. The risk management and analysis software should include the ability to manipulate data into risk patterns.

Are the "right" managers being provided with the appropriate information on a timely basis? A determination must also be made of the communication and distribution features of the software. The software should be flexible so that reports may be customized depending on the data needed and for whom. For example, a factory foreman or manager wants to know how many employee injuries occurred and of what nature. On the other hand, the accounting department manager wants to know the negative financial effects the accidents have on the company's financial position and operating performance.

Software may be used to evaluate safety statistical data by division, department, responsibility unit, geographic location, and manager. Potential difficulties may be highlighted. An example of a risk management software application is providing a report on how many employee injuries took place by department, operation, and activity. Is the client's incidence rate above or below expected ranges? How does the client injury rate compare to competitors and industry averages? There should be a software feature, such as an expert system, on how to correct the problem of a high rate of employee accidents and offer other relevant recommendations.

If a company is exchanging risk information with others (e.g., insurance company, investment banker, and government agencies), then software compatibility is needed. Further, there should exist appropriate operating systems and network support. A company may use its Intranet to expand risk management throughout the company. It is important that there be proper user interfaces.

RISK CONTROL

Risk control includes environmental compliance, periodic inspections, and alarm systems. Loss prevention and control must consider physical and human aspects. For example, "safer" machines may be used to prevent worker injury. Appropriate sprinklers may be installed to prevent fires. Consultants may be retained in specialized areas such as industrial hygiene.

Product labeling should be appraised as to appropriateness and representation. Any consumer complaints should be immediately investigated to avoid possible government action or litigation.

The financial manager must determine the best kind, term, and amount of insurance to carry to guard against losses. Insurance coverage may be taken out for losses to plant, property and equipment, product/service deficiencies, and employee conduct. The financial manager should consider insuring areas not typically insured against, such as industrial espionage, loss of intellectual property, or employee theft. An example of the latter is employment practice liability insurance (EPLI). This policy is available from many insurance companies such as Chubb and Lexington. Unfortunately even this type of policy often excludes coverage for bodily injury, workers' compensation, and infractions under ERISA. It is not unusual for an employee to sue because of an employer's promotion and hiring policies. The insurance premium may be lowered by increasing the deductible or changing to less expensive insurance carriers.

The financial manager must carefully monitor the entity's fiduciary responsibilities, working conditions, contractual commitments, and employment practices. Systems must be checked on an ongoing basis for defects in functioning such as fire alarm devices. The company must be certain that its employee policies are fair and in conformity with federal and local laws.

Risk control includes provisions against terrorist acts related to loss of life, product losses, and property damage. Security procedures including access controls must be strong in high-risk areas such as in a foreign country with extremist groups. Employees must be instructed to use safety precautions.

RISK SOFTWARE PACKAGES AND PRODUCTS

There are many risk management software packages available to financial managers. Some useful packages are described below.

Decision Support Systems' The Expert Business Impact Analysis System provides risk appraisal factors and protection strategy recommendations. It has a database of global threats, vulnerability assessments, comparative analysis, and reporting capabilities (including by location). It contains threat probabilities with documented statistical sources, outage durations, and regional segmentation. It has interactive "what-if" analysis features for scenario planning to evaluate the benefits of alternative solutions and to perform comparisons with the current and historical background. (For information telephone: (800) 788-6447, e-mail: BIAsys@aol.com or write to Decision Support Systems, 380 S. State Road 434, Suite 1004-117, Altamonte Springs, Florida 32714.)

Strohl Systems offers contingency planning software products to plan for unexpected disruptions on the company's operations. It is better to anticipate interruptions before they turn into major problems. BIA Professional is a business impact analysis tool allowing the company to quickly and easily define the effects of disaster and helps target critical functions for contingency planning. Living Disaster Recovery Planning Systems (LDRPS) is continuity (recovery) planning software including a question and answer feature, sample documents and diagrams, graphics, report writer, recover strategies and contingency planning, and presentation of recovery activities in the form of Program Evaluation and Review Technique (PERT) and Gantt charts. Plans and procedures cover emergency response, crisis management, notification, facilities relocation, security, asset management and retrieval, vital records, contamination, safety, and health. (For information write: Strohl Systems, 500 North Gulph Road, King of Prussia, PA 19406, telephone: (610) 768-4120, fax: (610) 768-4138, or Web: http://www.strohl-systems.com.)

CSCI's Recovery PAC is business recovery planning software including comprehensive business impact analysis and risk assessment. It identifies critical business functions and applications and sets priorities for recovery. It also identifies risk exposures that can potentially turn into a disaster. (For information telephone: (800) 925-CSCI.)

Business Foundations' Internal Operations Risk Analysis software evaluates a company's areas of risk and internal control structure. It is an expert system developed around 180 interview questions. Based on the answers to the questions, the software prepares a management report highlighting the strengths and weaknesses in the operations of the business. A risk rating (high, medium, and low) is assigned to categories of risk. Relevant management and analytical reports are generated. Operational areas evaluated by the software include working environment, objects, planning, and personnel. It has database capabilities. It recommends for problem areas corrective steps. There is an upgrade for industry-specific components.

Price Waterhouse's Controls assists in risk analysis by documenting, evaluating, and testing the company's internal controls. Areas of risk exposure are identified. Control weaknesses are highlighted with resultant recommendations for improvement. Control effectiveness may be evaluated at different levels within the company (e.g., by activity, by business unit). A comparison and analysis may be made of the relative control performance of different operating units. (For information fax: (201) 292-3800 or Web: http://www.pw.com.)

Pleier and Associates' ADM Plus performs risk management, planning, and analysis.

Corporate Systems' CS EDGE Series offers a risk management information system providing claim processing and evaluation, accident analysis, management of fixed assets, and risk reporting and appraisal. (For information telephone: (800) 9-CS-EDGE or Web: http://www.csedge.com.)

American International Group (AIG)'s IntelliRisk is a risk management information system providing claims information, asset management, risk reduction strategies, account information, payment history, report preparation, searches and sorting, and communication online features with underwriters, brokers, and adjusters. (For information telephone: Alan Louison, Director of Risk Management Information Services at (800) 767-2524 or write: American International Group, Department A, 70 Pine Street, New York, N.Y. 10270.)

Dorn Technology Group's RISK MASTER/WIN integration package has many features including incident reporting, claim adjustments and reporting, policy management, workers' compensation, actuarial reporting, and reserve analysis. (For information telephone (800) 587-1440 or (313) 462-5800; fax (313) 462-5809; or Web: http://dorn.com.)

Health Management Technologies' RETURN is software for workers' compensation, disability, and group health plans. It manages cases, channels information to network providers, monitors both work status and return to work, and documents activity and case outcome. It offers an electronic Rolodex of providers, treatment centers, resources, and contacts. The package evaluates provider performance and results in cost savings. The features include a standard letter generator, report writer, accounts receivable for case management, bill repricing, and job analysis. (For information telephone: (800) 647-7007 or write: Health Management Technologies, 1150 Moraga Way, Suite 150, Moraga, California 94556.)

California Interactive Computer's Claims and Risk Management Systems has modules for workers' compensation, group medical, property and casualty, disability management, and general risk management. The software can be customized for your particular needs by the vendor. (For information telephone: (805) 294-1300, fax: (805) 294-1310, write: California Interactive Computing, 25572 Avenue Stanford, Valencia, California 91355, Web: http://calinteractive.com.)

Conway Computer Group's Pabblo and Paccasso are a windows-based client/server solution for workers compensation and property/casualty insurance administration. (For information telephone: (601) 957-7400 or write: Conway Computer Group, P.O. Box 12801, Jackson, Mississippi 39211, Web: http://www.ccg.com.)

PC Solutions' Certifitra keeps track of insurance certificates, aids in insurance auditing, and prepares reports of insurance status (e.g., coverage, expiration dates). (For information telephone: (704) 525-9330, fax: (704) 525-9539, or e-mail: pcsoln@vnet.net.)

CCH Incorporated's Safety Compliance Assistant is interactive software to comply with the U.S. Occupational Safety and Health Administration (OSHA) General Industry Standards. It provides inspection and training checklists, detects OSHA compliance violations, maintains required documents, and corrects violations. (For information telephone: (800) 228-8353.)

CIC Incorporated's Back Track software verifies employees' background for hiring purposes. (For information telephone: (800) 321-HIRE extension 126, or fax: (813) 559-0232.)

QA Systems QASYS is innovative flexible risk management software for insurance companies. (For information telephone: (800) 946-1717 or (212) 599-1717, or write: QA Systems, 220 E. 42nd St., New York, N.Y. 10017.)

RISK MODELING SOFTWARE APPLICATIONS

Risk modeling is a decision-making aid to the financial manager. Models may be used in analyzing risks while financial models can evaluate the financial consequences arising from accidents or other adverse developments. Risk models may be developed for measuring the financial impact due to catastrophes (fire, flood, earthquake, nuclear). The probable loss arising from the accident, disaster, or other event may be estimated. The model may also determine the probable effects on business activities as well as possible competitive reactions. A contingency model may help in planning an appropriate strategy and response. A "what-if" scenario analysis may be formulated to see the end-result effects of changing input variables and factors. An example of a scenario modeling analysis is to simulate the possible operating and financial consequences on the company from various possibilities arising from a hurricane. The company's risk vulnerability from such an event may be "mapped" and appraised. The "best-case," "worst-case," and "likely" scenarios may be depicted and reviewed. The model simulation has the benefit of aiding the company in determining beforehand how to best minimize the damage operationally and financially and how to provide proper protective measures.

The software enables the company to determine the areas, types, and degrees of risk facing the business. A minimum-maximum range of loss figure may be derived.

Risk modeling may be used to identify and define the type and amount of risks related to various exposures. A priority ranking based on risk and uncertainty may also be prepared and studied. Risk problem areas may be analyzed along with a set of appropriate alternative responses.

RISK MANAGEMENT INFORMATION SYSTEMS (RMIS) TESTING LABORATORY

Deloitte and Touche, CPAs has started the first independent risk management systems testing laboratory that tests software, develops systems solutions, evaluates software usefulness, provides benchmarking information, and customizes applications. Deloitte and Touche, CPAs will compare software products, compare reporting and application features, and appraise effectiveness in meeting your needs. (For information contact David Duden, RMIS/Lab Director at telephone: (860) 543-7341, e-mail: dduden@ dttus.com, or Web: http://www.rmislab.com.)

ONLINE RISK MANAGEMENT DATA BASE SERVICES

There are many online services available providing important risk management information. For example, the National Council on Compensation Insurance (NCCI) Inc. provides an online InsNet Workers Compensation Characteristic Series containing claims data useful in having a cost-effective workers compensation system. The service aids in evaluating risks, determining and appraising workers compensation costs including frequency data, specifying injury claim characteristics, providing demographic and body claim characteristics, and specifying benefit type information. (For information about NCCI's InsNet online service telephone: (800) 622-4123, access the Web site: http://www.ncci.com, or write to National Council on Compensation Insurance, 750 Park of Commerce Drive, Boca Raton, Florida 33487.)

REENGINEERING AND OUTSOURCING THE BUSINESS

Reengineering includes downsizing and restructuring. It should be properly balanced. Outsourcing is contracting out production or service functions performed by the company to save on costs or to establish efficiencies. The financial manager must identify problems within the organization and recommend solutions. The financial manager must therefore understand what reengineering and outsourcing are about, how they affect the business, and how they may be implemented correctly. The financial manager needs to analyze, evaluate, offer suggestions, and comment on the company's existing or possible efforts to reengineer, downsize, restructure, and outsource the business.

REENGINEERING

A strategy is the implementation of a company's plans and tactics. A company may downsize or right size to its "core" to create value. Reengineering is defined as a multidisciplinary approach to making fundamental changes in how operations, activities, functions, and procedures are conducted within a business. The objective of such change is to improve performance, productivity, and profitability. Reengineering should be undertaken if the benefit exceeds the cost of doing so considering money and time. There should be a "road map" of the steps in the reengineering process. Reengineering may be for the company as a whole, one or more business units, and particular geographic locations. There is a risk in reengineering of not enough or too much change. For reengineering to succeed the following should be present: employee understanding and cooperation, good project planning and management, timely assessment, benchmarks, and realistic expectations. Reengineering may take different forms of approach including business process redesign (redesigning processes to achieve efficiencies and enhance service quality) and process innovation (making fundamental changes to improve the importance of processes). Reengineering attempts continual improvement in business procedures.

In reengineering, the focus should be on the current and potential customer and then corporate structure and processes designed accordingly. In other words, reengineering from the outside in. Managers must monitor and track the current and emerging satisfaction needs of customers and formulate the products and services they demand. New product innovation and creativity may be required. Reengineering must create "real value" to the customer. In so doing, consider if the current product/service line helps in keeping present customers and expanding the customer base.

Objectives for cost reduction should be established such as time for each job (task, operation, activity), expected maintenance, and compatibility.

Employees must understand the why to reengineering so their support, contribution, and continued morale to the process may be obtained. Cultural differences have to be taken into account. Disproportionate downsizing is a mistake. The company must be restructured logically and practically. Proper planning is required to avoid any surprises.

Reengineering may aid in developing new products and/or services, improving product distribution, and achieving growth. A successful strategy includes joint ventures and franchishing. The purposes of reengineering include:

- Cost control and reduction (e.g., employee costs)
- Revenue, profit, and rate of return maximization
- Growth and capacity therefor
- Reduction in risk
- Appreciation in stock and bond price
- Improvement in bond rating
- Lowering in the cost of financing
- Inventory reduction
- Improved market share
- Remaining competitive
- Reduction in headcount
- Change in corporate culture
- Additional flexibility
- Spinoff of a segment or operation

- Improved quality
- Improved integration
- Streamlining production and distribution
- Keeping up-to-date with the latest technology
- Improved productivity
- Improved interaction and communication
- Improved product delivery and service
- Change the product/service mix

In reengineering, consideration should be given to the cost and time of doing so, new ideas, developing products and services, managing operations and projects, portfolio management, retraining, acquisitions and mergers, joint ventures, automation, amount of restructuring needed, change to equipment, employee training, inspection requirements, infrastructure, risk profile, whether fundamental or incremental change is needed, reassignment (if any) of displaced employees, and legal and contractual provisions and limitations.

The right resources must be at the right places at the right time. Processes may be redesigned to improve service quality and promote efficiencies. Continuous improvement in processes and procedures, job descriptions, and work flow mandate commitment and follow-through. However, be careful not to make inappropriate or incorrect changes to the system or process. The effect of current changes on the future must be taken into account. A manager does not want to make a change now having just an immediate benefit but having a long-term negative effect. An example is laying off experienced supervisors who will be needed in the future to train employees when business picks up. Questions to be answered in reengineering follow:

- Should the reengineering effort be centralized or decentralized? If decentralized, how will integration be accomplished?
- Where does reengineering begin and end?
- What expectations are there to be achieved?
- What is the role of technology in the reengineering effort?
- What are the logistics throughout the project's life?
- What effect does reengineering efforts have on the environmental program of the business?
- How much value does the reengineering plan achieve?
- What uncertainties and risks does reengineering have and what steps have been undertaken to reduce such risks? The risks associated with

reengineering include financial, technological, operational, and political.

- What legal issues and contract commitments are raised because of the reengineering program?
- If, and to what extent, will outside consultants be involved?
- When, and how will periodic reviews (reports) take place?
- Is reengineering proceeding as scheduled? If not, what is the problem and how may it be rectified?
- Who will be assigned to the reengineering effort, and why? What are their qualifications and time commitment?

Before full-scale reengineering takes place at the entire company, a pilot program and prototyping should be conducted to identify problems, learn from mistakes, and formulate sound strategies and approaches based on experience. By developing solutions to expected problems before full scale implementation, the company may save in cost and time as well as reduce risks. It is best to complete one reengineering project before proceeding to the next because the manager becomes more focused and learns from experience.

Scenario analysis should be undertaken looking at high, low, and average situations. Probabilities, weights, and rankings may be assigned to alternative scenario situations as part of the evaluative process. There is a link between scenario planning and business reengineering. Scenario analysis considers uncertainties, range of possibilities (outcomes), what is critical and what is not, controllable and uncontrollable factors, the effect of implementing a strategy in one area on other areas, contingent possibilities (a course of action is valuable only in particular scenario settings). Scenario analysis considers advisable steps to take now or in the future, or if a particular change in circumstance occurs. It is similar to a simulation to determine what will happen in the "real world." "Red flags" should be recognized and corrective action taken. What are the positive and negative outcomes from implementing a particular procedure or strategy? Scenario analysis assists in reducing risk and focusing on reengineering efforts. The scenario program provides "visions" as to the future. Its results include what activities should be emphasized or deemphasized, and what actions should be eliminated. Scenario analysis looks at the alternative possibilities available and aids in timely implementation. A priority ranking of alternatives may be established.

Reengineering in the plant may take the form of automating operations, updating manufacturing approaches, and accomplishing greater flexibility. It may involve reorganizing the human resource function to achieve economies and eliminate duplication. Internal organizational processes and product/service deliveries may be redesigned.

One must be careful that reengineering does not result in "dumbsizing" when the entity's long-term financial position and operating results are adversely impacted. Does the reengineering program layoff experienced personnel, cut vital services, increase risk, result in legal liability, cause conflicts with vendors or customers, result in worker mistrust, cause injuries or malfunctioning of equipment, or cause other negative aspects that outweigh any benefits achieved? The authors are aware of instances when in fact a reengineering program that was improperly administered was counterproductive.

The reengineering team should consist of those who are representative of those to be affected within the department by the ultimate outcome of the proposed reengineering. The group should be a cross-section of individuals within the company. In other words, there should be organizational diversity. Determine who is responsible for what and how, and how often performance will be measured. If individuals are trying to sabotage the reengineering effort, take necessary steps to remove the roadblock such as dismissing uncooperative employees.

OUTSOURCING AND INSOURCING

A corporate policy must be established regarding outsourcing. Outsourcing is contracting to others work that was formerly done within the company. It includes buying goods and services from vendors. As a general rule, outsourcing is more appropriate for "core" activities than "noncore" operations. Companies more suitable for outsourcing are those that are decentralized, engaged in restructuring (e.g., downsizing), and are out-of-date.

There are many outsourcing service providers in areas such as finance, administration, engineering, manufacturing, buying, human resources, customer service, real estate management, computer systems, marketing and sales, investment management, maintenance, product procurement, distribution (e.g., shipping) and logistics, technology, and transportation. For example, information technology services are provided by Integrated Systems Solutions of White Plains, New York. Xerox Corporation offers many business services related to office work and duplication functions.

Before outsourcing, consideration should be given to whether it makes sense in light of expectations, company objectives and needs, business plans, major sources of revenue, cost (including conversion costs), risk (including business uncertainties), contract period, legal liability, availability, security, confidentiality, time constraints (including time to implement and schedule), capacity limitations, employee expertise and proficiency, employee morale, time concerns, nature of item (e.g., critical importance), compatibility, corporate culture, degree of control sought, innovation and creativity, logistics, and cost of redeployment and relocation. A company may be able to outsource an aspect of its operations for less than it costs to train and manage employees to conduct the same function within the business. If a function is "mission critical," it probably should not be outsourced because management would want to retain control over it. An activity that gives the company a significant competitive advantage (differentiation) should most likely stay within the company.

Outsourcing allows a business to be more efficient and effective, engage in subcontracting legacy systems, reduce costs (e.g., staff), reduce risk, streamline and simplify operations, improve quality, focus on core activities and competencies, free up capital and human resources, improve existing processes, improve delivery of activities, generate efficiencies and effectiveness, enhance flexibility, obtain a competitive advantage, redeploy staff and assets, achieve economies, enhance productivity, convert fixed costs to variable costs, and obtain improved up-to-date technology.

In selecting an outsourcing vendor, consider reputation, contacts, references, reliability, experience, specialty and focus, fees, flexibility, stability, expertise (specialized skills), cost, quality of service, creativity and innovation, upgrade potential, communications, commitment, contract provisions and restrictions (e.g., penalty and cancellation clauses), and "fit."

Ask the outsource vendor for a "trial period" to see how things are going before entering into a regular contract. However, avoid long-term contracts especially those that are rigid in its terms. You want flexibility and do not want to be locked in for the long-term. We recommend renewable short-term contracts. The contract should be updated as the environment and circumstances change.

Insist that outsourcing contracts contain provisions regarding performance expectations (e.g., service level goals) and measurement guidelines. Undertake periodic performance appraisals. Customer satisfaction with the outsourcer's services is crucial so surveys should be periodically conducted.

Insourcing is the self-manufacture of goods or services. Instead of buying the items from outside, the company produces the product or renders the service in an attempt to lower costs, improve quality, hasten availability, and be less reliant on outsiders. The cost-benefit of insourcing must be carefully evaluated.

FORECASTING AND FINANCIAL PLANNING

Financial management in private organizations typically operates under conditions of uncertainty or risk. Probably the most important function of business is forecasting. A forecast is a starting point for planning. The objective of forecasting is to reduce risk in decision making. In business, forecasts are the basis for capacity planning, production and inventory planning, personnel planning, planning for sales and market share, financial planning and budgeting, planning for research and development and top management's strategic planning. Sales forecasts are especially crucial aspects of many financial management activities, including budgets, profit planning, capital expenditure analysis, and acquisition and merger analysis.

Figure 1 illustrates how sales forecasts relate to various managerial functions of business.

WHO USES FORECASTS?

Forecasts are needed for marketing, production, purchasing, personnel, and financial planning. Further, top management needs forecasts for planning and implementing long-term strategic objectives and planning for capital expenditures. More specifically, marketing managers use sales forecasts to determine 1) optimal sales force allocations, 2) set sales goals, and 3) plan promotions and advertising. Other things such as market share, prices, and trends in new product development are required.

Production planners need forecasts in order to:

- Schedule production activities
- Order materials

Figure 1 Sales Forecasts and Managerial Functions

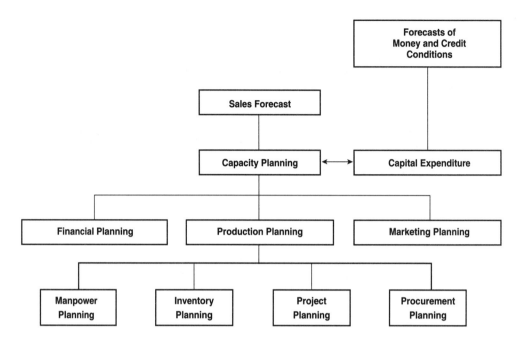

- Establish inventory levels
- Plan shipments

Some other areas which need forecasts include material requirements (purchasing and procurement), labor scheduling, equipment purchases, maintenance requirements, and plant capacity planning.

As shown in Figure 1, as soon as the company makes sure that it has enough capacity, the production plan is developed. If the company does not have enough capacity, it will require planning and budgeting decisions for capital spending for capacity expansion.

On this basis, the financial manager must estimate the future cash inflow and outflow. She must plan cash and borrowing needs for the company's future operations. Forecasts of cash flows and the rates of expenses and revenues are needed to maintain corporate liquidity and operating efficiency. In planning for capital investments, predictions about future economic activity are required so that returns or cash inflows accruing from the investment may be estimated.

Forecasts must also be made of money and credit conditions and interest rates so that the cash needs of the firm may be met at the lowest possible cost. The finance and accounting functions must also forecast interest rates to support the acquisition of new capital, the collection of accounts receivable to help in planning working capital needs, and capital equipment expenditure rates to help balance the flow of funds in the organization. Sound predictions of foreign exchange rates are increasingly important to financial managers of multinational companies (MNCs).

Long-term forecasts are needed for the planning of changes in the company's capital structure. Decisions as to whether to issue stock or debt in order to maintain the desired financial structure of the firm require forecasts of money and credit conditions.

The personnel department requires a number of forecasts in planning for human resources in the business. Workers must be hired and trained, and there must be benefits provided that are competitive with those available in the firm's labor market. Also, trends that affect such variables as labor turnover, retirement age, absenteeism, and tardiness need to be forecast as input for planning and decision making in this function.

The service sector which today accounts for 2/3 of the U.S. gross domestic product (GDP), including banks, insurance companies, restaurants, and cruiseships, need various projections for their operational and long-term strategic planning. Take a bank, for example. The bank has to forecast demands of various loans and deposits, as well as money and credit conditions so that it can determine the cost of money it lends.

TYPES OF FORECASTS

The types of forecasts used by businesses and other organizations may be classified in several categories, depending on the objective and the situation for which a forecast is to be used. Four types are discussed below.

Sales Forecasts

As discussed in the previous section, the sales forecast gives the expected level of sales for the company's goods or services throughout some future period and is instrumental in the company's planning and budgeting functions. It is the key to other forecasts and plans.

Financial Forecasts

Although the sales forecast is the primary input to many financial decisions, some financial forecasts need to be made independently of sales forecasts. This include forecasts of financial variables such as the amount of external financing needed, earnings, and cash flows and prediction of corporate bankruptcy.

Economic Forecasts

Economic forecasts, or statements of expected future business conditions, are published by governmental agencies and private economic forecasting firms. Business can use these forecasts and develop its own forecasts about external business outlook that will affect its product demand. Economic forecasts cover a variety of topics including GDP, levels of employment, interest rates, and foreign exchange rates.

Technological Forecasts

A technological forecast is an estimate of rates of technological progress. Certainly, software makers are interested in the rates of technological advancement in computer hardware and its peripheral equipment. Technological changes will provide many businesses with new products and materials to offer for sale, while other companies will encounter competition from other businesses. Technological forecasting is probably best performed by experts in the particular technology.

FORECASTING METHODS

There is a wide range of forecasting techniques which the company may choose from. There are basically two approaches to forecasting: qualitative and quantitative. They are as follows:

1. Qualitative approach—forecasts based on judgement and opinion.
   - Executive opinions
   - Delphi technique
   - Sales force polling
   - Consumer surveys
   - Techniques for eliciting experts' opinions—PERT-derived
2. Quantitative approach
   a) Forecasts based on historical data
      - Naive methods
      - Moving averages
      - Exponential smoothing
      - Trend analysis
      - Decomposition of time series
      - Box-Jenkins

b) Associative (Causal) forecasts
- Simple regression
- Multiple regression
- Econometric modeling

c) Forecasts based on consumer behavior—Markov approach

d) Indirect methods
- Market surveys
- Input-output analysis
- Economic indicators

Figure 2 summarizes the forecasting methods.

Quantitative models work superbly as long as little or no systematic change in the environment takes place. When patterns or relationships do change, by themselves, the objective models are of little use. It is here where the qualitative approach based on human judgment is indispensable. Because judgmental forecasting also bases forecasts on observation of exist-

Figure 2 Forecasting Methods

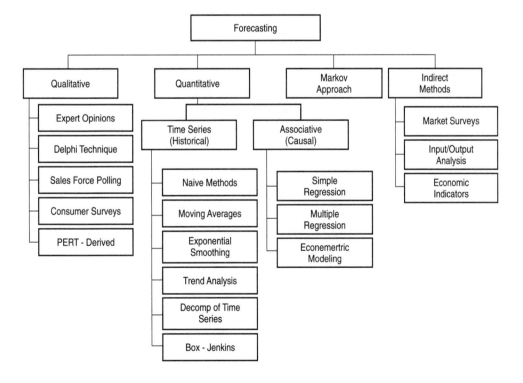

ing trends, they too are subject to a number of shortcomings. The advantage, however, is that they can identify systematic change more quickly and interpret better the effect of such change on the future.

We will discuss the qualitative method here in this chapter, while various quantitative methods along with their illustrations will be taken up in subsequent chapters.

SELECTION OF FORECASTING METHOD

The choice of a forecasting technique is significantly influenced by the stage of the product life cycle, and sometimes by the firm or industry for which a decision is being made.

In the beginning of the product life cycle, relatively small expenditures are made for research and market investigation. During the first phase of product introduction, these expenditures start to increase. In the rapid growth stage, considerable amounts of money are involved in the decisions; therefore a high level of accuracy is desirable. After the product has entered the maturity stage, the decisions are more routine, involving marketing and manufacturing. These are important considerations when determining the appropriate sales forecast technique.

After evaluating the particular stages of the product, and firm and industry life cycles, a further probe is necessary. Instead of selecting a forecasting technique by using whatever seems applicable, decision makers should determine what is appropriate. Some of the techniques are quite simple and rather inexpensive to develop and use, whereas others are extremely complex, require significant amounts of time to develop, and may be quite expensive. Some are best suited for short-term projections, whereas others are better prepared for intermediate- or long-term forecasts.

What technique or techniques to select depends on the following criteria:

1. What is the cost associated with developing the forecasting model compared with potential gains resulting from its use? The choice is one of benefit-cost trade-off.
2. How complicated are the relationships that are being forecasted?
3. Is it for short-run or long-run purposes?
4. How much accuracy is desired?
5. Is there a minimum tolerance level of errors?
6. How much data are available? Techniques vary in the amount of data they require.

THE QUALITATIVE APPROACH

The qualitative (or judgmental) approach can be useful in formulating short-term forecasts and also can supplement the projections based on the use of any of the qualitative methods. Four of the better known qualitative forecasting methods are Executive Opinions, the Delphi Method, Sales Force Polling, and Consumer Surveys.

Executive Opinions

The subjective views of executives or experts from sales, production, finance, purchasing and administration are averaged to generate a forecast about future sales. Usually this method is used in conjunction with some quantitative method such as trend extrapolation. The management team modifies the resulting forecast based on their expectations.

The advantage of this approach is that the forecasting is done quickly and easily, without need of elaborate statistics. Also, the jury of executive opinions may be the only feasible means of forecasting in the absence of adequate data. The disadvantage, however, is that of "group think." This is a set of problems inherent to those who meet as a group. Foremost among these problems are high cohesiveness, strong leadership, and insulation of the group. With high cohesiveness, the group becomes increasingly conforming through group pressure which helps stifle dissension and critical thought. Strong leadership fosters group pressure for unanimous opinion. Insulation of the group tends to separate the group from outside opinions, if given.

The Delphi Method

It is a group technique in which a panel of experts are individually questioned about their perceptions of future events. The experts do not meet as a group in order to reduce the possibility that consensus is reached because of dominant personality factors. Instead, the forecasts and accompanying arguments are summarized by an outside party and returned to the experts along with further questions. This continues until a consensus is reached by the group, especially after only a few rounds. This type of method is useful and quite effective for long-range forecasting.

The technique is done by "questionnaire" format and thus it eliminates the disadvantages of group think. There is no committee or debate. The experts are not influenced by peer pressure to forecast a certain way, as the answer is not intended to be reached by consensus or unanimity. Low reliability is cited as the main disadvantage of the Delphi Method, as well as lack of consensus from the returns.

Figure 3 An Example of the Use of the Delphi Method

1 Population (in Millions)	2 Midpoint	3 Number of Panelists	4 Probability Distribution of Panelists	5 Weighted Average (2×4)
30 and above	00	0	.00	0
20-30	25	1	.05	1.25
15-19	17	2	.10	1.70
10-14	12	2	.10	1.20
5-9	7	7	.35	2.45
2-4	3	8	.40	1.20
Less than 2	1	0	.00	0
Total		20	1.00	7.80

Case example: "In 1982, a panel of 20 representatives, with college educations, from different parts of the U.S.A., were asked to estimate the population of Bombay, India. None of the panelists had been to India since World War I.

"The population was estimated to be 7.8 million, which is very close to the actual population."

Source: Singhvi, Surendra. "Financial Forecast: Why and How?" *Managerial Planning.* March/April, 1984.

Sales-Force Polling

Some companies use as a forecast source sales people who have continual contacts with customers. They believe that the sales force who are closest to the ultimate customers may have significant insights regarding the state of the future market. Forecasts based on sales-force polling may be averaged to develop a future forecast. Or they may be used to modify other quantitative and/or qualitative forecasts that have been generated internally in the company. The advantages to this way of forecast are that (1) it is simple to use and understand, (2) it uses the specialized knowledge of those closest to the action, (3) it can place responsibility for attaining the forecast in the hands of those who most affect the actual results, and (4) the information can be easily broken down by territory, product, customer or salesperson.

The disadvantages include salespeople being overly optimistic or pessimistic regarding their predictions, and inaccuracies due to broader economic events that are largely beyond their control.

Consumer Surveys

Some companies conduct their own market surveys regarding specific consumer purchases. Surveys may consist of telephone contacts, personal interviews, or questionnaires as a means of obtaining data. Extensive statistical analysis is usually applied to survey results in order to test hypotheses regarding consumer behavior.

PERT-Derived Forecasts

A technique known as PERT (Program Evaluation and Review Technique) has been useful in producing estimates based on subjective opinions such as executive opinions or sales force polling. The PERT methodology requires that the expert provide three estimates: (1) pessimistic (a), (2) the most likely (m), and (3) optimistic (b). The theory suggests that these estimates combine to form an expected value, or forecast, as follows:

$$EV = (a + 4m + b)/6$$

with a standard deviation of

$$\sigma = (b - a)/6$$

where

EV = expected value (mean) of the forecast

σ = standard deviation of the forecast

For example, suppose that management of a company believes that if the economy is in recession, the next year's sales will be $300,000 and if the economy is in prosperity $330,000. Their most likely estimate is $310,000. The PERT method generates an expected value of sales as follows:

$$EV = (\$300,000 + 4(\$310,000) + \$330,000)/6 = \$311,667$$

with a standard deviation of

$$\sigma = (\$330,000 - \$300,000)/6 = \$5,000$$

Advantages:

1. It is often easier and more realistic to ask the expert to give optimistic, pessimistic and most likely estimates than a specific forecast value.

2. The PERT method includes a measure of dispersion (the standard deviation), which makes it possible to develop probabilistic statements regarding the forecast. For example, in the above example the forecaster is 95 percent confident that the true value of the forecasted sales lies between plus or minus two standard deviations from the mean ($311,667). That is the true value can be expected between $211,667 and $411,667.

A Word of Caution

It is also important to realize that forecasting is not an exact science like mathematics, it is an art. The quality of forecasts tends to improve over time as the forecaster gains more experience. Evidence, however, shows that forecasts using qualitative techniques are not as accurate as those using quantitative techniques:

> Humans possess unique knowledge and inside information not available to quantitative methods. Surprisingly, however, empirical studies and laboratory experiments have shown that their forecasts are not more accurate than those of quantitative methods. Humans tend to be optimistic and underestimate the future uncertainty. In addition, the cost of forecasting with judgmental methods is often considerably higher than when quantitative methods are used.[1]

Note: Therefore, a forecaster must use both qualitative as well as quantitative techniques to create a reasonable forecast.

COMMON FEATURES AND ASSUMPTIONS INHERENT IN FORECASTING

As pointed out, forecasting techniques are quite different from each other. But there are certain features and assumptions that underlie the business of forecasting. They are:

1. Forecasting techniques generally assume that the same underlying causal relationship that existed in the past will continue to prevail in the future. In other words, most of our techniques are based on historical data.

---

[1]"Science of Forecasting, *International Journal of Forecasting,* Vol. 2, 1986, p. 17.

2. Forecasts are very rarely perfect. Therefore, for planning purposes, allowances should be made for inaccuracies. For example, the company should always maintain a safety stock in anticipation of stockouts.

3. Forecast accuracy decreases as the time period covered by the forecast (that is, the time horizon) increases. Generally speaking, a long-term forecast tends to be more inaccurate than a short-term forecast because of the greater uncertainty.

4. Forecasts for groups of items tend to be more accurate than forecasts for individual items, since forecasting errors among items in a group tend to cancel each other out. For example, industry forecasting is more accurate than individual firm forecasting.

STEPS IN THE FORECASTING PROCESS

There are five basic steps in the forecasting process. They are:

1. Determine the what and why of the forecast and what will be needed. This will indicate the level of detail required in the forecast (for example, forecast by region, forecast by product, etc.), the amount of resources (for example, computer hardware and software, manpower, etc.) that can be justified, and the level of accuracy desired.

2. Establish a time horizon, short-term or long-term. More specifically, project for the next year or next five years, etc.

3. Select a forecasting technique. Refer to the criteria discussed before.

4. Gather the data and develop a forecast.

5. Identify any assumptions that had to be made in preparing the forecast and using it.

6. Monitor the forecast to see if it is performing in a manner desired. Develop an evaluation system for this purpose. If not, go to step 1.

Figure 4 The Forecasting Process

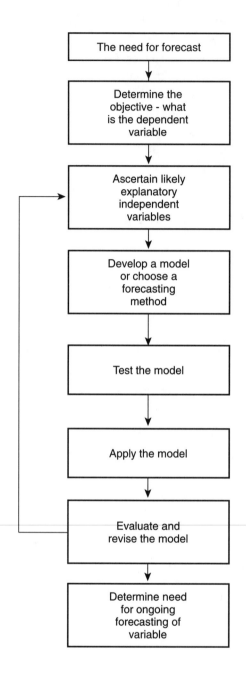

FINANCIAL AND EARNINGS FORECASTING

Financial forecasting, an essential element of planning, is the basis for *budgeting* activities. It is also needed when estimating future financing requirements. The company may look either internally or externally for financing. Internal financing refers to cash flow generated by the company's normal operating activities. External financing refers to capital provided by parties external to the company. You need to analyze how to estimate *external* financing requirements. Basically, forecasts of future sales and related expenses provide the firm with the information to project future external financing needs. The chapter discusses (1) the *percent-of-sales method* to determine the amount of external financing needed, (2) the CPA's involvement in prospective financial statements, and (3) earnings forecast.

THE PERCENT-OF-SALES METHOD

Percentage of sales is the most widely used method for projecting the company's financing needs. This method involves estimating the various expenses, assets, and liabilities for a future period as a percent of the sales forecast and then using these percentages, together with the projected sales, to construct pro forma balance sheets.

Basically, forecasts of future sales and their related expenses provide the firm with the information needed to project its future needs for financing. The basic steps in projecting financing needs are:

1. Project the firm's sales. The sales forecast is the initial most important step. Most other forecasts (budgets) follow the sales forecast.
2. Project additional variables such as expenses.

3. Estimate the level of investment in current and fixed assets required to support the projected sales.
4. Calculate the firm's financing needs.

The following example illustrates how to develop a pro forma balance sheet and determine the amount of external financing needed.

Example 1. Assume that sales for 19x1 = $20, projected sales for 19x2 = $24, net income = 5% of sales, and the dividend payout ratio = 40%. Figure 1 illustrates the method, step by step. All dollar amounts are in millions.

Figure 1 Pro Forma Balance Sheet (in millions of dollars)

	Present *(19X1)*	*% of Sales* *(19X1 Sales = $20)*	*Projected* *(19X2 Sales = $24)*	
ASSETS				
Current assets	2	10	2.4	
Fixed assets	4	20	4.8	
Total assets	6		7.2	
LIABILITIES AND STOCKHOLDERS' EQUITY				
Current liabilities	2	10	2.4	
Long-term debt	2.5	n.a.	2.5	
Total liabilities	4.5		4.9	
Common stock	0.1	n.a.	0.1	
Paid-in-capital	0.2	n.a.	0.1	
Retained earnings	1.2		1.92 (a)	
Total equity	1.5		2.22	
Total liabilities and stockholders' equity	6		7.12	Total financing provided
			0.08 (b)	External financing needed
			7.2	Total

(a) 19X2 retained earnings = 19X1 retained earnings + projected net income − cash dividends paid
= $1.2 + 5% ($24) − 40% [5% ($24)]
= $1.2 + $1.2 − $0.48
= $2.4 − $0.48
= $1.92
(b) External financing need = project total assets − (projected total liabilities + projected equity)
= $7.2 − ($4.9 + $2.22)
= $7.2 − $7.12
= $0.08

The steps for the computations are outlined as follows:

Step 1. Express those balance sheet items that vary directly with sales as a percentage of sales. Any item such as long-term debt that does not vary directly with sales is designated "n.a.," or "not applicable."

Step 2. Multiply these percentages by the 19x2 projected sales = $24 to obtain the projected amounts as shown in the last column.

Step 3. Simply insert figures for long-term debt, common stock and paid-in-capital from the 19x1 balance sheet.

Step 4. Compute 19x2 retained earnings as shown in (b).

Step 5. Sum the asset accounts, obtaining a total projected assets of $7.2, and also add the projected liabilities and equity to obtain $7.12, the total financing provided. Since liabilities and equity must total $7.2, but only $7.12 is projected, we have a shortfall of $0.08 "external financing needed."

Although the forecast of additional funds required can be made by setting up pro forma balance sheets as described above, it is often easier to use the following formula:

External funds needed (EFN)	=	Required increase in assets	−	Spontaneous increase in liabilities	−	Increase in retained earnings
EFN	=	$(A/S) \Delta S$	−	$(L/S) \Delta S$	−	$(PM)(PS)(1-d)$

where

A/S = Assets that increase spontaneously with sales as a percentage of sales.

L/S = Liabilities that increase spontaneously with sales as a percentage of sales.

ΔS = Change in sales.

PM = Profit margin on sales.

PS = Projected sales

d = Dividend payout ratio.

Example 2. In Example 1,

A/S = $6/$20 = 30%

L/S = $2/$20 = 10%

$\Delta S = ($24 - $20) = 4

PM = 5% on sales

PS = $24

d = 40%

Plugging these figures into the formula yields:

$$
\begin{aligned}
\text{EFN} &= 0.3(\$4) - 0.1(\$4) - (0.05)(\$24)(1 - 0.4) \\
&= \$1.2 - \$0.4 - \$0.72 = \$0.08
\end{aligned}
$$

Thus, the amount of external financing needed is $800,000, which can be raised by issuing notes payable, bonds, stocks, or any combination of these financing sources.

The major advantage of the percent-of-sales method of financial forecasting is that it is simple and inexpensive to use. One important assumption behind the use of the method is that the firm is operating at full capacity. This means that the company has no sufficient productive capacity to absorb a projected increase in sales and thus requires additional investment in assets. Therefore, the method must be used with extreme caution if excess capacity exists in certain asset accounts.

To obtain a more precise projection of the firm's future financing needs, however, the preparation of a cash budget may be required.

THE CPA'S INVOLVEMENT AND RESPONSIBILITY WITH PROSPECTIVE FINANCIAL STATEMENTS

The American Institute of Certified Public Accountants (AICPA) in *Statement of Position 45-4* provides guidelines for business enterprises which publish financial forecasts. Improved financial forecasting should be of concern to the AICPA and the Securities and Exchange Commission as a basis for financial decision making, security analysis, and in affecting the future market value of securities through investor expectations. Figure 2 presents an excerpt from the 1983 Annual Report of Masco Corporation which contains (1) a five-year cash flow forecast, (2) forecasts of a five-year growth rate for sales, and (3) key assumptions used in the forecasts.

There are three types of functions that CPAs can perform with respect to prospective financial statements that will be relied upon by third parties: examination, compilation, and application of agreed-upon procedures. CPAs must prepare prospective financial statements according to AICPA standards. There must be disclosure of the underlying assumptions.

Prospective financial statements may be for general use or limited use. General use is for those not directly dealing with the client. The general user

Figure 2 Management Forecast Disclosure by Masco Corporation

FIVE-YEAR FORECAST

We have included in the annual report a sales forecast for each of our major product lines and operating groups for 1988.

While we recognize that long-term forecasts are subject to many variables and uncertainties, our experience has been that our success is determined more by our own activities than by the performance of any industry or the economy in general. In addition, the balance and diversity of our products and markets have been such that a shortfall in expected performance in one area has been largely offset by higher than expected growth in another.

Although variations may occur in the forecast for any individual product line, we have a relatively high level of confidence that our overall five-year growth forecast is achievable.

ASSUMPTIONS USED IN FORECAST

1. Average 2-3 percent annual real growth in GNP.
2. Average inflation 5-7 percent.
3. Present tax structure to continue.
4. No change in currency exchange rates.
5. No acquisitions.
6. No additional financing.
7. Dividend payout ratio 20 percent.
8. Four percent after-tax return on investment of excess cash.
9. No exercise of stock options.

FIVE-YEAR CASH-FLOW FORECAST

(In thousands)	1984-1988
Net Income	$ 850,000
Depreciation	280,000
	1,130,000
	(230,000)
	(280,000)
	(260,000)
	(170,000)
Net Cash Change	190,000
Beginning Cash, 1-84	210,000
Cash, 12-31-88	$ 400,000

SALES GROWTH BY PRODUCTS

(In thousands)

	Sales Forecast		Actual Sales		
	5-Year Growth Rate 1984-1988	1988	5-Year Growth Rate 1979-1983	1983	1978
Products for the Home and Family	14%	$1,225,000	16%	$ 638,000	$308,000
Products for Industry	16%	875,000	9%	421,000	278,000
Total Sales	15%	$2,100,000	13%	$1,059,000	$585,000

SALES GROWTH BY SPECIFIC MARKETS AND PRODUCTS (1) (2)

(In thousands)

	Forecast		Actual		
	5-Year Growth Rate 1984-1988	1988	5-Year Growth Rate 1979-1983	1983	1978
Masco Faucet Sales (3)	15%	$490,000	9%	$243,000	$155,000
Faucet Industry Sales-Units	7%	35,000	(5)%	25,000	32,000
Masco Market Share-Units	2%	38%	5%	34%	27%
Housing Completions	4%	1,700	(4)%	1,400	1,700
Independent Cold Extrusion Industry Sales	13%	$580,000	1%	$310,000	$290,000
Masco Cold Extrusion Sales (3)	14%	$170,000	5%	$ 88,000	$ 70,000
Truck Production	7%	3,400	(8)%	2,400	3,700
Auto Production	4%	8,200	(6)%	6,800	92,00
Masco Auto Parts Sales	13%	$210,000	8%	$113,000	$ 76,000

(1) Excludes foreign sales.　(2) Industry data Masco estimates.　(3) Includes foreign sales.

Source: 1983 Annual Report of Masco Corporation, p. 42.

may take the deal or leave it. Limited use is for those having a direct relationship with the client.

Prospective financial statements may be presented as a complete set of financial statements (balance sheet, income statement, and statement of cash flows). However, in most cases, it is more practical to present them in summarized or condensed form. At a minimum, the financial statement items to be presented are:

- Sales
- Gross margin
- Nonrecurring items
- Taxes
- Income from continuing operations
- Income from discontinued operations
- Net income
- Primary and fully diluted earnings per share
- Material changes in financial position

Not considered prospective financial statements are pro-forma financial statements and partial presentations.

The American Institute of CPA's Code of Professional Ethics includes the following guidelines regarding prospective financial statements:

- Cannot vouch for the achieveability of prospective results
- Must disclose assumptions
- Accountant's report must state the nature of the work performed and the degree of responsibility assumed

CPAs are not permitted to furnish services on prospective financial statements if the statements are solely appropriate for limited use but are distributed to parties not involved directly with the issuing company. They are not allowed to use plain-paper services on prospective financial statements for third-party use.

A prospective financial statement may be classified as either a forecast or a projection.

Financial Forecast

A financial forecast presents management's expectations, and there is an expectation that all assumptions will take place. *Note:* A financial forecast encompasses a presentation that management expects to occur but that is not necessarily most probable. A financial forecast may be most useful to general users, since it presents the client's expectations. A financial forecast and not a financial projection may be issued to passive users, or those not negotiating directly with the client.

A financial forecast may be given a single monetary amount based on the best estimate, or as a reasonable range. *Caution:* This range must not be chosen in a misleading manner. ·

Irrespective of the accountant's involvement, management is the only one who has responsibility for the presentation because only management knows how it plans to run the business and accomplish its plans.

Financial Projection

A financial projection presents a "what-if" scenario that management does not necessarily expect to occur. However, a given assumption may actually occur if management moves in that direction. A financial projection may be most beneficial for limited users, since they may seek answers to hypothetical questions based on varying assumptions. These users may wish to alter their scenarios based on anticipated changing situations. A financial projection, like a forecast, may contain a range.

A financial projection may be presented to general users only when it supplements a financial forecast. Financial projections are not permitted in tax shelter offerings and other general-use documents.

Types of Engagements

The following five types of engagements may be performed by the CPA in connection with prospective financial statements:

Plain Paper.   The CPA's name is not associated with the prospective statements. This service can only be conducted if all of the following conditions are satisfied:

- The CPA is not reporting on the presentation.
- The prospective statements are on paper not identifying the accountant.
- The prospective financial statements are not shown with historical financial statements that have been audited, reviewed, or compiled by the CPA.

Internal Use. The prospective financial statements are only assembled, meaning mathematical and clerical functions are performed. Assembling financial data is permitted if the following two criteria exist:

- Third parties will not use the statements.
- The CPA's name is associated with the statement.

Note that assembling prospective financial statements is limited only to internal use. Appropriate language on the statements might be "For Internal Use Only."

Compilation. This is the lowest level of service performed for prospective financial statements directed for third parties. The compilation engagement involves:

- Assembling prospective data.
- The conduct of procedures to ascertain whether the presentation and assumptions are appropriate.
- Preparation of a compilation report.

With a compilation, no assurance is given regarding the presentation or assumptions, but rather it serves to identify obvious matters to be investigated further. Working papers have to be prepared to show there was proper planning and supervision of the work, as well as compliance with required compilation procedures. The CPA must also obtain a management letter from the client regarding representations given to him.

Warning: A compilation should not be made when the forecasted financial statements exclude disclosure of the significant assumptions or when the financial projections exclude the hypothetical assumptions.

Agreed-upon Procedures. This relates to applying procedures agreed to or requested by specific users, and issuing a report. The report identifies the procedures undertaken, gives the accountant's findings, and restricts distribution of the report to the particular parties. The specified users have to participate in establishing the nature and procedures. Also, the procedures undertaken must be more than just reading the prospective data.

Examination. The CPA appraises the preparation underlying the supporting assumptions and the presentation of prospective financial information in accordance with AICPA standards. A report is then issued on whether AICPA guidelines have been adhered to and whether the assumptions are reasonable. It is the highest level of assurance. An adverse opinion must be given if there is a failure to disclose a material assumption or if disclosed assumptions are unreasonable. For example, there may be not reasonable expectation that the actual figure will fall within the range of assumptions presented in a forecast having a range. A disclaimer opinion is necessary in the event of a scope limitation, such as when a required examination procedure cannot be performed because of client restrictions or inappropriate circumstances.

EARNINGS FORECAST

For many years, financial analysts have predicted earnings per share and stock price performance. Considerable emphasis has been placed on such forecasts in order to provide guidance to investors. Recently, management forecast disclosures in financial statements have placed greater emphasis on the development of forecasting methodology in this area. The accuracy of these earnings forecasts has been given much attention recently primarily due to the SEC's position on financial forecasts and issuance of a Statement of Position by the AICPA.

Security Analysts vs. Time-Series Models

Forecasts of earnings per share for business firms are published by both management and security analysts. Unfortunately, however, the accuracy of EPS forecasts by security analysts have been shown to be little if any better than that produced by some "naive" models such as extrapolating the past trend of earnings. Indeed, it increasingly appears that the change in EPS may be a random variable.

Projections of EPS are frequently made by independent security analysts. Examples of forecast sources include (1) Value Line Investment Survey, (2) Lynch, Jones and Ryan's Institutional Brokers Estimate System (IBES), (3) Standard & Poor's The Earnings Forecaster, and (4) Zacks Investment Research's Icarus Service. Figure 3 presents an excerpt from the monthly report from Lynch, Jones, and Ryan's IBES Service which contains various earnings forecasts by individual security analysts.

Figure 3 Extract from Monthly Summary Report of the IBES Service

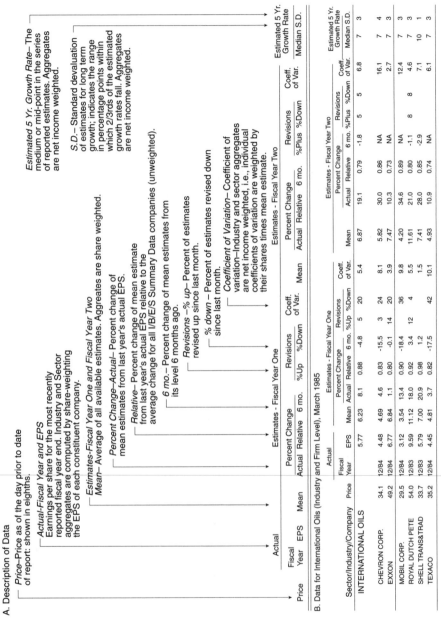

A. Description of Data

B. Data for International Oils (Industry and Firm Level), March 1985

Source: Lynch, Jones, and Ryan, IBES Monthly Summary Data (New York, N.Y.).

Figure 4 summarizes the pros and cons of both approaches.

Figure 4 Pros and Cons of Security Analyst and Univariate Time-Series Model Approaches to Forecasting

Security Analysts Approach to Forecasting

Pros

1. Ability to incorporate information from many sources.
2. Ability to adjust to structural change immediately.
3. Ability to update continually as new information becomes available.

Cons

1. High initial setup cost and high ongoing cost to monitor numerous variables, make company visits, and so on.
2. Heavy dependence on the skills of a single individual.
3. Analyst may have an incentive not to provide an unbiased forecast (e.g., due to pressure to conform to consensus forecasts).
4. Analyst may be manipulated by company officials (at least in the short run).

Univariate Time-Series Model Approach to Forecasting

Pros

1. Ability to detect and exploit systematic patterns in the past series.
2. Relatively low degree of subjectivity in the forecasting (especially given the availability of computer algorithms to identify and estimate models).
3. Low cost and ease of updating.
4. Ability to compute confidence intervals around the forecasts.

Cons

1. Limited number of observations available for newly formed firms, firms with structural change, and so on.
2. Financial statement data may not satisfy distributional assumptions of time-series model used.
3. Inability to update forecasts between successive interim or annual earnings releases.
4. Difficulty of communicating approach to clients (especially the statistical methodology used in identifying and estimating univariate models).

Source: Foster, George, *Financial Statement Analysis,* 2nd ed., Prentice Hall, Englewood Cliffs, N.J., 1986, p. 278.

Table 1 shows sources of earnings forecasting data preferred by financial analysts.

Table 1 What Are Your Present Sources of Earnings Forecasting Data?

	Rank	1	2	3	4	5
Company contacts		56	28	24	8	9
Own research		55	15	5	1	
Industry statistics		19	14	14	7	
Other analysis		12	17	2	8	11
Historical financial data		8	12	8	5	4
Economic forecasts		7	7	10	3	
Competition		1	7	2	6	1
Computer simulation						2
Field trips			1			
Government agencies				2		
Industry & trade sources		1	7	17	3	5
Public relations of a promotional nature						1
Retired directors						1
Rumor						2
Wall Street sources		1	4	9	3	4

Rank   1 = most preferred
        5 = least preferred

Source: Carper, Brent W., Barton Jr., Frank M., Wunder Haroldene F. "The Future of Forecasting." *Management Accounting.* August, 1997. pp. 27-31.

This section compares various forecasting methods using a sample drawn from the Standard and Poor's 400. It also examines the ability of financial analysts to forecast earnings per share performance based on the relationship of past forecasts of future earnings by financial analysts and through the use of recent univariate time-series models.

Our sample of Earnings Per Share (EPS) was drawn from the 1984 through 1988 time period using the quarterly *Compustat Industrial* data tapes available from S & P. Included in our sample are 30 firms randomly selected from the Standard & Poor 400 index for manufacturing firms over the period January 1984 to July 1988, using monthly data as reported to the public security markets. To collect data on financial analyst forecasts, we have selected the *Value Line Forecasting Survey* which is one of several reporting agencies that employ financial analysts and report their forecasts on a weekly basis.

In order to compare the forecasting ability of financial analysts with extrapolative models, seven time-series models were used to forecast earnings per share. The popular computer forecasting software *RATS* was used to estimate the models.

Data for the resulting sample of firms were used over the five-year time period studied (i.e., January, 1984-June, 1987) to estimate the models. This period was a relatively short time period to avoid the possibility of structural changes in the economy affecting the results of the study.

Next, forecasts were derived from July, 1987 to June, 1988 using monthly data. The accuracy of the forecasts from each of the models for the period were evaluated using the two measures: (1) MAPE (mean absolute percentage error) and (2) MSE (mean square error).

Forecasting Methodology

In this section, we present each forecasting model. These models relate to various models proposed by earnings forecasters in the accounting, finance, and forecasting literature. They are the following:

1. Exponential Smoothing Model with Additive Seasonal Effect.
2. Single Exponential Smoothing Model.
3. Exponential Smoothing Model with Linear Trend and Seasonal Additive Effects.
4. Exponential Smoothing Model with Exponential Trend and Seasonal Additive Effects.
5. Box-Jenkins Analysis SARIMA(1,0,0) (0,1,0) s = 12

   A seasonal autoregressive integrated moving average (SARIMA) model is identified with first order autoregressive parameters and a 12-month seasonal adjustment.

6. Box-Jenkins Analysis SARIMA(1,0,0) (0,1,1) s = 12

   A seasonal autoregressive integrated moving average (SARIMA) model is identified with first order autoregressive parameters and a 12-month seasonal adjustment. It also contains a seasonal moving average.

7. Linear Trend Analysis
8. Value Line Forecast

Forecasting Accuracy

In Table 1, the Sample Average Forecast Error was estimated for each of 12 months based on earlier data. From July 1987 through June 1988, the monthly forecast errors are presented using the MAPE measure. From this analysis there is some variation in forecasting accuracy. The exponential forecasting methods performed well for methods 1, 2, and 3. The Box-Jenkins approaches for methods 5 and 6, and the linear trend analysis for method 7 were reasonably successful. Overall, however, the monthly Value Line forecast resulted in the largest forecast errors.

Table 2 Sample Average Forecast Errors from 30 Companies Mean Absolute Percentage Error (MAPE)

Method 1	2	3	4	5	6	7	8
1987:7	0.28	0.30	0.39	1.54	0.42	0.64	0.57	1.77
1987:8	0.24	0.23	0.29	1.51	0.72	0.95	0.58	1.39
1987:9	0.19	0.22	0.16	1.51	1.00	1.23	0.56	0.70
1987:10	0.19	0.22	0.16	1.55	1.28	1.54	0.56	0.70
1987:11	0.24	0.43	0.46	1.48	1.72	1.98	0.56	1.73
1987:12	0.27	0.71	0.71	1.48	2.09	2.35	0.69	4.28
1988:1	0.42	0.83	1.11	1.46	2.47	2.60	0.55	4.97
1988:2	0.42	0.83	1.11	1.46	2.47	2.60	0.55	4.97
1988:3	0.67	2.15	2.10	2.00	3.31	3.45	0.73	6.01
1988:4	0.78	3.17	1.48	1.72	3.53	3.65	0.73	9.00
1988:5	0.81	1.44	1.44	1.80	0.86	0.99	0.68	8.62
1988:6	0.81	1.44	1.44	1.80	0.86	0.99	0.68	8.62

Table 2 presents the MSE results. Generally, the mean square error reflected similar conclusions (see Table 3).

Table 3 Sample Average Forecast Errors from 30 Companies Mean Square Error (MSE)

Method	1	2	3	4	5	6	7	8
1987:7	0.42	0.34	0.39	6.27	0.12	0.12	1.21	1.59
1987:8	0.31	0.23	0.40	6.17	0.13	0.13	1.26	1.63
1987:9	0.31	0.23	0.33	5.93	0.14	0.14	1.31	1.69
1987:10	0.31	0.21	0.33	5.93	0.14	0.14	1.31	1.69
1987:11	0.32	0.64	0.76	6.22	0.48	0.47	1.47	2.19
1987:12	0.34	0.78	0.87	5.93	0.55	0.53	1.62	2.39
1988:1	0.71	1.32	1.38	5.91	0.97	0.95	1.45	0.99
1988:2	0.71	1.32	1.38	5.91	0.97	0.95	1.45	0.99
1988:3	1.40	5.48	1.81	5.68	3.89	3.86	2.28	0.85
1988:4	1.20	6.10	1.40	5.33	3.45	3.43	1.95	0.82
1988:5	1.21	7.29	1.41	5.21	3.35	3.34	2.03	0.74
1988:6	1.21	7.29	1.41	5.21	3.35	3.34	2.03	0.74

CONCLUSION

Financial forecasting, an essential element of planning, is a vital function of financial managers. It is needed where the future financing needs are being estimated. Basically, forecasts of future sales and their related expenses provide the firm with the information needed to project its financing requirements. Furthermore, financial forecasting involves earnings forecasts which provide useful information concerning the expectations of a firm's future total market return. This is of interest to security analysts and investors. Different forecasting methods of earnings were compared in terms of their accuracy. Also presented was a CPA's involvement with prospective financial statements.

CASH FLOW FORECASTING

A forecast of cash collections and potential writeoffs of accounts receivable is essential in *cash budgeting* and in judging the appropriateness of current credit and discount policies. The critical step in making such a forecast is estimating the cash collection and bad debt percentages to be applied to sales or accounts receivable balances. This chapter discusses several methods of estimating *cash collection rates* (or *payment proportions*) and illustrates how these rates are used for cash budgeting purposes.

The first approach, which is based on the *Markov model,* involves the use of a probability matrix based on the estimates of what is referred to as transition probabilities. This method is described on a step-by-step basis using an illustrative example. The second approach involves a simple average. The third approach offers a more pragmatic method of estimating collection and bad debt percentages by relating credit sales and collection data. This method employs regression analysis. By using these approaches, a financial planner should be able to:

- Estimate future cash collections from accounts receivable
- Establish an allowance for doubtful accounts
- Provide a valuable insight into better methods of managing accounts receivable

MARKOV APPROACH

The Markov (probability matrix) approach has been around for a long time. This approach has been successfully applied by Cyert and others to accounts receivable analysis, specifically to the estimation of that portion of the accounts receivable that will eventually become uncollectible. The method requires classification of outstanding accounts receivable according to age categories that reflect the stage of account delinquency, e.g., current accounts, accounts one month past due, accounts two months past due, and so forth. Consider the following example. XYZ department store divides its accounts receivable into two classifications: 0 to 60 days old and 61 to 120 days old. Accounts that are more than 120 days old are declared uncollectible by XYZ. XYZ currently has $10,000 in accounts receivable: $7,000 from the 0-60-day-old category and $3,000 from the 61-120-day-old category. Based on an analysis of its past records, it provides us with what is known as the matrix of transition probabilities. The matrix is given as shown in Table 1.

Table 1 Probability Matrix

From To	Collected	Uncollectible	0-60 Days Old	61-120 Days Old
Collected	(1)	0	0	0
Uncollectible	0	1	0	0
0-60 days old	.3	[0]	.5	.2
61-120 days old	.5	.1	.3	.1

Transition probabilities are nothing more than the probability that an account receivable moves from one age stage category to another. We note three basic features of this matrix. First, notice the squared element, 0 in the matrix. This indicates that $1 in the 0-6-day-old category cannot become a bad debt in one month's time. Now look at the two circled elements. Each of these is 1, indicating that, in time, all the accounts receivable dollars will either be paid or become uncollectible. Eventually, all the dollars do wind up either as collected or uncollectible, but XYZ would be interested in knowing the probability that a dollar of a 0-60-day-old or a 61-120-day-old receivable would eventually find its way into either paid bills or bad debts. It is convenient to partition the matrix of transition probabilities into four sub-matrices, as follows.

$$\begin{matrix} I & O \\ R & Q \end{matrix}$$

so that

$$I = \begin{bmatrix} 1 & 0 \\ 0 & 1 \end{bmatrix} \qquad O = \begin{bmatrix} 0 & 0 \\ 0 & 0 \end{bmatrix}$$

$$R = \begin{bmatrix} .3 & 0 \\ .5 & .1 \end{bmatrix} \qquad Q = \begin{bmatrix} .5 & .2 \\ .3 & .1 \end{bmatrix}$$

Now we are in a position to illustrate the procedure used to determine:

- Estimated collection and bad debt percentages by age category
- Estimated allowance for doubtful accounts

Step-by-step, the procedure is as follows:

Step 1. Set up the matrix [I – Q].

$$[I - Q] = \begin{bmatrix} 1 & 0 \\ 0 & 1 \end{bmatrix} - \begin{bmatrix} .5 & .2 \\ .3 & .1 \end{bmatrix} = \begin{bmatrix} .5 & -.2 \\ -.3 & .9 \end{bmatrix}$$

Step 2. Find the inverse of this matrix, denoted by N.

$$N = [I - Q]^{-1} = \begin{bmatrix} 2.31 & .51 \\ .77 & 1.28 \end{bmatrix}$$

Note: The inverse of a matrix can be readily performed by spreadsheet programs such as *Microsoft's Excel, Lotus 1-2-3,* or *Quattro Pro.*

Step 3. Multiply this inverse by matrix R.

$$NR = \begin{bmatrix} 2.31 & .51 \\ .77 & 1.28 \end{bmatrix} \begin{bmatrix} .3 & 0 \\ .5 & .1 \end{bmatrix} = \begin{bmatrix} .95 & .05 \\ .87 & .13 \end{bmatrix}$$

NR gives us the probability that an account will eventually be collected or become a bad debt. Specifically, the top row in the answer is the probability that $1 of XYZ's accounts receivable in the 0-60-day-old category will end up in the collected and bad debt category will be paid, and a .05 probability that it will eventually become a bad debt. Turning to the second row, the two entries represent the probability that $1 now in the 61-120-day-old category will end up in the collected and bad debt categories. We can see from this row that there is a .87 probability that $1 currently in the 61-120-day-category will be collected and a .13 probability that it will eventually become uncollectible.

If XYZ wants to estimate the future of its $10,000 accounts receivable ($7,000 in the 0-60 day category and $3,000 in the 61-120 day category), it must set up the following matrix multiplication:

$$[7,000 \quad 3,000] \begin{bmatrix} .95 & .05 \\ .87 & .13 \end{bmatrix} = [9,260 \quad 740]$$

Hence, of its $10,000 in accounts receivable, XYZ expects to collect $9,260 and to lose $740 to bad debts. Therefore, the estimated allowances for the collectible accounts is $740.

The variance of each component is equal to

$$A = be \, (cNR - (cNR)_{sq})$$

where $c_i = b_i / \sum\limits_{i=1}^{2} b_i$ and e is the unit vector.

In our example, b = (7,000   3,000), c = (.7   .3). Therefore,

$$A = [7{,}000 \quad 3{,}000] \begin{bmatrix} 1 \\ 1 \end{bmatrix} \left\{ [.7 \quad .3] \begin{bmatrix} .95 & .05 \\ .87 & .13 \end{bmatrix} - [.7 \quad .3] \begin{bmatrix} .95 & .05 \\ .87 & .13 \end{bmatrix}_{sq} \right\}$$

$$= 10{,}000 \, [\, [.926 \quad .074] - [.857476 \quad .005476] \,]$$

$$= [685.24 \quad 685.24]$$

which makes the standard deviation equal to $26.18 ($\sqrt{\$685.24}$). If we want to be 95 percent confident about our estimate of collections, we would set the interval estimate at $9,260 + 2(26.18), or $9,207.64 -$9,312.36, assuming t = 2 as a rule of thumb. We would also be able to set the allowance to cover the bad debts at $740 + 2(26.18), or $792.36.

SIMPLE AVERAGE

The most straightforward way to estimate collection percentages is to compute the average value realized from past data, i.e.,

$$P'_i = AVE \, (C_{t+i}/S_t)$$

$$= \frac{1}{N} \sum_{t=1}^{N} \frac{C_{t+i}}{S_t}, \quad i = 0,1,2..$$

where

P'_t = an empirical estimate of collection percentages,

C_{t+i} = cash collection in month t+i from credit sales in month t,

S_t = credit sales in month t, and

N = the number of months of past data to compute the average.

LAGGED REGRESSION APPROACH

A more scientific approach to estimating cash collection percentages (or payment proportions) is to utilize *multiple regression*. We know that there is typically a time lag between the point of a credit sale and realization of cash. More specifically, the lagged effect of credit sales and cash inflows is distributed over a number of periods, as follows:

$$C_t = b_1 S_{t-1} + b_2 S_{t-2} + \ldots b_i S_{t-i}$$

where

C_t = cash collection in month t

S_t = credit sales made in period t

$b_1, b_2, \ldots b_i$ = collection percentages (the same as P'_i,) and

i = number of periods lagged

By using the regression method discussed previously, we will be able to estimate these collection rates. We can utilize "Regression" of Excel or special packages such as *SPSS, MicroTSP, SAS,* or *Systat.*

It should be noted that the cash collection percentages, $(b_1, b_2, \ldots, b_i)$ may not add up to 100 percent because of the possibility of bad debts. Once we estimate these percentages by using the regression method, we should be able to compute the bad debt percentage with no difficulty.

Table 2 shows the regression results using actual monthly data on credit sales and cash inflows for a real company. Equation I can be written as follows:

$$C_t = 60.6\%(S_{t-1}) + 24.3\%(S_{t-2}) + 8.8\%(S_{t-3})$$

This result indicates that the receivables generated by the credit sales are collected at the following rates: first month after sale, 60.6 percent; second month after sale, 24.3 percent; and third month after sale, 8.8 percent. The bad debt percentage is computed as 6.3 percent (100–93.7%).

It is important to note, however, that these collection and bad debt percentages are probabilistic variables; that is, variables whose values cannot be known with precision. However, the standard error of the regression coefficient and the 5-value permit us to assess the probability that the true percentage is between specified limits. The confidence interval takes the following form:

$$b \pm t\, S_b$$

where S_b = standard error of the coefficient.

Table 2 Regression Results for Cash Collection (C_t)

Independent Variables	Equation I	Equation II
S_{t-1}	0.606[a]	0.596[a]
	(0.062)[b]	(0.097)
S_{t-2}	0.243[a]	0.142
	(0.085)	(0.120)
S_{t-3}	0.088	0.043
	(0.157)	(0.191)
S_{t-4}		0.136
		(0.800)
R^2	0.754	0.753
Durbin-Watson	2.52[c]	2.48[c]
Standard Error of the estimate(S_e)	11.63	16.05
Number of monthly observations	21	20
Bad debt percentages	0.063	0.083

[a]Statistically significant at the 5% significance level.
[b]This figure in the parentheses is the standard error of the e estimate for the coefficient (S_b).
[c]No autocorrelation present at the 5% significance level.

Example 1. To illustrate, assuming t = 2 as rule of thumb at the 95 percent confidence level, the true collection percentage from the prior month's sales will be

60.6% ± 2(6.2%) = 60.6% ± 12.4%

Turning to the estimation of cash collections and allowance for doubtful accounts, the following values are used for illustrative purposes:

S_{t-1} = $77.6, S_{t-2} = $58.5, S_{t-3} = $76.4, and forecast average monthly net credit sales = $75.2

Then, (a) the forecast cash collection for period t would be

C_t = 60.6%(77.6) + 19.3%(58.5) + 8.8%(76.4) = $65.04

If the financial manager wants to be 95 percent confident about this forecast value, then the interval would be set as follows:

$C_t \pm t\, S_e$

where S_e = standard error of the estimate.

To illustrate, using t = 2 as a rule of thumb at the 95 percent confidence level, the true value for cash collections in period t will be

$$\$65.04 \pm 2(11.63) = \$65.04 \pm 23.26$$

(b) the estimated allowance for uncollectible accounts for period t will be

6.3% ($75.2) = $4.74

By using the limits discussed so far, financial planners can develop flexible (or probabilistic) cash budgets, where the lower and upper limits can be interpreted as pessimistic and optimistic outcomes, respectively. They can also simulate a cash budget in an attempt to determine both the expected change in cash collections for each period and the variation in this value.

In preparing a conventional cash inflow budget, the financial manager considers the various sources of cash, including cash on account, sale of assets, incurrence of debt, and so on. Cash collections from customers are emphasized, since that is the greatest problem in this type of budget.

Example 2. The following data are given for Erich Stores:

	September Actual	October Actual	November Estimated	December Estimated
Cash sales	$ 7,000	$ 6,000	$ 8,000	$ 6,000
Credit sales	50,000	48,000	62,000	80,000
Total sales	$57,000	$54,000	$70,000	$86,000

Past experience indicates net collections normally occur in the following pattern:

- No collections are made in the month of sale
- 80% of the sales of any month are collected in the following month
- 19% of sales are collected in the second following month
- 1% of sales are uncollectible

We can project total cash receipts for November and December as follows:

	November	December
Cash receipts		
Cash sales	$ 8,000	$ 6,000
Cash collections		
September sales		

50,000 (19%)	9,500	
October sales		
48,000 (80%)	38,400	
48,000 (19%)		9,120
November sales		
62,000 (80%)		49,600
Total cash receipts	$55,900	$64,720

CONCLUSION

Two methods of estimating the expected collectible and uncollectible patterns were presented. One advantage of the Markov model is that the expected value and standard deviation of these percentages can be determined, thereby making it possible to specify probabilistic statements about these figures. We have to be careful about these results, however, since the model makes some strong assumptions. A serious assumption is that the matrix of transition probabilities is constant over time. We do not expect this to be perfectly true. Updating of the matrix may have to be done, perhaps through the use of such techniques as exponential smoothing and time series analysis.

The regression approach is relatively inexpensive to use in the sense that it does not require a lot of data. All it requires is data on cash collections, and credit sales. Furthermore, credit sales values are all predetermined; we use previous months' credit sales to forecast cash collections, that is, there is no need to forecast credit sales. The model also allows you to make all kinds of statistical inferences about the cash collection percentages and forecast values.

Extensions of these models can be made toward setting credit and discount policies. Corresponding to a given set of policies, there is an associated transition matrix in the Markov model, and associated collection percentages in the regression model. By computing long-term collections and bad debts for each policy, an optimal policy can be chosen that maximizes expected long-run profits per period.

INTEREST RATE FORECASTING

While there have been a number of efforts devoted to evaluating the accuracy of forecasts of sales and earnings per share, there has been little attention given to the reliability of interest forecasts. Noting that interest rates and earnings are closely linked more than ever before, interest rates need to be forecast accurately.

Furthermore, many corporate financial decisions, such as the timing of a bond refunding, are dependent on anticipated changes in interest rates. Especially for financial institutions, changes in the level of interest rates can be one of the most important variables determining the success of the enterprise since both lending and investing decisions are influenced heavily by anticipated movements in interest rates. Clearly, the accuracy of interest rate forecasts is important from the perspective of the producer and the consumer of such forecasts.

Whether refinancing a mortgage, changing the mix of investment portfolios, or completing a multimillion-dollar acquisition, the future direction of interest rates is a key factor. It is important to develop a tracking and forecasting system that considers not only economic factors but also psychological and political forces.

INTEREST RATE FUNDAMENTALS

Today's supply of and demand for credit determines today's short-term interest rate. Expectations about the future supply of and demand for credit determine the long-term interest rate. Therefore, it is safe to say that short- and long-term interest rates are impacted by similar factors.

Then what are the specific factors that determine interest rates? The business cycle is one factor. The cycle tends to dictate credit demands by the government and businesses. Economic growth is "credit and liquidity driven" in our economy. As the demand for funds strengthens during an expansion, there is an upward pressure on interest rates. The reverse would occur during a business contraction.

Although the demand side is stressed in this explanation of the cyclical effect on interest rates, the supply side of credit and liquidity should not be ignored. For example, foreign credit supplies are certainly an important factor these days. The larger the trade deficit, the larger will be the trade deficit of foreign capital into the U.S.—which, all things being equal, helps lower interest rates.

Any gap between the demand and supply will be accentuated by monetary policy. The Federal Reserve is supposed to "lean against the wind." Thus, the Fed's net addition to liquidity (growth of the monetary aggregates) will tend to raise interest rates near cyclical peaks and diminish them at cyclical troughs.

In addition, inflation impacts short- and long-term interest rates. One key factor is compensation for anticipated inflation, which would otherwise erode the purchasing power of principal and interest and hence ruin the supply of savings.

The stage is set for interest rate forecasting. Interest rates are the dependent variable within a multiple regression framework in which the state of the business cycle, monetary policy, and inflation anticipations are the right-hand explanatory variables.

The difficulties, however, are that the correct measurement of the explanatory factors are hard to find. For example, how do you represent the business cycle? It can be characterized by a multitude of business conditions and their statistical representations. The Fed's monetary policy is another example. Finding the right "proxies" would be a burdensome task.

Furthermore, the interest rate as the dependent variable is also hard to define since there are short-term rates, intermediate-term rates, and long-term rates. Table 1 presents a guide to selecting the dependent variable and conceivable independent variables. This table is by no means an exhaustive list and is only a suggest guide, based on a review of past efforts at forecasting interest rates.

Table 2 provides a list of variables that emerged from some selected prior empirical testing by interest rate experts.

STATISTICAL METHODOLOGY AND A SAMPLE MODEL

Despite many difficulties, statistical forecasts of interest rates are commonly attempted by business economists and frequently structured along the lines of the sample equation shown in Table 3. Multiple regression analysis appears to be the dominant approach to building the model for interest rate forecasting.

Table 1 Commonly Used Variables in Interest Rate Forecasting

Dependent Variables

1. *Short-Term Rates*

   U.S. Treasury bill rates (notably three-month)

   Federal funds rate

   Prime rate

2. *Long-Term Rates*

   New AA utility bond yields

   20-year U.S. Treasury bond yields

   30-year U.S. Treasury bond yields

   10-year U.S. Treasury bond yields

   Commercial mortgage rates

   Residential mortgage rates

Independent Variables

1. *Real Economic Activity*

   Real GDP

   Change in real GDP

   Change in non-agricultural payroll employment

   Confidence index

   Leading economic indicators

2. *Capacity Utilization*

   Rate of growth in productivity

   Vendor performance

   New capacity utilization estimates

   Manufacturers capacity utilization

   Operating rates to preferred rates

   Utilization rate . . . Manufacturing

   Capacity utilization . . . Primary materials

   Capacity utilization . . . Advanced processing

   Buying policy

   Business equipment/consumer goods

   Help wanted/unemployment

   Number of initial jobless claims

   Change in unfilled orders

   Output/capacity

3. *Credit Demands by Government and Businesses*
   Income velocity (GDP/M-1)
   Federal budget deficit/GDP
   Change in mortgage debt
   Change in bank loans to business
   Change in installment debt
4. *Inflation Rate*
   Change in CPI (Consumer Price Index)
   Change in PPI (Producer Price Index)
5. *Monetary Aggregates*
   Change in money supply (M-1)
   Change in money supply (M-2)
   Real money base—Money supply in constant dollars (M-1)
6. *Liquidity*
   Money supply (M-1)/GDP
   Money supply (M-2)/GDP
7. *Banking*
   Member bank borrowing
   Loans/deposits . . . Commercial banks
   Loans/investments . . . Commercial banks
8. *Households*
   Change in household net worth (flow of funds)
9. *Corporations*
   Internal cash flow/business capital spending
10. *Foreign Credit Supplies and Foreign Influences*
    Size of current account (i.e., foreign trade) deficit/GDP
    Foreign interest rates
11. *Expectational-type Variables*
    Moving average of prior years of actual inflation
    Moving average of the change in the 3-month T-bill yield
    Polynomial distributed lag of the percentage change in the CPI

In Table 2, we show the 20-year U.S. Treasury bond yield as a function of the unemployment rate, the growth in money supply, a weighted average of past inflation, and volatility in the three-month Treasury bill.

Table 2 Key Variables in Interest Rate Forecasting Found in the Literature

Dependent Variable	Independent (Explanatory) Variables
1. *Roger Williams*[1]	
Federal fund rate	Vendor performance
	Change in money supply M-1 or M-2
	Rate of change in the CPI
New AA utility bond yields	Vendor performance
	Rate of change in the CPI lagged one period
	Ratio of bank loans to investments lagged one period
2. *The Prudential*[2]	
10-year Treasury bond yields	Government deficits/GDP
	Foreign trade/GDP
	Rate of growth in productivity
	Moving average of the five prior years of actual inflation
	Lagged change in GDP
	Foreign interest rates
	Variance and momentum indexes
3. *Schott*[3]	
20-year Treasury bond yields	Log (unemployment rate)
	Percentage change in M-1
	Polynomial distributed lag of the percentage change in the CPI
	Volatility = moving average of the change in the three-month T-bill.
4. *Horan*[4]	
New AA utility bond yield	Income volatility (GDP/M-1)
	Moving average of CPI change
	Commercial paper rate
	RHO (autoregressive error term)

[1]Roger Williams, "Forecasting Interest Rates and Inflation," *Business Economics,* January 1979, pp. 57-60.
[2]The Prudential, "Understanding Long-Term Interest Rates," *Economic Review,* July 1991, pp. 1-8.
[3]Francis H. Scott, "Forecasting Interest Rates: Methods and Application," *Journal of Business Forecasting,* Fall 1986, pp. 11-19.
[4]Lawrence J. Horan, "Forecasting Long-Term Interest Rates—A New Method," *Business Economics,* September 1978, pp. 5-8.

Table 3 Model and Values of Parameters

Model

20-Year T-Bond Yield =

$b_0 + b_1 \times \log$ (Unemployment Rate) $+ b_2 \times$ % Change in M-1
$+ b_3 \times$ Change in CPI, Annualized $+ b_4 \times$ Volatility

Value of Parameters

Independent Variable	Coefficient	t-Value*
1. Constant	11.137	4.36
2. Log (unemployment rate)	−3.297	−3.65
3. Percentage change in M-1	−0.026	−2.16
4. Polynomial distributed lag of the percentage change in the CPI annualized; lag of 4 quarters, 2nd degree polynomial	−0.24	2.73
5. Volatility; 4-year moving average of the absolute value of the change in the 3-month T-bill	1.726	2.05

n   = 47
S_e = 0.4709
R^2 = 0.975
Durbin-Watson = 1.64**

---

*Statistically significant at the 5 percent significance level.
**No autocorrelation (serial correlation) at the 1 percent level.
Source: Schott, Francis H., "Forecasting Interest Rates, Methods and Application," *Journal of Business Forecasting,* Fall 1986, p. 18.

CHECKLIST FOR SCREENING OUT EXPLANATORY FACTORS

In order to pick the best regression equation for interest forecasting, you should pretty much follow the same criteria as in Multiple Regression Analysis:

1. Many independent variables listed in Table 2 tend to be highly correlated with each other (*muticollinearity*). This will help lead to the elimination of a number of overlapping series.
2. Variables cannot be retained unless the positive or negative signs of regression coefficients are consistent with theoretical expectations.
3. Traditional yardsticks such as R^2, t-test, F-test, and Durbin-Watson test must be used to select preliminary equations.

4. The predictive performance of the preliminary models needs to be tested based on *ex ante* and *ex post* forecasts.

   a. It is usually measured by such metrics as MPE, RSME, MSE, MAD, and/or Henry Theil U Coefficient.

   b. Compare the forecasts with some "naive" (but much less costly) approach, such as assuming that rates in the future will be the same as today.

   c. Compare quantitative approaches such as econometric forecasting with judgmental forecasts. Judgment can be the overriding factor in interest rate forecasting.

   d. In addition to these evaluations, a separate evaluation of *turning point errors* needs to be made. A turning point error takes place when either you project an increase in interest levels when rates declined or when you anticipated its decline when rates increased. It often is argued that the ability of forecasters to anticipate reversals of interest rate trends is more important than the precise accuracy of the forecast. Substantial gains or losses may arise from a move from generally upward moving rates to downward rate trends (or vice versa), but gains or losses from incorrectly predicting the extent of a continued increase or decrease in rates may be much more limited.

A WORD OF CAUTION

No reasonable business planners should rely solely on statistical methods such as multiple regression. Other quantitative methods need to be attempted. It is important to realize that differences among forecasting methods and assumptions and in a choice of proxies regarding the explanatory variables can yield vastly different results from analyst to analyst. Judgments and expert opinions can help determine the future direction of interest rates. The right marriage between a quantitative evaluation and expert judgments is a must. Consensus forecasts such as those of the National Association of Business Economists (NABE), which receives wide coverage in the financial press, and econometric forecasts made by consulting firms such as The Wharton Econometric Associates, Chase Econometrics, and DRI/McGraw-Hill should be consulted as well.

The cost of errors in interest rate forecasting can be as severe as that of exchange rate forecasting mistakes. Schott at Equitable Life suggests that businesses use specific strategies and policies to reduce their exposure to interest rate forecasting mistakes (e.g., asset/liability maturity matching and hedging with futures).

CONCLUSION

Interest rate forecasting is as treacherous as other economic forecasting, such as the prediction of corporate earnings and foreign exchange rates. The chapter briefly touched upon fundamentals: business cycles, the outlook for the demand and supply of credits, monetary policy, and the inflation rate. It also presented a sample model that reflects on the fundamental theory. The forecasting ability of the model also should be judged in terms of its ability to anticipate major changes in the direction (or turning point) of rates.

FORECASTING FOREIGN EXCHANGE RATES*

This chapter addresses the problem of forecasting foreign exchange rates. It explores the need for managers to forecast the exchange rates. It then establishes a framework of the international exchange markets and explores the relationship between exchange rates, interest rate, and inflation rate. The chapter focuses on the different types of forecasting techniques used to predict the foreign exchange rates and concludes by setting up a framework within which forecasts can be evaluated.

WHY FORECAST EXCHANGE RATES?

Frequently companies are faced with a decision regarding forecasting foreign exchange rates. Some companies choose to ignore forecasting, while others often rely on their banks for the answer. Very few companies dedicate resources to forecast foreign exchange rate.

Many companies argue that the forecasts of international exchange rates are often inaccurate and hence invalid. Therefore, there is no need to forecast. These companies, however, fail to understand that forecasting is not an exact science but rather an art form where quality of forecasts generally tend to improve as companies and managers gain more experience in forecasting.

In today's global environment, companies trading across the national boundaries are often exposed to transaction risk, the risk that comes from fluctuation in the exchange rate between the time a contract is signed and when the payment is received. Historically, exchange rates have been fixed and there have been very few fluctuations within a short time period. However, most exchange rates today are floating and can easily vary as much as 5% within a week. Moreover, the recent crisis in the European

---

* This chapter was coauthored by Anique Qureshi, Ph.D., CPA, CIA, associate professor of accounting at Queens College, and an accounting consultant.

monetary market illustrates the need for accurate exchange rate information. There are four primary reasons why it is imperative to forecast the foreign exchange rates.

Hedging Decision

Multinational companies (MNCs) are constantly faced with the decision of whether or not to hedge payables and receivables in foreign currency. An exchange rate forecast can help MNC's determine if it should hedge its transactions. As an example, if forecasts determine that the Swiss franc is going to appreciate in value relative to the dollar, a company expecting payment from a Swiss partner in the future may not decide to hedge the transaction. However, if the forecasts showed that the Swiss franc is going to depreciate relative to the dollar, the U.S. partner should hedge the transaction.

Short-Term Financing Decision for MNC

A large corporation has several sources of capital market and several currencies in which it can borrow. Ideally, the currency it would borrow would exhibit low interest rate and depreciate in value over the financial period. For example, A U.S. firm could borrow in German marks; during the loan period, the marks would depreciate in value; at the end of the period, the company would have to use fewer dollars to buy the same amount of marks and would benefit from the deal.

International Capital Budgeting Decision

Accurate cash flows are imperative in order to make a good capital budgeting decision. In case of international projects, it is not only necessary to establish accurate cash flows but it is also necessary to convert them into an MNC's home country currency. This necessitates the use of a foreign exchange forecast to convert the cash flows and there after, evaluate the decision.

Subsidiary Earning Assessment for MNC

When an MNC reports its earnings, international subsidiary earnings are often translated and consolidated in the MNC's home country currency. For example, when IBM makes a projection for its earnings, it needs to project its earnings in Germany, then it needs to translate these earnings from Deutsche marks to dollars. A depreciation in marks would decrease a subsidiary's earnings and vice versa. Thus, it is necessary to generate an accurate forecast of marks to create a legitimate earnings assessment.

SOME BASIC TERMS AND RELATIONSHIPS

At this point, it is necessary to address some of the basic terminology used in foreign exchange as well as address the fundamental laws of international monetary economics. It is also necessary to establish a basic international monetary framework before forecasting.

Spot Rate

Spot rate can be defined as the rate that exists in today's market. Table 1 illustrates a typical listing of foreign exchange rates found in the *Wall Street Journal*. The British pound is quoted at 1.6708. This rate is the spot rate. It means you can go to the bank today and exchange $1.6708 for £1.00. How this works is, say, for example, your need £10,000 for a paying off an import transaction on a given day, you would ask your bank to purchase £10,000. The bank would not hand you the money, but instead it would instruct its English subsidiary to pay £10,000 to your English supplier and it would debit you account by (10,000 × 1.6708) $16,708.

Forward Rate

Besides the spot rate, Table 1 also quotes the forward rate. The 90-day forward rate for the pound is quoted as 1.6637. In forward market, you buy and sell currency for a future delivery date, usually, one, three, or six months in advance. If you know you need to buy or sell currency in the future, you can hedge against a loss by selling in the forward market. For example, let's say you are required to pay £10,000 in 3 months to your English supplier. You can purchase £10,000 today by paying $16,637 (10,000 × 1.6637). These pounds will be delivered in 90 days. In the meantime you have protected yourself. No matter what the exchange rate of pound or U.S. dollar is in 90 days, you are assured delivery at the quoted price.

As can be seen in the example, the cost of purchasing pounds in the forward market ($16,637) is less than the price in the spot market ($16,708). This implies that the pound is selling at a forward discount relative to the dollar, so you can buy more pounds in the forward market. It could also mean that the U.S. dollar is selling at a forward premium.

Interest Rate Parity Theory

The interest rate parity theory says that interest rate differential must equal the difference between the spot and the forward rate. The validity of this theory can be easily tested by a simple example. Lets assume that the interest rate in the U.S. is 10%. An identical investment in Switzerland yields 5%.

Table 1 Sample Listing of Foreign Exchange Rates

Thursday, April 30, 1998

The New York foreign exchange selling rates below apply to trading among banks in amounts of $1 million and more, as quoted at 4 p.m. Eastern time by Dow Jones and other sources. Retail transactions provide fewer units of foreign currency per dollar.

	U.S. $ equiv.		Currency per U.S. $	
Country	**Thu**	**Wed**	**Thu**	**Wed**
Argentina (Peso)	1.0001	1.0001	.9999	.9999
Australia (Dollar)	.6500	.6494	1.5385	1.5399
Austria (Schilling)	.07911	.07913	12.640	12.638
Bahrain (Dinar)	2.6525	2.6525	.3770	.3770
Belgium (Franc)	.02698	.02698	37.065	37.060
Brazil (Real)	.8744	.8736	1.1436	1.1447
Britain (Pound)	1.6708	1.6697	.5985	.5989
1-month forward	1.6682	1.6672	.5994	.5998
3-months forward	1.6637	1.6625	.6011	.6015
6-months forward	1.6575	1.6566	.6033	.6036
Canada (Dollar)	.6988	.6959	1.4310	1.4369
1-month forward	.6993	.6964	1.4301	1.4369
3-months forward	.7001	.6971	1.4284	1.4345
6-months forward	.7012	.6981	1.4261	1.4324
Chile (Peso)	.002208	.002209	452.85	452.65
China (Renminbi)	.1208	.1208	8.2781	8.2782
Colombia (Peso)	.0007322	.0007292	1365.72	1371.35
Czech. Rep. (Koruna)	....	....	....	....
Commercial rate	.03031	.03017	32.995	33.149
Denmark (Krone)	.1460	.1460	6.8475	6.8490
Ecuador (Sucre)	....	....	....	....
Floating rate	.0001996	.0001996	5010.00	5010.00
Finland (Markka)	.1836	.1835	5.4480	5.4490
France (Franc)	.1661	.1661	6.0195	6.0200
1-month forward	1.664	1.664	6.0088	6.0092
3-months forward	1.670	1.670	5.9886	5.9888
6-months forward	1.678	1.678	5.9605	5.9594

Furthermore, the exchange rate is .7097 dollar per franc. Now an investor can invest $100,000 in the U.S. and earn interest of $5,000 (100,000 × .10/2) in six months. The same investor can today purchase 140,905 francs (100,000/.7097) and invest in a Swiss bank to earn 144,428 francs. Now when the investor decides to transfer his currency to the U.S., what will be the exchange rate? If the investor has sold francs in the 180-day forward market, the exchange rate should be 0.7270 and investor earnings would transfer to $ 105,000. If the exchange rate were lower, i.e., 0.7100, the amount would be $102,543 and no one would be interested to invest in Switzerland. All Swiss investors would want to invest in U.S., so they would buy dollars and drive down the exchange rate until the exchange rate was 0.7270 and excess profits disappeared.

Fisher Price Effect

Fisher Price effect states that difference in interest rates must equal expected difference in inflation rates. Interest rate is made up several different components:

Interest Rate = $K_r + K_i + K_{drp}$

where

K_i = the inflation premium
K_{drp} = the default risk premium
K_r = the real interest rate

Fisher argued that the real interest rate remains the same for all countries. Thus the differences in exchange rate are a direct result of differences in inflation rate. (It is assumed that the investments are identical and therefore default risk would be the same.) If the real interest rates were different, it provides an excellent opportunity for currency arbitrage and eventually, the market would make the exchange rates such that the real interest rate was identical.

Purchasing Power Parity

The law of purchasing power parity states that the expected difference in inflation rate equals the difference between the forward and the spot rate. This can be easily proven. According to the interest rate parity theory, the difference in interest rate equals the difference between the forward and spot rate. According to the Fisher price effect, the difference between interest rates also equals the difference between inflation rates. Therefore, the difference between the inflation rates should equal the difference between the forward and spot rate.

The three previously described theories form the cornerstone of international finance. These theories are very important in that they are used in developing some fundamental forecasting models. These three models have been kept relatively simple although real life is not this simple. Frequently these models are modified to account for real world and market imperfections.

FORECASTING TECHNIQUES

The international financial markets are very complex. Therefore, a variety of forecasting techniques are used to forecast the foreign exchange rate. A certain method of forecasting may be more suited to one particular exchange rate or scenario. There are four major ways of forecasting foreign exchange rates: Fundamental forecasting, market-based forecasting, technical forecasting, and a mixture of the three.

Fundamental Forecasting

Fundamental forecasting is based on fundamental relationships between economic variables and exchange rates. Given current values of these variables along with their historical impact on a currency's value, corporations can develop exchange rate projections. In previous sections, we established a basic relationship between exchange rates, inflation rates, and interest rates. This relationship can be used to develop a simple linear forecasting model for the Deutsche mark.

$$DM = a + b\,(INF) + c\,(INT)$$

where

> DM = the quarterly percentage change in the German mark
>
> INF = quarterly percentage change in inflation differential (US inflation rate – German inflation rate)
>
> INT = quarterly percentage change in interest rate differential (US interest rate – German interest rate)

Note: This model is relatively simple with only two explanatory variables. In many cases, several other variables are added but the essential methodology remains the same.

Example 1. The following example illustrates how exchange rate forecasting can be accomplished using the fundamental approach. Table 2 shows the basic input data for the ten quarters. Table 3 shows a summary of the regression output, based on the use of *Microsoft Excel.*

Table 2

Period	US CPI	US INF	G CPI	G INF	US INT	G INT	DM/$	INF Diff	INT Diff
Apr 95	123.7	1.56%	104.0	0.87%	9.64%	6.97%	1.8783	0.69%	2.67%
Jul 95	124.7	0.81%	104.5	0.48%	9.51%	6.87%	1.8675	0.33%	2.64%
Oct 95	125.9	0.96%	105.2	0.67%	9.92%	7.40%	1.8375	0.29%	2.52%
Jan 96	128.1	1.75%	105.9	0.67%	10.82%	8.50%	1.6800	1.08%	2.32%
Apr 96	129.4	1.01%	106.4	0.47%	11.42%	8.87%	1.6820	0.54%	2.55%
Jul 96	131.6	1.70%	107.3	0.85%	11.25%	8.93%	1.5920	0.85%	2.32%
Oct 96	133.8	1.67%	108.4	1.03%	10.83%	9.00%	1.5180	0.65%	1.83%
Jan 97	134.9	0.82%	108.7	0.28%	10.06%	9.70%	1.4835	0.55%	0.36%
Apr 97	135.7	0.59%	108.7	0.00%	10.16%	8.40%	1.7350	0.59%	1.76%
Jul 97	136.6	0.66%	109.7	0.92%	9.84%	8.60%	1.7445	−0.26%	1.24%
Oct 97	137.8	0.88%	111.8	1.91%	9.62%	8.40%	1.6750	−1.04%	1.36%
Jan 98	138.8	0.73%	1112.7	0.81%	9.36%	8.00%		−0.08%	1.36%

	Quarterly % Change		
Period	INF Diff.	INT Diff.	DM/$
Jul 95	−0.5231	−0.01124	−0.00575
Oct 95	−0.1074	−0.04545	−0.01606
Jan 96	2.6998	−0.07937	−0.08571
Apr 96	−0.4984	0.099138	0.00119
Jul 96	0.5742	−0.0902	−0.05351
Oct 96	−0.2431	−0.21121	−0.04648
Jan 97	−0.1565	−0.80328	−0.02273
Apr 97	0.0874	3.888889	0.169532
Jul 97	−1.4329	−0.29545	0.005476
Oct 97	3.0346	−0.01613	−0.03984
Jan 98	−0.9234	0.114754	

Source: The raw data was derived from *International Economic Conditions,* August 1998.

Table 3 Microsoft *Excel* Repression Output

Analysis of Variance	df	Sum of Squares	Mean Square	F	Significance F
Regression	2	0.039325	0.01966	41.317	0.00013
Residual	7	0.003331	0.00048		
Total	9	0.042656			

	Coefficients	Standard Error	t-Statistic	P-value	Lower 95%	Upper 95%
Intercept	−0.0149	0.0072502	−2.057589	0.06975	−0.0321	0.00223
INF Diff.	−0.0171	0.0050964	−3.352584	0.00849	−0.0291	−0.005
INT Diff.	0.04679	0.0055715	8.39862	15E−05	0.0336	0.05997

Regression Statistics

Multiple R	0.9602
R Square	0.9219
Adjusted R Square	0.8996
Standard Error	0.0218
Observations	10

Our forecasting model that can be used to predict the DM/$ exchange rate for the next quarter is:

DM = −0.0149 − 0.0171 (INF) + 0.0468 (INT)

R^2 = 92.19%

Ex post predictions are summarized in Table 4 and plotted against actual values in Figure 1.

Assuming that INT = −0.9234 and INF = 0.1148 for the next quarter,

DM = −0.0149 − 0.0171 (-0.9234) + 0.0468 (0.1148) = 0.00623

DM/$ = (1 + 0.00623) × (1.6750) = 1.6854

According to the forecast, the exchange rate in first quarter of 98 should be 1.6854. The actual rate was 1.6392. The error in the forecast was .0462 (1.6854 − 1.6392) and the mean percentage error (MPE) of forecast was 2.78%.

This example presents a simple fundamental forecasting model for foreign exchange rates. This model is especially useful if the exchange rates are

Table 4

Observation	Predicted Y	Residuals	Standardized Residuals	Percentile	DM/$
1	−0.00651	0.000756	0.034667	5	−0.0857
2	−0.01521	−0.00085	−0.039159	15	−0.0535
3	−0.06476	−0.02095	−0.960496	25	−0.0465
4	−0.00176	0.002953	0.135359	35	−0.0398
5	−0.02895	−0.02456	−1.125773	45	−0.0227
6	−0.02065	−0.02584	−1.184324	55	−0.0161
7	−0.04983	0.027104	1.242462	65	−0.0057
8	0.165562	0.00397	0.181967	75	0.0012
9	−0.00426	0.009735	0.446276	85	0.0055
10	−0.06752	0.027684	1.269022	95	0.1695

Figure 1   Plot of Predicted and Actual Y Values

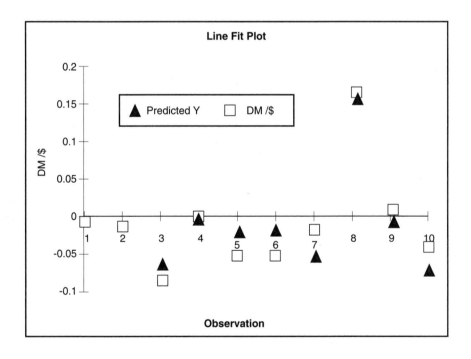

freely floating and there is minimum government or central bank intervention in the currency market. Note that this model relies on relationships between macro-economic variables.

However, there are certain problems with this forecasting technique. First, this technique will not be very effective with fixed exchange rates. This technique also relies on forecast to forecast. That is, one needs to project the future interest rate and the future inflation rate in order to compute the differentials that are the used to compute the exchange rate. Note: These estimates are frequently published in trade publications and bank reports. Second, this technique often ignores other variables that influence the foreign exchange rate.

Market-Based Forecasting

The process of developing forecasts from market indicators is known as *market-based forecasting*. This is perhaps the easiest forecasting model. While it is very simple, it is also very effective. The model relies on the spot rate and the forward rate to forecast the price. The model assumes that the spot rate reflects the foreign exchange rate in the near future. Let us suppose that the Italian lira is expected to depreciate vs. the U.S. dollar. This would encourage speculators to sell Lira and later purchase them back at the lower (future) price. This process if continued would drive down the prices of lira until the excess (arbitrage) profits were eliminated.

The model also suggests that the forward exchange rate equals the future spot price. Again, let us suppose that the 90-day forward rate is .987. The market forecasters believe that the exchange rate in 90 days is going to be .965. This provides an arbitrage opportunity. Markets will keep on selling the currency in the forward market until the opportunity for excess profit is eliminated.

This model, however, relies heavily on market efficiency. It assumes that capital markets and currency markets are highly efficient and that there is perfect information in the market place. Under these circumstances, this model can provide accurate forecasts. Indeed, many of the world currency markets such as the market for U.S. dollar, German mark, and Japanese Yen are highly efficient and this model is well suited for such markets. However, market imperfections or lack of perfect information reduces the effectiveness of this model. In some cases, this model cannot be used.

Technical Forecasting

Technical forecasting involves the use of historical exchange rates to predict future values. It is sometimes conducted in a judgmental manner, without statistical analysis. Often, however, statistical analysis is applied in technical forecasting to detect historical trends. There are also time series models that examine moving averages. Most technical models rely on the past to predict the future. They try to identify a historical pattern that seems to repeat and then try to forecast it. The models range from a simple moving average to a complex auto regressive integrated moving average (ARIMA). Most models try to break down the historical series. They try to identify and remove the random element. Then they try to forecast the overall trend with cyclical and seasonal variations.

A moving average is useful to remove minor random fluctuations. A trend analysis is useful to forecast a long-term linear or exponential trend. Winter's seasonal smoothing and Census XII decomposition are useful to forecast long-term cycles with additive seasonal variations. ARIMA (auto regressive integrated moving average) is useful to predict cycles with multiplicative seasonality. Many forecasting and statistical packages such as *Forecast Pro, Sibyl/Runner, Minitab,* and *SAS* can handle these computations. An example of technical forecasting follows.

Example 2. This example uses the past six years of monthly data of the German mark (DM/$) exchange rate to forecast the DM/$ for the first 9 months in 1998. The data is given Table 5 and plotted in Figure 2.

Table 5   Germany Currency 7-Year Monthly Closings

Month	1992	1993	1994	1995	1996	1997	1998
January	2.3892	1.8298	1.6785	1.8646	1.6805	1.4835	1.6190
February	2.2185	1.8268	1.6884	1.8296	1.6930	1.5195	1.6395
March	2.3175	1.8028	1.8219	1.8927	1.6947	1.7000	1.6445
April	2.1865	1.7985	1.6773	1.8783	1.6822	1.7350	1.6590
May	2.1327	1.8215	1.7015	1.9858	1.6913	1.7255	1.6080
June	2.1986	1.8249	1.8211	1.9535	1.6645	1.8120	1.5255
July	2.0940	1.8590	1.8810	1.8675	1.5920	1.7445	1.4778
August	2.0520	1.8145	1.8748	1.9608	1.5680	1.7425	1.4055
September	2.0207	1.8460	1.8798	1.8730	1.5650	1.6612	1.4105
October	2.0630	1.7255	1.7684	1.8353	1.5180	1.6750	
November	1.9880	1.6375	1.7354	1.7895	1.5030	1.6327	
December	1.9188	1.5713	1.7803	1.6915	1.4955	1.5175	

Source: The raw data was derived from *Business International,* December 1998.

Figure 2 Plot of 6-Year DM/$ Rate

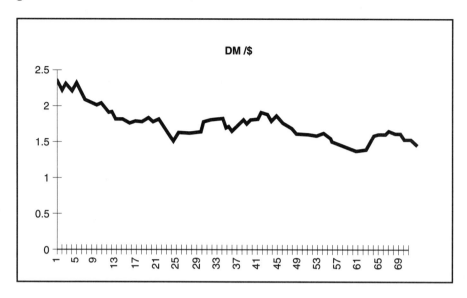

The data pattern seems to show a mild cycle with additive seasonality. Winter's seasonal smoothing is the ideal method under these situations. The data was run in *Forecast Pro for Windows,* a PC software package. The summary of the forecast is presented in Table 6 and plotted against actual values in Figure 3. Table 6 also summarizes the predictive performance of the model. The mean percentage error (MPE) was somewhat low (1.19%), which is generally indicative of a good forecast.

Table 6 Summary of Forecast

Forecast	Actual	Error	% Error
1.6080	1.6190	−0.0110	−0.68%
1.6507	1.6395	0.0112	0.68%
1.7248	1.6445	0.0803	4.77%
1.6593	1.6590	0.0003	0.02%
1.6079	1.6080	−0.0001	−0.01%
1.5879	1.5255	0.0624	4.01%
1.4863	1.4778	0.0085	0.57%
1.4526	1.4055	0.0471	3.30%
1.3834	1.4105	−0.0271	−1.94%
	Average:	0.0191	1.19%

Figure 3 Plot of Actual Versus Smoothed Values

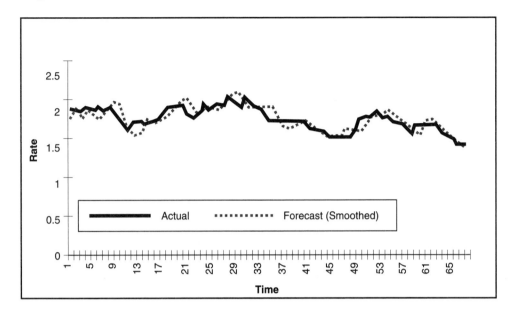

Mixed Forecasting

Mixed forecasting in not a unique technique but rather a combination of the three previously discussed methods. In some cases, a mixed forecast is nothing but a weighted average of a variety of the forecasting techniques. The techniques can be weighted arbitrarily or by assigning a higher weight to the more reliable technique. Mixed forecasting may often lead to a better result than relying on one single forecast.

A FRAMEWORK FOR EVALUATING FORECASTS

Forecasting foreign exchange is an ongoing process. Due to the dynamic nature of international markets, forecasts may not be accurate. However, the quality of a forecast does improve with a forecaster's experience. Therefore, it is necessary to set up some kind of framework within which a forecast can be evaluated.

The simplest framework would be to measure the errors in forecasting, which are discussed in detail in the next chapter (*Evaluation of Forecasts*). Several measures such as MAD, MSE, and MPE can be calculated and tracked. If more than one forecasting technique is used, i.e., a mixed forecast is used, a company may be able to decide which technique is superior. It may then adjust the weighting scale in a mixed forecast.

A good framework makes it easy for a company to predict errors in forecasting. For example, if a forecaster is consistently forecasting the foreign exchange rate for the German mark above its actual rate this would suggest that a forecaster needs to adjust the forecast for this bias. Furthermore, a tracking signal and the turning point error needs to be systematically monitored.

CONCLUSION

In reality, currency forecasting is neglected in many multinational firms. They often argue that forecasting is useless since it does not provide an accurate estimate. They do not even have a hedging strategy. Failure to accurately forecast currency can have a disastrous impact on earnings. Moreover, it is important to realize that forecasting is often undertaken so the corporation has a general idea about the overall trend of the future and that the companies are not caught off guard. While currency forecasts are not 100% accurate, they do provide some advance warning of future trends.

It is also important to realize that forecasting is not an exact science. The quality of forecasts tends to improve over time as the forecaster gains more experience. One cannot ignore the value of judgement and intuition in forecasting, although evidence shows that forecasts using qualitative techniques are not as accurate as those using quantitative techniques.

Note: An experienced forecaster uses both qualitative as well as quantitative techniques to create a reasonable forecast.

EVALUATION OF FORECASTS

The cost of a prediction error can be substantial. Forecasters must always find ways to improve their forecasts. That means that they might want to examine some objective evaluations of alternative forecasting techniques. This section presents the guidelines they need. Two evaluation techniques are presented here. The first is in the form of a checklist. A forecaster could use it to evaluate either a new model he or she is in the process of developing or an existing model. The second is a statistical technique for evaluating a model.

COST OF PREDICTION ERRORS

There is always a cost involved with a failure to predict a certain variable accurately. It is important to determine the cost of the prediction error in order to minimize the potential detrimental effect on future profitability of the company. The cost of the prediction error can be substantial, depending upon the circumstances. For example, failure to make an accurate projection on sales could result in poor production planning, too much or too little purchase of labor, and so on, thereby causing potentially huge financial losses.

The cost of the prediction error is basically the contribution or profit lost on an inaccurate prediction. It can be measured in terms of lost sales, disgruntled customers, and idle machines.

Example 1. Assume that a company has been selling a toy doll having a cost of $.60 for $1.00 each. The fixed cost is $300. The company has no privilege of returning any unsold dolls. It has predicted sales of 2,000 units. However, unforeseen competition has reduced sales to 1,500 units. Then the cost of its prediction error (that is, its failure of predict demand accurately) would be calculated as follows:

1. Initial predicted sales = 2,000 units.

   Optimal decision: purchase 2,000 units.

   Expected net income = $500 [(2,000 units × $.40 contribution) – $300 fixed costs]

2. Alternative parameter value = 1,500 units.

   Optimal decision: purchase 1,500 units.

   Expected net income = $300 [(1,500 units × $.40 contribution) – $300 fixed costs]

3. Results of original decision under alternative parameter value.

   Expected net income:

   Revenue (1,500 units × $1.00) – Cost of dolls (2,000 units × $.60) – $300 fixed costs

   = $1,500 – $1,200 – $300 = $0.

4. Cost of prediction error, (2) – (3) = $300.

CHECKLIST

Two main items to be checked are the data and the model with its accompanying assumptions. The questions to be raised are the following:

1. Is the source reliable and accurate?
2. In the case of use of more than one source that is reliable and accurate, is the source used the best?
3. Are the data the most recent available?
4. If the answer to question 3 is yes, are the data subject to subsequent revision?
5. Is there any known systematic bias in the data which may be dealt with?

The model and its accompanying assumptions should be similarly examined. Among other things, the model has to make sense from a theoretical standpoint. The assumptions should be clearly stated and tested as well.

MEASURING ACCURACY OF FORECASTS

The performance of a forecast should be checked against its own record or against that of other forecasts. There are various statistical measures that can be used to measure performance of the model. Of course, the performance is measured in terms of forecasting error, where error is defined as the difference between a predicted value and the actual result.

Error (e) = Actual (A) − Forecast (F)

MAD, MSE, RMSE, and MAPE

The commonly used measures for summarizing historical errors include the *mean absolute deviation* (MAD), the *mean squared error* (MSE), the *root mean squared error* (RMSE), and the *mean absolute percentage error* (MAPE). The formulas used to calculate MAD, MSE, and RMSE are

$$MAD = \Sigma |e| / n$$
$$MSE = \Sigma e^2 / (n - 1)$$
$$RMSE = \sqrt{(\Sigma e^2/n)}$$

Sometimes it is more useful to compute the forecasting errors in percentages rather than in amounts. The MAPE is calculated by finding the absolute error in each period, dividing this by the actual value of that period, and then averaging these absolute percentage errors, as shown below.

$$MAPE = \Sigma |e|/A / n$$

The following example illustrates the computation of MAD, MSE, and RMSE, and MAPE.

Example 2. Sales data of a microwave oven manufacturer are given below:

Period	Actual (A)	Forecast (F)	e (A−F)	|e|	e^2	Absolute Percent Error |e|/A
1	217	215	2	2	4	.0092
2	213	216	−3	3	9	.0014
3	216	215	1	1	1	.0046
4	210	214	−4	4	16	.0190
5	213	211	2	2	4	.0094
6	219	214	5	5	25	.0023
7	216	217	−1	1	1	.0046
8	212	216	−4	4	16	.0019
			−2	22	76	.0524

Using the figures,

$$MAD = \Sigma \, |e| \, /n = 22/8 = 2.75$$
$$MSE = \Sigma \, e^2 \, / \, (n-1) = 76/7 = 10.86$$
$$RMSE = \sqrt{\Sigma \, e^2 \, / \, n} = \sqrt{76/8} = \sqrt{9.5} = 3.08$$
$$MAPE = \Sigma \, |e|/A \, / \, n = .0524/8 = .0066$$

One way these measures are used is to evaluate forecasting ability of alternative forecasting methods. For example, using either MAD or MSE, a forecaster could compare the results of exponential smoothing with alphas and elect the one that performed best in terms of the lowest MAD or MSE for a given set of data. Also, it can help select the best initial forecast value for exponential smoothing.

THE U STATISTIC AND TURNING POINT ERRORS

There is still a number of statistical measures for measuring accuracy of the forecast. Two standards may be identified. First, one could compare the forecast being evaluated with a naive forecast to see if there are vast differences. The naive forecast can be anything; for instance, the same as last year, moving average, or the output of an exponential smoothing technique. In the second case, the forecast may be compared against the outcome when there is enough to do so. The comparison may be against the actual level of the variable forecasted, or the change observed may be compared with the change forecast.

The Theil U Statistic is based upon a comparison of the predicted change with the observed change. It is calculated as:

$$U = 1/n \; \Sigma \, (F - A)^2 \, / \, (1/n)\Sigma \, F^2 + (1/n)\Sigma \, A^2$$

As can be seen, U=0 is a perfect forecast, since the forecast would equal actual and $F - A = 0$ for all observations. At the other extreme, U=1 would be a case of all incorrect forecasts. The smaller the value of U, the more accurate are the forecasts. If U is greater than or equal to 1, the predictive ability of the model is lower than a naive no-change extrapolation. *Note:* Many computer software packages routinely compute the U Statistic.

Still other evaluation techniques consider the number of *turning point* errors which is based on the total number of reversals of trends. The turning point error is also known as "error in the direction of prediction." In a certain case, such as interest rate forecasts, the turning point error is more serious than the accuracy of the forecast. For example, the ability of forecasters to anticipated reversals of interest rate trends is more important—perhaps substantially more important—than the precise accuracy of the forecast. Substantial gains or losses may arise from a move from generally upward moving rates to downward rate trends (or vice versa) but gains or losses from incorrectly forecasting the extent of a continued increase or decrease in rates may be much more limited.

CONTROL OF FORECASTS

It is important to monitor forecast errors to insure that the forecast is performing well. If the model is performing poorly based on some criteria, the forecaster might reconsider the use of the existing model or switch to another forecasting model or technique. The forecasting control can be accomplished by comparing forecasting errors to predetermined values, or limits. Errors that fall within the limits would be judged acceptable while errors outside of the limits would signal that corrective action is desirable (See Figure 1).

Figure 1 Monitoring Forecast Errors

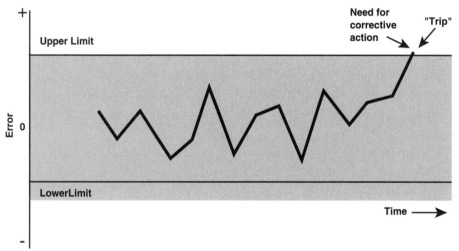

Forecasts can be monitored using either tracking signals or control charts.

Tracking Signals

A tracking signal is based on the ratio of cumulative forecast error to the corresponding value of MAD.

$$\text{Tracking signal} = \Sigma(A - F) / \text{MAD}$$

The resulting tracking signal values are compared to predetermined limits. These are based on experience and judgement and often range from plus or minus three to plus or minus eight. Values within the limits suggest that the forecast is performing adequately. By the same token, when the signal goes beyond this range, corrective action is appropriate.

Example 3. Going back to Example 2, the deviation and cumulative deviation have already been computed:

$$MAD = \Sigma |A - F| / n = 22 / 8 = 2.75$$
$$\text{Tracking signal} = \Sigma (A - F) / MAD = -2 / 2.75 = -0.73$$

A tracking signal is as low as -0.73, which is substantially below the limit (-3 to -8). It would not suggest any action at this time.

Note: After an initial value of MAD has been computed, the estimate of the MAD can be continually updated using exponential smoothing.

$$MAD_t = \alpha(A - F) + (1 - \alpha) MAD_{t-1}$$

Control Charts

The control chart approach involves setting upper and lower limits for individual forecasting errors instead of cumulative errors. The limits are multiples of the estimated standard deviation of forecast, S_f, which is the square root of MSE. Frequently, control limits are set at 2 or 3 standard deviations.

$$\pm 2 \text{ (or 3) } S_f$$

Note: Plot the errors and see if all errors are within the limits, so that the forecaster can visualize the process and determine if the method being used is in control.

Example 4. For the sales data below, using the naive forecast, we will determine if the forecast is in control. For illustrative purposes, we will use 2 sigma control limits.

Year	Sales	Forecasts	Error	Error^2
1	320			
2	326	320	6	36
3	310	326	−16	256
4	317	310	7	49
5	315	317	−2	4
6	318	315	3	9
7	310	318	−8	64
8	316	310	6	36
9	314	316	−2	4
10	317	314	3	9
			−3	467

Evaluation of Forecasts

First, compute the standard deviation of forecast errors

$$S_f = \sqrt{e^2 / (n - 1)} = \sqrt{467/(9 - 1)} = 7.64$$

Two sigma limits are then plus or minus 2(7.64) = -15.28 to +15.28

Note that the forecast error for year 3 is below the lower bound, so the forecast is not in control (See Figure 2). The use of other methods such as moving average, exponential smoothing, or regression would possibly achieve a better forecast.

Figure 2 Control Chart for Forecasting Errors

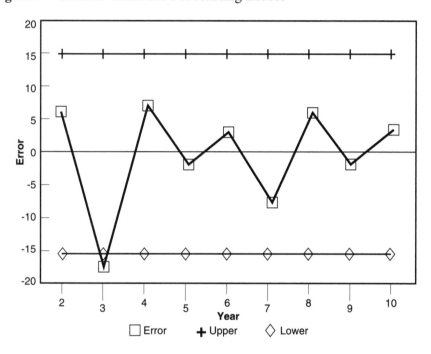

Note: A system of monitoring forecasts needs to be developed. The computer may be programmed to print a report showing the past history when the tracking signal "trips" a limit. For example, when a type of exponential smoothing is used, the system may try a different value of α (so the forecast will be more responsive) and to continue forecasting.

CONCLUSION

There is always a cost associated with a failure to predict a certain variable accurately. Because all forecasts tend to be off the mark, it is important to provide a measure of accuracy for each forecast. Several measures of forecast accuracy and a measure of turning point error can be calculated.

These quite often are used to help managers evaluate the performance of a given method as well as to choose among alternative forecasting techniques. Control of forecasts involves deciding whether a forecast is performing adequately, using either a control chart or a tracking signal. Selection of a forecasting method involves choosing a technique that will serve its intended purpose at an acceptable level of cost and accuracy.

FORECASTING TOOLS AND SOFTWARE

The life cycle of a typical new product is divided into four major stages: introduction, growth, maturity, and saturation (decline). Depending upon the nature of the market, a right choice of forecasting methodology is called for. Table 1 shows life cycle effects upon forecasting methodology. Table 2 summarizes the forecasting methods that have been discussed in this book. It is organized in the following format:

1. Description
2. Accuracy
3. Identification of turning point
4. Typical application
5. Data required
6. Cost
7. Time required to develop an application and make forecasts

Furthermore, in an effort to aid forecasters in choosing the right methodology, Table 3 provides rankings of forecasting methodology by:

1. Accuracy: Why do you need the forecast?
2. Cost: How much money is involved?
3. Timing: When will the forecast be used?
4. Form: Who will use the forecast?
5. Data: How much data are available?

Table 1   Life Cycle Effects on Forecasting Methodology

Introduction

Data:	No data available; Rely on qualitative methods.
Time:	Need long horizon.
Methods:	Qualitative (judgement) such as market surveys and Delphi.

Growth

Data:	Some data available for analysis.
Time:	Still need long horizon; trends and cause-effect relationships important.
Methods:	Market surveys still useful. Regression, time series and growth models justified.

Maturity

Data:	Considerable data available.
Time:	More uses of short-term forecasts; still need long-term projections, but trends change only gradually.
Methods:	Quantitative methods more useful. Time series helpful for trend, seasonal. Regression and exponential smoothing very useful.

Decline

Data:	Abundant data.
Time:	Shorter horizon.
Methods:	Continue use of maturity methods as applicable. Judgement and market surveys may signal changes.

Table 2 Summary of Commonly Used Forecasting Methods

Summary of Commonly Used Qualitative (Judgmental) Forecasting Techniques

Technique	*PERT-Derived*	*Sales Force Polling*	*Consumer Surveys*
Description	Based on three estimates provided by experts: pessimistic, most likely, and optimistic.	Based on sales force opinions; tend to be too optimistic.	Based on market surveys regarding specific consumer purchases.
Accuracy:			
Short-term (0-3 mon)	Fair	Fair to good	Fair to good
Medium-term (3 mon-2 yr)	Poor	Poor	Poor
Long-term (2 yr and over)	Poor	Poor	Poor
Identification of turning point	Poor to fair	Poor to good	Poor
Typical application	Same as expert opinions.	Forecasts of short-term sales forecasts.	Forecasts of short-term sales forecasts.
Data required	Same as expert opinions.	Data by regional and product line breakdowns.	Telephone contacts, personal interviews or questionnaires.
Cost of forecasting with a computer	Minimal	Minimal	Minimal
Time required to develop an application and make forecasts	Two weeks	Two weeks	More than a month

Continued on next page

Table 2   Summary of Commonly Used Forecasting Methods *(continued)*

Summary of Commonly Used Quantitative Forecasting Methods

Technique	PERT-Derived	Sales Force Polling	Consumer Surveys
Description	Functionally relates sales to other economic, competitive, or internal variables and estimates an equation using the least-squares technique.	A system of interdependent regression equations that describes some sector of economic sales or profit activity. The parameters of the regression equations are usually estimated simultaneously.	Models based on learned behavior: Consumers tend to repeat their part brand loyalty.
Accuracy:			
Short-term (0-3 mon)	Good to very good	Good to very good	Excellent
Medium-term (3 mon-2 yr)	Good to very good	Very good to excellent	Poor
Long-term (2 yr and over)	Poor	Good	Poor
Identification of turning point	Good	Excellent	Good
Typical application	Forecast of sales by product classes, forecasts of earnings, and other financial data.	Forecasts of sales by product classes, forecasts of earnings.	Forecasts of sales and cash collections.
Data required	At least 30 observations are recommended for acceptable results.	The same as for regression.	Data required for transaction probabilities.
Cost of forecasting with a computer	Varies with application	Expensive	Expensive
Time required to develop an application and make forecasts	Depends on ability to identify relationships	More than a month	More than a month

Continued on next page

Table 2 Summary of Commonly Used Forecasting Methods *(continued)*

Summary of Commonly Used Time Series Methods

Technique	*Classical Decomposition*	*Box-Jenkins*
Description	Decomposes a time series into seasonals, trend cycles, and irregular elements. Primarily used for detailed time-series analysis (including estimating seasonals)	Iterative procedure that produces an autoregressive, integrated moving average model, adjusts for seasonal and trend factors, estimates appropriate weighting parameters, tests the model, and repeats the cycle as appropriate.
Accuracy:		
Short-term (0-3 mon)	Very good to excellent	Very good to excellent
Medium-term (3 mon-2 yr)	Good	Poor to good
Long-term (2 yr and over)	Very poor	Very poor
Identification of turning point	Very good	Fair
Typical application	Tracking and warning, forecasts of sales and financial data.	Production and inventory control for large volume items, forecasts of cash balances and earnings.
Data required	A minimum of three years' history to start. Thereafter, the complete history.	Production and inventory control for large volume items, forecasts of cash balances and earnings.
Cost of forecasting with a computer	Minimal	Expensive
Time required to develop an application and make forecasts	One day	Two days

Source: Heavily adapted from Chambers, John, S. Mullick and D. Smith, "How to Choose the Right Forecasting Technique," *Harvard Business Review,* Vol. 49, no. 4, July-August 1971.

Table 3   The Forecasting Decision Matrix

Techniques	Timing: When Will the Forecast Be Used?	Rankings
Qualitative or Judgmental	Short Lead Time ↕ Long Lead Time	Expert Opinion Consensus Opinion Sales Force Polling Market Surveys Delphi
Time Series	Short Lead Time ↕ Long Lead Time	Trend Analysis Moving Average Exponential Smoothing Classical Decomposition Box-Jenkins
Causal, Markov, and Direct	Short Lead Time ↕ Long Lead Time	Markov Regression Leading Indicator Life Cycle Analysis Surveys Econometric Input-Outpur Analysis

Techniques	Form: Who Will Use the Forecast?	Rankings
Qualitative or Judgmental	Precise Forecast ↕ Imprecise Forecast	Market Surveys Expert Opinion Sales Force Polling Delphi
Time Series	Precise Forecast ↕ Imprecise Forecast	All Similar, Giving Precise Forecasts
Causal, Markov, and Indirect	Precise Forecast ↕ Imprecise Forecast	All Similar, Giving Precise Forecasts

Techniques	Data: How Much Are Available?	Rankings
Qualitative or Judgmental	Considerable Data Required ↕ Little Data Required	Generally All Similar, Little Historical Data Needed
Time Series	Considerable Data Required ↕ Little Data Required	All Similar, At Least Two Years' Data Usually Required
Causal, Markov, and Indirect	Considerable Data Required ↕ Little Data Required	Input-Out Analysis Econometric Life Cycle Analysis Markov Leading Indicator Regression Surveys

FORECASTING AND STATISTICAL SOFTWARE

There are numerous computer software that are used for forecasting purposes. They are broadly divided into two major categories: forecasting software and general purpose statistical software. Some programs are stand-alone, while others are spreadsheet add-ins. Still others are templates. A brief summary of some popular programs follows.

1. SALES & MARKET FORECASTING TOOLKIT

Sales & Market Forecast Toolkit is a *Lotus 1-2-3 template* that produces sales and market forecasts, even for new products with limited historical data. It provides eight powerful methods for more accurate forecasts, and includes spreadsheet models, complete with graph, ready-to-use with your numbers. The Sales & Market Forecasting Toolkit offers a variety of forecasting methods to help you generate accurate business forecasts, even in new or changing markets with limited historical data.

The forecasting methods include:

- Customer Poll
- Whole Market Penetration
- Chain Method
- Strategic Modeling
- Moving Averages, exponential smoothing, and linear regressions

The Customer Poll method helps build a forecast from the ground up, by summing the individual components such as products, stores, or customers. Whole Market Penetration, Market Share, and the Chain Method are top-down forecasting methods used to predict sales for new products and markets lacking sales data. The Strategic Modeling method develops a forecast by projecting the impact of changes to pricing and advertising expenditures. Statistical forecasting methods include exponential smoothing, moving averages, and linear regression.

You can use the built-in macros to enter data into your forecast automatically. For example, enter values for the first and last months of a 12-month forecast. The compounded-growth-rate macro will automatically compute and enter values for the other ten months.

It is available from:

Lotus Selects
P.O. Box 9172
Cambridge, MA 02139-9946
(800) 635-6887   (617) 693-3981

2. Forecast! GFX

Forecast! GFX is a *stand-alone* forecasting system that can perform five types of time-series analysis: seasonal adjustment, linear and nonlinear trend analysis, moving-average analysis, exponential smoothing, and decomposition. Trend analysis supports linear, exponential, hyperbolic, S-curve, and polynomial trends. Hyperbolic trend models are used to analyze data that indicate a decline toward a limit, such as the output of an oil well or the price of a particular model of personal computer. *Forecast! GFX* can perform multiple-regression analysis with up to 10 independent variables.

> Intex Solutions
> 35 Highland Cir.
> Needham, MA 01294
> (617)449-6222   (617)444-2318 (fax)

3. ForeCalc

ForeCalc, Lotus and *Symphony Add-in,* feature the following:

- Uses nine forecasting techniques and includes both automatic and manual modes
- Eliminates the need to export or reenter data

You can use it in either automatic or manual mode. In automatic mode, just highlight the historical data in your spreadsheet, such as sales, expenses, or net income; then *ForeCalc* tests several exponential-smoothing models and picks the one that best fits your data.

Forecast results can be transferred to your spreadsheet with upper and lower confidence limits. *ForeCalc* generates a line graph showing the original data, the forecasted values, and confidence limits.

ForeCalc can automatically choose the most accurate forecasting technique:

- Simple one-parameter smoothing
- Holt's two-parameter smoothing
- Winters' three-parameter smoothing
- Trendless seasonal models
- Dampened versions of Holt and Winters's smoothing

ForeCalc's manual mode lets you select the type of trend and seasonality-yielding nine possible model combinations. You can vary the type of trend (constant, linear, or dampened), as well as the seasonality (nonseasonal, additive, or multiplicative).

Business Forecast Systems, Inc.
68 Leonard St.
Belmont, MA 02178
(617)484-5050

4. StatPlan IV

StatPlan IV is a *stand-alone* program for those who understand how to apply statistics to business analysis. You can use it for market analysis, trend forecasting, and statistical modeling.

StatPlan IV lets you analyze data by range, mean, median, standard deviation, skewdness, kurtosis, correlation analysis, one- or two-way analysis of variance (ANOVA), cross tabulations, and t-test.

The forecasting methods include multiple regression, stepwise multiple regression, polynomial regression, bivariate curve fitting, autocorrelation analysis, trend and cycle analysis, and exponential smoothing.

The data can be displayed in X-Y plots, histograms, time-series graphs, autocorrelation plots, actual vs. forecast plots, or frequency and percentile tables.

It is available from:

Lotus Selects
P.O. Box 9172
Cambridge, MA 02139-9946
(800) 635-6887   (617) 693-3981

5. Geneva Statistical Forecasting

Geneva Statistical Forecasting, a *stand-alone* software, can batch-process forecasts for thousands of data series, provided the series are all measured in the same time units (days, weeks, months, and so on). The software automatically explores as many as nine different forecasting methods, including six linear and nonlinear regressions and three exponential-smoothing techniques, before picking the one that best fits your historical data.

The program incorporates provisions that simplify and accelerate the process of reforecasting data items. Once you complete the initial forecast, you can save a data file that records the forecasting method assigned to each line item. When it is time to update the data, simply retrieve the file and reforecast, using the same methods as before.

Geneva Statistical Forecasting tries as many as nine forecasting methods for each line item.

Pizzano & Co.
800 W. Cummings Park
Woburn, MA 01801
(617)935-7122

6. SmartForecasts

SmartForecasts, a *stand-alone* forecasting software, does the following:

- Automatically chooses the right statistical method
- Lets you manually adjust forecasts to reflect your business judgement
- Produces forecast results

SmartForecasts combines the benefits of statistical and judgmental forecasting. It can determine which statistical method will give you the most accurate forecast, and handle all the math.

Forecasts can be modified using the program's EYEBALL utility. You may need to adjust a sales forecast to reflect an anticipated increase in advertising or a decrease in price. *SmartForecasts* summarizes data with descriptive statistics, plots the distribution of data values with histograms, plots variables in a scattergram, and identifies leading indicators.

You can forecast using single- and double-exponential smoothing, and simple- and linear-moving averages. It even builds seasonality into your forecasts using Winters's exponential smoothing, or you can eliminate seasonality by using times series decomposition and seasonal adjustment.

In addition, *SmartForecasts* features simultaneous multiseries forecasting of up to 60 variables and 150 data points per variable, offers multivariate regression to let you relate business variables, and has an Undo command for mistakes.

Smart Software, Inc.
4 Hill Rd.
Belmont, MA 02178
(800)762-7899   (617)489-2748 (fax)

7. Tomorrow

Tomorrow, a *stand-alone* forecasting software, uses an optimized combination of linear regression, single exponential smoothing, adaptive rate response single exponential smoothing, Brown's one-parameter double exponential smoothing, Holt's two-parameter exponential smoothing, Brown's one-parameter triple exponential smoothing, and Gardner's three-parameter damped trend. Some of the main features include:

- There's no need to reformat your existing spreadsheets. *Tomorrow* recognizes and forecasts formula cells (containing totals and subtotals, for example). It handles both horizontally and vertically oriented spreadsheets. It accepts historical data in up to 30 separate ranges.
- Allows you to specify seasonality manually, or calculates seasonality automatically.
- Allows you to do several forecasts of different time series (for example, sales data from different regions) at once.
- Recognizes and forecasts time series headings (names of months, etc.).
- Forecast optionally becomes normal part of your spreadsheet.
- Undo command restores original spreadsheet.
- Browse feature allows you to look at any part of the spreadsheet (including the forecast) without leaving *Tomorrow*.
- Checks for and prevents accidental overlaying of nonempty or protected cells.
- Optional annotation mode labels forecast cells, calculates MAPE, and, when seasonality is automatically determined, describes the seasonality.
- Comprehensive context-sensitive on-line help.

Isogon Corp.
330 Seventh Ave.
New York, NY 10001
(212)967-2424

8. Forecast Pro

Forecast Pro, a *stand-alone* forecasting software, uses artificial intelligence. A built-in expert system examines your data. Then it guides you to exponential smoothing, Box-Jenkins, or regression, whichever method suits the data best.

Business Forecast Systems, Inc.
68 Leonard St.
Belmont, MA 02178
(617)484-5050   (617)484-9219

9. MicroTSP

MicroTSP is a *stand-alone* software that provides the tools most frequently used in practical econometric and forecasting work. It covers the following:

1. Descriptive statistics
2. A wide range of single equation estimation techniques including ordinary least squares (multiple regression), two-stage least squares, non-linear least squares, and probit and logit.

Forecasting tools includes:

1. Exponential smoothing including single exponential, double exponential, and Winters smoothing.
2. Box-Jenkins methodology.

Quantitative Micro Software
4521 Campus Drive, Suite 336
Irvine, CA 92715
(714) 856-3368

10. Sibyl/Runner

Sibyl/Runner is an interactive, *stand-alone* forecasting system. In addition to allowing the usage of all major forecasting methods, the package permits analysis of the data, suggests available forecasting methods, compares results, and provides several accuracy measures in such a way that it is easier for the user to select an appropriate method and forecast needed data under different economic and environmental conditions. For details, see Makridakis, S., Hodgsdon, and S. Wheelwright, "An Interactive Forecasting System," *American Statistician,* November 1974.

Applied Decision Systems
Lexington, MA 02173
(614) 424-9820

11. Forecast Plus

Forecast Plus, a *stand-alone* forecasting software, uses artificial intelligence. A built-in expert system examines your data. Then it guides you to thirteen forecasting methods including exponential smoothing, Box-Jenkins, or regression, whichever method suits the data best.
The software features the following:

- A simple to use menu system
- High resolution graphic capability

- An ability to choose an appropriate forecasting technique
- An ability to handle all phases of forecasting analysis
- An ability to save forecasted data
- Optimization of smoothing constants

StatPac, Inc.
3814 Lyndale Avenue South
Minneapolis, MN 55409
(612) 822-8252

12. Other Forecasting Software

There are many other forecasting software such as *Autocast II* and *4 Cast* (Delphus, Inc. 103 Washington St. #348 Morristown, NJ 07960, (201) 267-9269) and *Trendsetter Expert Version* (Concentric Data Systems 110 Turnpike Rd., Westborough, MA 01581, (800) 325-9035).

13. General Purpose Statistical Software

There are numerous statistical software widely in use that can be utilized in order to build a forecasting model. Some of the more popular ones include Systat, SAS Application System, Statgraphics, SPSS, PC-90, Minitab, RATS, and BMD.

CHOOSING THE RIGHT PACKAGE

Since different software packages apply different techniques for many of the same tasks, it is a good idea to select a package that explains which method it is using and why, so you can eventually learn the most appropriate technique for your specific forecasting task. Figure 3 spells out your options in choosing the right package.

CONCLUSION

Today's financial managers have some powerful tools at hand to simplify the forecasting process and increase its accuracy. Several forecasting models are available, and the automated versions of these should be considered by any manager who is regularly called upon to provide forecasts. A personal com-

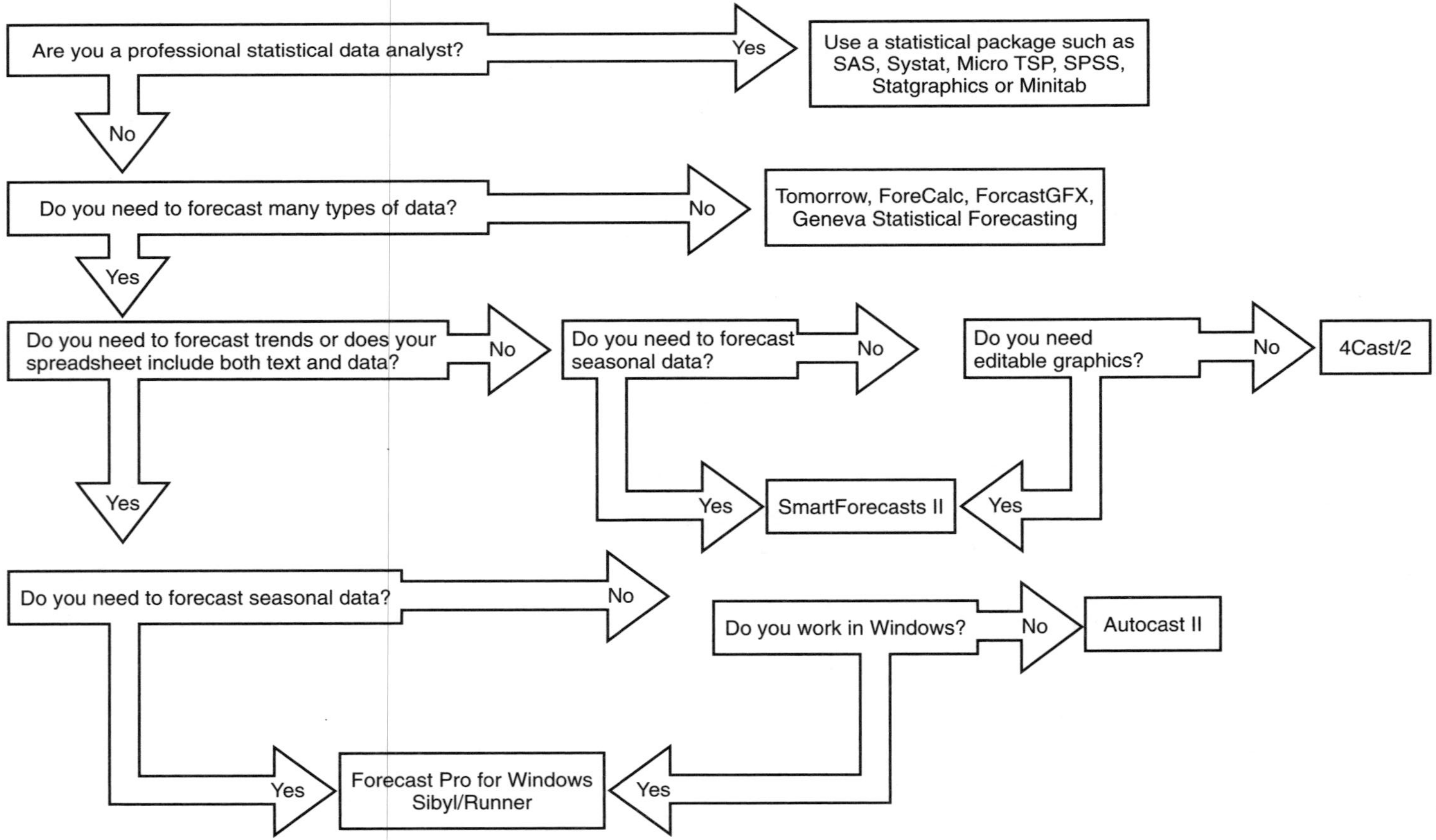

Figure 3 Which Forecasting Software Is Right for You? Know Your Options

puter with a spreadsheet is a good beginning, but the stand-alone packages currently available provide the most accurate forecasts and are the easiest to use. In addition, they make several forecasting models available and can automatically select the best one for a particular data set.

FINANCIAL STATEMENT ANALYSIS

VALUATION OF A BUSINESS

A company may need to be *valued* for many reasons including a purchase, sale, merger, buy-back agreement, litigation, attempt to expand the credit line, or tax matter. The valuation depends on the purpose at hand. The **valuation process** is an art and not a science since everyone's perception is slightly different. In litigation matters, the valuation method used should be logically consistent, reasonable, cost-effective, and simply explained. This chapter provides several *sound ways* to determine what a business is worth. The valuation methods may apply to any situation in which the value of a business must be made. Further, various Internal Revenue Service Revenue Rulings have been issued recommending specific valuation measures in the case of income taxes.

In valuing the business, the following factors should be considered: history of the business, nature of the company and its major activities, maturity of the business, economic and political conditions, health of the industry, financial position of the firm, degree of risk, growth potential, trend and stability of earnings, competition, marketing factors, customer base, quality of management, and ease of transferability of ownership.

As an initial step in valuation, the key financial information must be accumulated and analyzed including historical financial statements, forecasted financial statements, and tax returns. There must be a full familiarity with the business. Further, the major assumptions of the valuation must be clearly spelled out.

The valuation methods are based on the assumption that an entity is a "going concern." The valuation approaches may be profit- or asset-oriented. Adjusted earnings may be capitalized at an appropriate multiple. Future adjusted cash earnings may be discounted by the projected return rate. Assets may be valued at fair market value, such as through appraisal. Comparative values of similar companies may serve as excellent benchmarks.

Comparison with Industry Averages

Valid comparisons can be made between the entity being valued and others in the same industry. Industry norms should be noted. A good source of comparative industry data is Leo Troy, *Almanac of Business and Industrial Financial Ratios* (based on corporate tax returns to the Internal Revenue Service) published by Prentice Hall.

Valuation Methods

We now look at the various approaches to business valuation. A combination of these approaches may be used to obtain a representative value.

Capitalization of Earnings. Primary consideration should be given to profits when valuing a business. Analysis of historical earnings is typically the beginning point in applying a capitalization method to most business valuations. In general, historical earnings are a reliable predictor of future earnings.

The value of the business may be based on its adjusted earnings times a multiplier indicating what the business would sell for in the industry.

Net income may be multiplied by a multiplier to determine the value of a business. The multiplier should be higher for a low-risk business but generally not more than 10. The multiplier should be lower for a high-risk business, often only 1 or 2. Of course, an average multiplier would be used when average risk exists, such as 5. The P/E ratio for a comparable company would be a good benchmark. Typically, a five-year average adjusted historical earnings figure is used. The five years' profits up to the valuation date demonstrates past earning power. The computation is:

Value of a Business = Average adjusted earnings over 5 years × Multiplier

(P/E ratio) of 5 (based on industry standard)

Instead of a simple average, a weighted-average adjusted historical earnings figure is recommended. This gives more weight to the most recent years, which reflects higher currency prices and recent business performance. If a five-year weighted-average is used, the current year is given a weight of 5 while the first year is assigned a weight of 1. The multiplier is then applied to the weighted-average five-year adjusted earnings to determine the value of the business. An illustration follows:

Year	Net Income	×	Weight	= Total
19X9	$130,000	×	5	$650,000
19X8	100,000	×	4	400,000
19X7	120,000	×	3	360,000
19X6	80,000	×	2	160,000
19X5	105,000	×	1	105,000
			15	$1,675,000

Weighted-average 5 year earnings:
  $1,675,000/15 = $111,667

Weighted-average 5 year earnings	$111,667
× Multiplier	×5
Valuation	$558,335

Note: The multiplier may be based on the price-earnings ratio for a comparable publicly traded company or may be based on such factors as risk, stability, expected future earnings, liquidity, etc.

If the company's financial statements are not audited, you should insist on an audit to assure accurate reporting.

Has the business failed to record cash sales to hide income? One way of determining this is to take purchases and add a typical profit markup in the industry. To verify reported profit, the financial manager can multiply the sales by the profit margin in the industry. If reported earnings is significantly below what the earnings should be based on the industry standard, there may be some hidden income.

Capitalization of Excess Earnings.   The best method is to capitalize excess earnings. The normal rate of return on the weighted-average net tangible assets is subtracted from the weighted-average earnings to determine excess earnings. It is suggested that the weighting be based on a five-year period. The excess earnings figure is then capitalized to determine the value of the intangibles (primarily goodwill). The addition of the value of the intangibles and the fair market value of the net intangible assets equals the total valuation. As per IRS Revenue Ruling 68-609 (to be discussed in detail later), the IRS recommends this method to value a business for tax purposes. An illustration follows.

Weighted-average net tangible assets is computed below.

Year	Amount	T	Weight	= Total
19X1	$750,000	×	1	$750,000
19X2	1,100,000	×	2	2,200,000
19X3	1,300,000	×	3	3,900,000
19X4	1,500,000	×	4	6,000,000
19X5	1,400,000	×	5	7,000,000
			15	19,850,000

Weighted-Average Net Tangible Assets:
  $19,850,000/15 = $1,323,333

Weighted-Average Net Income (5 years)—assumed	$200,000
Minus Reasonable Rate of Return on Weighted-Average	
Tangible Net Assets ($1,323,333 × 10%)	132,333
Excess Earnings	$67,667
× Capitalization factor (25%)	× 4
Valuation of Intangibles	$270,668
Plus Fair Market Value of Net Tangible Assets	3,200,000
Capitalization-of-Excess-Earnings Valuation	$3,470,668

Capitalization of Cash Flow. Cash earnings may be capitalized in arriving at a value for the firm. An example follows:

Cash Earnings	$200,000
× Capitalization Factor (20%)	× 5
Capitalization of Cash Flow	$1,000,000
Less Liabilities	100,000
Capitalization-of-Cash-Flow Earnings	$900,000

Present Value (Discounting) of Future Cash Flows. A business is worth the discounted value of future cash earnings plus the discounted value of the expected selling price. Cash flow may be a more valid criterion of value than book profits because cash flow can be used for reinvestment. This approach is suggested in a third-party sale situation.

Step 1: Present Value of Cash Earnings. The earnings should be estimated over future years using an expected growth rate considering inflation. Once the future earnings are ascertained, they should be discounted. Future profits may be based on the previous years' earnings and the current profit margin applied to sales. Cash profits equals net income plus noncash expense adjustments such as amortization.

Step 2: Present Value of Sales Price. The present value of the anticipated selling price of the business at the sale date should be determined.

The financial manager should use as the discount rate the return rate earned by the business. The discount rate should consider the typical return rate for money, a risk premium, and perhaps a premium for the illiquidity of the investment. If the risk-free interest is 7% (on government bonds), the risk premium is 8%, and the illiquidity premium is 7%, the capitalization (discount) rate will be 22%. The risk premium may range from 5% to 10% while the illiquidity premium may range from 5% to 15%.

Illustration. In 19X1, the net profit is $200,000. Earnings are anticipated to grow at 8% per year. The discount rate is 10%. The financial analyst estimates that the business is worth the discounted value of future earnings. The valuation equals:

Year	Net Income (8% growth rate)		PV Factor (at 10% Interest)	Present Value
19X1	$200,000	×	.909	$181,800
19X2	216,000	×	.826	178,416
19X3	233,280	×	.751	175,193
19X4	251,942	×	.683	172,076
19X5	272,098	×	.621	168,973
Present Value of Future Earnings				$876,458

If the anticipated selling price at the end of year 19X5 is $600,000, the valuation of the business equals:

Present value of future profits	$876,458
Present value of selling price $600,000 × .621	372,600
Valuation	$1,249,058

Book Value (Net Worth). The business may be valued based on the book value of the net assets at the latest balance sheet date. However, this approach is unrealistic because it does not consider current values. It may only be acceptable when it is impossible to compute the fair value of net assets and/or goodwill.

Tangible Net Worth. The entity's valuation is its tangible net worth for the current year equal to stockholders' equity, less intangibles.

Economic Net Worth (Adjusted Book Value). Economic net worth equals: Fair market value of net assets, plus: Goodwill (as per contract).

Fair Market Value of Net Assets.   The fair market value of the net tangible assets of the entity may be based on independent appraisal. Expert appraisers for different kinds of tangible assets may be used, such as specialized appraisers for real estate, trucks, and equipment. Additionally, reference may be made to published values for specific assets, such as the "blue book" for business automobiles. Typically, the fair value of the net tangible assets (assets minus liabilities) exceeds book value. To this, we add the value of the goodwill (if any). Note that goodwill applies to such aspects as corporate reputation, customer base, and high quality goods. A business broker may be hired to appraise property, plant, and equipment for a smaller company. The general rule is to value inventory at a maximum value of cost.

Unrecorded liabilities should be taken into account when ascertaining the fair value of net assets since such off-balance sheet liabilities represent future commitments and contingencies. For example, one company the author consulted for had both an unrecorded liability for liquidated damages for non-union contract of $3,100,000 and an unrecorded liability for $4,900,000 related to the expected employer final withdrawal liability. Lawsuits and tax disputes are other examples of an unrecorded liability. As a result of unrecognized liabilities, the business valuation is reduced.

Unrecorded assets increase the value of the business such as high quality personnel.

Gross Revenue Multiplier.   The value of the entity may be computed by multiplying the revenue by the gross revenue multiplier customary in the industry. The industry norm gross revenue multiplier is based on the average ratio of market price to sales typical in the industry. Hence, if revenue is $15,000,000 and the multiplier is .3, the valuation is: $15,000,000 \times .3 = $4,500,000. This approach may be used when profits are questionable.

Profit Margin/Capitalization Rate.   The profit margin divided by the capitalization rate provides a multiplier which is then applied to revenue. A multiplier of revenue that a company would sell at is the company's profit margin. The profit margin may be based on the industry average. The formula is:

Profit margin/capitalization rate = Net income/sales divided by capitalization

rate = Multiplier

The capitalization rate in earnings is the return demanded by investors. In determining a capitalization rate, the prime interest rate may be considered.

The ensuing multiplier when multiplied by revenue is the amount the buyer is willing to pay. Assume sales of $16,000,000, a profit margin of 8%, and a capitalization rate of 22%. The multiplier is 25% (5%/20%). The valuation is:

Sales × 30%

$16,000,000 × 30% = $4,800,000

The Internal Revenue Service and the courts have considered current sales as a key factor.

Price-Earnings Factor. The value of an entity may be based on the price-earnings multiple applied to earnings per share. An example appears below.

Net Income	$600,000
Outstanding shares	100,000
EPS	$6
P/E ratio	×9
Estimated market price per share	$54
× Number of shares outstanding	×100,000
Price-earnings valuation	$5,400,000

MANAGEMENT ANALYSIS
OF OPERATIONS

This chapter discusses the analysis of a company's profit including the revenue and cost components. Means to control costs are included. There is a discussion of the cost of quality (COQ) and the cost of prediction errors. The chapter presents performance measures, productivity concerns, monitoring of sales efforts, appraising personnel, evaluating the efficiency of space utilization, and analysis of business processes. The corporate controller must also take into account life cycles and time considerations. Divestitures may be necessary to get rid of operations draining the firm such as those losing money and generating excessive risk levels.

ANALYSIS OF PROFIT

Profit margin (net income/net sales) measures the profitability of each sales dollar. Profitability should be determined by source (product, service, customer (including customer profiles), age group, industry segment, geographic area, channel of distribution, type of marketing effort, market segment, and responsibility center (division, plant, department, and units within the department). Profit variance analysis should be performed to identify causes for actual profit being less than expected. Problems should be immediately identified and corrected. Profit maximization strategies should be formulated. Reports should be prepared by profit-generating source (e.g., market, client). Profit planning including strategic pricing and volume plans should be undertaken.

ANALYSIS OF REVENUE

An analysis should be made of sales mix, product demand, order quantities, product obsolescence, manufacturing schedules, storage space, and competition. Appraise sales generated by different types of selling efforts (direct mail, television, newspaper). Also, compare sales and profit before and after product refinement. The amount of sales returns and allowances is a good indicator of the quality of merchandise. If returns and allowances are high relative to sales, buyer dissatisfaction exists having a negative effect on the company's reputation. Further, the company may have to pay the freight for returned goods.

Sales ratios include:

- Quality of sales = cash sales/total sales
- Days of sales backlog = backlog balance/sales volume divided by sales in period. This ratio helps to monitor sales status and planning.
- Sales per customer = net sales/average number of customers
- Order response rate = average number of transactions/average number of solicitations
- Sales response rate = average dollar sales/average solicitations
- Customer contact ratio = calls to customers/total calls

The ratio of sales to current debt looks at the degree to which short-term liabilities finances sales growth.

Determine the variability in volume, price, and cost of each major product or service.

Questions to be asked and answered are:

- Should products or services be more personalized?
- Which services or products are ineffective and/or excessively costly?
- How can products, services, manufacturing, or distribution be redesigned to make them more profitable?

A "close to the customer" strategy assures more useful customer information and improved sales, and lower distribution costs.

COST ANALYSIS AND CONTROL

Cost Analysis

A company's costs should be compared over the years to determine if there is a problem in cost incurrence. The reasons for unusual changes in costs should be noted and corrective steps taken when warranted.

Direct cost ratios may be used in analyzing operating costs such as (1) direct labor/sales, (2) direct travel/sales, and (3) computer usage/sales.

Determine if costs are excessive relative to production volume. The ratio of selling expenses to net sales reflects the cost of selling the product. Is such cost excessive?

Locked-in (designed) costs will be incurred in the "future" based on decisions already made. It is difficult to reduce locked-in costs. "Cost down" is reducing product costs but still fulfill customer expectations. Also, compare the number of project rejections due to high initial costs to total projects available.

Proper cost allocation should be made to responsibility centers, geographic areas, products, services, and customers.

Cost Control

Recommendations should be made on improving quality control. Expenses are often related to sales to determine if proper controls exist and if the expenditures are resulting in improved revenue and/or profitability. Examine the following ratios:

- Total operating expenses/net sales
- Specific expense/net sales
- Utilities expense/net sales
- Selling expenses/net sales

A cost-benefit analysis is crucial. Costs should be controlled by major type (e.g., manufacturing, selling, administrative, legal, insurance). Cost control reports should be prepared. Cost control may be evaluated by doing the following:

- Undertake a cost reduction program for projects, products, and services. Such a program may eliminate waste and inefficiency resulting in improved profitability. However, cost reductions must make sense.
- Evaluate leased premises to reduce rental charges.
- Consider joint ventures to reduce cost.
- Eliminate duplicate facilities and activities by streamlining operations.
- Implement an energy conservation program.
- Place "caps" on expense categories (e.g., telephone, travel and entertainment). Pinpoint those responsible for excessive costs (e.g., excessive telephone calls). Authorization will be needed on an employee basis for amounts exceeding ceiling levels.

- Assign each employee an identification number for xerox, fax, and computer use.
- Substitute cheaper sources of supply or self-manufacture the part.
- Undertake an engineering study to see if manufactured goods can be redesigned to save costs.
- Perform inspection at key points in the manufacturing cycle to correct problems early.
- Adjust output levels as needed.
- Contract for long-term purchase agreements.
- Obtain competitive bids and change suppliers, insurance companies, consultants, etc. when lower fees are obtained assuming similar levels of quality.
- Redesign the delivery system to reduce fuel costs.
- Tie salary increments to increased productivity.
- Subcontract work if lower costs arise.

COST OF QUALITY (COQ)

The cost of quality (COQ) is defined as any costs to correct poor quality or to enhance good quality. It takes into account the costs to "prevent" product defects (e.g., employee training, machine maintenance), appraisal costs (e.g., testing, inspecting), and the cost of the failure to control (e.g., scrap, rework, warranties). Problems must be detected and corrected in a timely fashion. There is also an opportunity cost of foregone earnings arising from customers switching to other suppliers because of the company's poor quality products or services. The following ratios may be enlightening: (1) cost of quality/total operating costs and (2) cost of quality/sales. The manager's objective is to minimize COQ subject to the constraints of corporate policy, customer requirements, and manufacturing limitations. Ultimately, the overall quality of the company's goods benefit.

COST OF PREDICTION ERRORS

The failure to accurately project sales could result in poor production planning, improper labor levels, etc. causing potentially huge financial losses. The cost of the prediction error is the profit lost because of the inaccurate prediction. It can be measured in lost sales, disgruntled customers, and idle machinery. It is important to determine the cost of the prediction error so as to minimize the potential negative affect on the business. Prediction relates to sales, expenses, and purchases.

PERFORMANCE MEASURES

Performance evaluation must consider the trend in a measure over time within the company, to competing companies, and to industry norms. Index numbers may be used to compare current-year figures to base-year (representative, typical year) figures. Revenue, cost, and profit may be tracked by division, department, product, service, process, contract, job, sales territory, and customer. Measures of performance include:

- Repeat sales to customers
- Backup of orders
- Number of skills per worker
- Number of complaints and warranty required services
- Rework costs relative to cost of goods manufactured
- Setup time relative to total manufacturing time
- Number and length of equipment breakdowns
- Number and duration of manufacturing delays
- Output per manhour
- Manufacturing costs to total costs
- Manufacturing costs to revenue
- Lead time
- Time per business process
- Time between receipt of an order and delivery
- Time between order placement and receipt
- Non-value added cost to total cost
- Percentage of declining and developmental products to total products

"Production run size" is an optimum production run quantity which minimizes the sum of carrying and setup costs.

STUDYING PRODUCTIVITY

Productivity is enhanced by minimizing direct labor cost. Also, an attempt should be made to reduce indirect costs relative to direct labor costs. Management might consolidate facilities and equipment to achieve a more efficient productivity level. A measure of productivity is the relationship between the cost, time, and quality of an "input" to the quality and units generated for the "output." A proper input-output balance is needed. Resources should be utilized in an optimum fashion.

SALES EFFORTS

An appraisal should be made of salesperson effectiveness (e.g., income generated by salesperson, cost per salesperson, salesperson incentives, call frequency, dollar value of orders obtained per hour spent), promotional and advertising effectiveness (marketing costs to sales, dollar expenditure by media compared to sales generated, media measures, comparison of profit before and after promotion), test market analysis (consumer vs. industry), and activity analysis (sales and marketing, customer support, order management). An analysis should also be made of product/service warranties and complaints.

LOOKING AT PERSONNEL

The ratio of sales to personnel represents a comparison of sales dollars and/or sales volume generated relative to the number of employees. It provides insight into levels of employee productivity. The following ratios should be computed: (l) sales/number of employees, (2) sales volume/number of employees, (3) sales/salaries expense. Other useful ratios are: (l) net income/manpower, (2) number of transactions/average number of employees, (3) total tangible assets/number of workers, (4) labor costs/total costs, (5) labor costs/sales, and (6) labor costs/net income. Another consideration as to employee efficiency and morale is employee turnover (number of employees leaving/average number of employees).

The ratio of indirect labor to direct labor monitors indirect labor planning and control. Labor planning and control are crucial at all supervisory levels to produce competitive products and/or to perform profitable services. Management uses this ratio to appraise indirect personnel requirements through the impact of these requirements on operations, earnings, and overhead costs. A declining ratio is unfavorable because it shows management has not maintained a desirable relationship.

Consider automation and up-to-date technology to decrease labor costs.

EFFICIENCY OF SPACE USE

The usefulness of space may be computed as follows:

- Revenue per square foot = net sales/square feet of space.
- Sales per square foot of machinery = net sales/square feet of space for machinery.

- Production per square foot = total units produced/square feet of space for machinery.
- Profit per square foot = net income/square feet of space.
- Customer space = number of customers/square feet of space
- Employee space = square feet of space/number of employees
- Parking lot space = square feet of parking lot space/number of customers.
- Rent per square foot = rent expense/square feet of space.
- Expenses per square foot for owned property = expenses of owning property/square feet of space.

BUSINESS PROCESSES

A business process is an operation, function, or activity that crosses among divisions or departments of a company to manufacture the product or render the service. By concentrating on the process itself (rather than each department separately) operations and product/service quality may be improved, costs slashed, and processing time reduced.

By analyzing a process itself it is easier to understand the complexities and interrelationships among units of the organization, and aid in better communication as to where each responsibility unit fits in. Concentrating on and improving the business process (as distinct from individual departments) results in greater efficiency and effectiveness. In appraising business processes, consider:

- What does the process cost and how long does it take?
- Does the process involve irrelevant and unneeded steps that can be cut?
- What is the quality associated with the process?
- What problems or bottlenecks exist?
- What is the work flow?

The financial manager should identify cases in which work performed at the client is redundant or unnecessary, or where such work is too costly or time consuming. Further, procedures, activities or policies may be unjustifiably complex and can be simplified. A process needs to be revamped when its cost or time does not add value to the customer. Therefore, a customer survey may be warranted. The CPA may decide to recommend modifying, adding, or dropping a process.

The business process might be improved by doing the following: reduce the number of employees involved or functions required, reduce cycle time, reduce the number of individuals required to approve the process or modification thereto, reorganize the procedures, eliminate illogical administrative steps, improve the sequence of the operation, prioritize strategies, cut out excessive paper work, improve training, clarify job descriptions and instructions, upgrade equipment, and use up-to-date technology.

Cycle time should be expressed as average and maximum. An example of cycle time is how long it takes to process a bill to a customer. The efficiency to which a cycle is performed may be expressed by the ratio of total processing time divided by total processing plus non-processing time. A lower ratio is unfavorable and requires corrective action.

"A value-added evaluation" should be conducted for each operation, function, or responsibility unit. How much is the value-added? Is it sufficient to justify that activity or business segment? If not, what should be done (e.g., improvements made, disbandonment)? Work improvement teams can be used in production, material handling, shipping, and accounting. Such teams should document the process flows, layouts, etc. and find ways to reorganize the process to make it better.

A business process analysis may be undertaken as a pre-emptive troubleshooter and should be on an ongoing basis. Examples of situations to which a business process analysis is crucial are when profit margins for a product line are shrinking, market share is dramatically declining, service quality is deteriorating, and customer response time is becoming prohibitive.

Operational audits should be performed examining corporate policies and procedures to assure that they are functioning properly.

LIFE CYCLES

There are different types of life cycles affecting a business. "Product-life cycle" is the time from the start of the R&D effort to the ending of customer support for the product. A "life cycle budget" of costs is for this time period and aids in formulating selling prices. Many costs occur even before production starts. The development product period may range from short to long. "Product life-cycle reporting" is not on a calendar year basis but rather tracks the revenue and costs for each product over several calendar years. Product cost analysis is done by product over each major stage in their life cycle (early, middle, late). There is a highlighting of cost interrelationships among major business functions. "Life-cycle costing" organizes costs based on the product or service life cycle. It monitors and computes the actual total costs of the product or service from beginning to end. Decisions are then made about the good or service based on its profile. "Customer life-cycle costs" concentrate on the total costs to a customer of buying and using a product over its life.

TIME CONSIDERATIONS

Time-based competition stresses the customer and considers product quality, timing, and cost/pricing. An example is how long it takes to design a new product model to meet customer demand. Another example is how long it takes to fill a customer's order. Such analysis strives to enhance productivity, improve market position, raise selling prices, and reduce risk. Efforts should be made to streamline operations.

The time between developing and marketing a product or service should be minimized to lower up-front costs (e.g., design, process, and promotion). Revenue must be generated as quickly as possible to recoup such costs.

DIVESTITURES

Divestitures may be made of unprofitable and/or risky business segments. Divestiture involves the complete or partial conversion, sale, or reallocation of capital or human resources as well as product/service lines. Freed resources may be used for some more productive business purpose. A business segment may qualify for divestiture if it is providing a poor rate of return, does not generate adequate cash flow, does not mesh with overall company strategy, has excessive risk (e.g., vulnerable to lawsuits), is in a state of decline, or where the pieces are worth more than the whole. The objectives of divestiture include repositioning the company in the industry, getting out of an industry, meeting market changes, obtaining needed funds, and cutting losses. Before a divestiture is made, a joint venture may be considered with another company.

MANAGEMENT OF ACCOUNTS RECEIVABLES

CASH DISBURSEMENT

The disbursement of cash is improved if based on controlled disbursement when the amount of money to be deposited on a daily basis to pay checks clearing that day is determined. Other effective means to disburse cash are using a positive pay service to reduce the incidence of fraud, and an accounts receivable reconcilement service.

Export receivables and foreign risk may be managed better by taking out export credit insurance coverage to assure payment for shipped goods. Credit coverage may be obtained via the U.S. Export-Import Bank or a letter of credit from a U.S. or foreign bank. Even though a letter of credit guards against customer default, it needs to be secured before each export transaction. In emerging markets, the multinational company should consider the following as part of its accounts receivable management program:

- Stability of the foreign country's banking system.
- Variability in foreign exchange rates.
- Variance in foreign payment schedules.
- Stability of political, economic and financial conditions.
- Astuteness of financial management by the country's trade representatives and other government officials.

Financial Derivative Products and Financial Engineering

FINANCIAL DERIVATIVES

A derivative is simply a transaction, or contract, whose value depends on (or, as the name implies, derives from) the value of underlying assets such as stocks, bonds, mortgages, market indexes, or foreign currencies. One party with exposure to unwanted risk can pass some or all of that risk to a second party. The first party can assume a different risk from the second party, pay the second party to assume the risk, or, as is often the case, create a combination.

The participants in derivatives activity can be divided into two broad types—dealers and end-users. Dealers, few in numbers, include investment banks, commercial banks, merchant banks, and independent brokers. In contrast, the number of end-users is large and growing as more organizations are involved in international financial transactions. End-users include business, banks, securities firms, insurance companies, governmental units at the local, state, and federal levels, "supernational" organizations such as the World Bank, mutual funds, and both private and public pension funds.

The objectives of end-users may vary. A common reason to use derivatives is so that the risk of financial operations can be controlled. Derivatives can be used to manage foreign exchange exposure, especially unfavorable exchange rate movements. Speculators and arbitrageurs can seek profits from general price changes or simultaneous price differences in different markets, respectively. Others use derivatives to *hedge* their position; that is, to set up two financial assets so that any unfavorable price movement in one asset is offset by favorable price movement in the other asset.

There are five common types of derivatives: options, futures, forward contracts, asset swaps, and hybrid. The general characteristics of each are summarized in Figure 1, although only two most common types—options and futures—are covered in detail in this chapter.

An important feature of derivatives is that the types of risk are not unique to derivatives and can be found in many other financial activities. The risks for derivatives are especially difficult to manage for two principal reasons: (1) the derivative products are complex, and (2) there are very real difficulties in measuring the risks associated derivatives. It is imperative for financial officers of a firm to know how to manage the risks from the use of derivatives.

Figure 1 General Characteristics of Major Types of Financial Derivatives

Type	Market	Contract	Definition
Option	OTC or Organized Exchange	Custom* or Standard	Gives the buyer the right but *not* obligation to buy or sell a specific amount at a specified price within a specified period.
Futures	Organized Exchange	Standard	*Obligates* the holder to buy or sell at a specified price on a specified date.
Forward	OTC	Custom	Same as futures
Swap	OTC	Custom	Agreement between the parties to make periodic payments to each other during the swap period.
Hybrid	OTC	Custom	Incorporates various provisions of other types of derivatives.

*Custom contracts vary and are negotiated between the parties with respect to their value, period, and other terms.

OPTIONS

An option is a contract to give the investor the right—but *not an obligation*—to buy or sell something. It has three main features. It allows you, as an investor to "lock in":

1. a specified number of shares of stock
2. at a fixed price per share, called strike or exercise price
3. for a limited length of time.

For example, if you have purchased an option on a stock, you have the right to "exercise" the option at any time during the life of the option. This means that, regardless of the current market price of the stock, you have the right to buy or sell a specified number of shares of the stock at the strike price (rather than the current market price).

Options possess their own inherent value and are traded in *secondary markets*. You may want to acquire an option so that you can take advantage of an expected rise in the price of the underlying stock. Option prices are directly related to the prices of the common stock they apply to. Investing in options is very risky and requires specialized knowledge.

KINDS OF OPTIONS

All options are divided into two broad categories: calls and puts. A call option gives you the right (but not the obligation) to buy:

1. 100 shares of a specific stock
2. at a fixed price per share, called the "strike or exercise price"
3. for up to 9 months, depending on the expiration date of the option.

When you purchase a call, you are buying the right to purchase stock at a set price. You expect price appreciation to occur. You can make a sizable gain from a minimal investment, but you may lose all your money if stock price does not go up.

Example 1. You purchase a 3-month call option on Dow Chemical stock for $4 1/2 at an exercise price of $50 when the stock price is $53.

On the other hand, a single put option gives you the right (but not the obligation) to sell:

1. 100 shares of a specific stock
2. at a fixed price, the strike price
3. for up to 9 months, depending on the expiration date of the option.

Purchasing a put gives you the right to sell stock at a set price. You buy a put if you expect a stock price to fall. You have the chance to earn a considerable gain from a minimal investment, but you lose the whole investment if price depreciation does not materialize.

The buyer of the contract (called the "holder") pays the seller (called the "writer") a premium for the contract. In return for the premium, the buyer obtains the right to buy securities from the writer or sell securities to the writer at a fixed price over a stated period of time.

Option Holder = Option Buyer = Long Position

Option Writer = Option Seller = Short Position

	Call Option	*Put Option*
Buy (long)	The right to call (buy) from the writer	The right to put (sell) from the writer
Sell (short)	Known as *writing a call,* being obligated to sell if called	Known as *writing a put,* if the stock or contract is put

Calls and puts are typically for widely held and actively traded securities on organized exchanges. With calls there are no voting privileges, ownership interest, or dividend income. However, option contracts are adjusted for stock splits and stock dividends.

Calls and puts are not issued by the company with the common stock but rather by option makers or option writers. The maker of the option receives the price paid for the call or put minus commission costs. The option trades on the open market. Calls and puts are written and can be acquired through brokers and dealers. The writer is required to purchase or deliver the stock when requested.

Holders of calls and puts do not have to exercise them to earn a return. They can trade them in the secondary market for whatever their value is. The value of a call increases as the underlying common stock goes up in price. The call can be sold on the market before its expiration date.

WHY INVESTORS USE OPTIONS

Why use options? Reasons can vary from the conservative to the speculative. The most common reasons are:

1. You can earn large profits with *leverage,* that is, without having to tie up a lot of your own money. The leverage you can have with options typically runs 20:1 (each investor dollar controls the profit on twenty dollars of stock) as contrasted with the 2:1 leverage with stocks bought on margin or the 1:1 leverage with stocks bought outright with cash. *Note:* Leverage is a two-edge sword. It works both ways. You can lose a lot, too. That is why it is a risk, derivative instrument.

2. Options may be purchased as "insurance or hedge" against large price drops in underlying stocks already held by the investor.

3. If you are neutral or slightly bullish in the short term on stocks you own you can sell (or write) options on those stocks and realize extra profit.

4. Options offer a range of strategies that cannot be obtained with stocks. Thus, options are a flexible and complementary investment vehicle to stocks and bonds.

HOW OPTIONS ARE TRADED

Options are traded on listed option exchanges (secondary markets) such as *the Chicago Board Options Exchange, American Stock Exchange, Philadelphia Stock Exchange, and Pacific Stock Exchange.* They may also be exchanged in the *over-the counter (OTC)* market. Option exchanges are only for buying and selling call and put options. Listed options are traded on organized exchanges. Conventional options are traded in the OTC market.

The *Options Clearing Corporation (OCC)* acts as principal in every options transaction for listed options contracts. As principal it issues all listed options, guarantees the contracts, and is the legal entity on the other side of every transaction. Orders are placed with this corporation, which then issues the calls or closes the position. Since certificates are not issued for options, a brokerage account is required. When an investor exercises a call, he goes through the Clearing Corporation, which randomly selects a writer from a member list. A call writer is obligated to sell 100 shares at the exercise price.

Exchanges permit general orders (i.e., limit) and orders applicable only to the option (i.e., spread order).

TERMS OF AN OPTION

There are three key terms you need to be familiar with in connection with options: the exercise or strike price, expiration date, and option premium. The *exercise price* is the price per share for 100 shares, which you may buy at (call). For a put, it is the price at which the stock may be sold. The purchase or sale of the stock is to the writer of the option. The striking price is set for the life of the option on the options exchange. When stock price changes, new exercise prices are introduced for trading purposes reflecting the new value.

In case of conventional calls, restrictions do not exist on what the striking price should be. However, it is usually close to the market price of the stock it relates to. But in the case of listed calls, stocks having a price lower than $50 a share must have striking prices in $5 increments. Stocks between $50 and $100 have striking prices in $20 increments. Striking prices are adjusted for material stock splits and stock dividends.

The *expiration date* of an option is the last day it can be exercised. For conventional options, the expiration date can be any business day; for a listed option there is a standardized expiration date.

The cost of an option is referred to as a *premium*. It is the price the buyer of the call or put has to pay the seller (writer). In other words, the option premium is what an option costs to you as a buyer. *Note:* With other securities, the premium is the excess of the purchase price over a determined theoretical value.

USING PROFIT DIAGRAMS

In order to understand the risks and rewards associated with various option strategies, it is very helpful to understand how the profit diagram works. In fact, it is essential to understanding how an option works. The profit diagram is a visual portrayal of your profit in relation to the price of a stock at a single point in time.

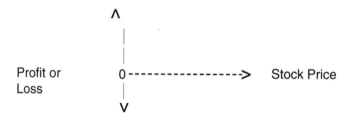

Example 2.

IBM Stock Price in 3 months	Profit (Loss)
$ 60	-$2000
$ 70	-$1000
$ 80	$ 0
$ 90	$1000
$ 100	$2000

The following shows the profit diagram for 100 shares of IBM stock if you bought them today at $80 per share and sold them in 3 months. (Commissions are ignored in this example.)

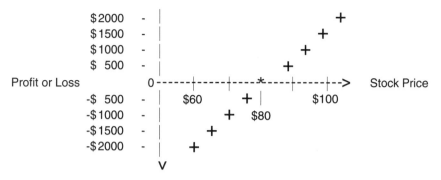

```
  $2000  - |                              +
  $1500  - |                          +
  $1000  - |                      +
  $ 500  - |                  +
Profit or Loss   0 -----+-----+----*----+-----+-->   Stock Price
  -$ 500  - |  $60      +  |         $100
  -$1000  - |         +   $80
  -$1500  - |      +
  -$2000  - |   +
            V
```

Note that all stocks have the same shape on the profit diagram at any point in the future. You will later see that this is *not* the case with options.

Example 3. Assume that on April 7, you become convinced that IBM stock which is trading at $80 a share will move considerably higher in the next few months. So, you buy one call option on IBM stock with a premium of $2 a share. Since the call option involves a block of 100 shares of stock, it costs you a total of $2 times 100 shares or $200. Assume further that this call option has a striking price of $85 and an expiration date near the end of September. What this means is that for $200 you have the right to buy:

1. 100 shares of IBM stock
2. at $85 a share
3. until near the end of September.

This may not sound like you're getting much for $200, but if IBM stock goes up to $95 a share by the end of September, you'd have the right to purchase 100 shares of IBM stock for $8500 ($85 times 100 shares) and to turn right around and sell them for $9500, keeping the difference of $1000, an $800 profit. That works out to 400% profit in less than five months.

However, if you are wrong and IBM stock goes down in price, the most you could lose would be the price of the option, $200. The following displays the profit table for this example.

If the IBM stock price in Sep. turns out to be:		The value of the call option would be:		And your profit would be:
$ 75	---->	$ 0	---->	-$ 200
$ 80		$ 0		-$ 200
$ 85		$ 0		-$ 200
$ 87		$ 200		$ 0
$ 90		$ 500		$ 300
$ 95		$1000		$ 800

The profit diagram will look like this:

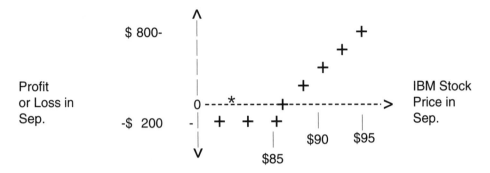

You are "long 1 IBM Sep 85 call" option.

Notice where the profit line bends—at $85, unlike stocks that have the same shape on the profit diagram at any point in the future. This is *not* the case with options. You start making money after the price of IBM stock goes higher than the $85 striking price of the call option. When this happens, the option is called "in-the-money."

On the other hand, the profit diagram for a put option looks like this:

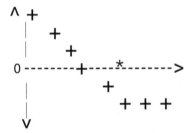

So, a put is typically used by an investor who is bearish on that particular stock. The put option can also be used as "insurance" against price drops for the investor with a long stock position.

OPTION COSTS

The premium for an option (or cost of an option) depends primarily on:

- Fluctuation in price of the underlying security. (A higher variability means a higher premium because of the greater speculative appeal of the option.)
- Time period remaining before the option's expiration. (The more time there is until the expiration, the greater the premium you must pay the seller.)

Financial Derivative Products and Financial Engineering

- Price spread between the stock compared to the option's strike price. (A wider difference translates to a higher price.)

Example 4. ABC stock is selling at $32 a share today. Consider two options: 1. Option X gives you the right to buy the stock at $25 per share and (2) Option Y gives you the right to buy the stock at $40 per share. Since you would rather have an option to pay $25 for a $32 stock instead of $32, Option X is more valuable than Option Y. Thus, it will cost you more to buy Option X than to buy Option Y.

Other factors that determine the cost of an option are:

- The dividend trend of the underlying security
- The volume of trading in the option
- The exchange the option is listed on
- "Going" interest rates
- The market price of the underlying stock

In-the-Money and Out-of-the-Money Call Options

Options may or may not be exercised, depending on the difference between the market price of the stock and the exercise price.

Let P = the price of the underlying stock

and S = the exercise price

There are three possible situations:

1. If $P > X$ or $P - X > 0$, then the call option is said to be *in the money*. (By exercising the call option, you, as a holder, realize a positive profit, $P - X$)

The value of the call in this case is:

Value of call = (market price of stock − exercise price of call) × 100

Example 5. Assume that the market price of a stock is $90, with a strike price of $80. The call has a value of $1,000.

2. If $P - X = 0$, then the option is said to be *at the money*.

3. If $P - X < 0$, then the option is said to be *out of the money*. It is unprofitable. The option holder can purchase the stock at the cheaper price in the market rather than exercising the option and thus the option is thrown away. Out-of-the-money call options have no intrinsic value.

If the total premium (option price) of an option is $14 and the intrinsic value is $6, there is an additional premium of $8 arising from other factors.

Total premium is comprised of the intrinsic value and speculative premium (time value) based on variables like risk, expected future prices, maturity, leverage, dividend, and fluctuation in price.

Total premium = intrinsic value + speculative premium (time value)

1. Intrinsic value = In the money option
i.e., $P - S > 0$ for a call and $S - P > 0$ for a put option
2. Time value—For in the money options, time value is the difference between premium and intrinsic value. For other options all value is time value.

Call option		Put option	
$		$	
:	Intrinsic value	:	
:		:	
:		:	
:		:	Intrinsic value
:		:	
:		:	
:		:	
:	Time value	:	Time value
:_____P		:_____P	
S		S	

In-the-Money and Out-of-the-Money Put Options

A put option on a common stock allows the holder of the option to sell ("put") a share of the underlying stock at an exercise price until an expiration date. The definition of in-the-money and out-of-the-money are different for puts since the owner may sell stock at the strike price. For a put option, the option is in the money if $P - X < 0$.

Its value is determined as follows:

Value of put = (exercise price of put − market price of stock) × 100

And the option is out of the money when $P - X > 0$ and has no value.

Example 6. Assume a stock has a market price of $100 and a strike price of the put is $116. The value of the put is $1,600.

If market price of stock exceeds strike price, an out-of-the money put exists. Because a stock owner can sell it for a greater amount in the market relative to exercising the put, no intrinsic value exists of the out-of-money put.

	ABC Calls at 60 Strike Price Stock Price	ABC Puts at 60 Strike Price Stock Price
In-the-money	Over 60	Under 60
At-the-money	60	60
Out-of-the-money	Under 60	Over 60

The theoretical value for calls and puts reflects the price the options should be traded. But usually they are traded at prices exceeding true value when options have a long period to go. This difference is referred to as investment premium.

$$\text{Investment premium} = \frac{\text{option premium} - \text{option value}}{\text{option value}}$$

Example 7. Assume a put with a theoretical value of $2,500 and a price of $3,000. It is therefore traded at an investment premium of 20% [($3,000 − $2,500)/$2,500].

THE RISKS AND REWARDS OF OPTIONS

Your risk in buying options is limited to the premium you paid. That is the downside risk for option investing. For example, assume you own a two-month call option to acquire 500 shares of ABC Company at $20 per share. Within that time period, you exercise the option when the market price is $38. You make a gain of $9,000 ($18 × 500 shares) except for the brokerage commission. Of course, the higher the stock's price goes, the more you can profit. However, if the market price had declined from $20 you would not have exercised the call option, and you would have lost the cost of the option. *Note:* If you owned the stock whose price fell $10 per share, you would have lost $10 a share. But if you had an option to buy that stock, you could have lost only the cost (premium) of that option, no matter how far the stock price fell.

How Do Calls Work?

By buying a call you can own common stock for a low percentage of the cost of buying regular shares. Leverage is obtained since a small change in common stock price can magnify a major move in the call option's price. An element of the percentage gain in the price of the call is the speculative premium related to the remaining time left on the call. Calls can also be viewed as a way of controlling 100 shares of stock without a large monetary commitment.

Example 8. Assume that a security has a present market price of $70. A call can be bought for $600 permitting the purchase of 100 shares at $70 per share. If stock price goes up, the call increases in value. Assume the stock goes to $95 at the call's expiration date. The profit is $25 per share in the call, or a total of $2,500 on an investment of $600. There is a return of 417%. When you exercise the call for 100 shares at $70 each, you can immediately sell them at $95 per share.

Note: You could have earned the same amount by investing directly in the common stock. However, you would have needed to invest $7,000 resulting in a much lower return rate.

How Do Puts Work?

The put holder may sell 100 shares at the exercise price for a specified time period to a put writer. A put is bought when a price decline is expected. Like a call option, the entire premium cost (investment) would be lost if the price does not drop.

Example 9. Assume that a stock has a market price of $80. You buy a put to sell 100 shares of stock at $80 per share. The put cost is $500. At the exercise date, the price of the stock goes to $70 a share. The profit is $10 per share, or $1,000. You just buy on the market 100 shares at $70 each and then sell them to the writer of the put for $80 each. The net gain is $500 ($1,000 − $500).

The following tables summarize payoffs, risks, and breakeven stock prices for various option participants.

Option Payoffs and Risks

	Call buyer	Call seller (writer)
Pay-off	$-c + (P - S)$ where c = the call premium For a break-even, $-c + (P - S) = 0$ or $P = S + c$.	$+c - (P - S)$
Risk	Maximum risk is to lose the premium because investor	No risk limit as the stock price rises above

	throws away the out-of-money option	the exercise price— Uncovered (naked) option
		To be covered, investor should own the underlying stock or hold a long call on the same stock

	Put buyer	Put seller (writer)
Pay-off	$-c + (S - P)$ where c = the put premium For a breakeven, $-c + (S - P)$ $= 0$ or $P = S - c$	$+c - (S - P)$
Risk	Maximum risk is to lose the premium	Maximum risk is the strike price when the stock price is zero— Uncovered (naked) To be covered, investor should sell the underlying stock short or hold a long put on the same stock

Breakeven Points for Option Parties

Option parties	Breakeven market price
A call-holder	the strike price + the premium
A put-holder	the strike price – the premium
A call-writer	the strike price + the premium
A put-writer	the strike price – the premium
A covered call-writer	the original cost of the security – the premium
A covered put-writer	the strike price + the premium (short the stock)

CALL AND PUT INVESTMENT STRATEGIES YOU MAY USE

Investment possibilities with calls and puts include (1) hedging, (2) specula-tion, (3) straddles, and (4) spreads. If you own call and put options, you can *hedge* by holding two or more securities to reduce risk and earn a profit. You may purchase a stock and subsequently buy an option on it. For instance, you may buy a stock and write a call on it. Further, if you own a stock that has appreciated you may buy a put to insulate from downside risk.

Example 10. You bought 100 shares of XYZ at $52 per share and a put for $300 on the 100 shares at an exercise price of $52. If the stock does not move, you lose $300 on the put. If the price falls, your loss offsets your gain on the put. If stock price goes up, you have a capital gain on the stock but lose your investment in the put. To obtain the advantage of a hedge, you incur a loss on the put. Note that at the expiration date, you have a loss with no hedge any longer.

You may employ calls and puts to *speculate*. You may buy options when you believe you will make a higher return compared to investing in the underlying stock. You can earn a higher return at lower risk with out-of-the-money options. However, with such an option, the price is composed just of the investment premium, which may be lost if the stock does not increase in price.

Here is an example of this kind of speculation.

Example 11. You speculate by buying an option contract to purchase 100 shares at $55 a share. The option costs $250. The stock price increases to $63 a share. You exercise the option and sell the shares in the market, recognizing a gain of $550 ($63 − $55 − $2.50 = $5.50 × 100 shares). You, as a speculator, can sell the option and earn a profit due to the appreciated value. But if stock price drops, your loss is limited to $250 (the option's cost). Obviously, there will also be commissions. In sum, this call option allowed you to buy 100 shares worth $5,500 for $250 up to the option's expiration date.

Straddling combines a put and call on the identical security with the same strike price and expiration date. It allows you to trade on both sides of the market. You hope for a substantial change in stock price either way so as to earn a gain exceeding the cost of both options. If the price change does materialize, the loss is the cost of the both options. You may increase risk and earning potential by closing one option prior to the other.

Example 12. You buy a call and put for $8 each on October 31 when the stock price is $82. There is a three-month expiration date. Your investment is $16, or $1,600 in total. If the stock increases to $150 at expiration of the options, the call generates a profit of $60 ($68 − $8) and the loss on the put is $8. Your net gain is $52, or $5,200 in total.

In a *spread,* you buy a call option (long position) and write a call option (short position) in the identical stock. A sophisticated investor may write many spreads to profit from the spread in option premiums. There is substantial return potential but high risk. Different kinds of spreads exist such as a *bull call spread* (two call's having the same expiration date) and *horizontal spread* (initiated with either two call options or two put options on the identical underlying stock). These two options must be with the same strike price but different expiration dates.

You may purchase straddles and spreads to maximize return or reduce risk. You may buy them through dealers belonging to the *Put and Call Brokers and Dealers Association.*

HOW OPTION WRITING WORKS

The writer of a call contracts to sell shares at the strike price for the price incurred for the call option. Call option writers do the opposite of buyers. Investors write options expecting price appreciation in the stock to be less than what the call buyer anticipates. They may even anticipate the price of the stock to be stable or decrease. Option writers receive the option premium less applied transaction costs. If the option is not exercised, the writer earns the price he paid for it. If the option is exercised, the writer incurs a loss, possibly significant.

If the writer of an option elects to sell, he must give the stock at the contracted price if the option is exercised. In either instance, the option writer receives income from the premium. (Shares are in denominations of 100.) An investor typically sells an option when he anticipates it not to be exercised. The risk of option writing is that the writer, if uncovered, must purchase stock or, if covered, loses the gain. As the writer, you can purchase back an option to end your exposure.

Example 13. Assume a strike price of $50 and a premium for the call option of $7. If the stock is below $50, the call would not be exercised, and you earn the $7 premium. If the stock is above $50, the call may be exercised, and you must furnish 100 shares at $50. But the call writer loses money if the stock price was above $57.

SELLING AN OPTION ON SOMETHING YOU DON'T OWN

Naked (uncovered) and *covered* options exist. Naked options are on stock the writer does not own. There is much risk because you have to buy the stock and then immediately sell it to the option buyer on demand, irrespective of how much you lose. The investor writes the call or put for the premium and will retain it if the price change is beneficial to him or insignificant. The writer has unlimited loss possibilities.

To eliminate this risk, you may write *covered options* (options written on stocks you own). For instance, a call can be written for stock the writer owns or a put can be written for stock sold short. This is a conservative strategy to generate positive returns. The objective is to write an out-of-the-money option, retain the premium paid, and have the stock price equal but not exceed the option exercise price. The writing of a covered call option is like hedging a position because if stock price drops, the writer's loss on the security is partly offset against the option premium.

OPTION STRATEGIES

Currently, about 90% of the option strategies implemented by investors are long call's and long put's only. These are the most basic strategies and are the easiest to implement. However, they are usually the riskiest in terms of a traditional measure of risk: variability (uncertainty) of outcomes. A variety of other strategies can offer better returns at less risk.

(1) *Long Call*
   This strategy is implemented simply by purchasing a call option on a stock. This strategy is good for a very bullish stock assessment.

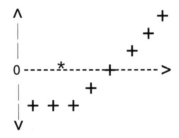

(2) *Bull Call Spread*
   This strategy requires two call's, both with the same expiration date. It is good for a mildly bullish assessment of the underlying stock.

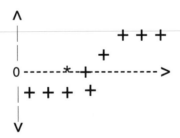

(3) *Naked Put Write*
   This strategy is implemented by writing a put and is appropriate for a neutral or mildly bullish projection on the underlying stock.

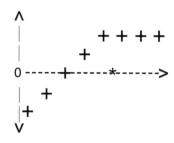

(4) Covered Call Write

This strategy is equivalent to the *naked put write*. This strategy is good as a neutral or mildly bullish assessment of the underlying stock.

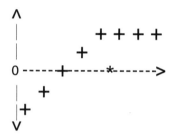

(5) Straddle

This strategy is implemented by purchasing both a call and a put option on the same underlying stock. This strategy is good when the underlying stock is likely to make a big move but there is uncertainty as to its direction.

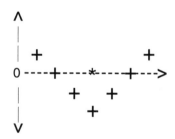

(6) Inverse Straddle

This strategy is implemented by writing both a call and a put on the same underlying stock. This strategy is appropriate for a neutral assessment of the underlying stock. A substantial amount of collateral is required for this strategy due to the open-ended risk should the underlying stock make a big move.

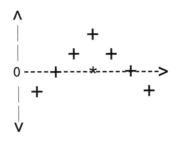

(7) Horizontal Spread

This strategy is implemented with either two call options or two put options on the same underlying stock. These two options must have the same striking price but have different expiration dates.

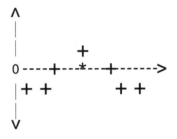

(8) Naked Call Write

This strategy is implemented by writing a call and is appropriate for a neutral or mildly bearish assessment on the underlying stock. A substantial amount of collateral is required for this strategy due to the open-ended risk should the underlying stock rise in value.

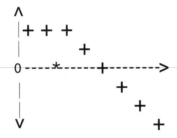

(9) Bear Put Spread

This strategy is the opposite of the bull call spread. It is implemented with two put's, both with the same expiration date. This strategy is appropriate for a mildly bearish assessment of the underlying stock.

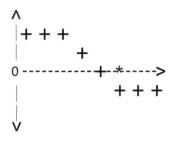

(10) *Long Put*

This strategy is implemented simply by purchasing a put option on a stock. It is good for a very bearish stock assessment.

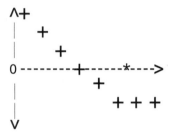

Note: Computer software such as *OptionVue* plots profit tables and diagrams and helps you evaluate large numbers of options for minimum risk and maximum reward.

HOW TO CHOOSE AN OPTION STRATEGY

The key question remains: Which option strategy should you choose? What factors should you consider? What would be a typical decision process? There are three major steps in the decision process:

(1) *Select the underlying stock*

First, you should decide which stock to consider and do a thorough analysis on the stock, including the effects of current market trends.

(2) *Choose the strategy*

You then determine the risk involved in the stock based on its volatility. Computer software can be of great help. Based on the assessment on the stock (bullish or bearish) and its volatility, a strategy is chosen. For example, a strongly bullish, high volatility stock would indicate a long call strategy since the underlying stock is likely to rise a substantial amount.

The ranking of strategies so far discussed, from bullish to bearish, is as follows:

Bullish	• Long Call • Bull Call Spread • Naked Put Write (Covered Call Write)
Neutral	• Straddle • Inverse Straddle • Horizontal Spread
Bearish	• Naked Call Write • Bear Put Spread • Long Put

Note: The key to choosing the specific option contracts to implement a strategy is to accurately forecast both the price of the underlying stock and the amount of time it will take to get to that price. This will facilitate choosing the striking price and expiration date of the options to be used.

(3) *Assess the risk*

Option strategies have some interesting risk/reward tradeoffs. Some strategies have a small chance of a very large profit while other strategies have a large chance of making a small profit.

You have to decide exactly how much to risk for how much reward.

INDEX OPTIONS

Options on stock indexes rather than on individual stocks have been popular among investors. Index options include ones on S&P 100, S&P OTC 250, S&P 500, Gold/Silver Index, and Computer Technology Index.

Index options offer advantages over stock options in several ways:

1. There is greater stability in a stock index due to *diversification.* Since an index is a composite of stocks, the effects of mergers, announcements, and reports are much milder in an index than with an individual stock.

2. Index options provide a wider selection of striking prices and expiration dates than stock options.

3. It appears easier to predict the behavior of the market than an individual stock.

4. More liquidity exists with index options. Due to the high volume of activity, it is easier to buy and sell index options for the price you want. This is especially helpful for far out-of-the-money or deep in-the-money options.

5. Index options are always settled in cash, never in shares of the underlying stock. This settlement is automatic at expiration and the cash settlement prevents unintended stock assignment.

A disadvantage of index options is that no covered writing is possible on index options.

SOFTWARE FOR OPTIONS ANALYSIS

The Value Line Options Survey (800-535-9643 ext. 2854-Dept. 414M10) recommends the few dozen buying and covered writing candidates (out of more than 10,000 options listed on the several exchanges), based on their computerized model.

The following is a list of popular options software:

Stock Option Analysis Program and Stock Options Scanner (DOS)
H&H Scientific, (301) 292-2958

An Option Valuator/An Option Writer (DOS)
Revenge Software, (516) 271-9556

Strategist (DOS)
Iotinomics Corp., (800) 255-3374 or (801) 466-2111

Advanced Stock Option Analyzer (DOS, Mac)
Option-80, (508) 369-1589

Optionvue IV (DOS)
Optionvue Systems International, Inc.,
(800) 733-6610 or (708) 816-6610

Option Pro (Windows)
Essex Trading Co., (800) 726-2140 or (708) 416-3530

Options and Arbitrage Software Package (DOS)
Programmed Press, (516) 599-6527

THE BLACK-SCHOLES OPTION PRICING MODEL (OPM)

The model provides the relationship between call option value and the five factors that determine the premium of an option's market value over its expiration value:

1. **Time to maturity.** The longer the option period, the greater the value of the option.
2. **Stock price volatility.** The greater the volatility of the underlying stock's price, the greater its value.
3. **Exercise price.** The lower the exercise price, the greater the value.
4. **Stock price.** The higher the price of the underlying stock, the greater the value.
5. **Risk-free rate.** The higher the risk-free rate, the higher the value.

The formula is:

$$V = P[N(d_1)] - Xe^{-rt}[N(d_2)]$$

where

V = current value of a call option

P = current price of the underlying stock

$N(d)$ = cumulative normal probability density function = probability that a deviation less than d will occur in a standard normal distribution.

X = exercise or strike price of the option

t = time to exercise date (For example, 3 months means t = 3/12 = 1/4 = 0.25)

r = (continuously compounded) risk-free rate of interest

e = 2.71828

$$d_1 = \frac{\ln(P/X) + [r + s^2/2]t}{s\sqrt{t}}$$

$$d_2 = \frac{\ln(P/X) + [r + s^2/2]t}{s\sqrt{t}} \ \text{or} = d_1 - s\sqrt{t}$$

s^2 = variance per period of (continuously compounded) rate of return on the stock

The formula, while somewhat imposing, actually requires readily available input data, with the exception of s^2, or volatility. P, X, r, and t are easily obtained. The implications of the option model are the following:

1. The value of the option increases with the level of stock price relative to the exercise price (P/X), the time to expiration times the interest rate (rt), and the time to expiration times the stock's variability (s^2t).
2. Other properties:

Financial Derivative Products and Financial Engineering

a. The option price is always less than the stock price.

b. The optional price never falls below the payoff to immediate exercise (P − EX or zero, whichever is larger).

c. If the stock is worthless, the option is worthless.

d. As the stock price becomes very large, the option price approaches the stock price less the present value of the exercise price.

Example 14. You are evaluating a call option which has a $20 exercise price and sells for $1.60. It has three months to expiration. The underlying stock price is also $20 and its variance is 0.16. The risk-free rate is 12 percent. The option's value is:

First, calculate d_1 and d_2:

$$d_1 = \frac{\ln(P/X) + [r + s^2/2]t}{s\sqrt{t}}$$

$$= \frac{\ln(\$20/\$20) + [0.12 + (0.16/2)](0.25)}{(0.40)\sqrt{0.25}}$$

$$= \frac{0 + 0.05}{0.20} = 0.25$$

$$d_2 = d_1 - s\sqrt{t} = 0.25 - 0.20 = 0.05$$

Next, look up the values for $N(d_1)$ and $N(d_2)$:

$$N(d_1) = N(0.25) = 1 - 0.4013 = 0.5987$$
$$N(d_2) = N(0.05) = 1 - 0.4801 = 0.5199$$

Finally, use those values to find the option's value:

$$V = P[N(d_1)] - Xe^{-rt}[N(d_2)]$$
$$= \$20[0.5987] - \$20e^{(-0.12)(0.25)}[0.5199]$$
$$= \$11.97 - \$19.41(0.5199)$$
$$= \$11.97 - \$10.09 = \$1.88$$

At $1.60, the option is undervalued according to the Black-Scholes model. The rational investor would buy one option and sell .5987 shares of stock short.

    Note: Under FASB Statement No. 123, *Accounting for Stock-Based Compensation,* companies are required to provide new footnote disclosures about employee stock options based on their fair value at the date of the grant. Since options granted to employees generally are not traded on an organized exchange, Statement No. 123 requires companies to use recognized option pricing models such as the Black-Scholes model to estimate the fair values.

FUTURES CONTRACTS

Futures is another derivative instrument. A futures is a contract to purchase or sell a given amount of an item for a given price by a certain date in the future (thus the name "futures market"). The seller of a futures contract agrees to deliver the item to the buyer of the contract, who agrees to purchase the item. The contract specifies the amount, valuation, method, quality, month, and means of delivery, and exchange to be traded in. The month of delivery is the expiration date; in other words, the date on which the commodity or financial instrument must be delivered.

Commodity contracts are guarantees by a seller to deliver a commodity (e.g., cocoa or cotton). Financial contracts are a commitment by the seller to deliver a financial instrument (e.g., a Treasury bill) or a specific amount of foreign currency.

What Is the Difference Between a Long and Short Position?

A long position is the purchase of a contract expecting the price to increase. A short position is selling expecting price to decrease. The position may be terminated by reversing the transaction. For example, the long buyer can subsequently engage in a short position of the commodity or financial instrument. Mostly all futures are offset (canceled out) prior to delivery. It is unusual for delivery to settle the futures contract.

How Are Futures Contracts Traded?

A futures contract is traded in the futures market. Trading is performed by specialized brokers. Some commodity firms deal exclusively in futures. The fee for a futures contract is tied to the amount of the contract and the item's price. Commissions vary depending on the amount and nature of the contract. The trading in futures is basically the same as with stocks, except the investor needs a commodity trading account. However, the margin buying and the types of orders are the same. You buy or sell contracts with desired terms.

FUTURES TRADING AND RISK

Futures trading may assist an investor handling inflation but is specialized with much risk. Your loss may be magnified due to *leverage*. Leverage (using of other people's money) means with minimal down payment you control something of much greater value. For instance, you can put down $2,000 to control a futures contract valued at $40,000. Each time the price of a commodity increases $1 you could earn or lose $20. With an *option*, you just lose the money invested. With a futures contract, you lose a lot more. Further, futures contract prices may be very unstable. However, many exchanges place per day price limits on each contract trading to insulate traders from huge losses.

COMMODITIES FUTURES

A commodity contract involves a seller who contracts to deliver a commodity by a specified date at a set price. The contract stipulates the item, price, expiration date, and standardized unit to be traded (e.g., 100,000 pounds). Commodity contracts may last up to one year. You must always appraise the impact of market activity on the contract's value.

Assume that you purchase a futures contract for the delivery of 2,000 units of a commodity six months from now at $5.00 per unit. The seller of the contract does not have to have physical custody of the item, and the contract buyer does not have to take possession of the commodity at the "deliver" date. Commodity contracts are typically reversed, or terminated, before consummation. For example, as the initial buyer of 5,000 bushels of wheat, you may engage in a similar contract to sell the same amount, in effect closing your position.

You may enter into commodity trading to achieve high return rates and hedge inflation. In times of increasing prices, commodities react favorably because they are tied to economic trends. However, there is high risk and uncertainty since commodity prices fluctuate and there is a lot of low-margin investing. You need a lot of cash in case of a margin call to cover losses. To minimize risk, hold a diversified portfolio. Futures contracts are only for knowledgeable and experienced investors.

The buyer of a commodity can opt to terminate the contract or continue holding on expectation of higher profits. Conversely, the investor may use the earnings to furnish margin on another futures contract (called an inverse pyramid in a futures contract).

Commodity futures enable buyers and sellers to negotiate cash (spot) prices. Cash is paid to immediately obtain custody of a commodity. Prices in the cash market depend partly upon prices in the futures market. There may be higher prices for the commodity over time, taking into account carrying costs and expected inflation.

Commodity futures are traded in the *Chicago Board of Trade (CBOT),* the largest exchange. There are other exchanges specializing in particular commodities such as *the New York Cotton Exchange (NCTN), Chicago Mercantile Exchange (CME),* and *Kansas City Board of Trade (KBOT).* Because of the possibility of substantial gains and losses in commodities, exchanges have caps on the highest daily price changes for a commodity. *The Federal Commodity Futures Trading Commission* regulates commodities exchanges. Commodity futures trading is accomplished through open outcry auction.

RETURNS AND RISKS FOR FUTURES CONTRACTS

The return on a futures contract stems from capital appreciation (selling price less acquisition cost) because no current income is earned. Significant capital gain may arise from price fluctuation in the commodity and the impact of leverage due to low margin. If things go against you, much of your investment may be lost. The return on investment in commodities (a long or short position) equals:

$$\text{Return on investment} = \frac{\text{Selling price} - \text{purchase price}}{\text{Margin deposit}}$$

Example 15. Assume you buy a contract on a commodity for $80,000, with a deposit of $10,000. Subsequently, you sell the contract for $85,000. The return is:

$$\frac{\$85,000 - \$80,000}{\$10,000} = 50\%$$

The margin requirement for commodity contracts is small, typically from 3% to 6% of the contract's value. (For stocks, recall that the margin requirement was 50%). Because in commodities trading there is no loan involved, there is no interest.

An *initial margin* deposit must be made on a futures contract so as to cover a drop in market price on the contract. Such deposit varies with the type of contract and the particular commodity exchange.

A *maintenance deposit* may also be required, which is lower than the initial deposit. It furnishes the minimum margin that must be kept in the account. It is typically about 80% of the initial margin.

Example 16. On September 1, you contract to purchase 50,000 pounds of sugar at $2 a pound to be delivered by December 31. The value of the total contract is $100,000. The initial margin requirement is 15%, or $15,000. The margin maintenance requirement is 80%, or $12,000. Assuming a contract loss of $2,500, you must pay $2,500 to cover the margin position. If not, the contract will be terminated with the ensuing loss.

WHO USES FUTURES?

Trading in futures is performed by hedgers and speculators. Investors employ hedging to protect their position in a commodity. For instance, a farmer (the seller) may hedge to obtain a higher price for his goods while a processor (or buyer) of the product will hedge to get a lower price. By hedging you reduce the risk of loss but forego earning a sizable profit.

Example 17. A commodity is presently selling at $160 a pound. The potential buyer (assume a manufacturer) anticipates the price to increase. To protect against higher prices, the purchaser buys a futures contract selling at $175 a pound. Five months later, the commodity price is $225. The futures contract price will similarly increase to say, $250. The buyer's profit is $75 a pound. If 10,000 pounds are involved, the total profit is $750,000. However, the cost on the market rose by only $65 pound, or $650,000. The producer has hedged his position, deriving a profit of $100,000, and has put a tip on the rising commodity costs.

Commodities may also be used for speculation in the market. Speculators engage in futures contracts to obtain capital gain on price increases of the commodity, currency, or financial instrument.

Example 18. You buy a September futures contract for 20,000 pounds of wheat at $2 a pound. If the price rises to $2.20, you'll gain $.20 a pound for a total gain of $4,000. The percent gain, assuming an initial margin requirement of 5%, is 200% ($.2/$.1). Assuming transactions occur over a three-month period, the annual gain would be 800% (200% × 12 months/3 months). This resulted from a mere 10% ($.2/$2.00) gain in the price of a pound of wheat.

HOW TO MINIMIZE RISKS

Spreading capitalizes on wide swings in price and at the same time limits loss exposure. Spreading is like stock option trading. You engage in at least two contracts to earn some profit while capping loss potential. You buy one contract and sell the other expecting to achieve a reasonable profit. If the worst occurs, the spread aids in minimizing the investor's loss.

Example 19. You buy Contract A for 20,000 pounds of commodity T at $300 a pound. Simultaneously, you sell short Contract B for 20,000 pounds of the identical commodity at $325 per pound. Later, you sell Contract A for $325 a pound and buy Contract B for $345 a pound. Contract A earns a profit of $25 a pound while Contract B has a loss of $20 a pound. The net effect is a profit of $5 a pound, or a total gain of $100,000.

FINANCIAL FUTURES

Financial futures include: (1) interest rate; (2) foreign currency; and (3) stock-index. Financial futures trading is similar to commodity trading. It represents about 70 percent of all contracts. Due to fluctuation in interest and exchange rates, financial futures can be used as a hedge. They may also be used to speculate having potential for wide price swings. Financial futures have a *lower* margin requirement than commodities do. For instance, the margin on a U.S. Treasury bill might be as low as 2%.

Financial futures are traded in the *New York Futures Exchange, Amex Commodities Exchange, International Monetary Market* (part of *Chicago Mercantile Exchange*), and *the Chicago Board of Trade.*

How Do Interest Rate Futures Work?

An interest rate futures contract gives the holder the right to a specified amount of the underlying debt security at a later date (typically not exceeding three years). They may be in such forms as Treasury bills, notes, and bonds, paper, "Ginnie Mae (GNMA)" certificates, CRB Index, Eurodollars, and U.S. Dollar Index.

Interest rate futures are expressed as a percentage of the face value of the applicable debt security. The value of interest rate futures contracts is linked to interest rates. For instance, as interest rates drop, the contract's value rises. If the price or quote of the contract increases, the buyer gains but the seller loses. A change of one basis point in interest rates causes a price change. A basis point equals 1/100 of 1%.

Those trading in interest rate futures do not typically take custody of the financial instrument. The contract is employed either to hedge or to speculate on future interest rates and security prices.

How Do Currency Futures Work?

A *currency futures contract* provides the right to a stipulated amount of foreign currency at a later date. The contracts are standardized, and secondary markets exist. Currency futures are stated in dollars per unit of the underlying foreign currency. They usually have a delivery not exceeding one year.

Currency futures may be used to either hedge or speculate. Hedging in a currency may lock you into the best possible money exchange.

WHAT IS A STOCK INDEX FUTURE?

A *stock-index futures contract* is linked to a stock market index (e.g., *the S & P 500 Stock Index, New York Stock Exchange Composite Stock Index*). But smaller investors can use the *S & P 100* futures contract which has a lower margin deposit. Stock-index futures allow you to participate in the overall stock market. You can buy and sell the "market as a whole" instead of one security. If you expect a bull market but are not certain which stock will increase, you should purchase (long position) a stock-index future. Since there is a lot of risk, trade in stock-index futures only to hedge.

TRANSACTING IN FUTURES

You may invest directly in a commodity or indirectly through a *mutual fund*. A third way is to buy a *limited partnership* involved with commodity investments. The mutual fund and partnership approaches are more conservative, because risk is spread and there is professional management.

Futures may be directly invested in as follows:

1. *Commodity pools.* Professional traders manage a pool. A filing is made with the *Commodity Futures Trading Commission (CFTC).*
2. *Full service brokers.* They may recommend something, when attractive.
3. *Discount brokers.* You must decide on your own when and if.
4. *Managed futures.* You deposit funds in an individual managed account and choose a *commodity trading advisor (CTA)* to trade it.

To obtain information on managed futures, refer to:

1. *ATA Research Inc.* provides information on trading advisors and manages individuals accounts via private pools and funds.
2. *Barclay Trading Group* publishes quarterly reports on trading advisers.
3. *CMA Reports* monitors the performance of trading advisers and private pools.
4. *Management Account Reports,* monthly newsletters, tracking the funds and furnishes information on their fees and track records.
5. *Trading Advisor* follows more than 100 trading advisers.

There are several drawbacks to managed futures, including:

1. High cost of a futures program, ranging from 15 to 20 percent of the funds invested.

2. Substantial risk and inconsistent performance of fund advisors. *Note:* Despite its recent popularity, management futures is still a risky choice and should not be done apart from a well-diversified portfolio.

PRINTED CHART SERVICE AND SOFTWARE FOR FUTURES

There are many printed chart services such as *Future Charts* (Commodity Trend Service, (800) 331-1069 or (407) 694-0960). Also, there are many computer software for futures analysis and charting services, including:

Strategist (DOS)
Iotinomics Corp., (800) 255-3374 or (801) 466-2111

Futures Pro (Windows)
Essex Trading Co., (800) 726-2140 or (708) 416-3530

Futures Markets Analyzer (DOS)
Investment Tools, Inc., (702) 851-1157

Commodities and Futures Software Package, Foreign Exchange Software Package (DOS)
Programmed Press, (516) 599-6527

FINANCIAL ENGINEERING

Closely related to the use of financial derivatives for risk management is *financial engineering*. Financial engineering, an obscure term in finance and investments, is based on financial economics, or the application of economic principles to the dynamics of securities markets, especially for the purpose of structuring, pricing, and managing the risk of financial contracts. In designing a risk-management strategy, the financial engineer, like the civil engineer designing a bridge, works within budgetary and physical restrictions. How much will it cost? How will it perform under present and future tax and accounting regulations and rules? Will it survive a financial earthquake, such as an opposite party's default? Will the strategy perform even if the market moves abruptly and severely? Basically, to be successful, the financial engineer must seek optimal solutions within many diverse and often conflicting constraints.

These varied restrictions lead to different solutions. Financial engineers can design different types of financial instruments or strategies to produce a desired outcome. Robert C. Merton has presented a concrete example of the financial engineer's ability to develop alternative routes to the same end, all basically similar but each with its pros and cons (*Journal of Banking and Finance,* June 1995). For instance, assume a corporate investor wishes to take a leveraged position in the S&P 500 basket of American stocks. Merton lists and dwells on eleven ways of accomplishing that goal. The first three are conventional ways: borrowing to buy stocks.

1. Buying each stock individually on the margin
2. Borrowing to buy shares in a S&P 500 index fund
3. Borrowing to purchase a basket of stocks such as AMEX's SPDR product.

The next three are products in which traditional financial intermediaries act as principals and offer payoffs that closely emulate the leveraged stock position; the actual products are structured as bank CDs, indexed notes, or variable rate annuities. The last five categories of alternatives deal with buying so-called financial derivatives, such as futures, forwards, swaps, or one of two options on the S&P index. They are so called in that their payoffs are a function (or are derived from) the value of an underlying index.

Each of the eleven instruments or strategies can give the investor exposure to the stock market, and each produces functionally similar payoffs. The multitude of solutions exist due to the differing constraints facing the financial engineer. It is important to realize that as bridges often collapse, financial engineered products can fail and examining their wreckage to determine culpability is equally difficult.

Nevertheless, financial managers need to benchmark and keep abreast of their rivals' successful uses of financial engineering. CPAs need to be familiar with financial derivative products. The issuance of FASB 123, *Accounting for Stock-Based Compensation,* means CPAs who prepare and audit the financial statements of the companies that issue employee stock options will need to become familiar with option pricing models—including the Black-Scholes model. The new standard says the fair value of options at the date of the grant must be disclosed in a footnote.

Option theory has many applications addressed to CFOs and other financial officers. Besides the Black-Scholes solution for a relatively simple option, many capital budgeting projects have option components, corporate debt is callable or convertible, the decision to prepay a mortgage, labor contracts may endow options on workers (e.g., the choice of early retirement), real estate leases can be renewed, a mine can be opened or closed, and bank line of credits often contain contingent elements. The correct valuations of so many interest rate-contingent securities depend on a satisfactory dynamic model of the interest rate process.

HOW TAXES AFFECT BUSINESS DECISIONS

DIVIDENDS-RECEIVED DEDUCTION

The application of the general rule may be illustrated as follows:

Sales	$300,000
Dividend income received from a less than 20%-owned corporation	100,000
	400,000
Operating expenses	310,000
Tentative taxable income	90,000
Dividends-received deduction; limited to 70% of $90,000	63,000
Taxable income	$ 27,000

On the other hand, had the corporation sustained an operating loss of $90,000, the "70% of tentative taxable income limitation" would not be applicable; accordingly, the dividends-received deduction would be 70% of $100,000, or $70,000, effectively increasing the net operating loss to $160,000.

Further, the following example illustrates that the "70% of tentative taxable income limitation" does not apply if the corporation sustains a net operating loss after the dividends-received deduction:

Sales	$300,000
Dividend income received from a less than 20%-owned corporation	100,000
	400,000
Operating expenses	390,000
Tentative taxable income	10,000
Dividends-received deduction; 70% of $100,000	70,000
Net operating loss	$ (60,000)

Investment strategies should be carefully monitored in order to secure the benefits of the dividends-received deduction. The wrong investment vehicles could easily result in the loss of the desired tax benefit. For example, the following dividends are not eligible for the dividends-received deduction:

1. Dividends from mutual savings banks, which in essence represent interest on bank accounts.
2. Dividends derived from real estate investment trusts.
3. Capital gains dividends passed through from mutual funds.
4. Dividends from money market funds which invest solely in interest-paying securities.

It should also be noted that the dividends-received deduction is allowed only if the dividend-paying stock is held at least 46 days during the 90-day period that commences 45 days before the stock became ex-dividend with respect to the dividend.

CHARITABLE CONTRIBUTIONS

There is a typographical error in the next to the last sentence of the first paragraph on page 909 of the main text. The sentence should read as follows: "Corporations using the accrual method of accounting may deduct charitable contributions authorized by the board of directors but paid after year-end as long as payment is made within *2 1/2* months after year-end."

NET OPERATING LOSS DEDUCTIONS

Under the Taxpayer Relief Act of 1997 (TRA), with respect to net operating losses arising in tax years beginning after August 5, 1997, the carryback period is reduced to two years and the carryforward period is increased to twenty years.

DEPRECIATION

As indicated on page 911 of the main text, automobiles are included in a special category of property referred to as "listed property." It should be noted that the annual deduction for such autos is dependent upon the year in which the auto was placed into service, since the Internal Revenue Services issues applicable tables annually. The annual deduction for autos placed into service in 1997 are as follows:

Year	Allowable Deduction
1	$3,160
2	5,000
3	3,050
Each Year Thereafter	1,775

The annual deduction for autos places into service in 1998 are as follows:

Year	Allowable Deduction
1	$3,160
2	5,000
3	2,950
Each Year Thereafter	1,775

THE ALTERNATIVE MINIMUM TAX

If a corporation is deemed to be a small corporation, then it may not be subject to the alternative minimum tax. To be treated initially as a small corporation, the corporation's average annual gross receipts for the most recent three-year period beginning after 1994 must be less than $5,000,000. Treatment as a small corporation will be lost in a particular year if the entity's average gross receipts for the preceding three years is in excess of $7,500,000.

THE PERSONAL HOLDING COMPANY TAX

The personal holding company tax is imposed on "undistributed personal holding company income," which is taxable income with the following adjustments, minus the dividends paid deduction:

1. Deduction is allowed for federal and foreign income and excess profits taxes.
2. Deduction is allowed for excess charitable contributions; in lieu of the normal 10% limit, the deduction may be as high as 50% of taxable income.
3. Deduction is allowed for net long-term capital gain less related federal income taxes.
4. The dividends-received deduction is not allowed.
5. Other than a special one-year net operating loss carryover deduction, no deduction is allowed for a net operating loss.

As indicated in the main text (page 915), corporations may plan to mitigate the personal holding company tax by paying sufficient dividends to their stockholders. It should be noted that the deduction for dividends paid includes the following:

1. Dividends actually paid during the tax year.
2. Consent dividends, which represent amounts not actually paid out as dividends but that are includible in the shareholder's income because such an election was made by consenting shareholders on the last day of the corporation's tax year.
3. With certain limitations, "late paid" dividends. "Late paid" dividends are dividends paid after year-end, but no later than the 15th day of the third month of the following year. In order to claim the deduction for "late paid" dividends, a proper election must be made.

On page 914 of the main text, reference is made to the stock ownership test. It should be noted that for purposes of determining the five individuals, the rules of constructive ownership are applicable. Pursuant to the constructive ownership rules, stock owned, directly or indirectly, by or for a corporation, partnership, estate, or trust shall be considered as being owned proportionately by its shareholders, partners, or beneficiaries. Additionally, an individual shall be considered as owning the stock owned, directly, or indirectly, by or for his or her family or by or for his or her partner. Family, for this purpose, is limited to brothers, sisters, spouse, ancestors (i.e., grandparents) and lineal descendants (i.e., children and grandchildren).

CORPORATE REORGANIZATIONS

It is important to note that a stock redemption (which occurs when a corporation cancels or redeems its own stock) is *not* a corporate reorganization.

STOCK REDEMPTIONS

A stock redemption, which occurs when a corporation cancels or redeems its own stock, may afford shareholders beneficial tax treatment.

In general, a stockholder will recognize capital gain or loss in connection with a stock redemption if one of the following conditions is satisfied:

1. The redemption is not essentially equivalent to a dividend; i.e., the redemption results in a meaningful reduction in the shareholder's voting power, interest in the earnings and assets of the corporation, etc.

2. The redemption is substantially disproportionate; i.e., immediately after the redemption (a) the ratio of the shareholder's voting stock to the total outstanding voting stock is less than 80% of that ratio immediately before the redemption, and (b) the shareholder owns less than 50% of the corporation's outstanding voting stock.

3. The redemption results in the complete termination of the shareholder's interest.

4. The redemption is a redemption of a noncorporate shareholder's stock in partial liquidation of the corporation.

5. The redemption occurred in order to pay a decedent's death taxes and administrative expenses.

Distributions received in connection with redemptions not meeting one of the conditions above will be treated as dividends; accordingly, such distributions will be taxed as ordinary income.

CONTROLLED GROUP OF CORPORATIONS

There are two types of controlled groups of corporations.

The first type is known as a brother-sister controlled group. A brother-sister controlled group exists when (1) five or fewer persons (which may be individuals, estates or trusts) own at least 80% of the total voting stock (or value of shares) of each of two or more corporations, and (2) these same persons own more than 50% of the total voting power (or value of shares) of each corporation. It should be observed that a particular person's stock is to be considered only to the extent that it is owned identically with respect to each corporation.

The second type of controlled group is known as the parent-subsidiary group. (See the discussion on affiliated corporations.)

It is important to recognize the existence of either type of controlled groups of corporations. A controlled group of corporations must generally apportion the preferential tax bracket amounts (on page 912 of the main text) equally among all members of the group. However, a valid election may be made by all members of the group to an apportionment plan. For example, assuming Corporation A and Corporation B are brother-sister corporations. Corporations A and B may (1) apportion the first $50,000 of taxable income (subject to the preferential 15% tax rate) equally between themselves or (2) apportion the first $50,000 of taxable income between themselves in any manner that is most beneficial to the group. Under the latter election, if Company A sustained a net operating loss of $50,000 and Company B generated a $50,000 profit, it would probably by prudent to allocate the entire $50,000 tax bracket (subject to the preferential tax rate of 15%) to Company B.

Further, a controlled group of corporations must apportion other tax attributes. For example, the annual Section 179 election must be apportioned amongst the corporations in the controlled group. In this case, if the apportionment rules were not applicable, establishing multiple corporations could easily enable the intent of the law's annual limit to be overridden.

AFFILIATED CORPORATIONS

An affiliated group of corporations is created when one or more chains of includible corporations is connected through stock ownership with a common parent corporation which is an includible corporation, but only if (1) the common parent corporation owns at least 80% of the total voting power and at least 80% of the total value of the stock of at least one includible corporation, and (2) stock meeting the 80% requirement in each of the includible corporations (but not the common parent corporation) is owned directly by one or more of the other includible corporations.

An includible corporation is defined as any corporation other than the following:

1. An exempt corporation.
2. A life insurance or mutual insurance company.
3. A foreign corporation.
4. A corporation deriving at least 80% of its income from possessions of the United States.
5. A regulated investment company.
6. A real estate investment trust.
7. Certain domestic international sales corporations.

If all of the corporations that were members of the affiliated group at any time during the tax year consent before the last day for filing the return, an election may be made to file consolidated tax returns for the period that they are affiliated. Accordingly, net operating losses of some members of the group may be used to offset taxable income of other group members; the net effect obviously results in a decrease in tax liability.

TAX FREE EXCHANGE OF PROPERTY FOR STOCK

Under Internal Revenue Code Section 351, if property is transferred to a corporation by one or more persons (which includes individuals, trusts, estates, partnerships and corporations) solely in exchange for stock in that corporation, and immediately after the exchange such person or persons are in control of the corporation to which the property was transferred, then no gain or loss will generally be recognized by the transferor or transferee.

For purposes of this Code section, control means that the person or persons making the transfer (i.e., transferor(s)) must own, immediately after the exchange, 80% or more of the total combined voting power of all classes of voting stock and 80% or more of the total number of outstanding nonvoting shares.

It should be noted that "property" includes cash or other property, but does not include services rendered to the corporation. If stock is received for services rendered, then a taxable event has occurred. The recipient will be required to recognize ordinary income measured by the fair market value of the stock.

In the event that a transferor receives cash or other property in addition to stock, then gain will be recognized by the transferor, but only to the extent of the cash and/or fair market value of the other property received in the exchange. However, a loss on the transaction may never be recognized.

If property encumbered by debt (e.g., a mortgage) is transferred to a corporation, gain will only be recognized to the extent that the debt assumed by the corporation is in excess of the adjusted basis of the property transferred.

The stockholder's basis in stock received is equal to the cash plus the adjusted basis of any property transferred to the corporation, increased by any gain to be recognized. The stockholder's basis is reduced by the cash and the fair market value of any property received by the shareholder as part of the exchange. Further, since debt assumed by the corporation is treated as cash, the shareholder's basis in the stock is reduced by any debt assumed by the corporation.

From the corporation's point of view, the basis of property it receives is generally equal to the shareholder's basis immediately prior to the transfer, increased by any gain recognized by the shareholder in connection with the transfer.

To illustrate the major points above, assume that on July 1 of the current year, Moose Inc. is formed by Katie and Michael. Katie transfers $200,000 in cash to Moose and Michael transfers land and a building that originally cost him 180,000, but have a fair market value of $250,000 on July 1. The building is subject to a $150,000 mortgage, which is assumed by Moose. Based on these facts, the following should be noted:

1. No gain or loss is to be recognized by Katie, Michael, or Moose Inc.
2. Katie's basis in her Moose stock is $200,000.
3. Michael's basis in his Moose stock is $180,000 less $150,000, or $30,000.
4. Moose's basis in the land and building received from Michael is $180,000.

PAYROLL TAXES

SOCIAL SECURITY AND MEDICARE TAXES

For 1998, social security must be withheld from the first $68,400 of employee wages. Accordingly, the maximum amount that can be withheld from an employee's wages during 1998 is $4,240.80.

FEDERAL WITHHOLDING TAXES

There is a typographical error on page 925 of the main text. The text should read, "Every employer is required to withhold federal withholding taxes from employee wage payments in accordance with the allowances claimed by the employee on Form W-4."

A blank Form W-4, along with related instructions, follows:

Form W-4 (1998)

Purpose. Complete Form W-4 so your employer can withhold the correct Federal income tax from your pay. Because your tax situation may change, you may want to refigure your withholding each year.

Exemption from withholding. If you are exempt, complete only lines 1, 2, 3, 4, and 7, and sign the form to validate it. Your exemption for 1998 expires February 16, 1999.

Note: You cannot claim exemption from withholding if (1) your income exceeds $700 and includes unearned income (e.g., interest and dividends) and (2) another person can claim you as a dependent on their tax return.

Basic Instructions. If you are not exempt, complete the Personal Allowances Worksheet. The worksheets on page 2 adjust your withholding allowances based on itemized deductions, adjustments to income, or two-earner/two-job situations. Complete all worksheets that apply. They will help you figure the number of withholding allowances you are entitled to claim. However, you may claim fewer allowances.

New-Child tax and higher education credits. For details on adjusting withholding for these and other credits, see **Pub. 919,** Is My Withholding Correct for 1998?

Head of household. Generally, you may claim head of household filing status on your tax return only if you are unmarried and pay more than 50% of the costs of keeping up a home for yourself and your dependent(s) or other qualifying individuals.

Nonwage Income. If you have a large amount of nonwage income, such as interest or dividends, you should consider making estimated tax payments using Form 1040-ES. Otherwise, you may owe additional tax.

Two earners/two jobs. If you have a working spouse or more than one job, figure the total number of allowances you are entitled to claim on all jobs using worksheets from only one W-4. Your withholding will usually be most accurate when all allowances are claimed on the W-4 filed for the highest paying job and zero allowances are claimed for the others.

Check your withholding. After your W-4 takes effect, use Pub. 919 to see how the dollar amount you are having withheld compares to your estimated total annual tax. Get Pub. 919 especially if you used the Two-Earner/Two-Job Worksheet and your earnings exceed $150,000 (Single) or $200,000 (Married). To order Pub. 919, call 1-800-829-3676. Check your telephone directory for the IRS assistance number for further help.

Sign this form. Form W-4 is not valid unless you sign it.

Personal Allowances Worksheet

A Enter "1" for **yourself** if no one else can claim you as a dependent . . . . **A** _____

B Enter "1" if:
- You are single and have only one job; or
- You are married, have only one job, and your spouse does not work; or
- Your wages from a second job or your spouse's wages (or the total of both) are $1,000 or less.

. . . . **B** _____

C Enter "1" for your **spouse.** But, you may choose to enter -0- if you are married and have either a working spouse or more than one job. (This may help you avoid having too little tax withheld.) . . . . **C** _____

D Enter number of **dependents** (other than your spouse or yourself) you will claim on your tax return . . . . **D** _____

E Enter "1" if you will file as **head of household** on your tax return (see conditions under **Head of household** above) . . . **E** _____

F Enter "1" if you have at least $1,500 of **child or dependent care expenses** for which you plan to claim a credit . . . . **F** _____

G New-Child Tax Credit: • If your total income will be between $16,500 and $47,000 ($21,000 and $60,000 if married), enter "1" for each eligible child. • If your total income will be between $47,000 and $80,000 ($60,000 and $115,000 if married), enter "1" if you have two or three eligible children, or enter "2" if you have four or more . . . . **G** _____

H Add lines A through G and enter total here. **Note:** This amount may be different from the number of exemptions you claim on your return . . . . ▶ **H** _____

For accuracy, complete all worksheets that apply.
- If you plan to **itemize or claim adjustments to income** and want to reduce your withholding, see the Deductions and Adjustments Worksheet on page 2.
- If you are **single,** have **more than one job,** and your combined earnings from all jobs exceed $32,000 OR if you are **married** and have a **working spouse or more than one job,** and the combined earnings from all jobs exceed $55,000, see the Two-Earner/Two-Job Worksheet on page 2 to avoid having too little tax withheld.
- If **neither** of the above situations applies, **stop here** and enter the number from line H on line 5 of Form W-4 below.

Cut here and give the certificate to your employer. Keep the top part for your records.

Form **W-4**

Department of the Treasury
Internal Revenue Service

Employee's Withholding Allowance Certificate

▶ **For Privacy Act and Paperwork Reduction Act Notice, see page 2.**

OMB No. 1545-0010

1998

1 Type or print your name and address	2 Your social security number

3 ☐ Single ☐ Married ☐ Married, but withhold at higher Single rate.
Note: If married, but legally separated, or spouse is a nonresident alien, check the Single box.

4 If your last name differs from that on your social security card, check here and call 1-800-772-1213 for a new card ▶ ☐

| 5 | Total number of allowances you are claiming (from line H above or from the worksheets on page 2 if they apply) . . | 5 | |
| 6 | Additional amount, if any, you want withheld from each paycheck . . . . | 6 | |

7 I claim exemption from withholding for 1998, and I certify that I meet **BOTH** of the following conditions for exemption:
- Last year I had a right to a refund of **ALL** Federal income tax withheld because I had **NO** tax liability **AND**
- This year I expect a refund of **ALL** Federal income tax withheld because I expect to have **NO** tax liability.
If you meet both conditions, enter "EXEMPT" here . . . . ▶ | 7 | |

Under penalties of perjury, I certify that I am entitled to the number of withholding allowances claimed on this certificate or entitled to claim exempt status.

Employee's signature ▶

Date ▶ _____ , 19____

8 Employer's name and address (Employer: Complete 8 and 10 only if sending to the IRS)	9 Office code (optional)	10 Employer identification number

EDA

Deductions and Adjustments Worksheet

Note: Use this worksheet only if you plan to itemize deductions or claim adjustments to income on your 1998 tax return.

1 Enter an estimate of your 1998 itemized deductions. These include qualifying home mortgage interest, charitable contributions, state and local taxes (but not sales taxes), medical expenses in excess of 7.5% of your income, and miscellaneous deductions. (For 1998, you may have to reduce your itemized deductions if your income is over $124,500 ($62,250 if married filing separately). Get Pub. 919 for details.) . . . . **1** _____

2 Enter:
{ $7,100 if married filing jointly or qualifying widow(er)
$6,250 if head of household
$4,250 if single
$3,550 if married filing separately }
. . . . **2** _____

3 **Subtract** line 2 from line 1. If line 2 is greater than line 1, enter –0– . . . . **3** _____

4 Enter an estimate of your 1998 adjustments to income, including alimony, deductible IRA contributions, and education loan interest . . . . **4** _____

5 **Add** lines 3 and 4 and enter the total . . . . **5** _____

6 Enter an estimate of your 1998 nonwage income (such as dividends or interest) . . . . **6** _____

7 **Subtract** line 6 from line 5. Enter the result, but not less than –0– . . . . **7** _____

8 **Divide** the amount on line 7 by $2,500 and enter the result here. Drop any fraction . . . . **8** _____

9 Enter the number from Personal Allowances Worksheet, line H, on page 1 . . . . **9** _____

10 **Add** lines 8 and 9 and enter the total here. If you plan to use the Two-Earner/Two-Job Worksheet, also enter this total on line 1 below. Otherwise, **stop here** and enter this total on Form W-4, line 5, on page 1 . . . . **10** _____

Two-Earner/Two-Job Worksheet

Note: Use this worksheet only if the instructions for line H on page 1 direct you here.

1 Enter the number from line H on page 1 (or from line 10 above if you used the Deductions and Adjustments Worksheet) . . . . . **1** _____

2 Find the number in **Table 1** below that applies to the **LOWEST** paying job and enter it here . . . . **2** _____

3 If line 1 is **GREATER THAN OR EQUAL TO** line 2, subtract line 2 from line 1. Enter the result here (if zero, enter –0–) and on Form W-4, line 5, on page 1. **DO NOT** use the rest of this worksheet . . . . **3** _____

Note: If line 1 is **LESS THAN** line 2, enter –0– on Form W-4, line 5, on page 1. Complete lines 4–9 to calculate the additional withholding amount necessary to avoid a year end tax bill.

4 Enter the number from line 2 of this worksheet . . . . **4** _____

5 Enter the number from line 1 of this worksheet . . . . **5** _____

6 **Subtract** line 5 from line 4 . . . . **6** _____

7 Find the amount in **Table 2** below that applies to the **HIGHEST** paying job and enter it here . . . . **7** _____

8 **Multiply** line 7 by line 6 and enter the result here. This is the additional annual withholding amount needed . . . . . **8** _____

9 Divide line 8 by the number of pay periods remaining in 1998. (For example, divide by 26 if you are paid every other week and you complete this form in December 1997.) Enter the result here and on Form W-4, line 6, page 1. This is the additional amount to be withheld from each paycheck . . . . **9** _____

Table 1: Two-Earner/Two-Job Worksheet

Married Filing Jointly				All Others			
If wages from **LOWEST** paying job are–	Enter on line 2 above	If wages from **LOWEST** paying job are–	Enter on line 2 above	If wages from **LOWEST** paying job are–	Enter on line 2 above	If wages from **LOWEST** paying job are–	Enter on line 2 above
0 – $4,000	0	38,001 – 43,000	8	0 – $5,000	0	70,001 – 85,000	8
4,001 – 7,000	1	43,001 – 54,000	9	5,001 – 11,000	1	85,001 – 100,000	9
7,001 – 12,000	2	54,001 – 62,000	10	11,001 – 16,000	2	100,001 and over	10
12,001 – 18,000	3	62,001 – 70,000	11	16,001 – 21,000	3		
18,001 – 24,000	4	70,001 – 85,000	12	21,001 – 25,000	4		
24,001 – 28,000	5	85,001 – 100,000	13	25,001 – 42,000	5		
28,001 – 33,000	6	100,001 – 110,000	14	42,001 – 55,000	6		
33,001 – 38,000	7	110,001 and over	15	55,001 – 70,000	7		

Table 2: Two-Earner/Two-Job Worksheet

Married Filing Jointly		All Others	
If wages from **HIGHEST** paying job are–	Enter on line 7 above	If wages from **HIGHEST** paying job are–	Enter on line 7 above
0 – $50,000	$400	0 – $30,000	$400
50,001 – 100,000	760	30,001 – 60,000	760
100,001 – 130,000	840	60,001 – 120,000	840
130,001 – 240,000	970	120,001 – 250,000	970
240,001 and over	1,070	250,001 and over	1,070

Privacy Act and Paperwork Reduction Act Notice. We ask for the information on this form to carry out the Internal Revenue laws of the United States. The Internal Revenue Code requires this information under sections 3402(f)(2)(A) and 6109 and their regulations. Failure to provide a completed form will result in your being treated as a single person who claims no withholding allowances. Routine uses of this information include giving it to the Department of Justice for civil and criminal litigation and to cities, states, and the District of Columbia for use in administering their tax laws.

You are not required to provide the information requested on a form that is subject to the Paperwork Reduction Act unless the form displays a valid OMB control number. Books or records relating to a form or its instructions must be retained as long as their contents may become material in the administration of any Internal Revenue Law. Generally, tax returns and return information are confidential, as required by Code section 6103.

The time needed to complete this form will vary depending on individual circumstances. The estimated average time is: Recordkeeping 46 min., Learning about the law or the form 10 min., Preparing the form 1 hr., 10 min. If you have comments concerning the accuracy of these time estimates or suggestions for making this form simpler, we would be happy to hear from you. You can write to the Tax Forms Committee, Western Area Distribution Center, Rancho Cordova, CA 95743-0001. DO NOT send the tax form to this address. Instead, give it to your employer.

Form **W-4** (1998)

TAX DEPOSITS

A copy of Form 941, Employer's Quarterly Federal Tax Return (along with related instructions) referred to on page 925 of the main text, follows:

Form 941
(Rev. January 1998)
Department of the Treasury
Internal Revenue Service

(1)

Employer's Quarterly Federal Tax Return

▶ See separate instructions for information on completing this return.
Please type or print.

OMB No. 1545-0029

Enter state code for state in which deposits were made ONLY if different from state in address to the right ▶ ☐ (see page 3 of instructions).

T	
FF	
FD	
FP	
I	
T	

If address is different from prior return, check here ▶ ☐

IRS Use

1	1	1	1	1	1	1	1	1	1		2		3	3	3	3	3	3	3		4	4	4		5	5	5
6		7		8	8	8	8	8	8	8		9	9	9	9	9		10	10	10	10	10	10	10	10	10	10

If you do not have to file returns in the future, check here ▶ ☐ and enter date final wages paid ▶
If you are a seasonal employer, see **Seasonal employers** on page 1 of the instructions and check here ▶ ☐

1	Number of employees in the pay period that includes March 12th . ▶ **1**	
2	Total wages and tips, plus other compensation	**2**
3	Total income tax withheld from wages, tips, and sick pay	**3**
4	Adjustment of withheld income tax for preceding quarters of calendar year	**4**
5	Adjusted total of income tax withheld (line 3 as adjusted by line 4—see instructions) . . .	**5**
6	Taxable social security wages **6a**	× 12.4% (.124) = **6b**
	Taxable social security tips **6c**	× 12.4% (.124) = **6d**
7	Taxable Medicare wages and tips . . . **7a**	× 2.9% (.029) = **7b**
8	Total social security and Medicare taxes (add lines 6b, 6d, and 7b). Check here if wages are not subject to social security and/or Medicare tax . . . . ▶ ☐	**8**
9	Adjustment of social security and Medicare taxes (see instructions for required explanation) Sick Pay $ _____ ± Fractions of Cents $ _____ ± Other $ _____ =	**9**
10	Adjusted total of social security and Medicare taxes (line 8 as adjusted by line 9—see instructions)	**10**
11	**Total taxes** (add lines 5 and 10)	**11**
12	Advance earned income credit (EIC) payments made to employees	**12**
13	Net taxes (subtract line 12 from line 11). **This should equal line 17, column (d) below (or line D of Schedule B (Form 941))**	**13**
14	Total deposits for quarter, including overpayment applied from a prior quarter	**14**
15	**Balance due** (subtract line 14 from line 13). See instructions	**15**
16	Overpayment, if line 14 is more than line 13, enter excess here ▶ $ _____	

and check if to be: ☐ Applied to next return **OR** ☐ Refunded.
- **All filers:** If line 13 is less than $500, you need not complete line 17 or Schedule B (Form 941).
- **Semiweekly schedule depositors:** Complete Schedule B (Form 941) and check here . . . . ▶ ☐
- **Monthly schedule depositors:** Complete line 17, columns (a) through (d), and check here . . . . ▶ ☐

17	Monthly Summary of Federal Tax Liability. Do not complete if you were a semiweekly schedule depositor.			
	(a) First month liability	(b) Second month liability	(c) Third month liability	(d) Total liability for quarter

Sign Here

Under penalties of perjury, I declare that I have examined this return, including accompanying schedules and statements, and to the best of my knowledge and belief, it is true, correct, and complete.

Signature ▶   Print Your Name and Title ▶   Date ▶

For Privacy Act and Paperwork Reduction Act Notice, see page 4 of separate instructions.   Cat. No. 17001Z   Form **941** (Rev. 1-98)

07JA180473

Instructions for Form 941

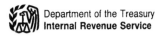
Department of the Treasury
Internal Revenue Service

(Revised January 1998)
Employer's Quarterly Federal Tax Return
Section references are to the Internal Revenue Code unless otherwise noted.

Changes To Note

Social security wage base for 1998. Stop withholding social security tax after an employee reaches **$68,400** in taxable wages.

Electronic deposit requirement. If your total deposits of social security, Medicare, railroad retirement, and withheld income taxes were more than $50,000 in 1996, you must make electronic deposits for **all** depository tax liabilities that occur after 1997. When determining whether you exceeded the $50,000 threshold, combine deposits of only the following tax returns you filed: Forms 941, 941–M, 941–PR, 941–SS, 943, 945, and CT–1. If you were required to deposit by electronic funds transfer in prior years, continue to do so throughout 1998. The **Electronic Federal Tax Payment System (EFTPS)** must be used to make electronic deposits. If you are required to make deposits by electronic funds transfer and fail to do so, you may be subject to a 10% penalty. However, if you were first required to use EFTPS on or after July 1, 1997, no penalties for failure to use EFTPS will be imposed prior to July 1, 1998. Taxpayers who are not required to make electronic deposits may voluntarily participate in EFTPS. To enroll in EFTPS, call 1–800–945–8400 or 1–800–555–4477. For general information about EFTPS, call 1–800–829–1040.

Educational assistance programs. The $5,250 exclusion for employer-provided educational assistance programs, which expired for courses beginning after June 30, 1997, has been extended retroactively for courses beginning before June 1, 2000. See section 5 of **Pub. 15–A**, Employer's Supplemental Tax Guide, for information on educational assistance programs.

Form 941 Color Change. Because Form 941 will not be processed by machine scanning, it is being printed with black ink rather than the red ink previously required for scanning.

General Instructions

Purpose of form. To report—
• Income tax you withheld from wages, including tips, supplemental unemployment compensation benefits, and third-party payments of sick pay.
• Social security and Medicare taxes.

Who must file. Employers who withhold income tax on wages, or who must pay social security or Medicare tax, must file Form 941 quarterly. After you file your initial Form 941, you must file a return for each quarter, even if you have no taxes to report (but see the *seasonal employer* and *final return* information below). If you filed Form 941 on magnetic tape or by electronic or TeleFile methods, do not also file a paper Form 941.

Seasonal employers are not required to file for quarters when they regularly have no tax liability because they have paid no wages. To alert the IRS that you will not have to file a return for one or more quarters during the year, check the **Seasonal employer** box above line 1 on Form 941. The IRS will mail two Forms 941 to you once a year after March 1. The preprinted name and address information will not include the date the quarter ended. You must enter the date the quarter ended when you file the return. The IRS generally will not inquire about unfiled returns if at least one taxable return is filed each year. However, you must check the **Seasonal employer** box on each quarterly return you file. Otherwise, the IRS will expect a return to be filed for each quarter.

Employers who report wages on *household employees,* see Circular E and Pub. 926, Household Employer's Tax Guide.

Employers who report wages on *farmworkers,* see **Form 943,** Employer's Annual Tax Return for Agricultural Employees, and **Circular A,** Agricultural Employer's Tax Guide (Pub. 51).

Business reorganization or termination. If you sell or transfer your business, both you and the new owner must file a return for the quarter in which the change took place. Neither should report wages paid by the other. (An example of a transfer is when a sole proprietor forms a partnership or corporation. The partnership or corporation is considered a new business and must apply for a new employer identification number (EIN). See section 1 of **Circular E,** Employer's Tax Guide.) If a change occurs, please attach to your return a statement that shows: new owner's name (or new name of the business); whether the business is now a sole proprietorship, partnership, or corporation; kind of change that took place (sale, transfer, etc.); and date of the change.

When a business is merged or consolidated with another, the continuing firm must file the return for the quarter in which the change took place. The return should show all wages paid for that quarter. The other firm should file a final return.

Final return. If you go out of business or stop paying wages, file a final return. Be sure to mark the final return checkbox and enter the date final wages were paid above line 1. See the **Instructions for Form W–2** *for information on the earlier due dates for the expedited furnishing and filing Form W–2 when a final Form 941 is filed.*

Preprinted name and address information. If any of the preprinted name, EIN, or address information on Form 941 is not correct, cross it out and type or print the correct information.

Generally, preprinted address information is from IRS records. However, if you filed a change of address card with the United States Postal Service (USPS), that address information may be preprinted on your Form 941 and 941 TeleFile Tax Record. If the preprinted address is from the USPS, your IRS address of record will be changed when your return is filed and properly processed.

Form preparation suggestions. The following suggestions will allow the IRS to process Form 941 faster and more accurately:
● Make dollar entries without the dollar sign and comma (0000.00).
● Enter negative amounts in parentheses.
● File the Form 941 that has your preprinted name and address.

Ordering forms and publications. After you file your first return, we will send you a Form 941 every 3 months. If you do not have a Form 941, get one by calling 1–800–TAX–FORM (1–800–829–3676) in time to file the return when due. Other IRS forms and publications also are available at this phone number. See Circular E for additional methods of obtaining forms and publications.

When to file. File starting with the first quarter in which you are required to withhold income tax or pay wages subject to social security and Medicare taxes.

Quarter	Ending	Due Date
Jan.-Feb.-Mar.	March 31	April 30
Apr.-May-June	June 30	July 31
July-Aug.-Sept.	Sept. 30	Oct. 31
Oct.-Nov.-Dec.	Dec. 31	Jan. 31

If you made deposits on time in full payment of the taxes for a quarter, you have 10 more days after the above due date to file. Your return will be considered timely filed if it is properly addressed and mailed First-Class or sent by an IRS designated delivery service on or before the due date. See Circular E for

Cat. No. 14625L

more information on IRS designated delivery services. If the due date for filing a return falls on a Saturday, Sunday, or legal holiday, you may file the return on the next business day.

Where to file. In the list below, find the state where your legal residence, principal place of business, office, or agency is located. Send your return to the **Internal Revenue Service** at the address listed for your location. No street address is needed.

Note: *Where you file depends on whether or not you are including a payment.*

Florida, Georgia, South Carolina

Return without payment:	**Return with payment:**
Atlanta, GA 39901-0005	P.O. Box 105703
	Atlanta, GA 30348-5703

New Jersey, New York (New York City and counties of Nassau, Rockland, Suffolk, and Westchester)

Return without payment:	**Return with payment:**
Holtsville, NY 00501-0005	P.O. Box 416
	Newark, NJ 07101-0416

New York (all other counties), Connecticut, Maine, Massachusetts, New Hampshire, Rhode Island, Vermont

Return without payment:	**Return with payment:**
Andover, MA 05501-0005	P.O. Box 371493
	Pittsburgh, PA 15250-7493

Illinois, Iowa, Minnesota, Missouri, Wisconsin

Return without payment:	**Return with payment:**
Kansas City, MO 64999-0005	P.O. Box 970007
	St. Louis, MO 63197-0007

Delaware, District of Columbia, Maryland, Pennsylvania, Virginia

Return without payment:	**Return with payment:**
Philadelphia, PA 19255-0005	P.O. Box 8786
	Philadelphia, PA 19162-8786

Indiana, Kentucky, Michigan, Ohio, West Virginia

Return without payment:	**Return with payment:**
Cincinnati, OH 45999-0005	P.O. Box 7329
	Chicago, IL 60680-7329

Kansas, New Mexico, Oklahoma, Texas

Return without payment:	**Return with payment:**
Austin, TX 73301-0005	P.O. Box 970013
	St. Louis, MO 63197-0013

Alaska, Arizona, California (counties of Alpine, Amador, Butte, Calaveras, Colusa, Contra Costa, Del Norte, El Dorado, Glenn, Humboldt, Lake, Lassen, Marin, Mendocino, Modoc, Napa, Nevada, Placer, Plumas, Sacramento, San Joaquin, Shasta, Sierra, Siskiyou, Solano, Sonoma, Sutter, Tehama, Trinity, Yolo, and Yuba), Colorado, Idaho, Montana, Nebraska, Nevada, North Dakota, Oregon, South Dakota, Utah, Washington, Wyoming

Return without payment:	**Return with payment:**
Ogden, UT 84201-0005	P.O. Box 7922
	San Francisco, CA 94120-7922

California (all other counties), Hawaii

Return without payment:	**Return with payment:**
Fresno, CA 93888-0005	P.O. Box 60407
	Los Angeles, CA 90060-0407

Alabama, Arkansas, Louisiana, Mississippi, North Carolina, Tennessee

Return without payment:	**Return with payment:**
Memphis, TN 37501-0005	P.O. Box 70503
	Charlotte, NC 28272-0503

If you have no legal residence or principal place of business in any state

All Returns:
Philadelphia, PA 19255-0005

Forms W–4. Each quarter, send with Form 941 copies of any **Forms W–4,** Employee's Withholding Allowance Certificate, received during the quarter from employees claiming (1) more than 10 withholding allowances or (2) exemption from income tax withholding if their wages will normally be more than $200 a week. For details, see section 9 of Circular E.

Form W–5. Each eligible employee wishing to receive any advance earned income credit (EIC) payments must give you a completed **Form W–5,** Earned Income Credit Advance Payment Certificate. The employer's requirement to notify certain employees about the EIC can be met by giving each eligible employee **Notice 797,** Possible Federal Tax Refund Due to the Earned Income Credit (EIC). See Circular E and **Pub. 596,** Earned Income Credit, for more information.

Employer identification number (EIN). If you do not have an EIN, apply for one on **Form SS–4,** Application for Employer Identification Number. Get this form from the IRS or the Social Security Administration (SSA). If you do not have an EIN by the time a return is due, write "Applied for" and the date you applied in the space shown for the number. Form SS–4 has information on how to apply for an EIN by mail or by telephone.

Note: *Always be sure the EIN on the form you file matches the EIN assigned to your business by the IRS. Do not show your personal social security number on forms calling for an EIN. Filing a Form 941 with an incorrect EIN or using another business' EIN may result in penalties and delays in processing your return.*

Penalties and interest. There are penalties for filing a return late and paying or depositing taxes late, unless there is reasonable cause. If you are late, please attach an explanation to your return. There are also penalties for failure to (1) furnish Forms W–2 to employees and file copies with the SSA, (2) keep records, and (3) deposit taxes when required. In addition, there are penalties for willful failure to file returns and pay taxes when due and for filing false returns or submitting bad checks. Interest is charged on taxes paid late at the rate set by law. See Circular E for additional information.

Caution: *A **trust fund recovery penalty** may apply if income, social security, and Medicare taxes that must be withheld are not withheld or are not paid to the IRS. The penalty is the full amount of the unpaid trust fund tax. This penalty may apply when these unpaid taxes cannot be immediately collected from the employer or business. The trust fund recovery penalty may be imposed on all persons who are determined by the IRS to be responsible for collecting, accounting for, and paying over these taxes, and who acted willfully in not doing so. A **responsible person** can be an officer or employee of a corporation, a partner or employee of a partnership, an accountant, a volunteer director/trustee, or an employee of a sole proprietorship. A responsible person also may include one who signs checks for the business or otherwise has authority to cause the spending of business funds. **Willfully** means voluntarily, consciously, and intentionally.*

Depositing taxes. If your net taxes (line 13) are $500 or more for the quarter, you must deposit your tax liabilities at an authorized financial institution with **Form 8109,** Federal Tax Deposit Coupon, or by using the Electronic Federal Tax Payment System (EFTPS). See page 1 for the electronic deposit requirements and section 11 of Circular E for information and rules concerning Federal tax deposits.

Page 2

Payroll Taxes

Reconciliation of Forms 941 and W-3. Certain amounts reported on the four quarterly Forms 941 for 1997 should agree with the **Form W-2,** Wage and Tax Statement, totals reported on **Form W-3,** Transmittal of Wage and Tax Statements, or with information filed with the SSA or equivalent magnetic media reports with the SSA (Form 6559). The amounts that should agree are income tax withholding, social security wages, social security tips, Medicare wages and tips, and the advance earned income credit. If the totals do not agree, the IRS will require you to explain any differences and correct any errors. You can avoid this by making sure correct amounts (including adjustments) are reported on Forms 941 and W-3. See section 12 of Circular E.

Specific Instructions

State code. If you made your deposits in a state other than that shown in your address on Form 941, enter the state code for that state in the box provided in the upper left corner of the form. Use the Postal Service two-letter state abbreviation as the state code. Enter the code "MU" in the state code box if you deposit in more than one state. If you deposit in the same state as shown in your address, do not make an entry in this box.

Line 1—Number of employees. Enter the number of employees on your payroll during the pay period including March 12 (on the January–March calendar quarter return only). Do not include household employees, persons who received no pay during the pay period, pensioners, or members of the Armed Forces. An entry of 250 or more on line 1 indicates a need to file Forms W–2 on magnetic media. Call the SSA at 1–800–772–1213 for more information on magnetic media filing requirements.

Line 2—Total wages and tips, plus other compensation. Enter the total of all wages paid, tips reported, taxable fringe benefits provided, and other compensation paid to your employees, **even if you do not have to withhold income or social security and Medicare taxes on it.** Do not include supplemental unemployment compensation benefits, even if you withheld income tax on them. Do not include contributions to employee plans that are excluded from the employee's wages (e.g., section 401(k) and 125 plans).

If you get timely notice from your insurance carrier concerning the amount of third-party sick pay it paid your employees, include the sick pay on line 2. If you are an insurance company, do not include sick pay you paid policyholders' employees here if you gave the policyholders timely notice of the payments. See Pub. 15–A for details.

Line 3—Total income tax withheld. Enter the income tax you withheld on wages, tips, taxable fringe benefits, and supplemental unemployment compensation benefits. An insurance company should enter the income tax it withheld on third-party sick pay here.

Line 4—Adjustment of withheld income tax. Use line 4 to correct errors in income tax withheld from wages paid in earlier quarters of the *same calendar year*. You may not adjust or claim a refund or credit for any overpayment of income tax that you withheld or deducted from an employee in a prior year. This is because the employee uses the amount shown on Form W-2 as a credit when filing his or her income tax return. Because any amount shown on line 4 increases or decreases your tax liability, the adjustment must be taken into account on line 17, Monthly Summary of Federal Tax Liability, or on **Schedule B (Form 941),** Employer's Record of Federal Tax Liability. For details on how to report adjustments on the record of Federal tax liability, see the instructions for line 17 (on page 4) or the instructions for Schedule B (Form 941). Explain any adjustments on **Form 941c,** Supporting Statement To Correct Information, or an equivalent statement. See section 13 of Circular E.

Do not adjust income tax withholding for quarters in earlier years unless it is to correct an administrative error. An administrative error occurs if the amount you entered on Form 941 is not the amount you actually withheld. For example, if the total income tax actually withheld was incorrectly reported on Form 941 due to a mathematical or transposition error, this would be an administrative error. The administrative error adjustment corrects the amount reported on Form 941 to agree with the amount actually withheld from the employees.

Line 5—Adjusted total of income tax withheld. Add line 4 to line 3 if you are reporting additional income tax withheld for an earlier quarter. Subtract line 4 from line 3 if you are reducing the amount of income tax withheld. If there is no entry on line 4, line 5 will be the same as line 3.

Line 6a—Taxable social security wages. Enter the total wages subject to social security taxes that you paid your employees during the quarter. Also include any sick pay and taxable fringe benefits subject to social security taxes. See section 5 of Circular E for information on types of wages subject to social security taxes. Enter the amount before deductions. Do not include tips on this line. Stop reporting an employee's wages (including tips) when they reach $68,400 for 1998. However, continue to withhold income tax for the whole year on wages and tips even when the social security wage base of $68,400 is reached. See the line 7a instructions for Medicare tax. **If none of the payments are subject to social security tax, mark the checkbox in line 8.**

Line 6c—Taxable social security tips. Enter all tips your employees reported during the quarter until tips and wages for an employee reach $68,400 in 1998. Do this even if you were not able to withhold the employee tax (6.2%). However, see the line 9 instructions.

An employee must report to you cash tips, including tips you paid the employee for charge customers, totaling $20 or more in a month by the 10th of the next month. The employee may use **Form 4070,** Employee's Report of Tips to Employer, or a written statement.

Do not include allocated tips on this line. Instead, report them on **Form 8027,** Employer's Annual Information Return of Tip Income and Allocated Tips. Allocated tips are not reportable on Form 941 and are not subject to withholding of income, social security, or Medicare taxes.

Line 7a—Taxable Medicare wages and tips. Report all wages and tips subject to Medicare tax. Also include any sick pay and taxable fringe benefits subject to Medicare tax. See section 5 of Circular E for information on types of wages subject to Medicare tax. There is no limit on the amount of wages subject to Medicare tax. **If none of the payments are subject to Medicare tax, mark the checkbox in line 8.**

Include all tips your employees reported during the quarter, even if you were not able to withhold the employee tax (1.45%). However, see the line 9 instructions below.

Line 9—Adjustment of social security and Medicare taxes. *Current period adjustments.* In certain cases, amounts reported as social security and Medicare taxes on lines 6b, 6d, and 7b must be adjusted to arrive at your correct tax liability. See section 13 of Circular E for information on the following:

• Adjustment for the uncollected employee share of social security and Medicare taxes on tips.

• Adjustment for the employee share of social security and Medicare taxes on group-term life insurance premiums paid for former employees.

• Adjustment for the employee share of social security and Medicare taxes withheld by a third-party sick pay payer.

• Fractions of cents adjustment.

Enter the adjustments for sick pay and fractions of cents in the appropriate line 9 entry spaces. Enter the amount of all other adjustments in the "Other" entry space, and enter the total of the three types of adjustments, including prior period adjustments (discussed below), in the line 9 entry space to the right. Provide a supporting statement explaining any adjustments reported in the "Other" entry space.

Prior period adjustments. Use line 9 to correct errors in social security and Medicare taxes reported on an earlier return. If you report both an underpayment and an overpayment, show only the net difference.

Because any prior period adjustments shown on line 9 increase or decrease your tax liability, the adjustments must be taken into account on line 17, Monthly Summary of Federal Tax

Page 3

Liability, or on Schedule B (Form 941). For details on how to report adjustments on the record of Federal tax liability, see the instructions for line 17 below or the instructions for Schedule B (Form 941).

Explain any prior period adjustments on Form 941c. **Do not** file Form 941c separately from Form 941. Form 941c is not an amended return but is a statement providing necessary information and certifications supporting the adjustments on lines 4 and/or 9 on Form 941. If you do not have a Form 941c, you may file an equivalent supporting statement with the return providing the required information about the adjustment(s). See section 13 of Circular E.

If you are adjusting an employee's social security or Medicare wages or tips for a prior year, you must file **Form W–2c,** Corrected Wage and Tax Statement with **Form W–3c,** Transmittal of Corrected Wage and Tax Statements.

Line 10—Adjusted total of social security and Medicare taxes. Add line 9 to line 8 if line 9 is positive (e.g., the net adjustment increases your tax liability). Subtract line 9 from line 8 if line 9 is negative.

Line 12—Advance earned income credit (EIC) payments made to employees. Enter advance EIC payments made to employees. Your eligible employees may elect to receive part of the EIC as an advance payment. Eligible employees who have a qualifying child must give you a completed Form W–5 stating that they qualify for the EIC. Once the employee gives you a signed and completed Form W–5, you must make the advance EIC payments. Advance EIC payments are generally made from withheld income tax and employee and employer social security and Medicare taxes. See section 10 of Circular E and Pub. 596.

If the amount of your advance EIC payments exceeds your total taxes (line 11) for the quarter, you may claim a refund of the overpayment or elect to have the credit applied to your return for the next quarter. Provide a statement with your return identifying the amount of excess payment(s) and the pay period(s) in which it was paid. See section 10 of Circular E.

Line 15—Balance due. You do not have to pay if line 15 is under $1. You should have a balance due only if your net tax liability for the quarter (line 13) is less than $500. (However, see section 11 of Circular E regarding payments made under the *accuracy of deposits rule*). If line 13 is $500 or more and you have deposited all taxes when due, the amount shown on line 15 (balance due) should be zero. **Caution:** *If you fail to make deposits as required and instead pay these amounts with your return, you may be subject to a penalty.*

Line 16—Overpayment. If you deposited more than the correct amount for a quarter, you can have the overpayment refunded or applied to your next return by checking the appropriate box. If you do not check either box, your overpayment will be applied to your next return. The IRS may apply your overpayment to any past due tax account under your EIN. If line 16 is under $1, we will send a refund or apply it to your next return only on written request.

Line 17—Monthly summary of Federal tax liability.

Note: *This is a summary of your monthly tax liability, not a summary of deposits made. If line 13 is less than $500, do not complete line 17 or Schedule B (Form 941).*

Complete line 17 only if you were a monthly schedule depositor for the entire quarter (see section 11 of Circular E for details on the deposit rules). You are a monthly schedule depositor for the calendar year if the amount of your Form 941 taxes reported for the lookback period is not more than $50,000. The lookback period is the four consecutive quarters ending on June 30 of the prior year. For 1998, the lookback period begins July 1, 1996, and ends June 30, 1997.

Caution: *If you were a semiweekly schedule depositor during any part of the quarter, do not complete columns (a) through (d) of line 17. Instead, complete Schedule B (Form 941).*

Reporting adjustments on line 17. If the net adjustment during a month is negative (e.g., correcting an overreported liability in a prior period) and it exceeds the total liability for the month, do not enter a negative amount for the month. Instead, enter -0- for the month and carry over the unused portion of the adjustment to the next month. For example, Pine Co. discovered on February 6, 1998, that it overreported social security tax on a prior quarter return by $2,500. Its Form 941 taxes for the 1st quarter of 1998 were: January $2,000, February $2,000, March $2,000. Pine Co. should enter $2,000 in column (a), -0- in column (b), $1,500 in column (c), and the total, $3,500, in column (d). The prior period adjustment ($2,500) offsets the $2,000 liability for February and the excess $500 must be used to offset March liabilities. Since the error was not discovered until February, it does not affect January liabilities reported in column (a).

If excess negative adjustments are carried forward to the next quarter, do not show these excess adjustments on lines 4 or 9. Line 17, column (d), must equal line 13.

Privacy Act and Paperwork Reduction Act Notice. We ask for the information on this form to carry out the Internal Revenue laws of the United States. We need it to figure and collect the right amount of tax. Subtitle C, Employment Taxes, of the Internal Revenue Code imposes employment taxes on wages, including income tax withholding. This form is used to determine the amount of the taxes that you owe. Section 6011 requires you to provide the ;requested information if the tax is applicable to you. Section 6109 requires you to provide your employer identification number (EIN). Routine uses of this information include giving it to the Department of Justice for civil and criminal litigation, and to cities, states, and the District of Columbia for use in administering their tax laws. If you fail to provide this information in a timely manner, you may be subject to penalties and interest.

You are not required to provide the information requested on a form that is subject to the Paperwork Reduction Act unless the form displays a valid OMB control number. Books and records relating to a form or its instructions must be retained as long as their contents may become material in the administration of any Internal Revenue law. Generally, tax returns and return information are confidential, as required by section 6103.

The time needed to complete and file this form will vary depending on individual circumstances. The estimated average time is:

Recordkeeping .... 11 hr., 43 min.

Learning about the law or the form .... 28 min.

Preparing the form .... 1 hr., 37 min.

Copying, assembling, and sending the form to the IRS... 16 min.

If you have comments concerning the accuracy of these time estimates or suggestions for making this form simpler, we would be happy to hear from you. You can write to the Tax Forms Committee, Western Area Distribution Center, Rancho Cordova, CA 95743-0001. **DO NOT** send the tax form to this address. Instead, see **Where to file** on page 2.

Page 4

Printed on recycled paper

*U.S. Government Printing Office: 1998 - 435-462

Payroll Taxes

DEPOSIT RULE

On June 3, 1998, the IRS announced a change to the deposit rule contained in the fourth paragraph of this section on page 925. The new rule should read as follows:

> "If an employer accumulates less than a *$1,000* tax liability during a calendar quarter, no deposits are required and the liability may be paid with the return for the period."

A copy of Form 8109, Federal Tax Deposit Coupon, (along with related instructions) referred to on page 926 of the main text, follows:

AMOUNT OF DEPOSIT (Do NOT type, please print.)

DOLLARS   CENTS

	Darken only one		i n d	Darken only one
	TYPE OF TAX			**TAX PERIOD**

TAX YEAR MONTH ➤

EMPLOYER IDENTIFICATION NUMBER ➤

BANK NAME/ DATE STAMP

Name _____

Address _____

_____

City _____

State _____ ZIP _____

Telephone number (_____)

IRS USE ONLY

941	945	1st Quarter
990-C	1120	2nd Quarter
943	990-T	3rd Quarter
720	990-PF	4th Quarter
CT-1	1042	
940		35

FOR BANK USE IN MICR ENCODING

Federal Tax Deposit Coupon

Form 8109-B (Rev. 10-96)

▲ SEPARATE ALONG THIS LINE AND SUBMIT TO DEPOSITARY WITH PAYMENT ▲ OMB NO. 1545-0257

Note: *Except for the name, address, and telephone number, entries must be made in pencil. Please use a soft lead (for example, a #2 pencil) so that the entries can be read more accurately by optical scanning equipment. The name, address, and telephone number may be completed other than by hand. You CANNOT use photocopies of the coupons to make your deposits. Do not staple, tape, or fold the coupons.*

Paperwork Reduction Act Notice.—We ask for the information on this form to carry out the Internal Revenue laws of the United States. You are required to give us the information. We need it to ensure that you are complying with these laws and to allow us to figure and collect the right amount of tax.

You are not required to provide the information requested on a form that is subject to the Paperwork Reduction Act unless the form displays a valid OMB control number. Books or records relating to a form or its instructions must be retained as long as their contents may become material in the administration of any Internal Revenue law. Generally, tax returns and return information are confidential, as required by Code section 6103.

The time needed to complete and file this form will vary depending on individual circumstances. The estimated average time is 3 min. If you have comments concerning the accuracy of this time estimate or suggestions for making this form simpler, we would be happy to hear from you. You can write to the Tax Forms Committee, Western Area Distribution Center, Rancho Cordova, CA 95743-0001. DO NOT send this form to this address. Instead, see the instructions on the back of this page.

Purpose of Form.—Use Form 8109-B to make a tax deposit only in the following two situations:

1. You have not yet received your resupply of preprinted deposit coupons (Form 8109); or

2. You are a new entity and have already been assigned an employer identification number (EIN), but you have not yet received your initial supply of preprinted deposit coupons (Form 8109).

Note: *If you do not receive your resupply of deposit coupons and a deposit is due or you do not receive your initial supply within 5–6 weeks of receipt of your EIN, please call 1-800-829-1040.*

If you have applied for an EIN, have not received it, and a deposit must be made, send your payment to your Internal Revenue Service Center. Make your check or money order payable to the Internal Revenue Service and show on it your name (as shown on Form SS-4, Application for Employer Identification Number), address, kind of tax, period covered, and date you applied for an EIN. Also attach an explanation to the deposit. Do not use Form 8109-B in this situation. Do not use Form 8109-B to deposit delinquent taxes assessed by the IRS. Pay those taxes directly to the IRS. See Circular E, Employer's Tax Guide, for information on depositing by Electronic Funds Transfer.

How To Complete the Form.—Enter your name exactly as shown on your return or other IRS correspondence, address, and EIN in the spaces provided. If you are required to file a Form 1120, 990-C, 990-PF (with net investment income), 990-T, or 2438, enter the month in which your tax year ends in the TAX YEAR MONTH boxes. For example, if your tax year ends in January, enter 01; if it ends in June, enter 06; if it ends in December, enter 12. Please make your entries for EIN and tax year month (if applicable) in the manner specified in Amount of Deposit below. Darken one box each in the TYPE OF TAX and TAX PERIOD columns as explained below.

Amount of Deposit.—Enter the amount of the deposit in the space provided. Enter the amount legibly, forming the characters as shown below:

Hand print money amounts without using dollar signs, commas, a decimal point, or leading zeros. The commas and the decimal point are already shown in the entry area. For example, a deposit of $7,635.22 would be entered like this:

DOLLARS					CENTS
		7	6	3 5	2 2

If the deposit is for whole dollars only, enter "00" in the CENTS boxes.

Types of Tax.—

Form 941 —Withheld income tax and both the employer and employee social security and Medicare taxes from wages and other compensation (includes Forms 941-M, 941-PR, and 941-SS).

Form 945 —Withheld Income Tax From Pensions, Annuities, IRAs, Gambling, Indian Gaming, and Backup Withholding.

Form 990-C —Farmers' Cooperative Association Income Tax.

Form 943 —Agricultural Withheld Income, Social Security, and Medicare Taxes (includes Form 943-PR).

Form 720 —Excise Tax.

Form CT-1 —Railroad Retirement Taxes.

Form 940 —Federal Unemployment (FUTA) Tax (includes Form 940-EZ and Form 940-PR).

Form 1120 —Corporate Income Tax (includes Form 1120 series of returns and Form 2438).

Form 990-T —Exempt Organization Business Income Tax.

Form 990-PF —Excise Tax on Private Foundation Net Investment Income.

Form 1042 —Withholding on Foreign Persons.

Marking the Proper Tax Period.—

Payroll Taxes and Withholding (Forms 941, 940, 943, 945, CT-1, and 1042. See the separate instructions for Form 1042.)

If your liability was incurred during:

- January 1 through March 31, darken the 1st quarter box
- April 1 through June 30, darken the 2nd quarter box
- July 1 through September 30, darken the 3rd quarter box
- October 1 through December 31, darken the 4th quarter box

Note: *If the liability was incurred during one quarter and deposited in another quarter, darken the box for the quarter in which the tax liability was incurred. For example, if the liability was incurred in March and deposited in April, darken the 1st quarter box.*

(Continued on back of page.)

Department of the Treasury
Internal Revenue Service

Cat. No. 61042S

Form 8109-B (Rev. 10-96)

Payroll Taxes

Excise Taxes.—For Form 720, follow the instructions on the front page for Forms 941, 940, etc. For Form 990-PF, with net investment income, follow the instructions below for Form 1120, 990-C, etc.

Income Taxes (Form 1120, 990-C, 990-T, and 2438).—To make a deposit for the current tax year for any quarter, **darken only the 1st quarter box.** This applies to estimated income tax payments.

Example 1: If your tax year ends on December 31, 1996, and a deposit for 1996 is being made between January 1 and December 31, 1996, darken the 1st quarter box.

Example 2: If your tax year ends on June 30, 1996, and a deposit for that fiscal year is being made between July 1, 1995, and June 30, 1996, darken the 1st quarter box.

To make a deposit for the prior tax year, **darken only the 4th quarter box.** This includes:

• Deposits of balance due shown on the return (Forms 1120, 990-C, and 990-T (corporate filers), and Forms 990-PF and 990-T (trust filers)).

• Deposits of balance due shown on **Form 7004,** Application for Automatic Extension of Time To File Corporation Income Tax Return (be sure to darken the 1120, 990-C, or 990-T box as appropriate).

• Deposits of balance due (Forms 990-T (trust filers) and 990-PF filers) shown on **Form 2758,** Application for Extension of Time To File Certain Excise, Income, Information, and Other Returns (be sure to darken the 990-PF or 990-T box as appropriate).

• Deposits of tax due shown on Form 2438 (darken the 1120 box).

Example 1: If your tax year ends on December 31, 1996, and a deposit for 1996 is being made after that date, darken the 4th quarter box.

Example 2: If your tax year ends on June 30, 1996, and a deposit for that fiscal year is being made after that date, darken the 4th quarter box.

How To Ensure Your Deposit Is Credited to the Correct Account.—

1. Make sure your name and EIN are correct;

2. Prepare only one coupon for each type of tax deposit;

3. Darken only one box for the type of tax you are depositing;

4. Darken only one box for the tax period for which you are making a deposit; and

5. Use separate FTD coupons for each return period.

Telephone Number.—We need your daytime telephone number to call if we have difficulty processing your deposit.

Miscellaneous.—We use the "IRS USE ONLY" box to ensure proper crediting to your account. Do not darken this box when making a deposit.

Note: *Do not deposit delinquent taxes assessed by the IRS. Pay those taxes directly to the IRS.*

How To Make Deposits.—Mail or deliver the completed coupon with the appropriate payment for the amount of the deposit to an authorized depositary (financial institution) for Federal taxes or to the Federal Reserve bank (FRB) servicing your geographic area. Make checks or money orders payable to that depositary or FRB. Federal agencies deposit at FRBs only. To help ensure proper crediting of your account, include your EIN, the type of tax (e.g., Form 940), and the tax period to which the payment applies on your check or money order.

Deposits at Depositaries.—Authorized depositaries must accept cash, postal money orders drawn to the order of the depositary, or checks or drafts drawn on and to the order of the depositary. You can deposit taxes with a check drawn on another financial institution only if the depositary is willing to accept that form of payment.

Deposits at FRBs.—If you want to make a deposit at an FRB, you should make that deposit with the FRB servicing your area with a check or payment for which immediate credit is given according to the funds availability schedule of the receiving FRB. A personal check is not an immediate credit item. The FRB servicing your area can provide information regarding what are considered immediate credit items.

Timeliness of Deposits.—The IRS determines whether deposits are on time by the date they are received by an authorized depositary or collected by an FRB. However, a deposit received by the authorized depositary or FRB after the due date will be considered timely if the taxpayer establishes that it was mailed in the United States at least 2 days before the due date.

Note: *If you are required to deposit any taxes more than once a month, any deposit of $20,000 or more must be made by its due date to be timely.*

When To Make Deposits.—See instructions for the returns. For deposit rules for employment taxes, see Circular E. You can get copies from most IRS offices or call 1-800-TAX-FORM.

Penalties.—You may be charged a penalty for not making deposits when due or in sufficient amounts, unless you have reasonable cause. This penalty may also apply if you mail or deliver Federal tax deposits to unauthorized institutions or IRS offices, rather than to authorized depositaries or FRBs. Additionally, a trust fund recovery penalty may **apply to any responsible person, including any responsible employee, who willfully fails to collect, account for, and pay over income, social security, and Medicare taxes that must be withheld. For more information on penalties, see Circular E.**

 Printed on recycled paper

★ U.S.GPO:1997-428-316

ELECTRONIC FEDERAL TAX PAYMENT SYSTEM

With respect to EFTPS, as discussed on page 926 of the main text, it should be noted that any business making deposits of more than $50,000 in employment taxes for calendar year 1997 must use EFTPS effective January 1, 1999. Businesses that were required to use EFTPS on July 1, 1997 (because their employment tax deposits for the calendar year 1995 exceeded $50,000) or on January 1, 1998 (because their employment tax deposits for the calendar year 1996 exceeded $50,000) have, on more than one occasion, been granted statutory relief from IRS penalties for failure to comply with the requirements of EFTPS.

It should also be understood that EFTPS provides for two payment methods; i.e., the ACH debit payment option and the ACH credit payment option.

The ACH debit payment option is very easy to use and puts the taxpayer in control of the payment. Before an ACH debit can be initiated, the taxpayer must report the tax payment into EFTPS at least one business day (but not more than 30 calendar days) before the due date of the tax payment. A touch tone phone or a personal computer may be utilized to report taxes to EFTPS. Taxpayers can use a warehousing capability which can store desired tax payment reports in the system for up to 30 calendar days in advance of the tax due date. The ACH debit tax payment is then initiated and posts against the taxpayer's bank account on the appropriate due date. Taxpayers must record the acknowledgement number received upon completion of their tax payment report. Taxpayers are also responsible for ensuring that they have sufficient funds in their bank account to cover the tax payment. Penalties will not be imposed as long as the taxpayer initiates a timely tax payment.

Under the ACH credit payment option, the taxpayer utilizes an ACH credit service offered by their financial institution. Taxpayers must first ascertain whether their financial institution offers a service to originate ACH credit tax payment transactions. The financial institution is responsible for originating the ACH credit tax payment on behalf of the taxpayer. The taxpayer is responsible for (1) originating payments through the financial institution prior to the financial institution's processing deadline. (This transaction must take place at least one business day prior to the due date of the tax.), (2) ensuring that the financial institution originates the tax payment transaction on their behalf, and (3) maintaining sufficient funds in their account to cover the tax payment.

UNEMPLOYMENT INSURANCE

Copies of Forms 940 and 940-EZ (along with related instructions) referred to on page 927 of the main text, follow:

Department of the Treasury
Internal Revenue Service (99)

Employer's Annual Federal Unemployment (FUTA) Tax Return

▶ **For Paperwork Reduction Act Notice, see separate instructions.**

OMB No. 1545-0028

1997

T	
FF	
FD	
FP	
I	
T	

Name (as distinguished from trade name)   Calendar year

Trade name, if any

Address and ZIP code   Employer identification number

A Are you required to pay unemployment contributions to only one state? (If "No," skip questions B and C.) . ☐ **Yes** ☐ **No**

B Did you pay all state unemployment contributions by February 2, 1998? ((1) If you deposited your total FUTA tax when due, check "Yes" if you paid all state unemployment contributions by February 10. (2) If a 0% experience rate is granted, check "Yes." (3) If "No," skip question C.) . . . . ☐ **Yes** ☐ **No**

C Were all wages that were taxable for FUTA tax also taxable for your state's unemployment tax? . . . . ☐ **Yes** ☐ **No**

If you answered "No" to any of these questions, you must file Form 940. If you answered "Yes" to all the questions, you may file Form 940-EZ, which is a simplified version of Form 940. (Successor employers see **Special credit for successor employers** in the **Instructions for Form 940.**) You can get Form 940-EZ by calling 1-800-TAX-FORM (1-800-829-3676).

If you will not have to file returns in the future, check here, and complete and sign the return . . . . ▶ ☐
If this is an Amended Return, check here   . . . . ▶ ☐

Part I **Computation of Taxable Wages**

1	Total payments (including payments shown on lines 2 and 3) during the calendar year for services of employees	**1**
2	Exempt payments. (Explain all exempt payments, attaching additional sheets if necessary.) ▶	Amount paid **2**
3	Payments for services of more than $7,000. Enter only amounts over the first $7,000 paid to each employee. Do not include any exempt payments from line 2. The $7,000 amount is the Federal wage base. Your state wage base may be different. **Do not use your state wage limitation** .	**3**
4	Total exempt payments (add lines 2 and 3) . . . . ▶	**4**
5	**Total taxable wages** (subtract line 4 from line 1) . . . . ▶	**5**

Be sure to complete both sides of this return, and sign in the space provided on the back.   Cat. No. 11234O   Form **940** (1997)

DETACH HERE

Form **940-V**

Department of the Treasury
Internal Revenue Service

Form 940 Payment Voucher

Use this voucher only when making a payment with your return.

OMB No. 1545-0028

1997

Complete boxes 1, 2, 3, and 4. Do not send cash, and do not staple your payment to this voucher. Make your check or money order payable to the **Internal Revenue Service.** Be sure to enter your employer identification number, "Form 940," and "1997" on your payment.

1 Enter the amount of the payment you are making	**2** Enter the first four letters of your last name (business name if partnership or corporation)	**3** Enter your employer identification number
▶ $		

Instructions for Box 2	**4** Enter your business name (individual name for sole proprietors)
—Individuals (sole proprietors, trusts, and estates)— Enter the first four letters of your last name.	Enter your address
—Corporations and partnerships—Enter the first four characters of your business name (omit "The" if followed by more than one word).	Enter your city, state, and ZIP code

Payroll Taxes

Part II   **Tax Due or Refund**

1	Gross FUTA tax. Multiply the wages in Part I, line 5, by .062	**1**
2	Maximum credit. Multiply the wages in Part I, line 5, by .054 . . .	**2**	
3	**Computation of tentative credit (Note:** *All taxpayers must complete the applicable columns.***)**

(a) Name of state	(b) State reporting number(s) as shown on employer's state contribution returns	(c) Taxable payroll (as defined in state act)	(d) State experience rate period		(e) State experience rate	(f) Contributions if rate had been 5.4% (col. (c) x .054)	(g) Contributions payable at experience rate (col. (c) x col. (e))	(h) Additional credit (col. (f) minus col.(g)). If 0 or less, enter -0-.	(i) Contributions actually paid to state
			From	To					

3a	Totals . . . ▶	
3b	**Total tentative credit** (add line 3a, columns (h) and (i) only—see instructions for limitations on late payments) ▶	
4		
5		
6	**Credit:** Enter the smaller of the amount in Part II, line 2 or line 3b	**6**
7	**Total FUTA tax** (subtract line 6 from line 1)	**7**
8	Total FUTA tax deposited for the year, including any overpayment applied from a prior year . .	**8**
9	**Balance due** (subtract line 8 from line 7). This should be $100 or less. Pay to the Internal Revenue Service. See page 4 of the **Instructions for Form 940** for details . . . . ▶	**9**
10	**Overpayment** (subtract line 7 from line 8). Check if it is to be: ☐ **Applied to next return** or ☐ **Refunded** . . . . ▶	**10**

Part III   **Record of Quarterly Federal Unemployment Tax Liability** *(Do not include state liability.)* Complete only if line 7 is over $100.

Quarter	First (Jan. 1–Mar. 31)	Second (Apr. 1–June 30)	Third (July 1–Sept. 30)	Fourth (Oct. 1–Dec. 31)	Total for year
Liability for quarter					

Under penalties of perjury, I declare that I have examined this return, including accompanying schedules and statements, and to the best of my knowledge and belief, it is true, correct, and complete, and that no part of any payment made to a state unemployment fund claimed as a credit was, or is to be, deducted from the payments to employees.

Signature ▶   Title (Owner, etc.) ▶   Date ▶

Department of the Treasury
Internal Revenue Service

Instructions for Form 940

Employer's Annual Federal Unemployment (FUTA) Tax Return

For Paperwork Reduction Act Notice, see page 4.
(Section references are to the Internal Revenue Code unless otherwise noted.)

General Instructions

Items to Note

FUTA tax rate and wage base. The FUTA tax rate is 6.2% through 2007 and the Federal wage base is $7,000. Your state wage base may be different.

Services performed by inmates. Services performed by an inmate of a penal institution in a private-sector job are not subject to FUTA. This applies to services performed after January 1, 1994. Services for a government agency performed by inmates of a penal institution continue to be exempt from FUTA.

Electronic deposit requirement. If your total deposits of social security, Medicare, railroad retirement, and withheld income taxes were more than $50,000 in 1996, you must make electronic deposits for **all** depository tax liabilities (including FUTA tax) that occur after 1997 using the Electronic Federal Tax Payment System (EFTPS). However, if you were first required to use EFTPS on or after July 1, 1997, no penalties for failure to use EFTPS will be imposed prior to July 1, 1998. To enroll in EFTPS, call 1-800-945-8400 or 1-800-555-4477. For general information about EFTPS, call 1-800-829-1040.

State unemployment information. Employers must contact their state unemployment insurance offices to receive their state reporting number, state experience rate, and details about their state unemployment tax obligations.

Other new law provisions for 1997. Generally,

• Employer payments to a medical savings account (MSA) are not subject to FUTA tax.

• Employer contributions under a SIMPLE retirement account are not subject to FUTA tax, but elective salary reduction contributions are subject to FUTA tax.

• Payments under adoption assistance programs are subject to FUTA tax.

For more information on these and other changes, see **Circular E,** Employer's Tax Guide (Pub. 15) and **Pub. 15-A,** Employer's Supplemental Tax Guide.

Household employers. If you have only household employees, do not make deposits of FUTA tax nor file Form 940. Instead, report and pay FUTA tax on **Schedule H (Form 1040),** Household Employment Taxes, with your individual income tax return (e.g., Form 1040 or 1040A), or estate or trust tax return (Form 1041).

Purpose of Form

File Form 940 to report your annual Federal unemployment (FUTA) tax. You, as the employer, must pay this tax. Do not collect or deduct it from your employees' wages.

Use **Form 940-EZ,** Employer's Annual Federal Unemployment (FUTA) Tax Return, a simpler version of Form 940, to report your annual FUTA tax if–

1. You paid unemployment contributions to only one state.

2. You paid all state unemployment by February 2, 1998 (February 10 if you deposited all FUTA tax when due).

3. All wages that were taxable for FUTA tax were also taxable for your state's unemployment tax. If, for example, you

paid wages to corporate officers (these wages are taxable for FUTA tax) in a state that exempts these wages from its unemployment tax, you cannot use Form 940-EZ.

Note: A successor employer claiming a credit for state unemployment contributions paid by the prior employer must file Form 940.

For details, get Form 940-EZ. **Do not file Form 940 if you have already filed Form 940-EZ for 1997.**

Use the current year form to avoid delays in processing.

Who Must File

In general, you must file Form 940 if either of the following tests applies **(household and agricultural employers see below):**

1. You paid wages of $1,500 or more in any calendar quarter in 1996 or 1997 or

2. You had one or more employees for at least some part of a day in any 20 or more different weeks in 1996 or 20 or more different weeks in 1997.

Count all regular, temporary, and part-time employees. A partnership should not count its partners.

Note: If there is a change in ownership or other transfer of business during the year, each employer who meets test 1 or 2 must file. Do not report wages paid by the other employer.

Nonprofit organizations. Religious, educational, charitable, etc., organizations described in section 501(c)(3) and exempt from tax under section 501(a) are not subject to FUTA tax and are not required to file.

Household employers. File a FUTA tax return **ONLY** if you paid total cash wages of $1,000 or more (for all household employees) in any calendar quarter in 1996 or 1997 for household work in a private home, local college club, or local chapter of a college fraternity or sorority. Individuals, estates, and trusts that owe FUTA tax for **household work** in a private home, in most cases, must file **Schedule H (Form 1040)** instead of Form 940 or 940-EZ. See the instructions for Schedule H.

In some cases, such as when you employ both household employees and other employees, you may have the option to report social security, Medicare, and withheld Federal income taxes for your household employee(s) on **Form 941,** Employers Quarterly Federal Tax Return, or **Form 943,** Employer's Annual Tax Return for Agricultural Employees, instead of on Schedule H. If you reported your household employee's wages on Form 941 or 943, you must use Form 940 or 940-EZ to report FUTA tax.

Agricultural employers. File Form 940 if either test below applies:

1. You paid cash wages of $20,000 or more to farmworkers during any calendar quarter in 1996 or 1997 or

2. You employed 10 or more farmworkers during at least some part of a day (whether or not at the same time) during any 20 or more different weeks in 1996 or 20 or more different weeks in 1997.

Count wages paid to aliens admitted on a temporary basis to the United States to perform farmwork, also known as "H-2(A)" visa workers, to see if you meet either test. However, wages paid to H-2(A) visa workers are not subject to FUTA tax.

Cat. No. 13660I

Magnetic Media Reporting

You may file Form 940 using magnetic media. See Rev. Proc. 96-18, 1996-1 C.B. 637, for the procedures and **Pub. 1314** for the tape specifications.

Penalties and Interest

Avoid penalties and interest by making tax deposits when due, filing a correct return, and paying all taxes when due. There are penalties for late deposits and late filing unless you can show reasonable cause. If you file late, attach an explanation to the return. Get Circular E for more information on penalties.

There are also penalties for willful failure to pay tax, keep records, make returns, and for filing false or fraudulent returns.

Not Liable for FUTA Tax

If you receive Form 940 and are not liable for FUTA tax for 1997, write "Not Liable" across the front, sign the return, and return it to the IRS.

Credit for Contributions Paid To a State Fund

You get a credit for amounts you pay to a state (including Puerto Rico and the U.S. Virgin Islands) unemployment fund by February 2, 1998 (or February 10, 1998, if that is your Form 940 due date). Your FUTA tax will be higher if you do not pay the state contributions timely.

"Contributions" are payments that a state requires an employer to make to its unemployment fund for the payment of unemployment benefits. However, contributions do not include:
- Any payments deducted or deductible from your employees' pay.
- Penalties, interest, or special administrative taxes not included in the contribution rate the state assigned to you.
- Voluntary contributions paid to get a lower assigned rate.

You may receive an additional credit if you have an experience rate lower than 5.4% (.054). This applies even if your rate is different during the year. This **additional** credit is equal to the difference between actual payments and the amount you would have been required to pay at 5.4%.

The total credit allowable may not be more than 5.4% of the total taxable FUTA wages.

Special credit for successor employers. A successor employer is an employer who received a unit of another employer's trade or business or all or most of the property used in the trade or business of another employer. The successor employer must employ one or more individuals who were employed by the previous owner immediately after the acquisition.

You may be eligible for a credit based on the state unemployment contributions paid by the previous employer. You may claim these credits if you are a successor employer and acquired a business in 1997 from a previous employer who was not required to file Form 940 or 940–EZ for 1997. **If you are eligible to take this credit, you must file Form 940; you may not use Form 940–EZ.** See section 3302(e). Enter in Part II, line 3, columns (a) through (i) the information of the previous employer as if you paid the amounts.

Successor employers may be able to count the wages that the previous employer paid to their employees to meet the $7,000 wage base. See the instructions for Part I, line 3 on page 3.

When To File

File Form 940 by February 2, 1998. However, if you deposited your total FUTA tax when due, you have until February 10, 1998, to file your return. Your form is considered timely filed if it is properly addressed and mailed First Class or sent by an IRS designated delivery service by the due date. See Circular E for a list of designated delivery services.

Caution: Private delivery services cannot deliver items to P.O. boxes.

Where To File

In the list below, find the state where your legal residence, principal place of business, office, or agency is located. Send your return to the **Internal Revenue Service** at the address listed for your location. No street address is needed.

Note: Where you file depends on whether or not you are including a payment.

Florida, Georgia, South Carolina

Return without payment:	**Return with payment:**
Atlanta, GA 39901-0006	P.O. Box 105887
	Atlanta, GA 30348-5887

New Jersey, New York (New York City and counties of Nassau, Rockland, Suffolk, and Westchester)

Return without payment:	**Return with payment:**
Holtsville, NY 00501-0006	P.O. Box 1365
	Newark, NJ 07101-1365

New York (all other counties), Connecticut, Maine, Massachusetts, New Hampshire, Rhode Island, Vermont

Return without payment:	**Return with payment:**
Andover, MA 05501-0006	P.O. Box 371307
	Pittsburgh, PA 15250-7307

Illinois, Iowa, Minnesota, Missouri, Wisconsin

Return without payment:	**Return with payment:**
Kansas City, MO 64999-0006	P.O. Box 970010
	St. Louis, MO 63197-0010

Delaware, District of Columbia, Maryland, Pennsylvania, Puerto Rico, Virginia, Virgin Islands

Return without payment:	**Return with payment:**
Philadelphia, PA 19255-0006	P.O. Box 8726
	Philadelphia, PA 19162-8726

Indiana, Kentucky, Michigan, Ohio, West Virginia

Return without payment:	**Return with payment:**
Cincinnati, OH 45999-0006	P.O. Box 6977
	Chicago, IL 60680-6977

Kansas, New Mexico, Oklahoma, Texas

Return without payment:	**Return with payment:**
Austin, TX 73301-0006	P.O. Box 970017
	St. Louis, MO 63197-0017

Alaska, Arizona, California (counties of Alpine, Amador, Butte, Calaveras, Colusa, Contra Costa, Del Norte, El Dorado, Glenn, Humboldt, Lake, Lassen, Marin, Mendocino, Modoc, Napa, Nevada, Placer, Plumas, Sacramento, San Joaquin, Shasta, Sierra, Siskiyou, Solano, Sonoma, Sutter, Tehama, Trinity, Yolo, and Yuba), Colorado, Idaho, Montana, Nebraska, Nevada, North Dakota, Oregon, South Dakota, Utah, Washington, Wyoming

Return without payment:	**Return with payment:**
Ogden, UT 84201-0006	P.O. Box 7024
	San Francisco, CA 94120-7024

California (all other counties), Hawaii

Return without payment:	**Return with payment:**
Fresno, CA 93888-0006	P.O. Box 60378
	Los Angeles, CA 90060-0378

Alabama, Arkansas, Louisiana, Mississippi, North Carolina, Tennessee

Return without payment:	**Return with payment:**
Memphis, TN 37501-0006	P.O. Box 1210
	Charlotte, NC 28201-1210

FUTA Tax Depositing

When to deposit. Although Form 940 covers a calendar year, you may have to make deposits of the tax before filing the return. Generally, deposit FUTA tax quarterly but only when your liability exceeds $100. Determine your FUTA tax for each of the first three quarters by multiplying by .008 that part of the first $7,000 of each employee's annual wages you paid during the quarter. If any part of the amounts paid are exempt from state unemployment tax, you may deposit more than the .008 rate. For example, in certain states, wages paid to corporate officers,

Page 2

Payroll Taxes

certain payments of sick pay by unions, and certain fringe benefits, are exempt from state unemployment tax.

If your FUTA tax liability for any of the first three quarters of 1997 (plus any undeposited amount of $100 or less from any earlier quarter) is over $100, deposit it by the last day of the month after the end of the quarter. If it is $100 or less, carry it to the next quarter; a deposit is not required. If your liability for the fourth quarter (plus any undeposited amount from any earlier quarter) is over $100, deposit the entire amount by February 2, 1998. If it is $100 or less, you can either make a deposit or pay it with your Form 940 by February 2. (If you deposit it by February 2, you may file Form 940 by February 10, 1998.)

The deposit due dates are shown in the following chart:

If undeposited FUTA tax is over $100 on—	Deposit it by—
March 31	April 30
June 30	July 31
September 30	October 31
December 31	February 2

How to deposit. Use **Form 8109,** Federal Tax Deposit Coupon, when you make each tax deposit (**Caution: See Electronic deposit requirement** under **Items to Note** on page 1.) The IRS will send you a book of deposit coupons when you apply for an employer identification number (EIN). Follow the instructions in the coupon book. If you do not have coupons, see **Section II** in Circular E.

Make your deposits with an authorized financial institution (e.g., a commercial bank that is qualified to accept Federal tax deposits) or the Federal Reserve bank for your area. To avoid a possible penalty, do not mail deposits directly to the IRS. Records of your deposits will be sent to the IRS for crediting to your business accounts.

Specific Instructions

Employer's name, address, and employer identification number. Use the preaddressed Form 940 mailed to you. If you must use a form that is not preaddressed, type or print your name, trade name, address, and EIN on it. If you do not receive your EIN by the time a return is due, write "Applied for" and the date you applied for the number.

Questions A through C. The answers to the questions will direct you to the correct form to file. If you answered "Yes" to all the questions, you may file Form 940-EZ, a simpler version of Form 940. If you answer "No" to any of the questions or you are a successor employer claiming a credit for state unemployment contributions paid by the prior employer, complete and file Form 940.

Final return. If you will not have to file returns in the future, check the box on the line below question C. Then complete and sign the return. If you start paying FUTA wages again, file Form 940 or 940-EZ.

Amended return. Use a new Form 940 to amend a previously filed Form 940. Check the Amended Return box above Part I. Enter all amounts that should have been on the original return, for the tax year you are correcting, and sign the form. Attach an explanation of the reason for the amended return. For example, you are filing to claim the 90% credit for contributions paid to your state unemployment fund after the due date of Form 940. File the amended return with the Internal Revenue Service Center where you filed the original return.

If you are filing an amended return after June 30 to claim contributions to your state's unemployment fund that you paid after the due date of Form 940, attach a copy of the certification from the state. This will expedite the processing of the amended return.

Part I—Computation of Taxable Wages

Line 1—Total payments. Enter the total payments you made during the calendar year for services of employees, even if the payments are not taxable for FUTA tax. Include salaries, wages, commissions, fees, bonuses, vacation allowances, amounts paid to temporary or part-time employees, the value of goods, lodging, food, clothing, and noncash fringe benefits, contributions to a 401(k) plan, payments to medical savings accounts (MSA), adoption assistance programs, and SIMPLE retirement accounts (including elective salary reduction contributions), section 125 (cafeteria) plan benefits and sick pay (including third party if liability transferred to employer). For details on sick pay, see Pub. 15-A. Include tips of $20 or more in a month reported to you by your employees. Also, include payments made by a previous employer if you are counting those payments for the $7,000 wage base as explained under **Successor employer** in the line 3 instructions below. Enter the amount before any deductions.

How the payments are made is not important to determine if they are wages. Thus, you may pay wages for piecework or as a percentage of profits. You may pay wages hourly, daily, weekly, monthly, or yearly. You may pay wages in cash or some other way, such as goods, lodging, food, or clothing. For items other than cash, use the fair market value when paid.

Line 2—Exempt payments. The amounts reported on line 2 are exempt from FUTA tax. For FUTA purposes, "wages" and "employment" do not include every payment and every kind of service an employee may perform. In general, payments excluded from wages and payments for services excepted from employment are not subject to tax. You may deduct these exempt payments from total payments only if you explain them on line 2. Amounts that may be exempt from your state's unemployment tax, for example, corporate officers' wages, may not be exempt from FUTA tax.

Enter payments such as the following on line 2:

1. Agricultural labor if you did not meet either of the tests under **Agricultural employers** on page 1.

2. Benefit payments for sickness or injury under a workers' compensation law.

3. Household service if you did not pay total cash wages of $1,000 or more in any calendar quarter in 1996 or 1997, and you included the amount on line 1.

4. Certain family employment.

5. Certain fishing activities.

6. Noncash payments for farmwork or household services in a private home that are included on line 1. Only cash wages to these workers are taxable.

7. Value of certain meals and lodging.

8. Cost of group-term life insurance.

9. payments attributable to the employee's contributions to a sick-pay plan.

10. Employer contributions to a SIMPLE retirement account (other than elective salary reduction contributions).

11. Employer payments to a medical savings account (MSA).

12. Benefits excludable under a section 125 (cafeteria) plan.

13. Any other exempt service or pay.

14. Certain statutory employees (see Pub. 15-A).

For more information, see **Special Rules for Various Types of Services and Payments** in Circular E.

Line 3—Payments for services of more than $7,000. Enter the total amounts over $7,000 you paid each employee. For example, if you have 10 employees and paid each $8,000 during the year, enter $80,000 on line 1 and $10,000 on line 3. **Only the first $7,000 paid to each employee is subject to FUTA tax. Do not use the state wage base for this entry. The state wage base may be different than the Federal wage base of $7,000. Do not include any exempt payments from line 2 in figuring the $7,000.**

Successor employer. If you acquired a business from an employer who was liable for FUTA tax, you may count the wages that employer paid to the employees who continue to work for you when you figure the $7,000 wage base. Include on line 3 the payments made by the previous employer. See section 3306(b)(1) and Regulations section 31.3306(b)(1)-1(b).

Page 3

Line 5—Total taxable wages. This is the total tax amount subject to FUTA tax. Use this amount in Part II to compute the maximum FUTA tax and the maximum credit.

Part II—Tax Due or Refund

Line 1—Gross FUTA tax. Multiply the total taxable wages in Part I, line 5, by .062. This is the maximum amount of FUTA tax.
Line 2—Maximum credit. Multiply the total taxable wages in Part I, line 5, by .054. This is the maximum credit against FUTA tax.
Line 3—Computation of tentative credit. You must complete all applicable columns to receive any credit. Your state will provide an experience rate. If you have been assigned an experience rate of 0% or more, but less than 5.4%, for all or part of the year, use columns (a) through (i). If you have **not** been assigned any experience rate, use columns (a), (b), (c), and (i) only. If you have been assigned a rate of 5.4% or higher, use columns (a), (b), (c), (d), (e), and (i) only. If you were assigned an experience rate for only part of the year or the rate was changed during the year, complete a separate line for each rate period.

If you need additional lines, attach a separate statement with a similar format. Also, if you are a successor employer, see **Special credit for successor employers** on page 2.

Column (a). Enter the two-letter abbreviation for the state(s) to which you were required to pay contributions (including Puerto Rico and the Virgin Islands).

Column (b). Enter the state reporting number that was assigned to you when you registered as an employer with each state. Failure to enter the correct number may result in unnecessary correspondence.

Column (c). Enter the state taxable payroll on which you must pay state unemployment taxes for each state shown in column (a). If your experience rate is 0%, enter the wages that would have been subject to state unemployment tax if the 0% rate had not been granted.

Column (d). Enter the beginning and ending dates of the experience rate shown in column (e).

Column (e). Your state experience rate is the rate the state assigned to you for paying your state unemployment tax. This rate may change based on your "experience" with the state unemployment fund, for example, because of unemployment compensation paid to your former employees. If you do not know your rate, contact your state unemployment insurance service. The state experience rate can be stated as a percent or a decimal.

Column (f). Multiply the amount in column (c) by .054.
Column (g). Multiply the amount in column (c) by the rate in column (e).

Column (h). Subtract column (g) from column (f). If zero or less, enter "0." This additional credit is the difference between 5.4% and your state experience rate.

Column (i). Enter the contributions actually paid to the state unemployment fund by the due date for filing Form 940. **Do not include amounts you are required to pay but have not paid by the Form 940 due date (see When To File on page 2).** See **Amended return** on page 3. If you are **filing after the due date,** include all payments made before the return is filed, and see the instructions for line 3b below. If you are **claiming excess credits** as payments of state unemployment contributions, attach a copy of the letter from your state. **Do not** include any penalties, interest, or special administrative taxes (such as surcharges, employment and training taxes, excise tax, and assessments which are generally listed as a separate item on the state's quarterly wage report) not included in the experience rate assigned to you.

Line 3a—Totals. Enter the totals of columns (c), (h), and (i).
Line 3b—Total tentative credit. Add line 3a, columns (h) and (i) only. However, if you **file Form 940 after its due date** and any contributions in column (i) were made after the due date for

filing Form 940, your credit for late contributions is limited to **90%** of the amount that would have been allowable as a credit if such contributions were paid on or before the due date for filing Form 940. For example, you paid $1,500 of state contributions on time and $1,000 after the due date for filing Form 940. There is no additional credit in column (h). Enter $2,500, your total state contributions, in column (i). Your total tentative credit on line 3b is $2,400 ($1,500 (timely payment) + $900 (90% of $1,000 paid late)). Because the 90% limit applies to part of your payment, explain below the signature line how you computed the amount on line 3b.

Note: If you are receiving an additional credit (column (h)) because your state experience rate is less than 5.4%, the additional credit is not subject to the 90% limit.

Line 6—Credit. Enter the smaller of Part II, line 2 or line 3b. This is the credit allowable for your payments to state unemployment funds. If you do not have to make payments to the state, enter zero on this line.

Line 9. If the amount on line 9 is under $1, you do not have to pay it. Write your EIN, "Form 940," and 1997 on your check or money order. This will help ensure proper crediting of your account. On payments of $100 or less, make your check or money order payable to the "Internal Revenue Service." Enter the amount of the payment in box 1 of Form 940-V at the bottom of Form 940. If the employer information is not preprinted on the payment voucher, enter the requested information. On payments over $100 that you are depositing, make your check or money order payable to the depositary or Federal Reserve bank where you make your deposit.

Line 10. If the amount on line 10 is under $1, we will send a refund or apply it to your next return only on written request.

Part III—Record of Quarterly Federal Unemployment Tax Liability

Complete this part if your total tax (Part II, line 7) is over $100. To figure your FUTA tax liability **for each of the first three quarters of 1997,** see **FUTA Tax Depositing** on page 2. Enter this amount in the column for that quarter. This is your tax liability, not your deposit.

Your liability for the fourth quarter is the total tax (Part II, line 7) minus your liability for the first three quarters of the year. The total liability must equal your total tax. If not, you may be charged a failure to deposit penalty.

Paperwork Reduction Act Notice. We ask for the information on this form to carry out the Internal Revenue laws of the United States. You are required to give us the information. We need it to ensure that you are complying with these laws and to allow us to figure and collect the right amount of tax.

You are not required to provide the information requested on a form that is subject to the Paperwork Reduction Act unless the form displays a valid OMB control number. Books or records relating to a form or its instructions must be retained as long as their contents may become material in the administration of any Internal Revenue law. Generally, tax returns and return information are confidential, as required by section 6103.

The time needed to complete and file this form will vary depending on individual circumstances. The estimated average time is: **Recordkeeping** – 11 hr., 43 min., **Learning about the law or the form** – 18 min., **Preparing and sending the form to the IRS** – 30 min.

If you have comments concerning the accuracy of these time estimates or suggestions for making this form simpler, we would be happy to hear from you. You can write to the Tax Forms Committee, Western Area Distribution Center, Rancho Cordova, CA 95743-0001. Do not send the tax form to this office. Instead, see **Where To File** on page 2.

Page 4

Form **940-EZ**

Department of the Treasury
Internal Revenue Service   (99)

Employer's Annual Federal Unemployment (FUTA) Tax Return

▶ **For Paperwork Reduction Act Notice, see page 4.**

OMB No. 1545-1110

1997

T	
FF	
FD	
FP	
I	
T	

Name (as distinguished from trade name)   Calendar year

Trade name, if any

Address and ZIP code   Employer identification number

*Follow the chart under **Who May Use Form 940-EZ** on page 2. If you cannot use Form 940-EZ, you must use Form 940 instead.*

A Enter the amount of contributions paid to your state unemployment fund. (See instructions for line A on page 4.) ▶ $ ....

B (1) Enter the name of the state where you have to pay contributions . . . . ▶   ....
      (2) Enter your state reporting number as shown on state unemployment tax return ▶

If you will not have to file returns in the future, check here (see **Who must file** on page 2) and complete and sign the return . . . . ▶ ☐

If this is an Amended Return, check here . . . . ▶ ☐

Part I   Taxable Wages and FUTA Tax

1	Total payments (including payments shown on lines 2 and 3) during the calendar year for services of employees	**1**		
2	Exempt payments. (Explain all exempt payments, attaching additional sheets if necessary.) ▶	Amount paid **2**		
3	Payments for services of more than $7,000. Enter only amounts over the first $7,000 paid to each employee. Do not include any exempt payments from line 2. Do not use your state wage limitation. The $7,000 amount is the Federal wage base. Your state wage base may be different	**3**		
4	Total exempt payments (add lines 2 and 3) . . . . ▶		**4**	
5	**Total taxable wages** (subtract line 4 from line 1) . . . . ▶		**5**	
6	**FUTA tax.** Multiply the wages on line 5 by .008 and enter here. (If the result is over $100, also complete Part II.)		**6**	
7	Total FUTA tax deposited for the year, including any overpayment applied from a prior year (from your records)		**7**	
8	**Amount you owe** (subtract line 7 from line 6). This should be $100 or less. Pay to "Internal Revenue Service." ▶		**8**	
9	**Overpayment** (subtract line 6 from line 7). Check if it is to be: ☐ **Applied to next return or** ☐ **Refunded** ▶		**9**	

Part II   Record of Quarterly Federal Unemployment Tax Liability (Do not include state liability.) Complete only if line 6 is over $100.

Quarter	First (Jan. 1 – Mar. 31)	Second (Apr. 1 – June 30)	Third (July 1 – Sept. 30)	Fourth (Oct. 1 – Dec. 31)	Total for year
Liability for quarter					

Under penalties of perjury, I declare that I have examined this return, including accompanying schedules and statements, and, to the best of my knowledge and belief, it is true, correct, and complete, and that no part of any payment made to a state unemployment fund claimed as a credit was, or is to be, deducted from the payments to employees.

Signature ▶   Title (Owner, etc.) ▶   Date ▶

DETACH HERE   Cat. No. 10983G   Form **940-EZ** (1997)

Form **940-EZ(V)**

Department of the Treasury
Internal Revenue Service

Form 940-EZ Payment Voucher

Use this voucher only when making a payment with your return.

OMB No. 1545-1110

1997

Complete boxes 1, 2, 3, and 4. Do not send cash, and do not staple your payment to this voucher. Make your check or money order payable to the **Internal Revenue Service.** Be sure to enter your employer identification number, "Form 940-EZ," and "1997" on your payment.

1 Enter the amount of the payment you are making	**2** Enter the first four letters of your last name (business name if partnership or corporation)	**3** Enter your employer identification number
▶ $		

Instructions for Box 2	**4** Enter your name (individual name for sole proprietors)
—Individuals (sole proprietors, trusts, and estates)— Enter the first four letters of your last name.	Enter your address
—Corporations and partnerships—Enter the first four characters of your business name (omit "The" if followed by more than one word).	Enter your city, state, and ZIP code

Who May Use Form 940-EZ

The following chart will lead you to the right form to use; however, if you owe FUTA tax only for **household work** in a private home, you generally must use Schedule H (see **Household employers** below).

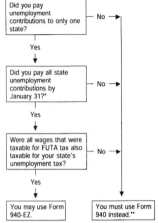

*If you deposited all FUTA tax when due, you may answer "Yes" if you paid all state unemployment contributions by February 10.

If you are a **successor employer** claiming a credit for state unemployment contributions paid by the prior employer, you must use Form 940.

**To get Form 940 or Schedule H (Form 1040), call 1-800-TAX-FORM (1-800-829-3676).

Note: *Do not file Form 940-EZ if you have already filed Form 940 for 1997.*

Changes To Note

FUTA rate. The FUTA rate of .008 shown on line 6 is effective through 2007.

Services performed by inmates. Services performed by inmates of a penal institution in a private-sector job are not subject to FUTA. This applies to services performed after January 1, 1994. Services for a government agency performed by inmates of a penal institution continue to be exempt from FUTA.

Electronic deposit requirements. If your total deposits of social security, Medicare, railroad retirement, and withheld income taxes were more than $50,000 in 1996, you must make electronic deposits for **all** depository tax liabilities (including FUTA tax) that occur after 1997 using the Electronic Federal Tax Payment System (EFTPS). However, if you were first required to use EFTPS on or after July 1, 1997, no penalties for failure to use EFTPS will be imposed prior to July 1, 1998. To enroll in EFTPS, call 1-800-945-8400 or 1-800-555-4477. For general information about EFTPS, call 1-800-829-1040.

General Instructions

Purpose of form. Use this form to report your annual Federal Unemployment Tax Act (FUTA) tax. FUTA tax, together with state unemployment systems, provides for payments of unemployment compensation to workers who have lost their jobs. Most employers pay both Federal and state unemployment taxes. **Only the employer pays this tax.** The tax applies to the first $7,000 you pay each employee in a year. The $7,000 amount is the Federal wage base. Your state wage base may be different.

When to file. File Form 940-EZ for 1997 by February 2, 1998. However, if you deposited all FUTA tax when due, you may file on or before February 10, 1998. Your return will be considered timely filed if it is properly addressed and mailed First Class or sent by an IRS designated delivery service by the due date. See **Cir. E,** Employer's Tax Guide, for a list of designated delivery services.

Caution: *Private delivery services cannot deliver items to P.O. boxes.*

Who must file. In general, you must file if either of the following tests applies (household and agricultural employers see below):

1. You paid wages of $1,500 or more in any calendar quarter in 1996 or 1997 or

2. You had one or more employees for some part of a day in any 20 or more different weeks in 1996 or 20 or more different weeks in 1997.

Count all regular, temporary, and part-time employees. A partnership should not count its partners. If a business changes hands during the year, each employer meeting test 1 or 2 must file. Do not report wages paid by the other.

Nonprofit organizations. Religious, educational, charitable, etc., organizations described in section 501(c)(3) of the Internal Revenue Code and exempt from tax under section 501(a) are not subject to FUTA tax and are not required to file.

Household employers. File a FUTA tax return **ONLY** if you paid total cash wages of $1,000 or more (for all household employees) in any calendar quarter in 1996 or 1997 for household work in a private home, local college club, or local chapter of a college fraternity or sorority. Individuals, estates, and trusts that owe FUTA tax for **household work** in a private home, in most cases must file **Schedule H (Form 1040),** Household Employment Taxes, instead of Form 940 or 940-EZ. See the instructions for Schedule H. In some cases, such as when you employ both household employees and other employees, you may have the option to report social security, Medicare, and withheld Federal income taxes for your household employee(s) on **Form 941,** Employer's Quarterly Federal Tax Return, **or 943,** Employer's Annual Tax Return for Agricultural Employees, instead of on Schedule H. If you choose to report on Form 941 or 943, you must use Form 940 or 940-EZ to report FUTA taxes.

Agricultural employers. File a FUTA tax return if either of the following tests applies:

1. You paid cash wages of $20,000 or more to farmworkers during any calendar quarter in 1996 or 1997 or

2. You employed 10 or more farmworkers during some part of a day (whether or not at the same time) for at least 1 day during any 20 different weeks in 1996 or 1997.

Count wages paid to aliens admitted on a temporary basis to the United States to perform farmwork, also known as workers with "H-2(A)" visas, to see if you meet either test. However, wages paid to H-2(A) visa workers are not subject to FUTA tax.

(Instructions continued on next page.)

Payroll Taxes

Not liable for FUTA tax? If you receive Form 940-EZ and are not liable for FUTA tax for 1997, write "Not Liable" across the front of the form, sign the return, and return it to the IRS.

Note: *If you will not have to file returns in the future, check the box on the line below B(2), complete and sign the return.*

Employer's name, address, and identification number. If you are not using a preaddressed Form 940-EZ, type or print your name, trade name, address, and employer identification number (EIN) on the form.

If you do not have an EIN, see Circular E for details on how to make tax deposits, file a return, etc.

Identifying your payments. When you pay any amount you owe to the IRS (line 8) or make Federal tax deposits, write the following on your check or money order: your EIN, "Form 940-EZ," and the tax year to which the payment applies. This helps us credit your account properly.

Penalties and interest. Avoid penalties and interest by making tax deposits when due, filing a correct return, and paying all taxes when due. There are penalties for late deposits and late filing unless you can show reasonable cause. If you file late, attach an explanation to the return. There are also penalties for willful failure to pay tax, keep records, make returns, and for filing false or fraudulent returns.

Credit for contributions paid to a state fund. You get a credit for amounts you pay to a state (including Puerto Rico and the U.S. Virgin Islands) unemployment fund by February 2, 1998 (or February 10, 1998, if that is your Form 940-EZ due date).

"Contributions" are payments that a state requires an employer to make to its unemployment fund for the payment of unemployment benefits. However, contributions do not include:

● Any payments deducted or deductible from your employees' pay.

● Penalties, interest, or special administrative taxes not included in the contribution rate the state assigned to you.

● Voluntary contributions you paid to get a lower assigned rate.

Note: *Be sure to enter your state reporting number on line B(2) at the top of the form. The IRS needs this to verify your state contributions.*

Where to file. In the list below, find the state where your legal residence, principal place of business, office, or agency is located. Send your return to the **Internal Revenue Service** at the address listed for your location. No street address is needed.

Note: *Where you file depends on whether or not you are including a payment.*

Florida, Georgia, South Carolina

Return without payment:	**Return with payment:**
Atlanta, GA 39901-0047	P.O. Box 105659
	Atlanta, GA 30348-5659

New Jersey, New York (New York City and counties of Nassau, Rockland, Suffolk, and Westchester)

Return without payment:	**Return with payment:**
Holtsville, NY 00501-0047	P.O. Box 210
	Newark, NJ 07101-0210

(Instructions continued on next page.)

New York (all other counties), Connecticut, Maine, Massachusetts,
New Hampshire, Rhode Island, Vermont

Return without payment:	**Return with payment:**
Andover, MA 05501-0047	P.O. Box 371324
	Pittsburgh, PA 15250-7324

Illinois, Iowa, Minnesota, Missouri, Wisconsin

Return without payment:	**Return with payment:**
Kansas City, MO 64999-0047	P.O. Box 970010
	St. Louis, MO 63197-0010

Delaware, District of Columbia, Maryland, Pennsylvania, Puerto Rico, Virginia,
U.S. Virgin Islands

Return without payment:	**Return with payment:**
Philadelphia, PA 19255-0047	P.O. Box 8738
	Philadelphia, PA 19162-8738

Indiana, Kentucky, Michigan, Ohio, West Virginia

Return without payment:	**Return with payment:**
Cincinnati, OH 45999-0047	P.O. Box 6796
	Chicago, IL 60680-6796

Kansas, New Mexico, Oklahoma, Texas

Return without payment:	**Return with payment:**
Austin, TX 73301-0047	P.O. Box 970017
	St. Louis, MO 63197-0017

Alaska, Arizona, California (counties of Alpine, Amador, Butte, Calaveras, Colusa,
Contra Costa, Del Norte, El Dorado, Glenn, Humboldt, Lake, Lassen, Marin,
Mendocino, Modoc, Napa, Nevada, Placer, Plumas, Sacramento, San Joaquin,
Shasta, Sierra, Siskiyou, Solano, Sonoma, Sutter, Tehama, Trinity, Yolo, and
Yuba), Colorado, Idaho, Montana, Nebraska, Nevada, North Dakota, Oregon,
South Dakota, Utah, Washington, Wyoming

Return without payment:	**Return with payment:**
Ogden, UT 84201-0047	P.O. Box 7028
	San Francisco, CA 94120-7028

California (all other counties), Hawaii

Return without payment:	**Return with payment:**
Fresno, CA 93888-0047	P.O. Box 60150
	Los Angeles, CA 90060-0150

Alabama, Arkansas, Louisiana, Mississippi, North Carolina, Tennessee

Return without payment:	**Return with payment:**
Memphis, TN 37501-0047	P.O. Box 1210
	Charlotte, NC 28201-1210

If you have no legal residence or principal place of business in any IRS district,
file with the Internal Revenue Service Center, Philadelphia, PA 19255.

Amended returns. Use a new Form 940-EZ to amend a previously filed
Form 940-EZ. Check the Amended Return box above Part I, enter all
amounts that should have been on the original return, and sign the
amended return. Attach an explanation of the reasons for amending the
original return.

If you were required to file Form 940 but filed Form 940-EZ instead,
file the amended return on Form 940. See Form 940 and its instructions.

Specific Instructions

*You must complete lines A and B and Part I. If your FUTA tax (line
6) is over $100, you must also complete Part II. Please remember to
sign the return.*

Line A. Enter the amount of state unemployment contributions. If your
state has given you a 0% experience rate, so there are no required
contributions, enter "0% rate" in the space.

Part I. Taxable Wages and FUTA Tax

Line 1—Total payments. Enter the total payments you made during the
calendar year for services of employees, even if the payments are not
taxable for FUTA tax. Include salaries, wages, commissions, fees,
bonuses, vacation allowances, amounts paid to temporary or part-time
employees, and the value of goods, lodging, food, clothing, and
noncash fringe benefits, contributions to a 401(k) plan, section 125
(cafeteria) plan benefits, and sick pay (including third party if liability
transferred to employer). Also, include tips of $20 or more in a month
reported to you by your employees. Enter the amount before any
deductions.

How you make the payments is not important to determine if they are
wages. Thus, you may pay wages for piecework or as a percentage of
profits. You may pay wages hourly, daily, etc. You may pay wages in
cash or some other way, such as goods, lodging, food, or clothing. For
items other than cash, use the fair market value when paid.

Line 2—Exempt payments. For FUTA purposes, "wages" and
"employment" do not include every payment and every kind of service
an employee may perform. In general, payments excluded from wages
and payments for services excepted from employment are not subject
to tax. Enter payments such as the following on line 2.

1. Agricultural labor if you did not meet either test under **Agricultural
employers** on page 2.

2. Benefit payments for sickness or injury under a worker's
compensation law.

3. Household service if you did not pay total cash wages of $1,000 or
more in any calendar quarter in 1996 or 1997, and you included the
amount on line 1.

4. Certain family employment.

5. Certain fishing activities.

6. Noncash payments for farmwork or household services in a private
home that are included on line 1. Only cash wages to these workers are
taxable.

7. Value of certain meals and lodging.

8. Cost of group-term life insurance.

9. Payments attributable to the employee's contributions to a
sick-pay plan.

10. Benefits excludable under a section 125 (cafeteria) plan.

11. Any other exempt service or pay.

For more information, see Special Rules for Various Types of Services
and Payments in Circular E.

Line 3—Payments for services of more than $7,000. Enter the total
amounts over $7,000 you paid each employee. For example, if you have
10 employees and paid each $8,000 during the year, enter $80,000 on
line 1 and $10,000 on line 3. The $10,000 is the amount over $7,000
paid to each employee. Do not include any exempt payments from line
2 in figuring the $7,000.

Lines 8 and 9.—If the amount on line 8 is under $1, you do not have to
pay it. If the amount on line 9 is under $1, we will send a refund or
apply it to your next return only on written request.

Part II. Record of Quarterly Federal Unemployment Tax Liability

Complete this part only if your FUTA tax on line 6 is over $100. To
figure your FUTA tax liability, multiply by .008 that part of the first
$7,000 of each employee's annual wages you paid during the quarter.
Enter the result in the space for that quarter. Your total liability must
equal your total tax. If not, you may be charged a failure to deposit
penalty.

Record your liability based on when you pay the wages, not on when
you deposit the tax. For example, if you pay wages on March 29, your
FUTA tax liability on those wages is $200, and you deposit the $200 on
April 30, you would record that $200 in the first quarter, not the second.

Depositing FUTA taxes.—Generally, FUTA taxes must be deposited
quarterly only when your liability exceeds $100. If you deposited the
right amounts, the amount you owe with Form 940-EZ will never be
over $100.

If your total deposits of social security, Medicare, railroad retirement,
and withheld income taxes exceeded $50,000 in 1996, you must
deposit taxes after 1997 using the Electronic Federal Tax Payment
System (EFTPS). See **Changes To Note** on page 2.

If you are not required to use EFTPS, use **Form 8109,** Federal Tax
Deposit Coupon, to deposit FUTA tax in an authorized financial
institution or the Federal Reserve bank for your area. Records of your
deposits will be sent to the IRS for crediting to your business accounts.

If your FUTA tax liability for any of the first three quarters of 1997
(plus any undeposited amount of $100 or less from any earlier quarter)
is over $100, deposit it by the last day of the month after the end of the
quarter. If it is $100 or less, carry it to the next quarter; a deposit is not
required. If your liability for the fourth quarter (plus any undeposited
amount from any earlier quarter) is over $100, deposit the entire amount
by February 2, 1998. If it is $100 or less, you can either make a deposit
or pay it with your Form 940-EZ.

Note: *The total amount of all deposits must be shown on line 7.*

Paperwork Reduction Act Notice.—We ask for the information on this
form to carry out the Internal Revenue laws of the United States. You
are required to give us the information. We need it to ensure that you
are complying with these laws and to allow us to figure and collect the
right amount of tax.

You are not required to provide the information requested on a form
that is subject to the Paperwork Reduction Act unless the form displays
a valid OMB control number. Books or records relating to a form or its
instructions must be retained as long as their contents may become
material in the administration of any Internal Revenue law. Generally, tax
returns and return information are confidential, as required by Code
section 6103.

The time needed to complete and file this form will vary depending on
individual circumstances. Estimated average time is: **Recordkeeping**—6
hr., 23 min., **Learning about the law or form**—7 min., and **Preparing
and sending the form to the IRS**—34 min.

If you have comments concerning the accuracy of these time
estimates or suggestions for making this form simpler, we would be
happy to hear from you. You can write to the Tax Forms Committee,
Western Area Distribution Center, Rancho Cordova, CA 95743-0001.
DO NOT send the form to this office. Instead, see **Where to file** on
page 3.

DIVESTITURE

APB OPINION NUMBER 29

According to APB Opinion Number 29, a gain or loss cannot be recorded on a corporate divestiture. However, footnote disclosure should be provided of the nature and provisions of the divestiture.

If there is an exchange of stock held by a parent in a subsidiary for stock of the parent company itself held by stockholders in the parent, there is a non-pro rata split-off of the business segment because a reorganization is recorded at fair value. However, if there is a split-off of a targeted company distributed on a proportionate basis to the one holding the applicable targeted stock, it should be recorded at historical cost provided the targeted stock did not arise in contemplation of the later split-off. If the contemplated situation did in fact exist, then the transaction is recorded at fair value. In a split-off, there is a distribution of shares being exchanged on a proportionate basis for the shares of the new entity. In a split-off, the transaction is in effect the acquisition of treasury stock. Retained earnings is not charged.

In a spin-off, there is a distribution of the segment's shares to the investor's shareholders without the holders surrendering their shares.

In some instances, a split-off or spin-off may be treated as a discontinued operation of a business segment.

In a split-up, there is a transfer of the operations of the original entity to at least two new entities.

Financial Management and Government Organizations

FINANCIAL MANAGEMENT (AND RELATED) ASSOCIATIONS

American Association of Artificial Intelligence
445 Burgess Drive
Menlo Park, CA 94025
Phone: 415-328-3123
FAX: 415-321-4457

American Association of Association Executives
1575 Eye Street NW
Washington, DC 20005

American Bar Association
750 N. Lake Shore Drive
Chicago, IL 60611
Phone: 312-988-5000
FAX: 312-988-6281

American Economic Association
2014 Broadway
Suite 305
Nashville, TN 37203
Phone: 615-322-2595
FAX: 615-343-7590

American Institute of Certified Public Accountants
Harborside Financial Center
201 Plaza III
Jersey City, NJ 07311-3881
Phone: 800-862-4272; 212-596-6200; 201-938-3301
FAX: 212-596-6213; 201-938-3329

American Institute for Computer Sciences
2101 Magnolia Ave.
Suite 200
Birmingham, AL 35205
Phone: 800-729-AICS
FAX: 205-328-2229

American Management Association
135 West 50th Street
New York, NY 10020
Phone: 800-262-9699; 212-903-8216
FAX: 212-903-8168

American Production and Inventory Control Society
500 W. Annandale Road
Falls Church, VA 22046
Phone: 800-444-2742; 703-237-8344
FAX: 703-237-1071

American Statistical Association
1429 Duke Street
Alexandria, VA 22314
Phone: 703-684-1221
FAX: 703-684-2036

Applied Business Telecommunications
P.O. Box 5106
San Ramon, CA 94583
Phone: 800-829-3400; 405-743-0320

Association for Investment Management and Research (AIMR). (Formed by a merger of the **Financial Analysts Federation** and the **Institute of Chartered Financial Analysts**)
5 Boar's Head Lane
P.O. Box 3668
Charlottesville, VA 22903
Phone: 804-977-6600
FAX: 804-977-1103

Canadian Institute of Chartered Accountants
277 Wellington Street, West
Toronto, Ontario, M5V 3H2, Canada
Phone: 416-977-3222
FAX: 416-977-8585

Chartered Institute of Management Accountants
63 Portland Place
London W1N 4AB, England

The Conference Board
845 Third Avenue
New York, NY 10022
Phone: 212-759-0900
FAX: 212-980-7014

Conference Board of Canada
255 Smyth Road
Ottawa, Ontario K1H8M7, Canada
(Also refer to **Canadian Business Infoworld** on the World Wide Web: http://csclub.uwaterloo.ca/u/nck-wan)

Financial Executives Institute
10 Madison Avenue
Morristown, NJ 07960
Phone: 800-336-0773; 201-989-4600
FAX: 201-898-4649

Financial Management Association
College of Business Administration
University of South Florida
4202 Fowler Avenue
Tampa, FL 33620
Phone: 813-974-2084
FAX: 813-974-3318

Institute of Internal Auditors
249 Maitland Avenue
Altamonte Springs, FL 32701
Phone: 407-830-7600
FAX: 813-974-3318

Institute of Management Accountants (formerly **National Association of Accountants**)
10 Paragon Drive
Montvale, NJ 07645
Phone: 800-638-4427; 201-573-9000

International Computer Training Association
Computer Learning Center
134 N. Peters Road
Knoxville, TN 37923
Phone: 800-354-3624

International Credit Association
243 North Lindbergh Blvd.
P.O. Box 27357
St. Louis, MO 63141-1757
Phone: 314-991-3030
FAX: 314-991-3029

National Association of Business Economists
1801 E. 9th Street
Suite 700
Cleveland, OH 44114
Phone: 202-463-6223
FAX: 202-463-6239

National Association of Credit Management
8815 Centre Park Drive
Suite 200
Columbia, MD 21045-2158
Phone: 410-740-5560
FAX: 410-740-5574

National Association for Female Executives
30 Irving Place
New York, NY 10003
Phone: 212-477-2200
FAX: 212-477-8215

National Society of Public Accountants
1010 North Fairfax Street
Alexandria, VA 22314-1574
Phone: 703-549-6400
FAX: 703-549-2984

National Tax Association
5310 E. Main Street
Columbus, OH 43213

New York Society of Security Analysts (NYSSA). (A local of the **Association for Investment Management and Research**)
1 World Trade Center
New York, NY 10048
Phone: 212-912-9249
FAX: 212-912-9310

North American Simulation and Gaming Association
c/o University of Wisconsin—La Crosse
203 Mitchell Hall
La Crosse, WI 54601
Phone: 608-785-8162

Risk and Insurance Management Society
655 Third Avenue
New York, NY 10017
Phone: 212-286-9292
FAX: 212-9865-9716

Society of Management Accountants of Canada
154 Main Street East
MPO Box 176
Hamilton, Ontario, Canada L8N 3C3
Phone: 905-524-4100

Tax Executives Institute
1001 Pennsylvania Avenue NW
Suite 320
Washington, DC 20004-2505
Phone: 202-638-5601
FAX: 202-638-5607

U.S. GOVERNMENT AGENCIES

Bureau of Economic Analysis
1441 L Street NW
Washington, DC 20230
Phone: 202-606-9900
FAX: 202-606-5310
World Wide Web: http://www.stat-usa.gov/BEN/Services/beahome.html

Department of Commerce
Fourteenth Street
Washington, DC 20230
Phone: 202-482-2000
World Wide Web Federal and Commerce Information Network: http://www.fedworld.gov

Director for Budget, Planning, and Organization
Herbert Hoover Building
14th Street and Constitution
Avenue NW
Room 5820
Washington, DC 20230
Phone: 202-482-3490

Director for Financial Management
Herbert Hoover Building
14th Street and Constitution
Avenue NW
Room 6827
Washington, DC 20230
Phone: 202-482-1207
World Wide Web (Finance Net): http://www.financenet.giv

Internal Revenue Service
1111 Constitution Avenue NW
Room 3000
Washington, DC 20224
Phone: 202-622-5000
World Wide Web: http://ustreas.gov/basic/cover.html

International Economic Policy
Office of Financial Management
Herbert Hoover Building
14th Street and Constitution
Avenue NW
Room 3866
Washington, DC 20230
Phone: 202-482-3022
FAX: 202-377-5444

International Trade Administration
Office of Financial Management
Herbert Hoover Building
14th Street and Constitution
Avenue NW
Room 4112
Washington, DC 20230
Phone: 202-482-3809
FAX: 202-377-5933

National Technical Information Service
Fourteenth Street
Room 1067
Washington, DC 20230
Phone: 202-377-0365

Office of Business Liaison
Herbert Hoover Building
14th Street and Constitution
Avenue NW
Room 5026
Washington, DC 20230
Phone: 202-482-1360
FAX: 202-377-4054

Office of Business and Industrial Analysis
Herbert Hoover Building
14th Street and Constitution
Avenue NW
Room 4875
Washington, DC 20230
Phone: 202-482-0096

Office of Financial Management Service
Liberty Center Building
401 14th Street SW
Room 548
Washington, DC 20227
Phone: 202-874-0700

Office of the Chief Economist
Herbert Hoover Building
14th Street and Constitution
Avenue NW
Room 4868A
Washington, DC 20230
Phone: 202-482-4885

Office of the General Counsel
1500 Pennsylvania Avenue NW
Room 3000
Washington, DC 20220
Phone: 202-622-0287

Office of the Secretary of the Treasury
Main Treasury
1500 Pennsylvania Avenue NW
Room 3330
Washington, DC 20220
Phone: 202-622-1100

Securities and Exchange Commission
450 5th Street NW
Room 6010
Washington, DC 20549
Phone: 202-942-4150
FAX: 202-272-7050
World Wide Web (SEC Edgar):
http://www.sec.gov/edgarhp.html

Note: The Federal Web Locator is http://www.law.vill.edu/fed-agency/fedwebloc.html.

APPENDIX B

PROFESSIONAL JOURNALS

AAII Journal
American Association of Individual
Investors
525 N. Michigan Ave.
Chicago, IL 60611
Phone: 312-280-0170
FAX: 312-280-1625

Academy of Management Journal
P.O. Box 39
300 S. Union St.
Ada, OH 45810
Phone: 419-772-1953
FAX: 419-772-1954

Academy of Management Review
P.O. Drawer KZ
Mississippi State University
Mississippi State, MS 39762
Phone: 419-772-1953
FAX: 419-772-1954

Across the Board
The Conference Board, Inc.
845 Third Ave.
New York, NY 10022
Phone: 212-759-0900
FAX: 212-980-7014

American Business Law Journal
Prof. Gregory J. Naples
Department of Accounting
College of Business Administration
Marquette University
Milwaukee, WI 53233
Phone: 513-529-2945
FAX: 513-529-6992

American Economic Review
American Economic Association
2014 Broadway
Suite 305
Nashville, TN 37203
Phone: 615-322-2595
FAX: 615-343-7590

Antitrust Law & Economic Review
P.O. Box 3532
Vero Beach, FL 32964-9990

Applied Financial Economics
Chapman & Hall
One Penn Plaza
41st Floor
New York, NY 10019
Phone: 0171-865-0066
FAX: 0171-522-9623

Association Management
American Society of Association
Executives
1575 Eye St. NW
Washington, DC 20005
Phone: 202-626-2735
FAX: 202-408-9635

Bankers Magazine
Warren, Gorham & Lamont, Inc.
31 St. James Ave.
Boston, MA 02116
Phone: 800-950-1252

Barron's
Dow Jones & Co., Inc.
200 Burnett Rd.
Chicopee, MA 01020
Phone: 212-416-2700
800-628-9320
FAX: 212-808-7282

**Business & Professional Ethics
Journal**
P.O. Box 15017
Gainesville, FL 32604
Phone: 904-392-2084
FAX: 904-392-5577

Business and Society Review
25-13 Old Kings Hwy. N
Suite 107
Darien, CT 06820
Phone: 212-399-1088
FAX: 212-245-1973

Business Credit
National Association of Credit
Management
8815 Centre Park Drive
Suite 200
Columbia, MD 21045-2158
Phone: 410-740-5560
FAX: 410-740-5574

Business Economics
National Association of Business
Economists
1233 20th St. NW, Suite 505
Washington, DC 20036
Phone: 202-463-6223
FAX: 202-463-6239

Business Horizons
Graduate School of Business
Indiana University
Bloomington, IN 47405
Phone: 812-855-5507

JAI Press, Inc.
Subscription Dept.
55 Old Post Rd., No. 2
P.O. Box 1678
Greenwich, CT 06836-1678
Phone: 203-661-7602

Business Insurance
Crain Communications
740 N. Rush Street
Chicago, IL 60611
Phone: 312-649-5286
FAX: 312-280-3174

Business Quarterly
The University of Western Ontario
1393 Western Rd.
London, Ontario N6A 3K7, Canada
Phone: 519-661-3309
FAX: 519-661-3838

Business Week
P.O. Box 430
Hightstown, NJ 08520
Phone: 212-512-2000

CA Magazine
Canadian Institute of Chartered
Accountants
277 Wellington St. W
Ontario M5V 3H2, Canada
Phone: 416-977-3222
FAX: 416-204-3409

California Management Review
University of California at Berkeley
5549 Haas School of Business, #1900
Berkeley, CA 94720-7159
Phone: 510-642-7159
FAX: 510-642-1318
E-mail: cmr@haas.berkeley.edu

Canadian Business Review
Conference Board of Canada
255 Smyth Road
Ottawa, Ontario K1H8M7, Canada
World Wide Web: http://csciub.uwa-terloo.ca/u/nckwan

Canadian Business
CB Media Ltd.
70 The Esplanade
2nd Floor
Toronto, Ontario M5E 1R2, Canada
Phone: 416-364-4266

CFO
CFO Publishing Company
253 Summer St.
Boston, MA 02210
Phone: 212-779-4469
FAX: 212-779-4277

CMA
Society of Management
Accountants of Canada
154 Main St. East
MPO Box 176
Hamilton, Ontario, Canada L8N 3C3
Phone: 905-524-4100

Columbia Journal of World Business
Columbia University
Uris Hall
3022 Broadway, Room 810
New York, NY 10027-7004
Phone: 203-661-7602
FAX: 203-661-0792

Compensation & Benefits Management
Panel Publishers, Inc.
Aspen Distribution Center
7201 McKinney Cir.
Frederick, MD 21701
Phone: 212-354-4545

Compensation and Benefits Review
American Management Association
Subscription Services
Box 408
Saranac Lake, NY 12983
Phone: 800-262-9699
212-903-8216
FAX: 2120-903-8168

Computers in Accounting
Warren, Gorham & Lamont
31 St. James Avenue
Boston, MA 02116
Phone: 800-950-1252

Corporate Cashflow
Intertec Publishing
6151 Powers Ferry Road NW
Atlanta, GA 30339
Phone: 770-955-2500

Corporate Controller
Faulkner & Gray
11 Penn Plaza
New York, NY 10001
Phone: 800-535-8403
212-867-7060

Corporate Finance (London, England)
Euromoney Publications PLC
Nestor House
Playhouse Yard
London EC4V 5EX, England
Phone: 0171-779-8935
FAX: 0171-779-8541

Corporate Finance
CF-VH Associates
415 Madison Ave.
New York, NY 10017
Phone: 212-432-0045

Corporate Taxation
Faulkner & Gray
11 Penn Plaza
New York, NY 10001
Phone: 800-535-8403
212-967-7060

CPA Journal
The New York Society of CPAs
530 5th Ave.
New York, NY 10036-5101
Phone: 212-719-8351
FAX: 212-719-3364

Credit Union Magazine
5710 Mineval Point Road
Madison, WI 53705
Phone: 608-231-4079
FAX: 608-231-4370

Credit World
International Credit Association
243 North Lindbergh Blvd.
P.O. Box 27357
St. Louis, MO 63141-1757
Phone: 314-991-3030
FAX: 314-991-3029
E-mail: bmurray@lmb.com

Economic Review
Federal Reserve Bank of Kansas City
Kansas City, MO 64198
Phone: 216-579-3079
FAX: 216-579-2477

Economist
25 St. James Street
London SW1A 1HG, England
Phone: 44-171-830-7000
FAX: 44-171-839-2968

Employer Benefit Plan Review
Charles D. Spencer & Associates, Inc.
250 S. Wacker Dr.
Suite 600
Chicago, IL 60606-5834
Phone: 312-993-7900

Employee Benefits Journal
International Foundation of
Employee Benefit Plans
18700 W. Bluemound Rd.
P.O. Box 69
Brookfield, WI 53005
Phone: 414-786-6700
FAX: 414-786-2990

Executive Accountant
Association of Cost & Executive
Accountants
Tower House
141-149 Fonthill Rd.
London N4 3HF, England
Phone: 44-71-272-3925
FAX: 44-71-281-5723

Executive Director
1801 E. 9th St.
Suite 700
Cleveland, OH 44114

Financial & Accounting Systems
Warren, Gorham & Lamont
31 St. James Avenue
Boston, MA 02116
Phone: 800-950-1252

Financial Analysts Journal
The Associates for Investment
Management and Research
P.O. Box 3668
Charlottesville, VA 22903
Phone: 804-980-9775
FAX: 804-977-1103
E-mail: faj@aimr.com

Financial Executive
Financial Executives Institute
10 Madison Ave.
P.O. Box 1938
Morristown, NJ 07960-1938
Phone: 800-336-0773
FAX: 201-898-4649

Financial Management
Financial Management Association
College of Business Administration
University of South Florida
4202 Fowler Ave.
Tampa, FL 33620
Phone: 813-974-2084
FAX: 201-898-4649

Financial Markets, Institutions & Instruments
Blackwell Publishers
238 Main St.
Suite 501
Cambridge, MA 02142, or
108 Cowley Rd.
Oxford OX41JF UK
Phone: 800-216-2522
617-547-7110
FAX: 617-547-0789

Financial Planning
P.O. Box 3060 C
Southeastern, PA 19398
Phone: 212-765-5311
FAX: 212-765-6123

Financial Review
c/o Prof. M. Carnes, Jr., School of Business
Georgia Southern College
L-B 8151
Statesboro, GA 30458
Phone: 912-681-5575
FAX: 912-244-3118

Financial World
Financial World Partners
1328 Broadway
New York, NY 10001
Phone: 212-594-5030
FAX: 212-629-1001

Forbes
60 Fifth Ave.
New York, NY 10011
Phone: 212-620-2200
800-888-9896

Fortune
P.O. Box 30604
Tampa, FL 33630-0604
Phone: 212-522-1212
800-621-8000

Harvard Business Review
Harvard Business School
Publishing Division
Soldiers Field
Boston, MA 02163
Phone: 800-988-0886
FAX: 617-495-6985

Industrial Management
Institute of Industrial Engineers
25 Technology Park-Atlanta
Norcross, GA 30092
Phone: 404-449-0460

Inc. Technology
Inc. Publishing Company
P.O. Box 54129
Boulder, CO 80322-4129
Phone: 800-234-0999

Industry Week
Penton Publishing Company
1100 Superior Ave.
Cleveland, OH 44114-2543
Phone: 216-696-7000
FAX: 216-696-7670

Internal Auditor
Institute of Internal Auditors
249 Maitland Avenue
Altamonte Springs, FL 32701
Phone: 407-830-7600
FAX: 407-831-5171

International Business
P.O. Box 5051
Brentwood, TN 37024-9736
Phone: 914-381-7700
FAX: 914-381-7713

International Economic Review
University of Pennsylvania
3718 Locust Walk
Philadelphia, PA 19104-6297
Phone: 215-898-5841
FAX: 215-573-2072

International Executive
John Wiley & Sons, Inc.
Susan Malawski, Director
Subscription Fulfillment and
Distribution
Subscriptions Dept.
605 Third Ave.
New York, NY 10158-0012
Phone: 212-850-6645

International Tax Journal
Panel Publishers, Inc.
Aspen Distribution Center
7201 McKinney Cir.
Frederick, MD 21701
Phone: 212-354-4545

Journal of Accountancy
American Institute of Certified
Public Accountants
Fulfillment Management
Harborside Financial Center
201 Plaza III
Jersey City, NJ 07311-3881
Phone: 201-938-3301
800-862-4272
FAX: 201-938-3329

**Journal of Accounting, Auditing &
Finance**
Greenwood Publishing Group, Inc.
88 Post Rd. W
P.O. Box 5007
Westport, CT 06881
Phone: 800-225-5800
203-226-3571

**Journal of Business & Economic
Statistics**
American Statistical Association
Subscriptions
1429 Duke St.
Alexandria, VA 22314-3402
Phone: 703-684-1221
FAX: 703-684-2036

**Journal of Business Finance &
Accounting**
Blackwell Publishers
238 Main St.
Suite 501
Cambridge, MA 01242, or
108 Cowley Rd.
Oxford OX41JF UK
Phone: 800-216-2522
617-547-7110

**Journal of Business Forecasting
Methods and Systems**
Graceway Publishing Co.
P.O. Box 159
Station C
Flushing, NY 11367
Phone: 718-463-3914
FAX: 718-544-9086

Journal of Business Strategy
Faulkner & Gray
11 Penn Plaza
New York, NY 10001
Phone: 800-535-8403
212-967-7000
FAX: 212-967-7155

Journal of Compensation & Benefits
Warren, Gorham & Lamont
31 St. James Avenue
Boston, MA 02116
Phone: 800-950-1252

Journal of Corporate Accounting and Finance
John Wiley and Sons, Inc.
Susan Malawski, Director
Subscription Fulfillment and Sales
605 Third Ave.
New York, NY 10158
Phone: 212-950-6000

Journal of Corporate Taxation
Warren, Gorham & Lamont
31 St. James Ave.
Boston, MA 02116
Phone: 800-950-1252

Journal of Cost Analysis
Society of Cost Estimating &
Accounting
101 S. Whiting St., Suite 313
Alexandria, VA 22304
Phone: 703-751-8069
FAX: 703-461-7328

Journal of Cost Management (formerly **Journal of Cost Management for the Manufacturing Industry**)
Warren, Gorham & Lamont
31 St. James Ave.
Boston, MA 02116-4112
Phone: 800-950-1205
FAX: 617-423-2026

Journal of Economics and Business
Elsevier Publishing Co., Inc.
Journals Fulfillment Department
665 Ave. of the Americas
New York, NY 10017
Phone: 212-989-5800

Journal of Finance
New York University
Graduate School of Business
100 Trinity Place
New York, NY 10006

Journal of Financial and Quantitative Analysis
University of Washington
Graduate School of Business
Administration
Makenzie Hall, DJ-10
Seattle, WA 98195
FAX: 206-543-6872

Journal of Financial Economics
Elsevier Science S.A.
P.O. Box 564
CH-1001
Lausanne 1, Switzerland
Phone: 212-989-5800

Journal of Financial Planning
Institute of Certified Financial
Planners
7600 E. Eastman Ave., Suite 301
Denver, CO 80231
Phone: 303-751-7600
FAX: 303-751-1037

Journal of Financial Research
Editor
Dept. of Finance
College of Business
Arizona State University
Tempe, AZ 85287-3906
Phone: 703-231-7699
FAX: 703-231-4706

Journal of Industrial Economics
Basil Blackwell Ltd.
108 Cowly Rd.
Oxford, OX4 1JF, England
Phone: 0865-791100
FAX: 0865-791347

Journal of International Financial Management and Accounting
Basil Blackwell Ltd.
108 Cowly Rd.
Oxford, OX4 1JF, England

Journal of International Taxation
Warren, Gorham & Lamont
31 St. James Ave.
Boston, MA 02116
Phone: 800-950-1252

Journal of Management
Graduate School of Business
Indiana University
10th & Fee Lane
Bloomington, IN 47405
Phone: 812-855-9209

JAI Press Inc.
Subscription Dept.
55 Old Post Rd., No. 2
P.O. Box 1678
Greenwich, CT 06836-1678

Journal of Money, Credit and Banking
Ohio State University Press
1070 Carmack Rd.
Columbus, OH 43210
Phone: 614-292-6930
E-mail:
mcgrothers@magnus.acs.ohio-state.edu

Journal of Portfolio Management
The Institutional Investor, Inc.
488 Madison Ave.
New York, NY 10022
Phone: 212-303-3300
FAX: 212-303-3527

Journal of Risk and Insurance
Dept. of Finance
College of Business

University of Central Florida
Orlando, FL 32816

Journal of Taxation
Warren, Gorham & Lamont
31 St. James Ave.
Boston, MA 02116
Phone: 800-950-1252

Journal of World Trade
P.O. Box 5134
1211 Geneva 11, Switzerland
Phone: 022-3103422
FAX: 022-3114592

Long Range Planning
Elsevier Science, Inc.
660 White Plains Rd.
Tarrytown, NY 10591-5153
Phone: 212-989-5800
914-524-9000
FAX: 914-333-2444

Management Accounting
Institute of Management
Accountants
10 Paragon Dr.
Montvale, NJ 07645-1760
Phone: 800-638-4427
201-573-9000
201-573-6269
FAX: 201-573-0639

Management Review
American Management
Association, Inc.
P.O. Box 408
Saranac Lake, NY 12983-0408
Phone: 800-644-2464
FAX: 212-903-8168

Management Today
Management Publications Ltd.
174 Hammersmith Road
London W671P, England
Phone: 0171-4134566

Managerial Auditing Journal
MCB University Press
60/62 Toller Lane
Bradford, West Yorkshire, England
BD89BY
Phone: 44-1274-777700

Mergers and Acquisitions
IDD Enterprises, L.P.
2 World Trade Center
18th Floor
New York, NY 10048
Phone: 212-432-0045
215-790-7000
FAX: 215-790-7005

Money
P.O. Box 30607
Tampa, FL 33630-0607
Phone: 800-633-9970

National Public Accountant
National Society of Public
Accountants
1010 N. Fairfax St.
Alexandria, VA 22314
Phone: 703-549-6400
FAX: 703-549-2984

National Tax Journal
National Tax Association-Tax
Institute of America
5310 Main St.
Columbus, OH 43213
Phone: 614-864-1221

Newsweek
251 West 57th Street
New York, NY 10019
Phone: 212-445-6000
800-631-1040

PC Magazine
Ziff-Davis Publishing Co.
P.O. Box 53131
Boulder, CO 80322-3131
Phone: 303-447-9330
800-289-0429

PC Week
Customer Service Department
P.O. Box 1770
Riverton, NJ 08077-7370
Phone: 609-461-2100

Pension Management
Argus Integrated Media
6151 Powers Ferry Road NW
Atlanta, GA 30339
Phone: 770-955-2500
FAX: 770-955-0400

Pensions & Investments
Circulation Dept.
965 E. Jefferson
Detroit, MI 48207
Phone: 212-210-0100
FAX: 212-210-0799

Planning Review
The Planning Forum
5500 College Corner Pike
P.O. Box 70
Oxford, OH 45056
Phone: 513-523-4185
FAX: 513-523-7539

Practical Accountant
Faulkner & Gray
11 Penn Plaza
New York, NY 10001
Phone: 800-535-8403
212-967-7060
FAX: 212-629-7885

Price Waterhouse Review
Price Waterhouse
1251 Avenue of the Americas
New York, NY 10020

Production and Inventory Management Journal
American Production and
Inventory Control Society
500 W. Annandale Rd.
Falls Church, VA 22046-4274
Phone: 800-444-2742
FAX: 703-237-1071

Public Finance
3 Robert Street
London, WCZN 6B4
Phone: 0171-895-8823
FAX: 0171-895-8825

Quarterly Review of Economics and Finance
JAI Press
P.O. Box 1678
55 Old Post Rd., No. 2
Greenwich, CT 06836-1678
Phone: 203-661-7602
FAX: 203-661-0792

Review of Financial Economics
JAI Press
55 Old Post Rd., No. 2
Greenwich, CT 06836-1678
Phone: 504-286-6240
FAX: 504-286-6094

Risk Management
Risk Management Society
Publishing
655 Third Ave.
New York, NY 10017
Phone: 212-286-9292
FAX: 212-986-9716

Sales & Marketing Management
335 Park Avenue South
New York, NY 10010
Phone: 212-592-6200

Simulation & Gaming
Sage Publications, Inc.
2455 Teller Rd.
Newbury Park, CA 91320
Phone: 805-499-0721

Sloan Management Review
P.O. Box 55255
Boulder, CO 80322-5255
Phone: 800-876-5764
617-253-7170
FAX: 617-253-5584

Small Business Controller
Warren, Gorham & Lamont
31 St. James Avenue
Boston, MA 02116
Phone: 800-950-1252
212-971-5000
FAX: 212-971-5113

Strategic Management Journal
John Wiley & Sons, Ltd.
Baffins Lane
Chichester, Sussex PO 19IUD,
England
Phone: 212-850-6000

Survey of Current Business
Superintendent of Documents
U.S. Government Printing Office
Washington, DC 20402
Phone: 202-606-9900
202-512-1800
FAX: 202-512-2250

Tax Advisor
AICPA
Harborside Financial Center
201 Plaza III
Jersey City, NJ 07311-3881
Phone: 800-862-4272
FAX: 201-938-3329

Tax Executive
Tax Executive Institute
1001 Pennsylvania Ave.
Washington, DC 20004-2505
Phone: 202-638-5601
FAX: 202-638-5607

Taxation for Accountants
Warren, Gorham & Lamont, Inc.
31 St. James Ave.
Boston, MA 02116
Phone: 800-950-1252

Taxes
Commerce Clearing House, Inc.
4025 W. Peterson Ave.
Chicago, IL 60646
Phone: 312-583-8500

World Economy
Blackwell Publishers
238 Main St.
Cambridge, MA 02142
Phone: 800-216-2522
617-547-7110

World
KPMG Peat Marwick
767 Fifth Ave.
New York, NY 10153

Worth
575 Lexington Avenue
New York, NY 10022
Phone: 212-751-4550

INDEX

Alternative minimum tax (AMT), 913-14
American Association of Artificial Intelligence, **S321**
American Association of Association Executives, **S321**
American Bar Association, **S321**
American Business Law Journal, **S327**
American Economic Association, **S321**
American Economic Review, **S327**
American Institute for Computer Sciences, **S321**
American Institute of Certified Public Accountants, **S321**
American International Group (AIG), **S146**
American Management Association, **S321**
American Production and Inventory Control Society, **S322**
American Statistical Association, **S322**
Americans with Disabilities Act, **S39**
AMERI-FAX, **S23**
Amortization:
    of intangible assets, 95-97
    of organization costs, 909
AMPS, 794
An Option Valuator/An Option Writer, **S277**
Analytical and control reports, 27
Antitrust Law & Economic Review, **S327**
Antitrust laws, 704
Appendices, internal audit reports, 549
Applied Business Telecommunications, **S322**
Applied Computer Services, **S10**
Applied Financial Economics, **S327**
Appraisal costs, **S129, S130, S133**
Appropriation of retained earnings, 108
Approved distribution lists, 36
Arbitrary cost allocations, 298
Arbor Software, **S2**
Armstrong Laing, **S9**
Asset profile, in balance sheet analysis, 651-52
Asset quality, appraising, 640
Assets, 81-97
    accounts receivable, 82-84
    fixed assets, 89-94
    intangibles, 94-97
        amortization of, 95
    inventory, 85-89
        dollar value LIFO, 88
        inventory stated at market value in excess of cost, 89
        inventory valuation difficulties, 89

losses on purchase commitments, 88-89
lower of cost or market value method, 85-86
retail LIFO, 87-88
retail lower of cost or market value method (conventional retail), 86-87
retail method, 86
Asset spin-off, 951
Asset utilization, in balance sheet analysis, 650-51
Association for Investment Management and Research (AIMR), **S322, S323**
Association Management, **S328**
ATA Research Inc., **S285**
Attribute sampling, 625-26
Audit attention, and financial statement analysis, 638-39
Audit tool, 543
Audit trail, 555
Authorization, types of, 556
Automobile insurance, 702
Automatic Consulting, **S10**
Axism Project Manager, **S6**

Back Track, **S147**
Background, internal audit reports, 548
Balance of payments, as monetary indicator, 722
Balance reporting system, 739
Balance sheet, 81-117
    assets, 81-97
        accounts receivable, 82-84
        fixed assets, 89-94
        intangibles, 94-97
        inventory, 85-89
    budgeted, 324-26
    liabilities, 97-106
        accounting for compensated absences, 103-4
        accounting for special termination benefits to employees 104
    bonds payable, 98-101
    disclosure of long-term purchase obligations, 105-6
    early extinguishment of debt, 101-2
    estimated liabilities (contingencies), 102-3
    obligations callable by the creditor, 105
    refinancing short-term debt to long-term debt, 104-5
    manufacturer, 217-18
    stockholders' equity, 106-17
        appropriation of retained earnings, 108
        dividends, 111-12

fractional share warrants, 116-17
preferred stock, 106-8
quasi-reorganization, 110
stock options, 113-16
stock split, 113
stock warrants, 116-17
treasury stock, 108-9
See also Balance sheet analysis; Income statement
Balance sheet analysis:
    accounts receivable, 641-43
    appraising asset quality, 640
    asset profile, 651-52
    asset utilization, 650-51
    avenues of financing, 654-55
    cash, 641
    deferred charges, 650
    fixed assets, 646-48
        management of, 648
    funds flow ratios, 657-61
    intangible assets, 648-49
    inventory, 643-45
    investments, 645-46
    liabilities, 652-54
        management of, 655
    liquidity analysis, 656-57
    overstated liabilities, 654
    solvency appraisal, 661-63
    stockholders' equity, 655-56
    undervalued/unrecorded liabilities, 654
Bank account analysis, 739
Bankers' acceptances (BAs), 788-89, 803
Bankers Magazine, **S328**
Banking relationships, 739-40
Bank loans, 799-804
    bankers' acceptances, 803
    dealing with the banker, 804
    installment loans, 801-2
    interest on, 802-3
    letter of credit, 801
    line of credit, 800-801
    revolving credit, 801
    secured loans, 800
    unsecured loans, 800
Bank reconciliation, 739-40
Bankruptcy, 987, **S51-S4**
Bankruptcy Reform Act of 1999, **S51**
Bankruptcy reorganization, 989-92
    exchange of obligations, 991-92
    recapitalization, 991
    valuation, 990
Barclay Trading Group, **S285**
Barron's, **S328**
Barton, R., **S11**
Basic earnings per share, **S71-S2**
Basic Information Package (BIP), 16
Basic standards, 356-57
Batch totals, 35
Bear put spread, **S274**

Cost of equity capital (*cont.*)
CAPM Approach, 868
Gordon's Growth Model, 867-68
Cost management:
and JIT costing, 503-5
and just-in-time (JIT) manufacturing, 497-98
Cost, management analysis of, **S246-S48**
Cost method, treasury stock, 108-9
Cost objective, 295
Cost point, **S6**
Cost of prediction errors, **S213-S14**
management analysis of, **S248**
Cost pools, 302-4
Costs:
by management function, 211-13
classifications, 210-11
common costs, 213
controllable costs, 216
definition of, 210
differential costs, 216
direct costs, 213
fixed costs, 213, 256-57
incremental costs, 216
indirect costs, 213
joint costs, 213
manufacturing costs, 211
mixed costs, 213, 256
noncontrollable costs, 216
nonmanufacturing costs, 211
opportunity costs, 217
out-of-pocket costs, 217
period costs, 213
for planing/control/decision making, 216-17
prime costs, 211
processing costs, 211
product costs, 213
relevant costs, 217
service department
allocation procedure, 233-34
allocation to production departments, 232-35
basis of assigning, 232-33
direct method of allocation, 233
reciprocal method of allocation, 234
step method of allocation, 234
standard costs, 216
sunk costs, 216-17
total costs, 215
unit costs, 215
variable costs, 213, 255-56
Cost variances, 359-60
Cost-volume formula, 257-58
Cost-volume-profit analysis (CVP), 269-82, **S99-S114**
applications of, and what-if analysis, 274-75
assumptions underlying, 278
break-even analysis, 271, **S104**

nonprofit organizations, **S99-S114**
break-even chart, 271
cash break-even point, 273
contribution margin (CM), 270
income taxes, impact of, 273
management options, **S114**
margin of safety, 273-74
profit-volume (P-V) chart, 271
program mix analysis, **S111-S13**
questions answered by, 269-77, **S100**
sales mix analysis, 275-77
target income volume, determining, 271-72
under conditions of uncertainty, 278-82
Cost-volume-revenue analysis, and nonprofit organizations, 277-78
Co-sureties, **S43-S4**
Coverage ratios, 877-79
Covered call write, **S273**
Covered option securities (COPs), 195, **S271-S72**
CPA Journal, **S330**
Creditor
obligations callable by, 105
rights of, **S44-S45**
Credit policy, 746-49
Credit rating:
bond funds, 786
corporate bonds, 780-81
Credit references, 742
Credit system, attributes of, 744-45
Credit Union Magazine, **S330**
Credit World, **S330**
Cross rates, 889-91
CS EDGE Series, **S145**
CSCI's Recovery PAC, **S145**
Currently attainable standards, 357
Current ratio, 1016
Current yield, 782-83

Daily labor mix report, 368
Daily material usage report, 365
DARTS, 794
Data base administrator, EDP department, 34
Data base management software (DBMS), 46-49
applications, 49
basic operations of, 47
desirable features of, 47-49
Data bases, online, **S15**
Data control group, EDP department, 35
Data entry operators, 34
DDS Financial, **S2**
DDS Work Order Management, **S6**
Debentures, 779, 828, 831
Debt:
cost of, 866

early extinguishment of, 101-2
Decentralization, advantages/disadvantages of, 452
Decision making:
decision matrix, 509-10
decision tree, 511-12
expected value of perfect information, 510-11
under uncertainty, 509
Decision support system (DSS), 328, 507, **S144**
Decision trees, 443-45, 511-12
Deep discount bonds, 828-30, 831
Deferred charges, in balance sheet analysis, 650
Deferred interest bonds, 830
Deferred tax liability vs. deferred tax asset, 183-84
Deficient rate of return, 987
Defined benefit pension plan, 172, 173-79
disclosures, 177
minimum pension liability, 175-77
trustee reporting for, 178-79
Defined contribution pension plan, 172, 173
Definitional equations, 333
Delphi Method, in forecasting, **S161-S62**
Degree of completion, estimating, 228
Degree of Relative Liquidity (DRL), 1012, 1016-17
Deloitte and Touche, **S10, S147-S48**
Deltzk Systems, **S6**
Demand function, 706
Department of Commerce, **S324**
Deposit collection float, 731
Deposit rule, **S205**
Depreciation, 910-12
fixed assets, 90
Derivative products, 193-95
disclosure of, **S88**
hedging, 193-94
types of, 194-95
Design Data System, **S2, S6**
Development state companies, disclosure requirements, 144
Differential costs, 216
Diluted earnings per share, **S72-S3**
Direct connection of intranet, **S27**
Direct costs, 213, 295
Direct financing method, leases, 165-67
Direct fixed costs, 305
Direct labor, 211, 219
Direct labor budget, 319-20
Direct quote, 889
Director for Budget, Planning, and Organization, **S324**
Director for Financial Management, **S324**
Disability coverage, 702
Disability insurance, 926-27

Index